Gender and Sexuality in Stoic Philosophy

Malin Grahn-Wilder

Gender and Sexuality in Stoic Philosophy

Malin Grahn-Wilder
New York, NY, USA

ISBN 978-3-030-09608-3   ISBN 978-3-319-53694-1 (eBook)
https://doi.org/10.1007/978-3-319-53694-1

© The Editor(s) (if applicable) and The Author(s) 2018
Softcover re-print of the Hardcover 1st edition 2018
This work is subject to copyright. All rights are solely and exclusively licensed by the Publisher, whether the whole or part of the material is concerned, specifically the rights of translation, reprinting, reuse of illustrations, recitation, broadcasting, reproduction on microfilms or in any other physical way, and transmission or information storage and retrieval, electronic adaptation, computer software, or by similar or dissimilar methodology now known or hereafter developed.
The use of general descriptive names, registered names, trademarks, service marks, etc. in this publication does not imply, even in the absence of a specific statement, that such names are exempt from the relevant protective laws and regulations and therefore free for general use.
The publisher, the authors and the editors are safe to assume that the advice and information in this book are believed to be true and accurate at the date of publication. Neither the publisher nor the authors or the editors give a warranty, express or implied, with respect to the material contained herein or for any errors or omissions that may have been made. The publisher remains neutral with regard to jurisdictional claims in published maps and institutional affiliations.

Cover credit: Engin Korkmaz/Alamy Stock Photo

Printed on acid-free paper

This Palgrave Macmillan imprint is published by Springer Nature
The registered company is Springer International Publishing AG
The registered company address is: Gewerbestrasse 11, 6330 Cham, Switzerland

*In memory of my philosophy teachers Juha Eerolainen (1962–2007)
and Juha Sihvola (1957–2012)*

Preface

This book arouse out of a twofold interest. On the one hand, I was guided by genuine scholarly curiosity to understand how past philosophers theorized about gender. I remember how years ago, as a philosophy student at the University of Helsinki, I was trying to find material on the Stoic views on gender and was shocked to realize that there was no monograph or any systematic study on the topic. When I was invited to join the Antiquity group of the *Philosophical Psychology, Morality, and Politics* Center of Excellence as a doctoral researcher, I wanted to fill this lacuna and started to scrutinize Stoic philosophy through the prism of gender and sexuality. This research laid the foundations for this book.

On the other hand, my interest in gender is essentially practical and present-day oriented. In my professional work both as a teacher at the university level and a dance educator working with children and youth, I constantly encounter the urgency of critically rethinking the normative notions of gender that still shape our contemporary world. The binary conception of gender, different forms of political and economic inequality, and beauty ideals causing distress and setting unrealistic expectations are just a few examples of problems we are still struggling with today. I believe that at best, systematic scrutiny of past thinking can increase the awareness of our present-day conceptions and ideas. By exploring Ancient views on gender, we also learn about the origins and development of Western thought.

Furthermore, as this book demonstrates, past thinkers can provide us with arguments that still today are thought-provoking. For those readers primarily interested in Ancient philosophy and Stoicism, I wish to show that the perspective of gender sheds new light on the Stoic philosophical enterprise on the whole. My topic has allowed me to pose new and original research questions to my source material, and highlight topics that previously have, at their best, been marginal in the scholarship. For those readers with a general interest in gender as a philosophical question, I provide a systematic and detailed account of the Stoic views that I wish to be helpful for theorizing these very topics today.

The investigation of Ancient Stoic philosophy has taken me on a historical journey, but also on a geographical one as I have worked on this project in many different countries and places. I developed the final version of this book as a visiting scholar at the Columbia University in the City of New York in 2016–2017, and I am profoundly grateful to Prof. Katja Vogt and the entire Department of Philosophy for the unique opportunity to focus on this work in a thriving scholarly environment. I wholeheartedly thank the Department of Social Sciences and Philosophy at the University of Jyväskylä, where I had the position of a postdoctoral scholar in 2015–2016. I also want to express my gratitude to my research community at the Academy of Finland's *Philosophical Psychology, Morality, and Politics* Center of Excellence at the University of Helsinki, where I worked as a doctoral researcher and received my doctorate in 2013. The present book is based on my work in this center, and I am deeply grateful for Profs. Simo Knuuttila and Juha Sihvola for their forward-looking leadership and for sharing their scholarly expertise with me. I want to express my gratitude to Prof. Miira Tuominen who, as a supervisor of my doctoral dissertation, has been a longtime companion on my philosophical journey and seen the development of this work from its very beginnings. I could not thank her enough for her truly philosophical character, her help and encouragement. Thank you Prof. Eyjólfur Kjalar Emilsson, Håvard Løkke, and the entire community of Ancient scholars at the University of Oslo, where I worked as a visiting scholar in 2007–2008 and had the chance to develop and present certain parts of this study. I thank the staff in the disciplines of Theoretical Philosophy, Gender Studies and Social and Moral Philosophy at the University of Helsinki. A special thank you to Prof. Gabriel Sandu for his support.

I would like to express my wholehearted gratitude to Profs. Julia Annas and Pauliina Remes. I truly appreciate their support for this project, and all of their feedback, critical questions as well as our wonderful philosophical conversations. I want to thank Profs. Sara Heinämaa and Johanna Oksala who have had a great influence on my thinking and understanding of feminist philosophy and Michel Foucault. I have worked as a teacher at the Departments of Philosophy and Gender Studies at the University of Helsinki since 2007, and as it is often said, teaching is the best way of learning. I am grateful for my students for all the inspiring classroom discussions, and for reinforcing my faith that philosophy is fundamentally a living, collective process. Thank you Maria Svanström for having been a fantastic co-teacher in our gender studies classes over many years. I thank wholeheartedly The Kone Foundation and The Finnish Cultural Foundation for financially supporting my research.

Even if none of the parts of this book have been previously published, I have had the privilege to present early versions of many chapters of this book in different seminars and conferences, and receive invaluable comments and questions that have been significant for the development of this work. In particular, I would like to thank the participants of the *History of Philosophy Research Seminar* at the University of Helsinki, where, over the years, I had the opportunity to present drafts of several chapters of this book. The chapters on Aristotle's and Galen's embryologies benefitted greatly from the comments I received for my colloquium lecture at the University of Arizona and my presentation in the *Gender, Nature, and Culture* gender studies conference at the University of Helsinki in 2010. I want to thank the participants at the research seminars at the Universities of Jyväskylä, Oslo, Uppsala, where I presented material on Plato's and Stoics' political thought and views on marriage. I thank the participants of Columbia University graduate seminar for a discussion on my chapter on Stoic metaphysics.

Finally, I wish to thank the anonymous reviewer of this work for insightful comments on my manuscript and for pointing out the fascinating research area opened up by the expressly gendered rivalry between the Stoics and the Epicureans. However, after serious contemplation, I decided to leave most of this area to be explored by future research and only scratch a surface of this wide area in this study that is already extensive as it is. I am extremely grateful for my collaboration with Palgrave Macmillan and I owe deep thanks to editor Philip Getz and assistant editor Amy Invernizzi for their professionalism and inspirational cooperation.

This work is dedicated to the memory of my teachers, mentors, and friends Juha Eerolainen (1962–2007) and Juha Sihvola (1957–2012), both of whom I was sad to see passing away so prematurely, and both of whom have had an important impact on my philosophical development and career. I thank my philosophy teacher Juha Eerolainen at Etu-Töölö High School in Helsinki for opening up the world of philosophy for me. I will always remember his pedagogical style and the fantastic ways in which he challenged his students to think further. Being his substitute teacher was my very first teaching job as an undergraduate student, and thus, I thank him for finding my passion both for studying and teaching philosophy. I thank Prof. Juha Sihvola for philosophical companionship and for being an extremely encouraging supervisor of my doctoral dissertation. As Seneca said that a good philosophy teacher should do, Sihvola "met me halfway," sharing his expertise with me and presenting his critical comments, while also encountering me as an equal partner of discussion. As a teacher, he always urged me to develop as the individual thinker I am. Both Eerolainen and Sihvola have been inspirational role models for philosophical pedagogy and applying philosophical traditions to a critical examination of what is happening in the world right now.

Finally, I would like to express my deepest gratitude to my husband Clyde Wilder. I thank him for being my partner in philosophical conversation, in love and in life, and for his unlimited support during the process of working on this book.

New York, USA
November 5 2017

Malin Grahn-Wilder

Contents

1 Introduction 1
   1.1 Mapping the Terrain: Gender in Stoic Sources
       and Scholarship 3
   1.2 Some Qualifications 5
   1.3 The Structure and Main Arguments 8
References 12

Part I The Body: Gender From Generation to Decoration

2 The Origin of Gender: Myths and Biology 17
   2.1 Plato's Philosophical Myths of Gender and Sexuality 17
       2.1.1 Genders, Planets, and Lust: Aristophanes'
             Speech 18
       2.1.2 Noble Birth Without Sex—Pausanias
             and Socrates 23
       2.1.3 Women as Former Vicious Men—Plato's
             Timaeus 26
   2.2 When Hot Meets Cold and Form Meets
       Matter—Gender and Generation in Aristotle's Biology 29
       2.2.1 Why Are Higher Animals Gendered? 30
       2.2.2 Gender and Form: Sameness and Difference 32
       2.2.3 Aristotelian Metaphysics of Gender 34
       2.2.4 Hot Men and Cold Women 38

2.3	Galen on Gender: Scientific, Medical, and Philosophical Perspectives		45
	2.3.1	Two Genders, Four Elements and the Problem of Gender Resemblance	46
	2.3.2	From Agricultural Analogy to Dual-Seed Theory	49
	2.3.3	On Cold and Idle Women	52
Appendix			53
References			56

3 **Semen, Zeus, and the Birth of Cosmos: Gender in Stoic Cosmogony and Cosmology**   59
   3.1   *Gender and the Two Principles*   60
   3.2   *Fire and Sperm: Generation in a Material World*   62
   3.3   *On the Sexual Encounter Between Zeus and Hera—A Biological Myth?*   64
   3.4   *Sexual Analogies in Stoic Cosmology*   69
   Appendix   72
   References   73

4 **The Metaphysical Insignificance of Gender**   75
   4.1   *The Stoic Theory of Categories: Gender and Substance*   76
   4.2   *Gender and the Qualified: Common and Individual Features*   78
   4.3   *The Disposed and the Relatively Disposed: Gender and Relations*   83
   4.4   *Reproduction and Rational Capacities: The Stoic Theory of Pneuma*   85
   4.5   *Stoic Notions of Embryology*   88
   4.6   *From Genital Difference to Good Life*   94
   Appendix   97
   References   99

5 **Perfumed Men and Bearded Philosophers—The Stoics on Signs of Gender**   101
   5.1   *Hair,* Prohairesis, *and Human Flourishing*   102
   5.2   *On Hairy Bodies and the Works of Nature*   106
   5.3   *The Philosopher's Beard*   111

	5.4	Gendered Signs and Effeminate Vanity—Early and Roman Stoics Compared	117
	Appendix		119
	References		122
6	Fiery and Cold Natures—Stoic Physiognomics of Gender		123
	6.1	Beautiful Souls in Beautiful Bodies	125
	6.2	Seneca on the Elements and Gendered Characteristics	128
	Appendix		131
	References		133

Part II Character: Education of Gender and Therapy of Sexuality

7	Gender, Character, and Education from Classic to Hellenistic Thought		137
	7.1	Character as a Philosophical Problem	137
	7.2	Equal Education and Gendered Characteristics—Critical Assessments on Plato's Republic	139
		7.2.1 Educability of Men and Women	140
		7.2.2 The Seed and the Soil—On the Origin of Gendered Characteristics	141
		7.2.3 Philosophers, Lovers, and the End of Gender Dimorphism?	143
		7.2.4 Beyond the Republic—On Uniformity of Virtue and Female Happiness	145
	7.3	Aristotle on the Education of Young Men: Habituation of Character and Political Goals	147
		7.3.1 Aristotle on Childhood and Habituation	148
		7.3.2 Gender, Virtue, and the Politics of Education	150
		7.3.3 Female Virtue and Happiness	152
	Appendix		155
	References		157
8	The Stoics on Equal Educability of Girls and Boys, and the Origin of Gendered Characteristics		159
	8.1	Musonius on Why Girls Should Be Educated	161

8.2   Inborn Capacities, Cultural Impact, and the Question
      Concerning Gendered Characteristics   164
      8.2.1   Nonrationality and Moral Irresponsibility—
              Stoic Views on Children   165
      8.2.2   Oikeiōsis and the Theory of Preconceptions:
              Arguments for Equal Educability
              of Girls and Boys   169
      8.2.3   Gendered Characteristics and Cultural
              Corruption   172
Appendix   176
References   179

9   To Become Properly Manly—Gender, Happiness, and the Figure of the Sage   181
9.1   Manly Stoics, Effeminate Epicureans   183
9.2   The Sage, Apatheia, and the Feminine   185
9.3   Female Idealizations and Exemplifications   188
9.4   Genders and Personae   193
Appendix   196
References   197

10   How to Take "Certain Spasms" Calmly—Sexuality in Stoic Philosophical Therapy   199
10.1   Making Friends Through Erotic Love   200
10.2   Sexuality and Inner Freedom   204
10.3   Philosophical Exercises on Sexuality 1: Impressions   206
10.4   Philosophical Exercises on Sexuality 2: Abstinence   210
Appendix   213
References   215

Part III   Community: Marriage, Family, and Human Bonding

11   Gender, Politics, and Economics: From Plato's Utopianism to Cynic Radicalism   219
11.1   Marriage and Private Ownership from Plato
       to the Cynics   219

		11.1.1	End of Monogamy and (Other Forms of) Private Ownership in Plato's Republic	220
		11.1.2	Sexual Control and the Problem of Equality	223
	11.2	The Economics of the Free Man's Household: Wife, Property, Slaves, and Cattle		225
	11.3	Cynic Upheavals of Gender and Family Roles		227
	Appendix			230
	References			232
12	"Holding Women in Common"—Gender in Early Stoic Utopias			235
	12.1	Stoic Abolishment of Marriage and Other Social Institutions		236
	12.2	Platonic, Cynic, and Stoic Ideals of Polygamy Compared		238
	12.3	Wives, Pork, and Theater Seats—Stoic Views on Women and Common Property		241
	12.4	Marriage and Non-Marriage, Incest, and Virtue—Contradictory and Controversial Elements in Early Stoicism		246
	Appendix			251
	References			252
13	Is It Possible to Marry and Be Happy? The Later Stoics on Matrimony and Modes of Life			253
	13.1	Learning to Lose One's Love		254
	13.2	Not Every Wife Is like Hipparchia—Epictetus on Conjugal and Parental Responsibilities		257
	13.3	Marriage as a Natural Way of Life: Partnership and Sociability		260
	13.4	The Roles of Wife and Husband		264
	13.5	Should the Wife Stay by Her Loom? Gender and the Division of Labor		268
	Appendix			273
	References			276
14	Gender and Stoic Cosmopolitanism			277
	14.1	A Spouse, a Human, a Citizen of the Cosmos— The Stoic Theory of Extending Circles		278

14.2 The Importance of the Inner Circle	281
Appendix	284
References	285
15 Conclusion	287
Index	295

CHAPTER 1

Introduction

The Ancient Stoic thinkers discuss problems related to gender and sexuality in various contexts of their philosophy: from cosmology to cosmopolitanism, from metaphysics to moral psychology, and from physics to the philosophy of life. These discussions relate to many fundamental doctrines such as their views of body and reason, theory of emotions, and political utopias. Furthermore, the sources also provide detailed accounts of specific topics such as generation, bodily beauty, cosmetics, marriage, and philosophical exercises for dealing with sexual impulses. This book explores these views and their significance in Ancient Stoic philosophy.

More specifically, my aim in this book is to scrutinize what features in humans (or in animals, or even in the entire cosmos) the Stoics discuss as gendered or sexual, and the role of these phenomena in the Stoic theory of a human being. Further, I will analyze how gender and sexuality are related to the Stoic ethics and the ideals of virtue and wisdom. Finally, I investigate how the Stoics view these phenomena in terms of interpersonal relationships that also affect society and politics. In order to arrive at a fuller understanding of Stoic arguments and to position them in a philosophical context, I also consider their background in the Ancient philosophical traditions of Plato and Aristotle. As I will show, the Stoics often take an exceptionally bold line in departing both from their predecessors' theoretical views, as well as from the notions on gender embedded in their contemporary culture. I also draw evidence from other Ancient sources such as Galen's medical treatises and texts by

Skeptic, Epicurean, and other rivaling schools of philosophy. However, a more systematic comparison between the Stoics and other schools of the Hellenistic and Roman era will unfortunately fall outside of the scope of this study.

Given that all areas of philosophy are systematically related in Stoicism, and that the discussions on gender and sexuality are scattered throughout the sources, I will investigate Stoic philosophy as a whole, covering their metaphysics, physics, ethics, and political thought. Furthermore, in scrutinizing specific related topics (such as Stoic views on embryology, or the female exemplifications and idealizations used in the sources) I wish to broaden our understanding of Stoic philosophy and to introduce new topics into Ancient philosophical scholarship. I believe that this comprehensive approach corresponds to the nature of Stoicism, but also to the complexity of the problem itself. The question of gender and sexuality is, on the one hand, a theoretical one: it concerns how we conceive of human beings, their capacities, bodies, and characters. On the other hand, it is highly practical, concerning how we grow up and form our identities in a certain cultural and historical situation. Gender and sexuality affect our moral agency and our choices in relation to other humans, and in relation to ourselves and our bodies. They affect intimate choices such as how we dress, present ourselves or embellish our looks, or how we act as sexual subjects. The question is also political given the implications related to the position of gender and sexual ethics in the society in which we live, or as we imagine it to be in an ideal society.

The Stoics were concerned with all of these sides of the problem (including the questions of dressing and beautification), and they are all of relevance in today's world, contemporary philosophy, and feminism. I hope my study will open up new perspectives not only for readers with a general interest in Stoicism and Ancient philosophy, but also for those interested in gender and sexuality as current philosophical questions. Through a systematic discussion of Stoic views I wish to shed light on these very questions: their philosophical relevance, their complexity as a subject of philosophical inquiry, and problems related to defining central concepts such as "equality" in current gender-related debates. Through Ancient Stoic views, this book provides a historical background and a detailed philosophical analysis, which I believe is also relevant to the contemporary debate on gender and sexuality.

1.1 Mapping the Terrain: Gender in Stoic Sources and Scholarship

The Stoic school of philosophy flourished from the time of its founder Zeno of Citium (ca. 334–262 BCE) to the late Stoic thinker and emperor of Rome, Marcus Aurelius (121–180 CE). This book covers the entire era of Ancient Stoicism, including both Hellenistic and Roman materials. Unavoidably, there is much more textual material from the later Roman Stoics, since none of the original works of the early thinkers have survived, and the research, therefore, has to rely on secondhand sources such as the testimony of other Ancient philosophers or doxographers. However, our sources both on early and Roman Stoicism include highly relevant arguments on gender, and there are both important continuums and differences between the early and the late school. Indeed, certain later Stoic arguments on gender make sense precisely against the backdrop of earlier Stoic theories, and therefore I find it both interesting and necessary to discuss Ancient Stoicism on the whole. All of these sources must be treated with terminological and historical accuracy and read within their own cultural, historical, and philosophical contexts. Particularly, in the case of such potentially controversial issues as sexuality, translations of the original texts can sometimes be inaccurate, or even misleading. However, even though I make several remarks on the Greek and Latin terminology, the focus of this book is primarily philosophical, not philological.

The original Stoic sources include fascinating discussions on gender and sexuality, and these topics are highly relevant in today's world and philosophy. Therefore it is surprising how little attention these topics have attracted in the scholarship on Stoicism. Before this book, there was no monograph focusing specifically on gender and/or sexuality in Stoicism, nor is there a systematic account of their roles in Stoic philosophy as a whole. Thus, one of the important tasks of this book is to fill this lacuna and shift the focus in our way of approaching Ancient Stoicism. As this book demonstrates, when it comes to gender, the lacuna in Stoic scholarship is not due to lack of relevant material in the original sources. Rather, it reflects those questions that the readers pose to the sources and how they evaluate their findings: what is considered central and what marginal. The prism of gender, I claim, opens fresh perspectives to the entire Stoic philosophical enterprise.

Even though there are no extensive studies precisely on gender and sexuality, there are important scholarly contributions to specific parts of this topic, in particular, concerning the relevant questions in Stoic ethics, philosophical practice, and political theory. Of particular importance to my discussion in this book are Julia Annas, who has analyzed the significance of close human relations such as family ties in Stoic ethics (1993), Martha Nussbaum, who has discussed the role of gender in Stoic moral education and philosophical therapy, and scrutinized Musonius Rufus' views on gender from a feminist point of view (1994, 2002), and Gretchen Reydams-Schils, who has investigated Roman Stoic views on marriage and family life, and highlighted the gendered aspects of these views (2005). Malcolm Schofield's reading of Stoic social utopias also pays attention to gender, and this work has an established position in the scholarly discussion on Stoicism whenever gender is mentioned (1991). Katja Vogt discusses gender and sexual ethics in her analysis of the Stoic cosmic city (2008). Brad Inwood's article, "Why do fools fall in love?" focuses on Stoic views of *erôs* (1997), and Elizabeth Asmis discusses gender in Stoic political thought in her article, "Stoics on Women" (1996). I also found it useful for the feminist scope of this book to look at how contemporary feminist thinkers such as Michèle LeDoeuff (2003) approach history of philosophy even if they usually don't explicitly discuss the Stoics.

As important as all of these mentioned scholarly contributions are, with the exception of Inwood's and Asmis' articles, none of them focus on the philosophical questions of gender and sexuality as such. Further, Stoic scholarship almost exclusively discusses these issues in the context of ethics and politics and neglects their role in metaphysics and physics. David E. Hahm (1977) and Kathy Gaca (2003) refer to the sexual myths found in Stoic cosmology but do not enter into a more systematic discussion of sexuality and gender in Stoic metaphysics and physics.

I also noticed that there is a tendency in the scholarship to present the Stoic position on gender through a comparison to Plato and Aristotle, usually by pointing out a similarity to the former or a difference to the latter, but without entering a detailed analysis. Since Plato, Aristotle, and the Stoics represent remarkably different types of philosophy, I found it necessary to take a closer look at the theoretical context in which each of them present their views on gender and sexuality. My analysis usually emphasizes the originality of the Stoic position in relation to their predecessors.

Finally, my approach derives inspiration from Michel Foucault's reading of Ancient Stoicism. Foucault turned to study of Antiquity, paying special attention to Stoicism, in his late philosophy of the 1980s, particularly in his *History of Sexuality* volumes II and III and his 1981–1982 lectures at the Collège de France published as *The Hermeneutics of the Subject*. Although he was not a Stoic scholar, he offers an interesting assessment of the role of sexuality in Stoicism. Even more important, as far as the present investigation is concerned, is his insight that a reading of Ancient thinking is also a project of rethinking our own era.[1] When investigating Ancient views on sexuality and gender, one also becomes aware of the historicity of the ways of thinking about these phenomena, and indeed of how they are constituted in their very materiality, as in the case of Stoic physical exercises for controlling sexuality.

Many scholars have criticized Foucault for historical inaccuracy, and also my reading takes a critical stance to several of his conclusion. Nevertheless, I would claim in a Foucauldian spirit that the reading of Ancient philosophical views with historical sensitivity and philosophical precision offers insights into the historical process in which the current thinking on gender and sexuality, as well as the practices and customs for dealing with them, were formed. I hope that the reader of this study, whether interested primarily in Ancient thinking or the philosophy of gender and sexuality, will find it useful not only in enhancing understanding of the Stoic views but also in facilitating a critical rethinking of present-day conceptions, as well as our ways of approaching Ancient philosophical texts.

1.2 Some Qualifications

What do we actually study when we study gender and sexuality in Ancient Stoic philosophy? One might also ask why I have chosen to connect the two concepts, "gender" and "sexuality," instead of focusing on one or the other. Further, the two concepts might sound suspiciously modern and thus anachronistic in the context of Ancient thought. For example, a reader of Michel Foucault's *History of Sexuality* might point out that the concept of "sexuality" first arose in the nineteenth century

---

[1] Foucault presents his genealogical method, or his "history of the present," e.g., in the preface to Foucault 1990b: 1–13; cf. Foucault 1988: 262.

medical discourse and thus did not, as such, occur in Ancient texts. I will first address the question concerning the two main terms I use in this study, and then explain why I chose to bring them together.

The practice of observing genital and other physical differences between the female and the male and having human beings called "women" and "men" obviously existed before the concept of "gender" was introduced, as did the experiencing of lust and desire, and the performing of acts such as caressing and making love. Ancient thinkers, including the Stoics, observed not only the existence of these phenomena but also the power they have in human life, affecting emotions, choices, self-control as well as the goals and conditions of life. Moreover, Ancient thinkers, in general, gave considerable attention to gender and sexuality as philosophical problems, specifically with regard to how they influence people's bodies, minds, lives, and happiness. Given this central role in everyday life and self-understanding, they also had considerable philosophical relevance in Ancient philosophy, not least in Stoicism that explicitly aimed to serve a therapeutic purpose in offering guidance on living a happy, everyday life.

Nevertheless, neither "gender" nor "sexuality" has a specific equivalent in Greek or Latin terminology, and the Stoics (as well as other Ancient thinkers) used a range of notions to refer to similar phenomena. I use "sexuality" (in Greek often *aphrodisia*; or different concepts derived from *erós*) to refer to sexual conduct, lust, and pleasure. I use "gender" to refer to the Stoic conception of men and women, including the discussion of their physical differences, their respective characteristics, distinctive social roles, and spheres of life. Even if the binary view of gender is dominant in the sources, it should also be noted that at least some Ancient thinkers acknowledged that gender is more complicated than a straightforward distinction into exactly two groups, men and women. For example, Aristotle and Galen discuss transgressions of binary gender categories in different animal species that are not sexually dimorphic. The authors of the original texts sometimes refer to "the male and the female" (*arren, thêly*), particularly, but not exclusively in biological discussions, and sometimes to "men and women" (*anêr, gynê*), and study of gender often takes place within the general philosophical theories on human beings (*anthrôpos*). Some sources specifically use the concept of *genos* (in the general meaning "a kind" or "genus") in referring to gender. However, my research is not restricted to these concepts.

The Ancient thinkers were obviously unaware of the terminological distinction between "sex" and "gender" that is central to the contemporary feminist philosophy, and in this book I also use "gender" in a broad sense, encompassing biology, hygiene, and clothing as well as education and social life. As we shall see, the Ancient Stoic view comprehends both sides since they discuss gender as not only natural or biological (in the sense of what many contemporary thinkers understand as "sex") but importantly as socially and culturally constructed (the modern sense of "gender"). The sources do not reveal how exactly the Stoics understood the relationship between these different aspects of gender, but their general tendency is to emphasize the inborn similarity between men and women, and claim that many gendered features are produced by the surrounding culture.

In order to counter possible objections concerning the connection between these two terms, I wish to draw attention to the phenomena themselves. Gender roles are often understood in terms of sexual roles (and vice versa), and it would be difficult, and often artificial, to distinguish between them. This is also clear in my sources. As an obvious example, in Ancient embryological theories, "being a male" and "being a female" are defined sexually in terms of their different functions in procreation. On the other hand, Ancient sexual ethics deals with questions such as whether a good man should prefer the erotic love of boys or of women. These are only two examples of how discussions on gender and sexuality coincide in the sources, and why I find it relevant to discuss them together. Moreover, the very connection between gender and sexuality raises further interesting and more detailed questions, such as whether sexual ethics are the same for men and women.

Finally, I wish to address possible objections concerning the scope of this work. I already commented why I chose to look at the Stoic sources through a wide lens. Since this is, to my knowledge, the first systematic research on the topic, I did not want to narrow my scope down to scrutinize gender and sexuality in only one part of Stoic philosophy. One could ask, however, why I have dedicated so many pages to Plato and Aristotle while my discussion of many other non-Stoic thinkers, such as Galen and Epicurus, is much more limited. In the final phase of finishing this book, it was pointed out to me how many fascinating research questions would arise from a more detailed comparison between the Stoic and Epicurean schools of philosophy whose rivalry in their own days was often expressed in explicitly gendered terms: Stoicism was commonly considered "masculine" and Epicureanism "feminine" type of philosophy. Whereas I do dedicate Sect. 9.1, "Manly Stoics, Effeminate Epicureans" to the gendered images of these two schools of philosophy, I decided to leave a more extensive discussion of this topic for future research. Entering a vast and largely unexplored area as my research has been, I came to realize that it would be impossible to turn each and every stone along the way. I also wanted to maintain a clear focus on analyzing the Stoic metaphysical conception of gender and how this view is reflected in their discussions on children, education, character, family, and politics. To accomplish this task, it was important for me to include chapters on Plato and Aristotle since as predecessors of the Stoic school, they provide us with invaluable evidence of philosophical theories, debates, and concepts concerning gender and sexuality that existed already before the Stoics. Indeed, we can see how the Stoics often partake into these preexisting discussions, sometimes adapting views of their predecessors but more often than not, as I many times emphasize in this book, expressing a largely original position on gender and sexuality. Furthermore, I will show that against the backdrop of earlier theories it is possible to make sense of certain fragmentary Stoic arguments that may be confusing in their own right. I have included passages on authors like Xenophon, Galen, and Epicurus as far as this has helped me to articulate the Stoic position. However, even though I have aimed my research to be systematic, it is by no means exhaustive (as no philosophical work can be), and I wholeheartedly wish that it will inspire future research to fill in the gaps.

1.3 The Structure and Main Arguments

This book consists of three parts, an introductory, and a concluding chapter. The three parts are divided into chapters, subchapters, and sections. I start each part by briefly placing the Stoic views into a historical and philosophical continuum by introducing some of the most important theoretical discussion that their views dialogue with.

Part I, entitled *The Body: Gender from Generation to Decoration*, investigates the role and importance of gender and sexuality in Stoic metaphysical views on the human body and the soul (understood in Stoicism as corporeal). By way of a philosophical background, Chap. 2, *The Origin of Gender: Myths and Biology*, examines explanations of gender dimorphism among earlier Ancient thinkers: Plato's philosophical myths, and the scientific/medical models of Aristotle and Galen.

Some scholars read the Stoic cosmology as a "biological myth" and maintain that the origin of the Stoic *kosmos* was sexual. The sources illustrate the two principles of Stoic metaphysics, understood as active and passive, by a sexual encounter between Zeus and Hera. In Chap. 3, *Semen, Zeus, and the Birth of Cosmos: Gender in Stoic Cosmogony and Cosmology*, I argue that the sexual and gendered illustrations should be understood as analogies helping us to understand the Stoic metaphysical principles, not as indicating that the Stoics understood these principles in gendered or sexual terms as such. Interestingly, then, the dichotomy between the "passive" and "active" elements did not receive a gendered interpretation in Stoicism (as it did e.g., in Aristotle, as well as a great part of Western philosophy after him).

Through a detailed discussion of a wide range of relevant passages in Chap. 4, *The Metaphysical Insignificance of Gender*, I show that Stoic metaphysics considers gender to be insignificant (*adiaphoron*). On the level of rationality, which for the Stoics is the most essential human feature, there is no difference between men and women. Furthermore, I scrutinize the position of gender in the categories of Stoic metaphysics, and posit that genderedness should be understood as a "common quality" (*koinos poion*), in other words, something all human beings have, but whether one is of a specific gender, for example, a woman, is to be understood as an individual quality (*idios poion*). According to the Stoics, the reproductive capacity is one of the rational capacities of the human soul, which makes gender appear as comparable to the senses. Thus, one's gender is as irrelevant for human rationality as, say, eye color is for the sight. This view has radical and far-reaching consequences for the ethical and political theories explored in parts II and III.

Chapter 5, entitled *Perfumed Men and Bearded Philosophers—The Stoics on Signs of Gender*, investigates gender as it appears on the surface of the body: in cosmetics, hairs, and the like. Original Stoic sources include extensive discussions of physical beauty and gendered signs such as beards. I argue that the Roman Stoic thinkers give considerable philosophical attention to hairs, beards, and scents because of their general focus on everyday life, in which they take existing customs and social expectations seriously. For these reasons, "indifferent things" such as beards could have something they call "selective value." Finally, in Chap. 6, *Fiery and Cold Natures—Stoic Physiognomics of Gender*, I analyze the Stoic notions of distinct feminine and masculine characteristics, such as "women are prone to weeping," which I relate to Ancient physiognomics, a theory that assumes a genuine connection between the body and personal characteristics. The traces of physiognomic thought found both in early and later Stoic texts lead me to investigate gender not just as a bodily phenomenon but also as something potentially affecting people's characters and emotional lives.

Part II, entitled *Character: Education of Gender and Therapy of Sexuality* discusses gender and sexuality in Stoic views on education and character. The main philosophical problems in this part concern the origin of gendered characteristics, the educability of girls and boys, the ideal of happiness, and the role of sexuality in Stoic philosophical therapy. I propose that, in addition to discussing physical masculine and feminine features (as in the context of physiognomy), the Stoics also considered gendered characteristics as products of cultural habituation. In terms of Stoic ethics, the philosophical weight is on the latter, in other words socially and culturally produced gendered characteristics.

Chapter 7, *Gender, Character, and Education from Classic to Hellenistic Thought*, provides background for the Stoic views by discussing critically the educational models of Plato's *Republic* and Aristotle's ethics. Against this background, we can also see how radical the Stoic position on girls' education and female happiness was in its time. Chapter 8, *The Stoics on Equal Educability of Girls and Boys, and the Origin of Gendered Characteristics*, shows how in Stoicism, childhood is considered, for the most part, a gender-neutral phase of human life. The assumption in the discussion is that girls and boys are equally educable for the highest purpose of life, which is to become fully rational, virtuous, and happy (which go together in Stoicism). The Roman Stoic Musonius argued that girls and boys should be educated in exactly the same manner. I show that this position follows naturally from premises commonly accepted by Stoic thinkers from Zeno to the Romans.

It is also crucial to examine critically the goal of Stoic philosophy, that is, the character of the sage, and whether this ideal is gendered or not. As I show in Chap. 9, *To Become Properly Manly—Gender, Happiness, and the Figure of the Sage*, the Ancient sources often contrast the Stoic "masculinity" with Epicurean "femininity," and thus these two different styles of philosophy with their respective goals (rationality versus pleasure) are presented in gendered terms. I suggest that the Stoic sage must indeed get rid of certain "effeminate" characteristics (given that characteristics such as vanity are classified as feminine), but that it does not follow from this that it was easier for men to become sages than it was for women. On the contrary, I will show that both men and women undergo several radical changes in Stoic philosophical therapy in order to become happy, and that the Stoic position is also critical about several traditional traits of masculinity.

Even though the Stoics considered sexuality as such ethically neutral, they give it an important role in their ethical theory. For the purpose of providing practical tools for striving toward happiness, Stoicism introduces philosophical exercises, some of which are explicitly related to sexuality. I analyze these exercises in Chap. 10, *How to Take "Certain Spasms" Calmly—Sexuality in Stoic Philosophical Therapy*. I show that even though several thinkers recommend abstinence from sexual relations, it does not follow that sexuality would be absent from the life of the sage. Abstinence is not a goal in itself, but a means of striving for freedom: so that one can control one's acts and emotions and thus make a free choice in any circumstances. The central ethical problem thus concerns virtuous erotic agency, and the goal is to control one's impressions and act right in one's intimate relationships.

Part III, entitled **Community: Marriage, Family, and Human Bonding** scrutinizes gender and sexuality in Stoic social and political philosophy, highlighting the roles of marriage, family life, and cosmopolitanism. Stoic ideas on social philosophy fall roughly into two categories: those concerning the ideal society and the community of sages, and those concerning real societies, which are far from perfect but in which one must still strive for happiness and to take care of ones social obligations. Gender is a prominent topic in both contexts.

Chapter 11, *Gender, Politics, and Economics: From Plato's Utopianism to Cynic Radicalism*, provides a background and a theoretical context for the Stoic views by analyzing the drastically different ways marriage and family were discussed in Plato, Cynic philosophy, and in the Ancient science of economics (*oikonomia* or *oikonomikē*). Similar to Plato and the Cynics, the utopias of Zeno and Chrysippus reverse traditional sexual norms and abolish monogamous marriage, promoting polygamy instead. In Chap. 12 *"Holding Women in Common"—Gender in Early Stoic Utopias*, I propose that the arguments concerning the utopian state should be read as a thought experiment of what a perfectly virtuous society would be like. One significant result of this experiment is the realization that many of the traditional customs and institutions, such as institutionalized marriage and the external control of sexual relations, are irrelevant to true happiness and would not exist among perfectly virtuous individuals. There are also potential problems arising from the exclusively male perspective of the Stoic proposal (as well as of Plato, who famously promoted the "common ownership of wives" in his *Republic*). My analysis shows, however, that even though the early Stoics did not explicitly promote gender equality, this idea follows naturally from some generally accepted Stoic premises. In fact, the idea of a rational and equal community of male and female sages is inbuilt in the utopian ideal.

The Roman Stoics aimed primarily at guiding people toward a happy everyday life in a society they considered utterly corrupt. In this context, the philosophers were concerned with the question of whether marriage and family life were good choices for anyone aiming at living happily in a depraved world. As I will show in Chap. 13, entitled *Is it Possible to Marry and Be Happy? The Later Stoics on Matrimony and Modes of Life*, there were different Stoic stances on this problem, but all of them hold in common the idea that for those who do marry and start a family, their spouse, and children should form a crucial sphere in which to exercise virtue. One's family and spouse are in a privileged position also in the Stoic view of ethical growth, according to which general other-concern arises from the love experienced in close human relations. Finally, in Chap. 14, *Gender and Stoic Cosmopolitanism*, I will demonstrate that family and intimate human relationships provide the model for the acquisition of a comprehensive ethical outlook that finally encompasses the entire human kind.

References

Annas, Julia. 1993. *The Morality of Happiness*. Oxford: Oxford University Press.
Asmis, Elizabeth. 1996. The Stoics on Women. In *Feminism and Ancient Philosophy*, ed. Julie K. Ward. New York and London: Routledge.
Foucault, Michel. 1986. *History of Sexuality, volume 3: The Care of the Self*, trans. Robert Hurely. New York: Vintage Books.
Foucault, Michel. 1988. The Concern for Truth. In *Michel Foucault—Politics, Philosophy, Culture*, (1977–1984), trans. Alan Sheridan et al and ed. Lawrence D. Kritzman, 255–267. New York and London: Routledge.
Foucault, Michel. 1990a. *History of Sexuality, volume 1: An Introduction*, trans. Robert Hurely. New York: Vintage Books.
Foucault, Michel. 1990b. *History of Sexuality, volume 2: The Use of Pleasure*, trans. Robert Hurely. New York: Vintage Books.

Foucault, Michel. 2005. *The Hermeneutics of the Subject*. New York: Palgrave Macmillan.

Gaca, Kathy. 2003. *The Making of Fornication—Eros, Ethics and Political Reform in Greek Philosophy and Early Christianity*. Berkley and Los Angeles: The University of California Press.

Hahm, David E. 1977. *The Origins of Stoic Cosmology*. Columbus: Ohio State University Press.

Inwood, Brad. 1997. Why do fools fall in love? In *Aristotle and After*, ed. Richard Sorabji, Bulletin of the Institute of Classical Studies, Supplement 68.

LeDoeuff, Michèle. 2003. *The Sex of Knowing*, trans. Kathryn Hamer & Lorraine Code. New York and London: Routledge.

Nussbaum, Martha. 1994. *The Therapy of Desire: Theory and Practice in Hellenistic Ethics*. Princeton: Princeton University Press.

Nussbaum, Martha. 2002. The Incomplete Feminism of Musonius Rufus. In *The Sleep of Reason—Erotic Experience and Sexual Ethics in Ancient Greek and Rome*, ed. Martha Nussbaum and Juha Sihvola, 283–326. Chicago and London: The University of Chicago Press.

Reydams-Schils, Gretchen. 2005. *The Roman Stoic—Self, Responsibility, and Affection*. Chicago and London: The University of Chicago Press.

Schofield, Malcolm. 1991. *The Stoic Idea of the City*. Cambridge: Cambridge University Press.

Vogt, Katja. 2008. *Law, Reason, and the Cosmic City*. Oxford: Oxford University Press.

PART I

The Body: Gender From Generation to Decoration

CHAPTER 2

The Origin of Gender: Myths and Biology

2.1 Plato's Philosophical Myths of Gender and Sexuality

What is the origin of gender? One way for a philosopher to approach this question is to tell a myth: a fabulous story that fabricates an account of the creation of humans as gendered and sexual beings. The Ancient culture was rich in mythology, and this heritage is present also in the philosophical texts. Even though it is often stated that Ancient philosophy distanced itself from the mythical world and searched for rational explanations instead, philosophers frequently both allude to the traditional myths of their times and create myths of their own for comprising their views. Particularly, such topics as passion and love, which powerfully affect our emotions and courses of life, often seem to escape plain theoretical arguments, and call for mythical and poetic expressions.

Among Ancient thinkers, Plato (ca. 428–347 BCE) in particular is famous for intertwining imaginative myths and rational arguments, and recent scholarship tends to emphasize the importance of the mythical form for his philosophical thinking.[1] In this chapter, I will analyze mythical explanations of gender dimorphism and sexual lust in Plato's *Symposium* and *Timaeus*. These myths form a fruitful backdrop for my

---

[1] See, e.g., Catalin Partenie (2009: 1–26), Kristin Sampson (2004: 17–34), Cynthia Freeland (2004: 33–49).

later analysis of the Stoic theories, but they are also highly valuable in their own right as they neatly condense many underlying philosophical problems concerning gender and sexuality.

2.1.1 Genders, Planets, and Lust: Aristophanes' Speech

Probably the most famous Ancient philosophical myth of gender and sexuality originates in Aristophanes' speech in *Symposium*. The comedian Aristophanes begins his eulogy to Eros, understood both as the personified male god of love and generally erotic passion, with an account of the origin of mankind.[2] At the beginning, Aristophanes narrates, humans did not look the same as they do now but were round like balls, each with two faces and two pairs of hands and legs on each side.[3] They also had two sets of genitals, and thus the number of genders was not two but three because a person could have two male or two female genitals or one of each. The third group, those having both types of genitals, was called androgynies, stemming from the Greek words *anêr*, signifying man, and *gynê*, signifying woman.[4] Aristophanes explains the number and respective natures of the genders by stating that the man is the offspring of the Sun, the woman of the Earth and the androgyny of the Moon. (*Symp.* 190b.) In traditional Greek mythology, Helios, the Sun, is personified as a god, and Gaea is the primordial goddess of the earth—as we shall see, the connection between the female gender and the earth prevails throughout Ancient thinking.[5] Selene, the Moon, is depicted as a goddess and the sister of Helios. It is remarkable that despite the association to the planets, Aristophanes' myth does not describe the round people as significantly different from each other, and we are invited to imagine that their bodies were of similar sizes and strengths.

According to Aristophanes, the division into two genders—as we know human beings today—occurred when the round people became

---

[2] On *erós* in Antiquity, see also David Halperin (2002a, b); Shadi Bartsch and Thomas Bartscherer (2005); Nussbaum and Sihvola (eds.) (2002).

[3] In Plato's *Timaeus*, it is stated that the round form is most perfect and self-similar (33b).

[4] Here, the Greek term *androgynos* signifies a combination of the male and the female, but in other contexts the term could also denote an effeminate man. Aristophanes' speech mentions that the term generally is used as an insult (189e).

[5] On the Ancient myths of the earth goddess Gaea, cf. Marilyn Skinner (2013: 31–36).

impudent and defied their gods. This led Zeus and the other gods to decide to weaken their power by cutting them in two—as one might divide an apple or an egg with a hair (*Symp.* 190e). By so doing, the gods gave birth to humans walking on two legs and possessing only one pair of genitals, those of a man or of a woman. The split humans tried desperately to find their missing halves. However, when two lonesome halves finally found each other, they wanted nothing but to stay in a close embrace, and the human kind started to die of starvation. At this stage, their genitals were on the back, but in order not to let the human race die out, the gods decided to move their genitals to the front in order to allow sexual intercourse. Now the halves could at least momentarily feel fulfillment, but still go on in their lives as separate entities. Thus, the splitting and moving of the genitals to the front side of their bodies also gave rise to sexual lust, which the myth depicts as a person's longing to find her or his "other half" (*Symp.* 191a–d).

This is also when sexual reproduction between a male and a female is introduced, since previously humans had reproduced by sawing directly on the ground "like cicadas." The dialogue is not specific on exactly what role gender played in the reproduction of the first humans. The comparison to cicadas would seem to suggest that the female laid down fertilized eggs, and thus both the male and the female produced a seed of some kind.[6] As I will show later in the context of biological theory, the Ancient embryologies had different ways of depicting the male and the female reproductive roles, and one specific debate concerned whether or not the female produced seed—or provided anything at all but a "hollow space" in reproduction.

Aristophanes' speech is fascinating as its vivid storytelling provides a mythical explanation both of the birth of gender dimorphism and the nature of sexual desire. Interestingly, both of these are initially presented as a form of a punishment of the disobedience of the first humans.[7]

---

[6] Kevin Corrigan and Elena Glazov-Corrigan point out that the cicada (*tettiges*) was the symbol of Athenian autochthony, and suggest that this association might have been intuitive for the participants of the symposium (2004: 78–79). Gary Alan Scott and William Welton read the comparison to cicadas as suggesting that the male/male and female/female combinations needed each other to reproduce (2008: 68). A chorus of cicadas appears also in Plato's *Phaedrus* (230c).

[7] Aristophanes' myth has also been compared to the myth of the Fall of the man in *Genesis*, cf. Scott and Welton (2008: 66).

When Zeus cut the round people in two, this not only weakened their physical power but also reduced the number of genders to two and condemned the individuals to a state of wanting and need. The original round people were self-satisfied and autonomous—apparently also in terms of sexuality. One the one hand, we could assume that the round people were utterly asexual and thus were free of lust and wanting.[8] One the other hand, we could assume that the round people were autoerotic, and received sexual pleasure from their two sets of genitals. Thus, they would not have needed anybody else for providing happiness or sexual satisfaction (or in the case of the androgynies, it seems, even to reproduce with).[9] By contrast, after being split into two, the humans are not any longer autonomous in relation to their happiness, but in a constant state of longing.

However, whereas sexual lust appears as a punishment, Aristophanes' myth presents sexual intercourse as an act of mercy. By this gift, the gods decided to save the human kind. Intercourse allows people, the former halves, to get relief from their desire which otherwise would literally make their lives unlivable (*Symp.* 191a–c). Thus, the view on sexuality in Aristophanes' myth is radically different from that of the later Christian thinkers who also discussed sexuality in terms of punishment. For example, the medieval philosopher St Augustine regards sexuality as both a punishment and a sin: It is a punishment because of the original sin of Adam and Eve, but lust in each person is also a source of sin in its own

---

[8] Gary Alan Scott and William Welton seem to imply this kind of a reading when they suggest that the reproduction of the round humans would have been a passionless, cool and rational act, dictated by instinct (2008: 68–69).

[9] The myth of Aristophanes has inspired artistic imagination and love narratives, as well as psychological theory all the way to our days. I recommend the reader trying to imagine what the original round people might have looked like to consult *La Petite Bibliothèque Philosophique, vol 1: Platon, Le Banquet* by the French cartoon artist Joann Sfar (2002), as well as a short French animation film *Discours d'Aristophane* by Pascal Szidon (2005). Both Sfar's and Szidon's visual works offer a vivid interpretation of Aristophanes' speech in general, and of the questions concerning gender and sexuality it raises in particular. They also give two different interpretations of the sexual activity of the round people. Szidon's film does not suggest that they copulated, but indicates that sexual conduct took place only after they had been split in two. Sfar, in contrast, illustrates how a round person could have copulated with its own other half. This reading, even if not based on any specific passage of the original text, is intuitive and also gives another reason why already the original, round human species had genitals—they used them as a medium for sexual pleasure.

right. As an example of this punishment, St Augustine discusses "the disobedience" of the (male) genitals, in other words the fact that a man's willpower might turn too weak to control his penis.[10] However, the view of sexuality as inherently sinful is absent from Aristophanes' account (and, as we shall see, from Ancient sexual ethics in general). The core of the punishment in Aristophanes' story is that as a consequence of sexual lust, the person is no longer self-sufficient. In the case of St Augustine, however, sexuality is always a punishment, and therefore also the ethical nature of sexual intercourse remains problematic.

Furthermore, it is worth noting that Aristophanes' myth does not take any moral stance to the different sexual preferences. By contrast, all the forms of sexual desires are presented on the same level: a man who desires a man or a woman, and a woman who desires a man or a woman. In this respect, the myth is exceptional even among Ancient sources which mostly do not discuss lesbian love—with the notable exception of the lyric poet Sappho from the island of Lesbos (c. 610–570 BCE). On the other hand, the Ancient thinkers commonly refer to pederasty, in other words, erotic relationships between an older man and a younger boy, referred to in the sources as *erastés* (lover) and *erómenos* (the loved one).[11] Even though these relations are widely discussed in the sources, they are rarely presented as morally equal with male–female relationships: For example, in Plato's *Symposium*, Pausanias' speech ranks pederastic relations categorically higher than male–female relationships. Aristophanes also alludes to this hierarchy when he states that the best of men are those who love other men, and calls them most "manly,"

---

[10] On St Augustine's views on sexual desire, see, e.g., his *Marriage and Virginity* and *Answer to the Pelagians II: Marriage and Desire*, which includes the passages entitled "To Blame Carnal Desire Is Not to Condemn Marriage," "On the Disease of Carnal Desire," and "The Disobedience of the Members is Punishment for Sin." The last mentioned deals with the question of involuntary movement of the penis. As just these few titles indicate, the view on sexuality is largely negative.

[11] The Greek categories and practices, as well as moral sensibilities concerning sexuality remarkably differed from ours, and therefore it has become somewhat commonplace in scholarship to point out the anachronism of calling the pederastic practices "homosexuality." Marilyn Skinner gives the following definition: "Pederasty designated the social custom whereby adult male Greeks courted citizen youths, as sexual objects but also as (...) protégés" (2013: 14). Indeed, pederastic relations often served a pedagogical function. On scholarship on pederasty, see K.J. Dover (1989), Marilyn Skinner (2013), James Davidson (2007).

referring to the Greek virtue of courage (*andreia*, literally "manliness"). He also mentions that adulterers most often originate from the former androgynies. Yet he does not argue that there was a natural hierarchy between men and women as such, or that lesbian love was less natural than other sexualities. Interestingly, the logical consequence of Aristophanes' myth is that what we would today call heterosexuality stems from what originally was the androgyny, and that consequently, only one-third of the people would originate from this alternative (assuming that there was a fairly equal amount of all of the three original genders) (*Symp.* 191d–192b).

Aristophanes' speech has often been read as merely bringing comic relief to the conversation of the *Symposium*. However, it seems to portray the human lot as a fundamentally tragic one: The source of our happiness is somewhere outside of ourselves, in something that is not completely up to us to find or to keep. Yet our lives seem to be dictated by this desperate search for "the right one." So what is his story, really—a piece of tragedy, or a piece of comedy?

I tend to agree with Martha Nussbaum who finds Aristophanes' story comic because it describes creatures that are physically different from us, but we cannot but recognize that it is still about us. According to her, the myth asks us to look at ourselves from a distance, as if we were observing another species, and by so doing to question our familiar anthropocentric perspective. As Nussbaum points out, Aristophanes' myth makes us wonder about the nature of our own bodies and desires, even the rationale of lovemaking since the biological act of generation was more functional when the first humans still saw directly on the ground (Nussbaum 1986/2001: 172).

Building on Nussbaum's interpretation, I consider Aristophanes' speech to be a truly philosophical myth since in a vivid and entertaining form, it introduces vital philosophical questions concerning gender, sexuality, love, and the human existence in general.[12] Furthermore, it invites the reader to enter a philosophical investigation on the myth's hidden meanings, and thus the myth appears to be a helpful tool of philosophical inquiry. To understand the mysteries of love and sexuality, philosophical argument alone might not be enough, and sometimes there is a need

---

[12] Also Corrigan and Glazov-Corrigan discuss Aristophanes' speech as a case in point of a philosophical myth that leads to logical analysis (2004: 224).

for presentations that make us laugh or cry. The very end of *Symposium* seems to release the tension between comedy and tragedy by declaring that these two genres fundamentally require the same qualities from the poet (*Symp.* 223d). Implicitly, this resolution also suggests that these qualities are required from the philosopher, as well.

I will return to the question concerning the relationship between tragedy and philosophy in the context of Stoic ethics. As I will show, Aristophanes' story illustrates exactly the kind of a view that the Stoic ethics attempts to deny: In other words, that something or somebody else was truly necessary for our happiness, and that consequently, our lives would constantly be on the verge of tragedy.

2.1.2 Noble Birth Without Sex—Pausanias and Socrates

Also Pausanias' speech in *Symposium* relates a myth in its account on *erôs*. Pausanias distinguishes between two different kinds of love, the good and the bad, and connects the former with the heavenly (*ourania*) and the latter with the common (*pandêmon*) Eros and Aphrodite, Greek gods of love. The myth depicts the heavenly Aphrodite as a motherless daughter of Uranus, the god of the heavens, and the younger, common Aphrodite as the daughter of Zeus and a mortal woman named Dione. Pausanias states that the heavenly Aphrodite is greater than her common sister because *she is not born of a female* (*Symp.* 181a–e). Pausanias thus presupposes that the greatest things do not have a sexual origin, nor do they emanate from the female gender.[13] The distinction between good and bad *erôs* is interesting because the Stoic sources later present an apparently similar standpoint.[14]

---

[13] Phaedrus' speech in *Symposium* makes a similar point in claiming that Eros is the greatest of all the gods because *he has no parents* (in Greek mythology, Eros is depicted both as a primordial God and son of Chaos, and as the son of the goddess of love Aphrodite). Thus, he supposes that the god who causes sexual lust in people does not have a sexual origin himself (*Symp.* 178b). Here, again, is an interesting parallel to Christianity, according to which Adam and Eve were born without a sexual origin, and sexuality and sexual birth were introduced in human life only after the fall. Also Jesus has no sexual origin since he was born of a virgin.

[14] Ancient scholar Brad Inwood even claims that Pausanias' views "actually inspired the early Stoics in their reflections of love" (1997: 56). Whether or not the Stoics were inspired by Pausanias' speech is a highly speculative question, and in Sect. 10.1. I will a present reading according to which, despite of certain similarities, Pausanias' and the Stoics' positions on erotic love are significantly different.

Pausanias connects love in general and sexual lust in particular with the works of Eros. Pausanias asserts that sexual lust (the "bad *erôs*") results from the common Eros, who drives people to fulfill their bodily desires without caring whether or not they do it virtuously. He also claims that it is this kind of love that makes men desire boys and women equally: the main thing being to get pleasure, no matter what kind or with whom. By contrast, the heavenly and good Eros makes people want to love and be loved beautifully. A lover like this wants to become a good person, and to help others to become good through love. This kind of love is directed toward a steady object, namely the person's soul and character, rather than something changing like the physical body. However, Pausanias also claims that the heavenly Eros makes men love other men, not women. In other words, it makes older men desire to become lovers and younger men desire to be loved (i.e., take up the roles of *erastês* and *erômenos* in a pederastic relationship). According to Pausanias, this is due to the fact that men, by nature, constitute the physically stronger (*to physei errômenos*) gender and have greater minds (*noun mallon ekhon*).[15]

Socrates' speech also ascribes a mythical origin to erotic love. This speech is original in the Ancient sources, because here Socrates reports a philosophical account of love as was taught to him by a woman named Diotima. Diotima's character brings up the important question concerning the relationship between wisdom, love, and gender, and whether or not both genders are considered to be equally capable of being virtuous lovers in erotic life, or lovers of wisdom in philosophical life.

According to Socrates/Diotima, Eros has the most peculiar origin: He is the child of Poros and Penia, richness and poverty. Penia had entered the gods' drinking party, found Poros asleep and took the advantage of the man by having him beget a child to her. Thus, Eros is a truly ambiguous figure, a mixture of two different inheritances: half-human and half-god, half-mortal and half-immortal; a mixture of extreme wealth and total poverty. Eros affects humans and animals by creating sexual desire that spurs them on to procreate. This desire is about reaching toward something more lasting than oneself, and finally seeking immortality. Animals and many (possibly most) humans seek immortality by conceiving and giving birth to new members of the species that come to replace those who die. However, Eros also makes some people surpass

---

[15] There is a pun here with the words *errômenos* (stronger) and *erômenos* (the loved one).

their mortality through immortal acts such as writing poetry or—even better—admiring the everlasting idea of beauty.[16]

Like Pausanias, Socrates/Diotima also differentiates between pederastic and male–female relations, suggesting that men "who are pregnant in their bodies" seek the company of women, whereas men who are "pregnant in their souls" prefer the company of other men. The noblest effects of love are reached through pederastic love where the lover ascends from loving the body of the beloved to loving his soul, and finally to love the idea of beauty itself (*Symp.* 207a–211c). As with Pausanias, this account seems to presuppose that the erotic subject is a man, not a woman—or at least they fail to specify that what they say holds reciprocally for women as well. However, if it were the case that the highest level of love was not possible for women, it would seem odd that Plato created a female character, Diotima, to express this view. The dialogue clearly presumes that she is a sage who has knowledge (*epistêmê*) and not only beliefs (*doxa*) about love. But why should she, as a woman, then prefer pederastic relations? I suggest that the hierarchy between pederasty and male–female relations may arise from the different social natures of these relationships. In the Ancient context, pederastic relations were not merely sexual (even though this was not excluded), but had importantly a pedagogic function, whereas male–female relations (with a great likelihood) would lead to reproduction. This is particularly true in the context of a society in which, first, even if there were some means of contraception, they could not be considered particularly reliable, and second, women were almost without exception left uneducated. Thus, the preference of pederastic

---

[16]Scholars have been debating how the conception of love in *Symposium* should be understood. According to Gregory Vlastos, the dialogue implies that particular individuals cannot be proper objects of love because they are imperfect, and only perfect beings can be both loved and known in the proper sense of the word (Vlastos 1973: 1–34). Martha Nussbaum challenges this reading, and focusing specifically on the final speech of *Symposium*, that of the young Alcibiades who is passionately in love with Socrates, she draws attention to the importance of unique individuals as objects of love (Nussbaum 1986/2001). More recently, Lorelle D. Lamascus has emphasized the importance of the myth of Poros and Penia for the philosophical account of love in *Symposium* (Lamascus 2016). Miira Tuominen offered an insightful reading in her yet unpublished manuscript on how love toward unique individuals is present also in the genealogy of Eros as a son of Poros and Penia (Tuominen, presentation at the University of Helsinki 2011/ unpublished manuscript). On the pedagogic function of *erôs* in *Symposium*, see Frisbee C.C. Sheffield (2006).

relations might denote a more general idea of preferring the cultivation of virtue in love relations, and thereby a preference of philosophical life over family life.[17] As we shall see, this type of a distinction is absent particularly in later Stoicism, and the later Stoics explicitly discuss the marriage between a man and a woman as a relationship that, at best, involves mutual philosophical development.

The myths discussed in this chapter turn to the works of gods and mythical events in order to explain the origin of lust. However, apart from Aristophanes' speech, gender difference is not really problematized in the dialogue: The Greek gods, to which the myths refer, were already gendered, and thus the myths already presuppose the notion of gender. Consequently, gender is viewed as a feature not only of mortal humans and animals, but also of the immortal gods. Thus, a philosophical inquiry concerning gender has to also take the underlying cosmological questions in account.

2.1.3 Women as Former Vicious Men—Plato's Timaeus

Plato's *Timaeus* is an exceptionally rich source of cosmological myths, or mythical cosmology. I will here only focus on a few parts of this complex dialogue, and draw attention to certain specific arguments on gender and sexuality that are particularly fruitful for forming a philosophical backdrop for my discussion of the Stoic views in the coming chapters.

The dialogue presents a mythical story of the creation of the universe through a gendered analogy: The source of creation is compared to the father, the recipient (*deksomenon*) to the mother, and what is engendered to the offspring. The role of the mother is presented in terms of void, like the empty space where the creation takes place (*Tim.* 50d–51a).

---

[17] My sources have surprisingly little to say on contraception or abortion. Aristotle possibly means some kind of pessaries when he mentions, in *GA*, a certain *prosthêta* that is evidently applied inside the vagina. According to Aristotle, the *prosthêta* shows that the uterus draws moisture into it, since the equipment in question is, in Aristotle's words, wet when applied but dry when removed (*GA* 739b5). I have not seen any scholarly comment on this passage that would give a better insight into what exactly Aristotle is discussing here. According to Galen, the Greek physician Hippocrates (ca. 460–375 BCE) wrote of a self-made abortion tactic he had advised for a singer "who kept company with men and who was obliged not to become pregnant, so that her price would not be lowered." Hippocrates had advised the girl to jump and kick her buttock, and after seven kicks, the girl had allegedly ejected the embryo (Galen, *On Semen*, I.4.28–33, transl. de Lacey).

Interestingly, this view of the mother, or the womb as a mere "container," to be filled by the male, is reflected also in Ancient embryological theories, to be discussed in the next subchapter.[18]

Furthermore, the dialogue also specifically addresses the question concerning gender dimorphism in humans, stating that the two genders correspond to the twofold human nature: men to the good part and women to the bad part. This also makes men the superior gender (*genos*) in the natural hierarchy of things (*Tim.* 42a–c). Gender division is presented as a process of degeneration where vicious and cowardly men are, as it were, punished of their bad lives by giving them a womanish nature (*gynaikos fysin*) in the second birth. Apparently, the dialogue indicates that this means being born in a female body, as well (*Tim.* 90e). Timaeus further states that a person who still does not lead a righteous life will be reborn as an animal which corresponds to the nature of his vices: for example, light-minded men would be reborn as birds (*Tim.* 42c; 91c). Thus, it seems, only a soul residing in the body of a man can be saved from the chain of reincarnation and return to its "home star," and the best thing that can happen to a woman is to be reborn as a man in the next reincarnation.

The mythical explanation of gender leads to a mythical explanation of sexual desire. In men, this desire arises in the genitals (*aidoion*), which become rebellious, maddened with desire (*epithymia*), and disobey reason (*Tim.* 91b). The corresponding desire in women resides in the womb (*métra*), which longs to be impregnated. If this desire is not fulfilled, "the animal inhabiting the womb" becomes restless and wanders through the body, causing various physical and mental disorders.[19] When a man and woman come together for reproduction, the male sows his seed in the woman's womb "as in the field" (*Tim.* 91c–d). However, in

---

[18]On feminist readings of this passage (*Tim.* 50c–52e), cf. Kristin Sampson (2004: 17–32); Cynthia Freeland (2004: 33–49).

[19]The image of a wandering womb, causing insanity in women, can be found in the Hippocratic tradition as well. This image reappears throughout the history of mental illness, and as Michel Foucault points out in *History of Madness*, the connection between the womb and the diagnosis of hysteria had a profound role in the conception of madness in the classic age. This connection stems from the Greek term *hystera* (womb) (Cf. Foucault 2006/1961: 277–290). Again, when *Timaeus* describes the male genitals as "becoming rebellious and masterful," there is a parallel to Christianity. As mentioned above, St Augustine discussed the "disobedience" of male genitals.

the cosmological context, Timaeus warns against comparing the mother to earth or any of the other elements, since the first recipient must be understood as being invisible and formless, and thus empty of any positive content (*Tim.* 50d–51d).

It is not clear, however, what we are supposed to understand as the "original" gender in *Timaeus*. If we read the dialogue as stating that vicious men's punishment was a rebirth as women, this would imply that the original gender is male and that the female gender is a deviation and a degenerated form. Is the ideal, then, that if everybody lived a good life, there would only be men? This question evokes a problem of the status of gender in Plato's metaphysics. Is there also a gender difference in the world of ideas, or is gender limited to the sensual world?[20]

If we read the myth with these questions in mind, we might notice that *Timaeus* discusses gender explicitly with reference to the sensual world. He does not mention gender among the everlasting things (such as the soul) that the demiurge created. When the gods were creating living beings, they decided to divide humans into two groups, men and women, in accordance with the "twofold human nature" (*Tim.* 42a). When the human species was created, the demiurge implanted understanding in the soul and placed the soul into the body (*Tim.* 30b). However, it is also suggested in the dialogue that the demiurge created the human soul but not the body, which was molded by younger gods. Within the body, the younger gods implanted "a mortal soul" which is subject to earthly affections (*Tim.* 42a–d). Timaeus states that the immortal soul is situated in the head, whereas the different parts of the mortal soul are scattered around the body below the throat. The marrow has a mediating function between the parts, and it is also called "the seed" and identified with the lust to reproduce (*Tim.* 72a–d). Underlying this physiological description, however, seems to be a view

---

[20] In his classic reading of Plato's *Timaeus*, Francis M. Cornford denies the interpretation that the male was the "original gender." He emphasizes that this myth should not be read as a historical account suggesting that men came about first, and women only later. He points out that *erôs* is implanted in men and women alike and is physically connected to the seed that is situated in the marrow (1937/1997: 291–209; 355–357). However, this reading does not provide any alternative explanation of how we should understand gender division in *Timaeus*, or why it is presented through this myth which Cornford calls "embarrassing" and entailing "the use of very vague language" (1937/1997: 295).

similar to the one presented in Socrates/Diotima's speech: Sexual desire is only the lowest form of surpassing one's mortality, and the noblest way to strive for immortality is through philosophy when the immortal soul contemplates everlasting things (*Tim.* 98a–d).

It becomes clear that lust and sexuality belong to the mortal part of the soul, together with the body (*Tim.* 69c–71d). Thus, both gender and sexual reproduction appear to belong to the sensual world, not to the ideal toward which humans should direct themselves. Apparently, among immortal souls, there would be no gender dimorphism, but gender is something that defines us specifically as living (and mortal) beings. Indeed, the Ancient thinkers theorized gender specifically in the context of their science of life (*bios*). This inquiry leads us from the mythical to the natural world.

2.2 When Hot Meets Cold and Form Meets Matter—Gender and Generation in Aristotle's Biology

Whereas the gendered and sexual myths appealed to gods and ancestral events, Ancient biology and medicine attempted to formulate scientific explanations of gender and sexuality and back up their claims with logical thinking and empirical observations.[21] Ancient embryological theories provide perhaps the most extensive and systematic discussion on gender in the original sources. These debates form also an indispensable background for understanding arguments on gender that occur in Ancient philosophical sources from the Classic thinkers to the Stoics. Indeed, as we shall see, the scientific, philosophical, and mythical explanations of gender often intertwine.

In this chapter, I will analyze gender, generation, and sexuality in Aristotle's (384–322 BCE) influential embryological theory. Aristotle was not only a remarkable philosopher, but he is also often recognized as the originator of biology, i.e., scientific study of life (literally study, *logos*, of life, *bios*) and I will scrutinize his embryology in light of his central metaphysical distinctions and the Ancient theory of elements, paying particular attention to the counterpart hot–cold for his account of

---

[21] In his biological investigations, Aristotle uses a research method that he justifies in his methodological works (named by later commentators the *Organon*): A combination of induction from empirical observation (*epagôgê*) and deduction (*syllogismos*). Yet we can see how elements of mythical thinking affect also his scientific theory formation.

gender. I will show that both his metaphysical distinctions and the idea of natural temperatures support a hierarchical view of the sexes, positing male naturally above the female.

2.2.1 Why Are Higher Animals Gendered?

It is notable how important a role sex plays in Aristotle's biological works. He discusses sexual dimorphism in various places in *Parts of Animals* (*PA*), but deliberately avoids a systematic discussion of male and female genitals in this work in order to dedicate a separate investigation to them, namely the *Generation of Animals* (*GA*). He also makes numerous remarks on the topic in his extensive study *History of Animals* (*HA*). Indeed, sex is so central for his biological theory that he bases his classification of animals specifically on modes of generation. This, he claims, provides a more natural criterion than any other difference such as in locomotion (walking, swimming, flying) (*GA* 732b25).[22] In Aristotle's biology, the basic division goes between viviparous, oviparous, and larviparous animals (i.e., those giving birth to living offspring, producing eggs, and multiplying through larvae; see e.g. *HA* I.v.489a34–489b15). Aristotle also calls generation the most common function (*ergon*) of nature: It demarcates living from non-living beings (*GA* 731a30).[23]

In his biological works, Aristotle frequently defines the male and the female as the *arkhai* of generation. In the Aristotelian metaphysic, *arkhê* can be read as "principle" or "starting point," but in this context, it could be understood as simply signifying "cause." Indeed, as we will see, Aristotle specifically discusses sexual dimorphism in terms of causes. He emphasizes, however, that even if the two genders are understood as *arkhai*, they are nevertheless not *necessary* for generation. Generation is

---

[22] A classification based on modes of locomotion was proposed e.g., in Plato's *Timaeus* (39e–40a). Aristotle also classifies animals on the basis of their natural temperature (hot versus cold), their constitutive elements (e.g., earthy versus fluid), and their stage of perfection (higher versus lower animals). These apparently different classes are interconnected and overlapping in that all of them are related to differences in procreation. Aristotle claims that more perfect and hotter animals (*teleótera kai thermotera*) produce living offspring. The lowest and coldest class of all species is that of larvae (*GA* 733b1–15).

[23] In *De Anima*, Aristotle writes that *soul* demarcates living from non-living beings. This is really putting the same idea in other words, because the lowest kind of soul is the nutritive one (which is common to all living beings including the most primitive, such as plants) and reproduction is a function of the nutritive soul (*De An.* 1.4).

possible without gender, which he demonstrates with numerous examples of plants and animals, such as amoebas.[24] According to Aristotle, in nature things are as they are either out of necessity (*ex anankês*) or "for the better" (*beltion*).[25] Since sexual dimorphism is not necessary for generation, some species must thus have distinct genders because it is *naturally better* for them. According to Aristotle, this is true of all of the so-called higher animals—that is, all that have the capacity of movement and are on the top of the natural hierarchy (*GA* 730b30–35).

What Aristotle means with the remark "naturally better" can be clarified in light of his influential metaphysical theory of four causes: material, efficient, formal, and final or teleological.[26] According to this theory, if we really wish to understand what an object of investigation is, we should look not only at the material it is made of, or at the causal process behind it, or even at its form (even if all of these are important), but should primarily consider what it is *for*, in other words, what is its end, *telos*. According to Aristotle, in animals the *telos* of sex is generation. Thus, even though there is generation without gender, there would be no gender without the goal of generation. Aristotle states that the *telos* of any particular species (*eidos*) is to strive for eternity and immortality. Given that any species consists of individual members, all of them mortal, the only way to strive for this goal is to constantly produce new members to replace the dying ones (*GA* 723a5). We encountered a similar view above in Socrates/Diotima's speech that presents conception and childbirth as a means of overcoming one's mortality, even though they discuss the idea from the point of view of an individual, not of a species (*Symp.* 206b–212a).[27]

---

[24] Aristotle discusses amoebas e.g., in *GA* 731b7–15. The Skeptic philosopher Sextus Empiricus (2nd and 3rd century CE) also makes interesting remarks on the variation in the ways animals generate (*PH* I: 42). Sextus also notes the exceptional case of the mule, which has "parents of two different species." Aristotle discusses mules in *GA* 747a23–748b40.

[25] Aristotle distinguishes between "out of necessity" and "for the better" in numerous places in his biological works (e.g., *GA* 717a15–25, 738a35 etc.).

[26] Cf. *Anal. Post.*, where Aristotle states that knowing something signifies knowing the *causes* of that something and that there are four causes altogether (*Anal. Post.* II. 11.94a 20). Aristotle's teleology is a complex topic and a matter of scholarly debate in its own right; see e.g., Monte Ransome Johnson (2005).

[27] A similar statement occurs in the pseudo-Aristotelian work *Economics*, claiming that nature created procreation in order to preserve the kind (*eidos*) because it was unable to preserve the individual (*Econ.* 1343b20). However, the *telos* of a species is usually understood from the special nature of that particular species (for a discussion of this problem, see Johnson 2005).

It is worth noting, however, that even if generation is a goal for every species, it is not necessarily the only or the uppermost goal. The more complicated the species, the more goals apart from procreation its life can serve. Aristotle maintains that the function (*ergon*) of plants is simply to sustain life through nutrition, to produce seeds and thereby to generate. He categorizes generation as an aspect of the nutritive soul, in other words, the lowest kind of soul, which is common to plants, animals, and humans (*De An.* 415a25; 416a20). Animals, however, also have other functions on the top of this: All of them have sense perception (*aisthêsis*) and, at least to some extent, understanding (*gnôsis*) (*GA* 731a25–b35). The highest form of understanding is in a human being, whose final goal is connected to rationality. Thus, even if generation is a *telos* in every living creature, in the case of higher animals, life also serves other purposes. This is true of both males and females. Especially from the point of view of a human being, procreation is only one of the many possible goals for which to strive and is not even included in the highest goals discussed in *Nicomachean Ethics*.

2.2.2   Gender and Form: Sameness and Difference

Aristotelian biology thus ascribes certain essential similarities to males and females: Both are understood as "starting-points" or "causes" of generation, and for neither is procreation the only or highest goal in life. Furthermore, Aristotle claims that there is no difference between the male and female soul (*psykhê*, *GA* 741a8). In *Metaphysics*, Aristotle wonders why males and females (or men and women) are of the same species, even if masculinity and femininity are contrary concepts. He explains that "being a male" or "being a female" is a characteristic of an animal, not because of its substance but because of its body and the matter it consists of (*Met.* 1058a30–b25). Since the soul, according to Aristotle, contains the being (*ousia*) of the animal, the male and the female consequently have the same being (e.g., *PA* 641a20). This account makes gender seem like a merely bodily difference, and an accidental rather than an essential characteristic.

Yet it is not clear how exactly we should understand the position of gender in Aristotelian metaphysics. When he discusses animal species (*eidos*), he states that males and females belong to the same *eidos*, just as both men and women are humans and both stallions and mares are horses. However, in another context, he claims that males and females "differ in form (*eidei*) and in *logos*" (*GA* 729a25). In Aristotle, *eidos* is a versatile concept that can signify a species or a form.[28] A plausible reading would be that he here uses *eidos* as a parallel concept to *morphê*, which specifically signifies the outer, visible form. The idea, then, would simply be that even if both men and women are humans, their bodies are of different "shapes".

Aristotle's numerous remarks on the respective *morphê* of males and females support this reading. He lists the following features as typical of females: They are small in size, pale, and their veins are not prominent (*GA* 727a25). They tend to be more knock-kneed and have less and finer bodily hair (or its counterparts such as feathers in non-haired animals). They have softer flesh, and a weaker and higher pitched voice (with the exception of the cow) (*HA* IV 538b1–15). Males characteristically share the opposite features. In this context, Aristotle also makes his notorious assertion that females have fewer teeth than males in the case of humans, pigs, sheep, and goats. All these statements apply to the outer form of the genders, in other words, the form that can be grasped through empirical observation (quite apart, of course, from the question of how convincing the empirical element in each of these statements is).

Aristotle also maintains that when animals are castrated, not only is a certain organ destroyed, but their whole *morphê* undergoes a change. By way of explanation, he points out that males and females differ in the shape (*skhêma*) of their genitals, but when "a small principle (*arkhê*) changes, usually many of the things which depend upon it undergo an accompanying change." (*GA* 716b5, transl. A.L. Peck)[29] This notion is intended to support his argument that male and female are principles, *arkhai*—you cannot remove a creature's gender without causing a fundamental alteration in its whole being.

---

[28]The versatility in Aristotle's notion of *eidos* is a much-debated problem in *Met*. VII (even though the problem in that paragraph is slightly different from the one I am discussing here).

[29]The Neo-Platonic thinker Porphyry (c. 232–304 CE) makes a similar point in *On Abstinence from Animal Food*, claiming that castrated animals become more effeminate which affect, for example, their voice (III.7). Galen refers to castrated animals as a "third gender" (to be discussed in Sect. 2.3). Aristotle's remarks on castration illustrate his general idea that many observable qualities follow from some more fundamental metaphysical factors. See also Aristotle's remarks on eunuchs in *GA* 728a17; 746b20; 766a25.

But what did Aristotle mean in his above statement that the male and female differ not only in their (outer) form, but also in their *logos*? In this context, *logos* does clearly not signify reason or rationality, but indicates the different ways in which the two sexes function as causes (or *arkhai*) of generation. Aristotle states that males and females differ *kata ton logon* because of the difference between their reproductive capacities: "The male is that which has the power (*to dynamenon*) to generate in another, while the female is that which can generate in itself (*eis auto*) and out of which the generated offspring, which is present in the generator, comes into being." (*GA* 716a20, A.L. Peck's translation slightly modified) However, as I will show, when clarifying this difference, Aristotle makes gender not only a biological but also a metaphysical question.[30]

2.2.3 *Aristotelian Metaphysics of Gender*

Aristotle's embryology builds on some of his most central metaphysical concepts. The first essential distinction is his above-mentioned theory of four causes. Aristotle names the female as the material and the male as the formal cause (*ho logos tês ousias*) of generation: "The female always provides the material and the male provides that which fashions the material into shape; this, in our view, is the specific characteristic of each of the genders: that is what it means to be a male or a female." (*GA* 738b20, transl. A.L. Peck) By way of illustration, he uses the analogy of coagulating milk with fig juice. In his words, milk and menstrual fluid are of the same nature: Both serve as the body (*sôma*) or the matter (*hylê*) out of which something is being produced. Similarly, the sperm of the male is compared to the fig juice, both of which function as the starting point of the alteration process which shapes material into a new form.[31]

In addition to being the formal cause, the male is also the *efficient cause* of generation, in other words "the origin of movement" (*hê arkhê tês kinêseôs*).[32] Aristotle uses his famous metaphysical distinction between actuality (*energeia, entelekheia*) and potentiality (*dynamis*) to explain this, as follows. The human form is in the man's sperm, but only potentially

---

[30] Marguerite Deslauriers also makes this point in 1998: 140.

[31] Aristotle repeats the analogy to milk and fig juice throughout *GA*, see e.g., 729a10–15; 737a15; 739b21ff.; 771b20.

[32] See e.g., *GA* 716a5; 737a20; cf. *De An.* 417b16.

and not actually, just as the woman's menstrual fluid potentially includes the human body.[33] After fertilization the embryo starts gradually to take on the human form. The movement (*kinēsis*) that catalyzes the development of the embryo comes from the male's sperm, as suggested in the analogy to fig juice.[34] In sum, generation requires both the male and the female factor, but for different reasons: the female because she provides the matter, the male, because he gives the form and movement. This idea goes well with Aristotle's assertion that the male gender is by its essence active, and the female passive (*GA* 729a25–30).

Consistent with this, Aristotle claims that the body of the embryo comes from the female, whereas the soul originates from the "generating parent" (*genēsanios*), in other words, the male (*GA* 738b20–25). This idea derives from his analysis of female and male secretions: sperm and menstrual fluid. According to Aristotle, sperm consists of a mixture of water and *pneuma*. *Pneuma* is a technical term that was widely used in Ancient philosophy and medicine, and which also became a central notion in Stoic philosophy, even though there is some difference in usage. Aristotle defines *pneuma* as a warm substance that facilitates fertility and is analogical to the essence of stars. However, he denies that sperm is identical to fire, or that it could be reduced to any of the four elements and claims that it is rather to be identified with the heavenly substance of ether.

We saw above that Aristophanes' myth in *Symposium* connected men to the Sun and women to the Earth. This archaic, mythical dichotomy occurs also in Aristotle's biology. He compares the sperm to the Sun since both have the capacity to give rise to new life, and claims that this is the reason why the heavens and the Sun are referred to as "Father" and "creator," whereas the Earth is often called "Mother" and "woman" (*GA* 716a10–15; 737a20).[35] It is noteworthy that here Aristotle

---

[33] Aristotle formulates this idea slightly differently in *Met.* IX: 7: Semen is not yet potentially a human being, but becomes one only after being altered "in another" (apparently in the womb). Analogically earth is not a potential sculpture because it must first be made into bronze (*Met.* 1049a10–15).

[34] However, the female also gives her own specific movements (*dynamei de hai tou thēleos; GA* 768a13). For a scholarly discussion on the female movements, see Devin Henry (2007, 2009).

[35] The idea that sperm includes *pneuma* (which is warm by nature) probably lay behind Aristotle's somewhat puzzling claim that "sperm does not freeze when exposed to frost in the open air" (unlike water, which is supposed to show that sperm is not water) (*GA* 735a35).

explicates genders and their respective secretions through analogies derived not only from the natural but also from the superlunary world. This is odd in that he generally considers the science of heavens and the science of living beings to be distinct fields of research, and this is one of the few places in his zoology in which superlunary entities are used to clarify sublunary phenomena.[36] (*GA* 738a17ff)

Many feminist critics have paid attention to the idea of the female as the material and male as the formal cause of generation and concluded that Aristotle's biology is entirely misogynistic.[37] However, other scholars, while admitting that there unquestionably are sexist elements in Aristotle's biology, have pointed out the fact that he still gives females a far more substantial role than many earlier theories, since by providing the matter the female functions as a genuine cause in reproduction (e.g., Sihvola 2006: 58).[38] It is true that many thinkers before Aristotle supported a theory that in later scholarship came to be named *preformationism*. According to this theory, the semen of the father contains everything that is needed for the creation of a new living being. Plato's *Timaeus* can be read as illustrating this theory since it depicts conception as "sowing into the womb," and the womb as a "hollow space" (*Tim.* 91c–d; cf. Preus 1977). As the example from *Timaeus* shows,

---

[36] Other examples of explaining sublunary phenomena with reference to the superlunary world include the timing of women's periods and the determination of the fetus' gender, both of which, according to Aristotle, can be affected by the position of the Moon. In passages like this, he might have been alluding to traditional myths that he adapted to fit his own theory. He also mentions in his work *On Dreams* the odd notion that a clean mirror turns red when a menstruating woman looks into it (*On Dreams* 459b30). Also this might refer to an archaic folk belief.

[37] Maryanne Cline Horowitz defended this kind of a position in her article of 1976, which started a debate on sexism in Aristotle's biology.

[38] Also Devin Henry defends the position that Aristotle unquestionably accepts gendered prejudices of his time and adapts them as a part of his theory. However, Henry claims that the misogynist arguments are somewhat separate parts of his theory, and this sexism does not characterize his biology on the whole (2007: 19). I disagree with this reading in that, as I demonstrate in this chapter, the sexist elements are imbedded in the very premises of the Aristotelian theory and are thus not just an isolated part of it. On a recent, comprehensive analysis on feminist readings on Aristotle's biology, see Sophia M. Connell (2016). Connell presents a detailed argument for why Aristotle's biology is unquestionably sexist—and why defending this position requires careful Ancient scholarship, which has been absent in many radical feminist interpretations (cf. 2016: 45–52).

preformationism is often illustrated through an agricultural analogy: Semen is presented as similar to seed, and the womb as similar to earth, which serves as a place for the seed to grow without affecting whether a seed will grow into a rose or a thorn bush.

It should be borne in mind, however, that Aristotle did not only reject preformationism but also another competing theory, so-called *dualseed theory* according to which an embryo is formed as a mixture of two seeds, one stemming from the father and the other from the mother. This was apparently supported in the Hippocratic School and was later defended by Galen (to be discussed later in this chapter). Thus, Aristotle rejected both a theory that presented the female as nothing but a hollow container and one that presented her as making an important or even equal contribution to reproduction.

Moreover, even though the female is considered to be the material and thus a genuine cause in procreation, this as such does not have a very high status in Aristotle's metaphysics. Pure matter without form cannot give rise to anything specific—we can hardly even imagine what a chaotic mess a material world without forms would be. Aristotle considers formal and efficient causes more important and explanatory than the material cause. If we wish to know what a chair is, for example, we would not get much of a picture from being told, "It is made of wood," which applies just as much to boats and wooden horses. We would get a much better idea if someone demonstrated what a chair looks like— and, even better, also explained what we are supposed to do with it. Hence, form and purpose say more about what a given thing is than the matter it is made of. Similarly, the soul says more about what a creature is than the body because the soul comprehends its being (*ousia*). According to Aristotle, the body exists *for* the soul just as a saw exists for sawing, not vice versa (*PA* 640b20–30; 641a20; 645b15). Not even males' and females' respective secretions are discussed neutrally: As noted above, Aristotle considered sperm nobler than menstrual fluid—a fact he justified with reference to the sperm's white and foamy consistency and the myth of Aphrodite who was born from the foam of the ocean (*GA* 736a20).[39] All in all, the different features Aristotle attributes to males and females do not have equal status in his theory but are, on

---

[39] Galen also points out that Aristotle "did not find fault with the myth that says that Aphrodite was born from foam." (*On Semen* I.5.18, transl. de Lacy) This, again, is one example of how the Ancient myth and biology sometimes intertwine.

the contrary, presented as hierarchical, and he systematically attributes higher features to males and lower to females. This is further demonstrated by his account of the natural temperatures of males and females.

2.2.4 Hot Men and Cold Women

Aristotle calls hot, cold, dry, and moist the basic principles of nature (*arkhai tôn physikôn*). These are the qualities of the four elements: fire, earth, air, and water, and they function as causes (*aitia*) that control life and death, as well as sleep and wakefulness, youth and oldness, health and illness (*PA* 648b10). The binary opposition between hot and cold is particularly important. As the previous analogy between the male sperm and the fiery planet of the Sun suggested, Aristotle asserts that males are naturally hot whereas females are naturally cold. The idea of respective hotness and coldness of the two sexes is an essential premise in Aristotle's argumentation: He draws on this distinction throughout his biological investigations and assigns it important explanatory functions.

In asserting that males are naturally warmer than females, Aristotle was contributing to a prevailing debate during that time. He reports, for example, that philosopher Parmenides (late 6th cn.–mid. 5th cn. BCE) was among those defending the view that women were naturally more warm-blooded than men, for one thing because they have periods. Philosopher Empedocles (ca. 495–435 BCE), however, held the contrary (and according to Aristotle the correct) view that females were naturally colder than males (*PA* 648a30). Aristotle refutes Empedocles' theory explaining the origin of gender difference in terms of hotness and coldness during pregnancy, however. Empedocles had claimed that a female infant is conceived when the semen enters a cold womb (and, accordingly, a male if the womb is warm), which Aristotle rejects by pointing out that twins can be of different genders even though they were in the uterus together. Aristotle also refutes the earlier theories that explain gender difference with reference to the right and left sides of the body. Some thinkers held the view that female offspring were produced on the left and male offspring on the right side of the uterus, whereas others claimed that males were born from semen produced in the right testicle and females correspondingly from semen from the left testicle.[40] (*GA* 764a1–b5)

---

[40] Aristotle mentions Leophanes (a Greek scientist, ca. 430–470 BCE) as a supporter of the view of the left and the right testicle, which was possibly also Hippocrates' view

Even though Aristotle rejects Empedocles' theory, he also refers to heat and coldness in his causal explanation for why a fetus develops into a male or a female.[41] When discussing the capacities of movement and action inherent in the male sperm, Aristotle states:

> When the principle (*arkhê*) can neither rule (*kratê*) nor, **due to lack of heat**, effect concoction (*pepsai*) and make it into its proper form (*eis to idion eidos autou*), but on the contrary fails in doing this, it necessarily changes (*metaballein*) into its opposition (*tounantion*). (*GA* 766a18–22, translation A.L. Peck, my emphasis)

Aristotle's argument is that when conception proceeds normally, the male principle (being, by virtue of its heat, naturally stronger than its feminine counterpart) should "rule" and make the fetus into its "proper" or "own" form—that is, another male. When it develops into a female, however, nature has failed to follow its normal course and produced a deformity. Aristotle lists different reasons why the fertilization process might be disturbed and give rise to female infants: The parents are either very young or old (i.e., not of prime fertile age), or they have excess of fluids in their bodies or (in the case of the father) in their sperm. The gender of the infant might also be affected by the wind, the climate, or the position of the Moon (*GA* 766b35–767a35).[42]

When Aristotle refers to deformities or monstrosities (in other words cases in which nature "strays from the generic type," e.g., *GA* 767b7) he names the female as the first kind of "monster" (*teras*) that nature

---

(cf. Preus 1977: 68). In her work on Ancient physiognomy, Maud Gleason points out that masculinity in Ancient thought is often connected to the right-hand side of the body (1995: 59). Aristotle mentions also in *EN* that the right hand is naturally better than the left hand (*EN* 1134 b 35).

[41] Present-day science recognizes the phenomenon called "temperature-dependent sex-determination" (TSD) in several reptile species. For example, the crocodile eggs develop into males in higher temperatures, whereas in most turtles the relationship between sex and temperature is the opposite, and higher temperature produces female hatchlings. See J.D. Murray (2002: 119–123).

[42] It is difficult to see, however, how Aristotle's own theory can avoid the problem he points out in Empedocles: Why twins sometimes have different genders? How should we understand the claim that in some cases the stronger element shapes one of the infants and the weaker element the other infant? Obviously the other conditions Aristotle lists (e.g., the wind or the Moon) are the same for both twins, as well.

created.⁴³ The idea is perplexing, not only from a feminist but also from an Aristotelian perspective. First, in his biological works, Aristotle supports the view of nature as a well-organized whole that does not produce anything superfluous or meaningless (e.g., *GA* 744a35). Why, then, should there be "flaws of nature?" In particular, why should a flaw be given such a specific and indispensable function as birth giving? Second, how can his theory explain the fact that females are born so regularly, in more or less half of the cases? This seems problematic in light of his comment on scientific explanations: He explicitly criticizes attempts to explain a regularly occurring phenomenon in terms of accidental or unpredictable events. The paragraphs on female deformity seem to be in conflict with the Aristotelian views on nature and scientific explanations.⁴⁴

It is worth emphasizing, however, that Aristotle does not claim that females are superfluous; on the contrary, he states that they are a necessity of nature (*anankaia tê physei; GA* 767b9). This differentiates them from the other types of monsters he describes, such as a calf with a child's head or a sheep with an ox's head (cf. *GA* 769b10ff.). Creatures of this kind are not only deformations, but they are also useless for the purposes of nature.⁴⁵

---

⁴³ Liddell and Scott's lexicon translates the concept *teras* as "(1) a sign, wonder, marvel, and (2) in concrete sense, a monster." I follow the custom in the secondary literature of translating *teras* as "monster," which is also consistent with the fact that Aristotle uses it later in the same chapter in *GA* to describe "creatures that have the head of another" and other such deformities (*GA* 769a15). In another context, he states that "female is as it were a deformed male" (*thêly hôsper arren esti pepêrômenon*) (*GA* 737a25–30). Here, he uses the word *pepêrômenon* derived from *pêroó*, which Liddle and Scott's dictionary translates as "to lame, maim, mutilate," and the substantive form *pêros* accordingly signifies "disabled in a limb, maimed." Yet I do not think that the term should lead us to associate with monsters of Hollywood horror movies as Kathleen Long seems to be doing when discussing continuations and parallels between Aristotle's notion of monstrosity and the TV-Show *X-Files* (Long 2012).

⁴⁴ Aristotle, for example, rejects Empedocles' theory that the backbone consists of many pieces because the fetus has been shaken in the womb. Aristotle found this explanation absurd because the backbone always consists of pieces, but "shaking during pregnancy" is accidental and random (*PA* 640a20–25).

⁴⁵ Cf. Henry, who points out that, "females have teleological value in Aristotle's developmental biology" (2007: 11). I think Henry is right in pointing out that in terms of generation, there is no teleological reason why any specific individual should be a male or a female (Henry 2007: 12). Interestingly, my reading of the status of gender in Stoic metaphysics proposes, in essence, a similar model where it is only important for the individual to be gendered but insignificant whether this is in the form of the male of the female (or whether the individual does not clearly fall under either category). Of course, in the context of Stoic metaphysics, the reasoning leading to this conclusion is very different than in Aristotle. Cf. Chap. 4.

Females are obviously needed for the goal of generation. Aristotle's idea seems to be that because nature needs females for the *telos* of the species, nature ensures that there will be enough of them. However, even if this provides a *teleological* explanation of why females are born so regularly, I still consider it problematic in terms of giving a plausible *causal* explanation of why a fetus is born either male or female, both having very nearly the same likelihood.

I should also point out that monstrosity, in Aristotle, refers not only to deformations or marvels, but also more generally to deviation and disresemblance. As Devin Henry points out, for Aristotle, "anything that does not resemble its generator is in a way a kind of monster." This is why he also refers to puppies as monsters, because they are blind, unlike their parents (Henry 2007: 13). Thus, Aristotle's reasoning for calling the female a "monster" is that she is the result of a fertilization process in which the naturally weaker element (matter) is dominant. The underlying presupposition is that the male is the "generating parent" and the stronger principle, and thus the offspring should naturally receive the form (*morphê*) of the male and thus resemble its generator.

Furthermore, Aristotle explicitly connects natural heat to a higher stand in the natural hierarchy which further supports the idea of the male's superiority over the female. He explicitly states that the maintenance of the natural hierarchy between the genders gives another rationale for sexual dimorphism: The female sex is needed for being subordinated to males. By way of justification, he points out that males sometimes fail to rule by virtue of other qualities such as youth, and hence "female offspring must by necessity be produced by animals." (*GA* 767b10)[46]

Aristotle also claims that animals "with hot, thin, and clear blood" stand higher (than cold-blooded animals) in the natural hierarchy, since they have more courage (*andreia*) and understanding (*phronêsis*). He then states that this difference (*diaphora*) also occurs between the upper and lower parts of the body, right and left sides of the body, and between the male and the female (*PA* 618a10–13).[47] Also the Pythagorean table

---

[46] He uses the same term *kratein* here as when he referred to sperm taking sway over menstrual fluid in fertilization.

[47] A.L. Peck translates the term *diaphora* in this paragraph not neutrally as "difference" (like Lennox), but as "pre-eminence." It is interesting to notice that in this passage, Aristotle also assumes that hot and cold can influence, not only bodily features (or *morphê*) but also character features (and indeed, in the case of humans, ethically relevant

of oppositions, to which Aristotle refers in *Metaphysics* I: 5, puts forward a similar list of binary oppositions, including also the pairs "paired–unpaired," "light–darkness" and "good–bad" (*Met.* 986a22). As the pair "good–bad" in particular demonstrates, these oppositions are not neutral, but imply a hierarchy between the compared things. He calls the efficient cause "better and more divine" (*beltionos kai theioteras*) than the matter, and concludes that the "superior one should be separate from the inferior one" (*GA* 732a5). He also explicitly draws the gendered implications of this standpoint:

> That is why whenever possible and so far as possible the male is separate from the female, since it is something better and more divine in that it is the principle of movement for generated things (*arkhê tês kinêseôs tois ginomenois*), while the female serves as their matter. The male, however, comes together with the female and mingles with it for the business of generation (*pros tên ergasian tês geneseôs*), because this is something that concerns both of them. (*GA* 732a5–10, A.L. Peck's translation slightly modified)

In my view, this passage clearly shows that Aristotle does not simply posit that female and male have different *morphê* and different reproductive functions. Indeed, this would not present a sexist position if one argued (a) that these differences are irrelevant to what is really important in an animal or human and (b) that they do not (and should not) justify any idea of a hierarchy between the two genders.[48] Many scholars emphasize

---

ones such as courage and fear, also discussed in *EN*). In another context, he mentions that whereas warm-blooded creatures are prone to being courageous, cold-blooded ones tend to be timid (*deilotera*) (*PA* 659 b 30–35). Similarly in *HA*, he claims that the female is less spirited than the male, with the exceptions of the leopard and the bear, and continues by stating that a wife is more compassionate and liable to cry than the husband, but also more lying, jealous and complaining, among other things (*HA* 608a32–b19). Thus, the discussions of gendered bodies and characteristics sometimes overlap. I will elaborate more on this connection in the context of Ancient physiognomics in Chap. 6.

[48] This is, in a nutshell, the ultimate idea in the chapter entitled "Biological Facts" in Simone de Beauvoir's classic feminist work *Second Sex*. She points out several biological differences between males and females—facts in light of which the female appears as the weaker and more fragile of the two genders. However, her point is specifically to criticize biological reductionism, which would explain or justify the moral and social realm of gender with its (alleged) biological foundations. Her point in discussing biological differences is to illustrate their moral and political insignificance, and thus she shows clearly that

the passages in Aristotle in which he apparently supports (a), such as the above-mentioned metaphysical assertions that male and female have the same soul, the same *ousia* and the same *eidos* (in the meaning of species).[49] However, there is evidence in Aristotle's theory such as the above passage that clearly speaks contrary to both (a) and (b). Aristotle refers to the male as the "better and more divine" gender and suggests that the relationship between males and females is (and should be) hierarchical. What Aristotle seems to imply is that given all these fine things that males posses and females lack, it is only right that males have as little to do with females as possible.[50] This passage from *GA* is quite exceptional in Aristotle's writing on zoology; however, in that he here discusses the *behavior* of males and females instead of their bodily features. He appears to assume that the essential difference in reproductive roles also implies a difference in life spheres: Males live separately from females, and procreation is the only thing that concerns both and brings them together. It is not quite clear, however, whether this remark is intended to be

---

pointing them out—even if this would seem to favor the male—does not in itself have to be antifeminist: What makes it antifeminist is the evaluation of these differences, or the justification of political inequalities based on them. It is nevertheless interesting to note that de Beauvoir's description of the female biology does not always seem to be much more positive than Aristotle's (Chapter I.1. in de Beauvoir: 2011).

[49] See, e.g., Deslauriers (1998), Henry (2007), Sihvola (2006).

[50] Devin Henry and Sophia M. Connell also draw attention to this paragraph and claim that Aristotle's position here is undeniably sexist, which his defenders cannot plausibly explain away (Henry 2007: 16–19; Connell 2016: 43). Particularly Robert Mayhew has defended Aristotle against the feminist charges, stating that his biological views originate from "observations of the facts of generation that were available to him" (2004: 38). Mayhew, even though admitting that Aristotle's views on females were often erroneous, dismisses the idea of any inherent misogynic ideology. He maintains that Aristotle arrived at these views as a scientist, not as a prejudiced advocate of the sexist opinions of his contemporary culture, and that there were thus rational reasons behind the claims. A similar position was earlier defended by Johannes Morsink (1979). The problem with this position is, however, that it has a strong tendency to explain away content in Aristotle that, from present-day point of view, seems questionable and unfavorable. Further, this position tends to mix the possible sexist motivations of an author with the sexist content. Even if it were possible to prove that Aristotle did not have sexist *motivations* behind his theory, it would be irrelevant in terms of evaluating the possible sexist elements in its *content*—like in passage *GA* 732a5–10.

descriptive or prescriptive: In other words, is he (allegedly) reporting observed behavior of animals, or an ideal?

It is worth noting, however, that the idea of hierarchy and separate life spheres is not present in books VIII–IX of *Nicomachean Ethics*. Furthermore, even though I claim that Aristotle's biology is unquestionably sexist, I would like to draw attention to another aspect of his theory, namely the lack of biological reductionism in his thinking. In other words, even if his biological works advocate the natural supremacy of males over females, and his political works posit political supremacy of men over women, he does not claim that the former view would lead to or justify the latter.

Here I agree with Marguerite Deslauriers, who explains in detail why it would be inconsistent of Aristotle to base political differences on biology, or vice versa to base biological differences on politics. In brief, I take the core of her argument to be that it would not be coherent in his thinking to assume that the lower functions of the soul (e.g., reproduction) would determine the higher functions (e.g., rationality). From Aristotle's teleological perspective, the lower-level functions are *for the sake of* the higher-level functions, just as the body is *for the sake of* the soul. I remarked at the beginning of this section that the highest goal of human life cannot be connected to the fulfillment of biological functions. Thus, it is rather the higher functions that determine the lower ones, not vice versa. As Deslauriers shows, however, Aristotle does not argue either that the reason for the biological weakness of females is to facilitate the political subordination of women.[51] She points out that Aristotle presents his idea of sexual reproduction as common to all higher animals without making a distinct case for humans (who, however, are the only animals who have social virtues). She concludes that the difference between males and females in Aristotle's biological works and the difference between men and women in his political works are not connected (Deslauriers 2009: 215–231).[52]

---

[51] Xenophon (c. 430–354 BCE) seems to support this line of thinking in his assertion that the gods created man and woman *for the sake of* the separate duties of indoor and outdoor labor (*Oec.* X).

[52] A similar reading has recently been defended by Sophia M. Connell who, for example, analyzes fallacies in many standard feminist readings of Aristotle: Among these she counts the assumption that his biology and politics are linked, and that he would justify subordination of actual women in his biological work (Connell 2016: 25–34) Cf. Devin Henry (2007: 2).

I would like to add that this holds not only for politics, but also for ethics and moral education in general: He does not discuss the development of virtues in his biology, nor does he refer to his biological theory in his discussion of virtues in *Nicomachean Ethics*. This, of course, is not to dismiss the fact that he was all in the favor of the social subordination of women and separate spheres of life in *Politics* and was exclusively thinking about boys in his view of education in *Nicomachean Ethics* (cf. Sect. 7.3). My point here is just to demonstrate that he does not justify men's political superiority with reference to his views of biological male superiority. Yet, as the next section demonstrates, Aristotle was criticized already in Antiquity for not giving the female a more active and important role in his theory of reproduction.

2.3 Galen on Gender: Scientific, Medical, and Philosophical Perspectives

Galen (ca. 130—ca. 210 CE) was one of the most influential commentators on Aristotle's embryology. Although he was a later thinker than most of the Stoics (he was the doctor of the Stoic emperor Marcus Aurelius), I discuss him here because his theories build directly on Aristotle. Galen was, first of all, a doctor, and thus his interests were primarily those of a natural scientist who investigates the human body with the practical aim of healing illnesses. Moreover, he was a doctor who emphasized the close connection between philosophy and medicine, and who combined a wide range of philosophical material in order to formulate a plausible basis for his medical theory and practice (e.g., in his treatise *The Best Doctor is also a Philosopher*, hereafter referred to as *BD*).[53] His scientific method, based on a combination of empirical observations and reasoning, resembles that of Aristotle. However, Galen was also an eclectic thinker who combines empirical data with philosophical arguments. For example, in his attempt to explain the development of the embryo he recollects empirical material on abortions (either observed by himself or as reported by others) as well as dissections of pregnant animals, and combines this data with a discussion of earlier theories and philosophical sources such as Plato's *Timaeus* and the Stoics

---

[53] On the life and philosophical background of Galen, see, e.g., R.J. Hankinson (1991). For more information on Galen's medical theories and his philosophy, see R.J. Hankinson (ed.) (2008). On Galen's embryology, see also Michael Boylan (1986).

(cf. *The Construction of the Embryo*, or *CE*). Sometimes he also uncritically appeals to the authority of earlier thinkers or some unidentified "everybody who know anything about this subject."

In his major study on generation entitled *On Semen* (*Peri Spermatos*, *De Semine*), Galen articulates particularly clearly (much more so than Plato or Aristotle) why gender is a tricky philosophical problem: It requires consideration of distinctly human features, individualizing characteristics as well as resemblances between different individuals. In his discussion on similarity and difference, Galen neatly explicates the following philosophical problem: How does gender function as a category which seems to divide human population into two basic groups? What do all members of one gender group have in common?

2.3.1 Two Genders, Four Elements and the Problem of Gender Resemblance

Galen wonders why there are different kinds of similarities or resemblances (*homoiotêtes*) between humans. First, there is the similarity "in kind of the entire substance" (*ousias eidos*)—the similarity we can observe between a human and a human, or between a horse and a horse. Second, there is a similarity created by the difference between animals of the same kind (*eidesi diaphora*). What Galen is referring to is that a certain *difference* actually creates a *similarity* since it connects all individuals who share the same differentiating principle. This type of a similarity could be observed between a parent and a child who share similar features. The third kind of similarity is that which can be observed between any individuals of the same sex. He wonders what this third kind of resemblance is and how it can be explained (*On Semen* II.5.19–22).

Galen claims that gender resemblance cannot be attributed solely to genital difference, as men have more in common than similar genitals—and their difference from women is also more fundamental than genital difference. Indeed, for him genital difference is merely a difference in degree, not in kind. According to Galen, the male and female genitalia (*ta gennêtika*) are essentially the same, except that they are turned inward in the female and outward in the male. Thus, they differ in position and in size, but both have all the corresponding parts; in Galen's terminology, both males and females have a penis (*posthês*) and testicles (*orkheis*). Galen thus counts the vagina as an inward-turned penis, and he suggests that the "female testicles" (i.e., the ovaries) are situated on each side of the womb (for which he uses both *hystera* and *mētra* interchangeably) (*On Semen* II: 5.41–51). Galen concludes that the generative parts belong to both males and females, "and neither set has more than the other in any respect at all" (*On Semen* II.5.51). However, he mentions in passing that males do not have any part that corresponds to the womb.

Since differences between the sexes cannot be reduced to the genitals (*gennētikois*), Galen suggests that we have to consider the entire body: "A person who sees a bull from a distance recognizes it immediately as male, without examining its organs of generation (*ta gennētika moria*)" (*On Semen* II: 5.8–10, transl. De Lacy). Similarly, Galen continues, we can distinguish between a male and female lion or a man and a woman just by looking at them. Galen's idea comes close to what I suggested earlier was Aristotle's position: That man and woman have the same *eidos* in the sense of kind, but different outer or visual forms (*morphē*). According to both thinkers, gender affects not only certain parts of human anatomy but also, more often than not, the whole shape and size of the body. However, Galen denies that these types of resemblances could be explained by the dominance (*kratēsē*) of the seed in fertilization (which would basically be the Aristotelian solution). Galen takes the resemblances between parents and offspring as evidence that the child is a total mixture of the two parents (not form coming from one and matter from the other), and points out that this resemblance is not gender-related in that a boy may also resemble his mother or a girl her father. And obviously this explanation cannot give any reason for finding a resemblance between any two unrelated males or females (*On Semen* II.5.16, 23).

Galen's solution to the problem derives from the notion of natural temperature. He claims that animals consist of mixtures of the four elements (water, air, earth, and fire), the qualities of which are distributed between the sexes so that males naturally have a greater proportion of both dryness and heat, whereas females have a greater portion of moisture and lack heat (*On Semen* II.4.24–25; *M* I.1.509). Galen thus agrees with Aristotle on the respective hotness and coldness of males and females but denies many of the conclusions Aristotle derives from this difference. Galen's emphasis is on the word *mixture*—no animal consists solely of one element, even though one of them (such as "hotness") can be dominant (*M* I.1). Hot and cold are not merely magnitudes that a thermometer could measure, and thus the female is not cold in the absolute sense, but relatively colder than the male since coldness is more dominant in her mixture than the other qualities.

Galen claims that this proportional difference in natural temperature characterizes fetuses already during pregnancy: "Among the fetuses themselves the male appears immediately from the start to be not only hotter but also drier than the female" (*On Semen* II.5.26, transl. De Lacy). He states further that evidence from abortions and dissections of pregnant animals, as well as the testimony of Hippocrates and other authorities, shows that the male fetus develops faster than the female (*On Semen* II.5. 26–28). He takes this to support his claim of differences in temperature and dryness/moistness in males and females and illustrates his idea with an analogy to shaping clay or making cheese: Wet clay is difficult to mold, and similarly curled milk has to be adequately firm before it can be molded to cheese. Similarly, a drier embryo is more quickly shaped, and thus males must be considered drier from the very beginning (*On Semen* II.5. 28–32). Of course, this explanation is rather odd: If clay, milk, or a fetus must be dry enough in order to be molded, the implication is that they are also wet enough, because obviously one cannot mold totally dry clay or milk, either. Further, the explanation already presumes, rather than explains, gender. Why are some fetuses, right from the start, drier or warmer?

Galen's solution stems from an archaic embryological theory (one that Aristotle had denied as superstitious), based on the binary opposition between left and right. Galen claims that male offspring is developed in the right and the female in the left side of the uterus, and moreover that "if the right testicle is better nourished and the first to be aerated in puberty, the animal produces male offspring." (*On Semen* II: 5. 33–37, transl. De Lacy) Galen thus connects the left–right theory with the elemental explanation by stating that there is agreement among "all who have written anything about temperaments" that the right side (apparently at least when it comes to the uterus and the testicles) is naturally drier and hotter than the left side. Galen's account leaves many questions open, but the main idea is that females are born if the right testicle is "less nourished" and develops later than the left testicle (he was presumably only referring to male testicles here even though, as indicated above, he also introduced the notion of female testicles). Moreover, the female embryo develops on the left side of the uterus, which is also moister and colder than the right side. As a result, from the start the female embryo is moister and colder and develops more slowly than the male embryo.

This moistness and coldness (and possibly even the slower development), then, explains in Galen's theory why females resemble each other and differ from males.

2.3.2   From Agricultural Analogy to Dual-Seed Theory

Galen apparently did not hold a uniform position on generation throughout his oeuvre. In *On Natural Faculties* and *On the Construction of the Embryo* (*CE*), he adapts the Aristotelian view of the male as the formal and the female as the material cause. Applying the common Ancient agricultural analogy, he describes how the "seed is cast into the womb or into the earth (for there is no difference)," hence assuming the semen to be the core of the future human (*CE* I. 6; II.3). He makes it clear that inherent semen is the activity and potential of becoming something new, in the same manner as the artist, not his material, possesses the potential of shaping and creating (cf. Aristotle's analogy with the carpenter: It is not the wood but the carpenter who shapes the bed). Unlike Aristotle, however, Galen endows sperm with yet another specific function. According to him, the fertilization and development of an embryo requires three things: semen, blood, and a faculty that knows how much blood to draw so that the semen will be properly nourished but not drowned (*CE* II.3). Galen illustrates this with an analogy with the artist Phidias, comparing semen with the artist himself and woman's menstrual blood with the wax to be sculpted, and concludes: "Now, it is not for the wax to discover for itself how much of it is required; that is the business of Phidias. Accordingly the artificer will draw to itself as much blood as it needs." (*CE* II.3) Interestingly, a similar idea occurs later in the thinking of the Stoic Hierocles.

However, in *On Semen*, Galen rejects the Aristotelian view and introduces the notion of female sperm (*thêleos sperma*). Galen argues that generation results from a mixture of male and female sperms that stem from their respective testicles. He criticizes Aristotle for "not permitting the menstrual blood to share in the quality from the semen," and thus for underrating the female role in generation (*On Semen* I.5.24). Galen adopts the position that in order to understand the complex process of generation, we must assign the female a more active role in the process than she receives in the theories of both Hippocrates and Aristotle (and, one might add, in Galen's own theory as presented in *CE* and *On Natural Faculty*).

It must be noted, however, that even though Galen introduces the notion of female sperm, he also follows Aristotle in considering the male sperm secretion of the purest and most highly developed kind. According to Galen, the female sperm "becomes nutriment for the semen of the male; for it is thinner than the male semen, and colder, and more suitable than all else for nourishment." (*On Semen* I.6.7.5–6) Nevertheless, the notion of female sperm plays a major role in Galen's embryology. It also helps to specify his position to the above-discussed problem of the different types of resemblances. Galen suggests that in handing down the first kind of resemblance, namely "the resemblance of the kind" (that occurs, e.g., between all horses), the female plays at least as important a role as the male. He defends this position by pointing out that if only the male sperm handed down the kind or the *eidos* (as Aristotle claimed), then when a male donkey mated with a mare, it should result in another donkey—which is not the case, since their offspring is a mule (ibid. II.1.40–50).[54] According to Galen, the second resemblance, that between parents and offspring, also supports the idea of female sperm: If this resemblance was solely attributable to male sperm, then all offspring should only resemble the father, and if it was attributable to menstrual blood, then they should only resemble the mother (ibid. II.1.55–66). As we saw above, his explanation of gender resemblance was that it follows from having the same constituting elements and developing in a similar way during pregnancy.

Galen does not apply his theory only to explaining generation, but also sexual lust. With reference to Plato's *Timaeus*, Galen describes the uterus as "active" in "desiring" to drag the semen into itself and to procreate. He claims that men often "clearly perceive this very thing, the uterus drawing in the genital (*aidion*) like a physician's suction cup" (*On Semen* I.2.12). He also compares the uterus to an octopus, which "seizes what it touches with its suckers" (ibid. I.7.10). Even if Galen introduces the concept of a "female penis," he here follows the common tendency in Ancient medical, biological, and philosophical texts to identify the female reproductive organs specifically with the uterus, without naming the genitalia.

---

[54] Somewhat illogically, Aristotle claims that the offspring of two animals of different species assumes the body of the mother (*GA* 738b25–35). This seems to be in contrast to the notion that the male sperm provides the soul, which includes the form. Galen attempts to correct Aristotle on this point.

Galen also remarks that when female swine are castrated through the removal of their (female) testicles, they not only lose the capacity to generate, they also "forget about sexuality (*aphrodisia*) altogether" (ibid. II.4.18; cf. I.15.27–33). Likewise, he claims, castrated males lose not only their ability to produce semen, but also their virility (*andreia*) and masculinity (*arrenotês*) (ibid. I.15.28). These remarks are notable for two reasons. First, here the anatomical notions on genitalia are used to explain sexual desire. Second, Galen draws attention to yet a new kind of resemblance: that between castrated males and females. In Galen's word, they form "a third gender," which is different from both male and female (ibid. I.16.18). However, this account seems to raise a problem compared with his account of gender resemblance: Now he seems to attribute it, after all, to the reproductive organs (particularly the testicles). How does this fit with his claim that the cause of gender resemblance was supposed to be the natural temperature, not the genitals?

The two apparently different explanations for manliness (heat on the one hand and testicles on the other) are, finally, connected. Galen blames his predecessors for having overlooked such an important topic as "the very great power of the testicles" (ibid. I.15.34). Having referred to castrated swine, he draws further evidence for his claim from Olympic athletes who would be willing to let a part of their body to be cut off in order to win (ibid. I.15.36).[55] However, Galen warns his readers that even if some men might consider it a good idea to avoid sexual indulgence by allowing their testicles to be amputated, this kind of operation is not entirely safe as it also deprives the entire body of masculinity and strength (*arrenotêta kai iskhun*) (ibid. I.15.37–8). Galen claims that those (presumably males) who are castrated are also chilled, which he compares to aging. He concludes that in addition to the heart, the testicles are the main source of inner heat, manliness, strength, and sexual desire (ibid. I.15.41–42). The last of these is peculiar to the testicles, and something even the heart cannot produce: "The heart is the source only of living, but the testicles the source of living well" and thus, "as much as living well is better than plain and simple living, by so much, among animals, are the testicles to be preferred to the heart" (ibid. I.15.48–50).

However, the combination of these two explanations seems only to apply to males whom Galen takes to be naturally warmer and thus

---

[55] Epictetus discussed a similar scenario in the context of human characters and ways of life; cf. my discussion of this passage in Sect. 5.3.

to lose a source of inner heat in the loss of the testicles. How, then, are we to understand his claim that not only do castrated males become more effeminate, but also castrated females become more masculine? Presumably, then, he takes the "female testicles" to be a weaker source of heat than the testicles in males. Galen does not elaborate on this, however. He only remarks that in both females and males, the testicles distribute power (*dynamis*) into the entire body, and this power further causes masculinity in males.

2.3.3   On Cold and Idle Women

Natural hotness or coldness is Galen's prime premise in his views on gender resemblance. He also refers to the natural temperatures of males and females, or men and women, outside of his embryology, and applies it to explaining not only mating but also other types of behavior. When discussing body fat, Galen states that naturally warmer animals usually are fleshier and consume the fat, whereas hibernating animals frequently have a greater amount of fat—as do women who are colder by nature and mostly stay at home. He goes on to state that sometimes fat is found inside of the veins of thin and small-veined people and that this condition is rare in men but "quite common in women; it is an indication of a comparatively cold nature and idle lifestyle." (*M* II.4.606–607).

Here, Galen is referring not only to women's natural (proportional) coldness, but also to their way of life: They are idle and spend a lot of time in their homes. How, then, are these things supposed to connect? One reading would be that Galen assumed that coldness causes idleness. This would imply that women are idle and prone to staying at home because of their coldness; for example, they lack the necessary strength, which is connected to heat, to lead more active lives. As pointed out above, Galen's embryological theory discusses female coldness as something that is already present in the embryos, which would support this reading. However, in the same chapter in which he discusses the idleness of women, he draws attention to the power of habituation, mentioning labor, worries, emotions, self-indulgence, and idleness as examples of factors that affect the balance between the bodily mixtures. Here, "idleness" serves as an example of habituation, not an inborn characteristic (*M*.II.).

Thus, an alternative reading would suggest that the causal connection functions the other way around: That women are cold *because* the traditional lifestyle restricts them to stay at home so much. In this case, the implication could be that because women do not exercise, their bodies do not warm up and create the necessary energy for active life. One could also suggest that both explanations are at stake: That women already have an inborn tendency to be colder than men, but idleness makes this condition worse.

The second and third reading are interesting because they show that one could plausibly assert, even on the basis of Galen's own premises, that culturally determined gender roles also concretely affect the bodies and health. Indeed, he could draw the conclusion that women *should* lead more active lives in order to have a healthier mixture of their body fluids. The same could even be said of their mental health, and Ancient sources give indications of the negative effects of women's restricted spheres of life on their psyche. For example, the Hippocratic treatise *On Diseases of Young Girls* (*Peri parthenión*) discusses how being forced to stay at home negatively affects the bodily fluids of young, unmarried girls and might even make them suicidal.[56] All of these examples show the potential damage that staying indoors might cause to the physical and mental well-being of girls and women, and that at least some Ancient authors were aware of this connection, too. Even if Galen did not problematize the connection between women's inborn capacities and habituation, let alone make any political claims of liberation with regard to women's spheres of life, his views are indicative of the fact that, in order to understand gender, we must scrutinize both the body, characteristics, habituation, and social roles, and the connections between these.

Appendix

Aristotle

An.Post.   *Posterior Analytics*
De An.   *De Anima*
Econ.   *Economics*
EN   *Nicomachean Ethics*
GA   *Generation of Animals*

---

[56] Cf. the sourcebook *Women's Life in Greece & Rome* (Lefkowitz and Fant 1982: 95–96). Van Hooff finds evidence that there was a wave of suicides among young girls in Miletus in 227 BCE (Van Hooff 1990: 98). On gender in Stoic views on suicide, see Malin Grahn (2014).

HA   History of Animals
Met. Metaphysics
On Dreams
PA   Parts of the Animals
Pol. Politics

The Complete Works of Aristotle. The Revised Oxford Translation. Jonathan Barnes (revised). Princeton, NJ: Princeton University Press, 1984.
De anima. W.D. Ross (ed.). Oxford: Clarendon Press, 1956.
Generation of animals. A.L. Peck (transl.). Cambridge, MA: Harvard University Press and London: W. Heinemann, 1979.
Parts of animals. A.L. Peck (transl.). Cambridge, MA: Harvard University Press and London: W. Heinemann, 1983.
Historia animalium. A.L. Peck (ed. and transl.). 3 vols. Cambridge, MA: Harvard University Press and London: Heinemann, 1965.
Metaphysics. W.D. Ross (ed.). Oxford: Clarendon Press, 1924.
Metaphysics, Oeconomica, Magna Moralia. C.G. Armstrong and H. Tredinnick (ed. and transl.). Cambridge, MA: Harvard University Press and London: Heinemann, 1996.

St Augustine

The Works of Saint Augustine. 2nd release, electronic edition, vol, 1/24, Past Masters, InteLex Corporation, Charlottesville, 2001.

Galen

BD   The Best Doctor is also a Philosopher
CE   The Construction of the Embryo
De Placitis Hippocratis et Platonis
De Semine
M   Mixtures
On Natural Faculties

Claudii Galeni Opera Omnia. C.G. Kühn (ed.). C. Cnobloch, Leipzig, 1821–1833, 1964–5.
On the Doctrines of Hipporcates and Plato. Philipp de Lacy (ed. and transl.). Berlin: Akademie Verlag, 1978.
On Semen. Philipp de Lacy (ed. and transl.). Berlin: Akademie Verlag, 1992.
Selected Works. P.N. Singer (transl.). Oxford: Oxford University Press, 1997.

Plato

Gorg.   *Gorgias*
Meno
Tim.   *Timaeus*
Symp.   *Symposium*

Platonis Opera (Oxford Classical Texts):
Vol. 1, ed. E.A. Duke et al. 1995.
Vol. 2, ed. J. Burnet 1922.
Vol. 3, ed. J. Burnet 1922.
Vol. 4, ed. J. Burnet 1922.
Respublica, ed. S.R. Slings 2003.

Complete Works. John M. Cooper (ed.). D.S. Hutchinson (associate ed.). Indianapolis: Hackett Publishers, 1997.
The Dialogues of Plato, Vol. 2: Republic, Gorgias, Parmenides. Oxford: Clarendon Press, 1953.
The Symposium. Christopher Gill (transl.). London and New York: Penguin Books, 1999.

Porphyry

On Abstinence from Killing Animals. Gilliam Clark (transl.). Ithaca: Cornell University Press, 2000.

Sextus Empeiricus

PH I-III Outlines of Pyrrhonism

Sexti Empirici Opera. H. Mutschmann and J. Mau (eds.). In: *Bibliotheca scriptorum Graecorum et Romanorum.* Lipsiae: Teubner, 1962.
Sextus Empiricus, *Outlines of Scepticism.* Julia Annas and Jonathan Barnes (eds.). Cambridge: Cambridge University Press, 1994.

Xenophon

Oec.   *Oeconomicus*

Oeconomicus—A Social and Historical Commentary. Sarah B. Pomeroy (transl.). Oxford: Clarendon University Press, 1994.

References

Bartsch, Shadi, and Thomas Bartscherer (eds.). 2005. *Erotikon—Essays on Eros, Ancient and Modern*. Chicago: The University of Chicago Press.

Boylan, Michael. 1986. Galen's Conception Theory. *Journal in the History of Biology* 19 (1) (Spring), 47–77.

Connell, Sophia M. 2016. *Aristotle on Female Animals*. Cambridge: Cambridge University Press.

Cornford, Francis M. (1937/1992). *Plato's Cosmology—The Timaeus of Plato*. Indianapolis, Cambridge: Hackett.

Corrigan, Kevin, and Elena Glazov-Corrigan. 2004. *Plato's Dialectic at Play: Argument, Structure, and Myth in the Symposium*. University Park, PA: Pennsylvania State University Press.

Davidson, James. 2007. *The Greeks and Greek Love: A Radical Reappraisal of Homosexuality in Ancient Greece*. London: Weidenfeld and Nicolson.

Deslauriers, Marguerite. 1998. Sex Difference and Essence in Aristotle's *Metaphysics* and Biology. In *Re-reading the Canon: A Series Devoted to Feminist Interpretations of Major Philosophers: Aristotle*, ed. Cynthia Freeland, 138–167. University Park: Pennsylvania State University Press.

Deslauriers, Marguerite. 2009. Sexual Difference in Aristotle's *Politics* and His Biology. *Classical World* 102 (3).

Dover, K.J. 1989. *Greek Homosexuality*. New York: MJF Books.

Foucault, Michel. 2006. *History of Madness*. London, New York: Routledge.

Freeland, Cynthia. 2004. Schemes and Scenes of Reading the *Timaeus*. In *Feminist Reflections on the History of Philosophy*, ed. Lilli Alanen and Charlotte Witt. Dordrecth, Boston, and London: Kluwer.

Gleason, Maud W. 1995. *Making Men—Sophists and Self-Presentation in Ancient Rome*. Princeton: Princeton University Press.

Grahn, Malin. 2014. Free Philosophers and Tragic Women—Stoic Perspectives on Suicide. In *Culture, Suicide, and the Human Condition*, ed. Marja-Liisa Honkasalo and Miira Tuominen, 105–128. New York: Berghahn Books.

Halperin, David. 2002a. Forgetting Foucault: Acts, Identities, and the History of Sexuality. In *The Sleep of Reason—Erotic Experience and Sexual Ethics in Ancient Greek and Rome*, ed. Martha Nussbaum and Juha Sihvola, 21–54. Chicago, London: The University of Chicago Press.

Halperin, David. 2002b. *How to Do the History of Homosexuality*. Chicago: The University of Chicago Press.

Hooff, Van, and J.L. Anton. 1990. *From Autothanasia to Suicide—Self-Killing in Classical Antiquity*. London, New York: Routledge.

Hankinson, R.J. 1991. Introduction. In *On the Therapeutic Method*, ed. Galen. Oxford: Clarendon Press.

Hankinson, R.J. (ed.). 2008. *Cambridge Companion to Galen*. Cambridge: Cambridge University Press.
Henry, Devin. 2007. How Sexist Is Aristotle's Developmental Biology? *Phronesis* 52: 1–19.
Henry, Devin. 2009. Aristotle's Generation of Animals. In *A Companion to Aristotle*, ed. Georgios Anagnostopoulos. Chichester and Malden, MA: Blackwell-Wiley.
Horowitz, Maryanne Cline. 1976. Aristotle and Woman. *Journal of the History of Biology*, Springer.
Inwood, Brad. 1997. Why Do Fools Fall in Love?. In *Aristotle and After*, ed. Richard Sorabji. Bulletin of the Institute of Classical Studies, Supplement 68. London: University of London.
Johnson, Monte Ransome. 2005. *Aristotle on Teleology*. Oxford: Oxford University Press.
Lamascus, Lorelle D. 2016. *Poverty of Eros in Plato's Symposium*. London and New York: Bloomsbury Academic.
Lefkowitz, Mary R., and Maureen B. Fant. (eds. and trans.). 1982. *Women's Life in Greece and Rome*. London: Duckworth.
Long, Kathleen. 2012. 'Nature Abhors Normality': Theories of the Monstrous from Aristotle to the X-Files (1993–2002). In *Speaking of Monsters*, ed. C.J.S. Picart et al. New York: Palgrave Macmillan.
Mayhew, Robert. 2004. *The Female in Aristotle's Biology—Reason or Rationalization*. Chicago: The University of Chicago Press.
Morsink, Johannes. 1979. Was Aristotle's Biology Sexist? *Journal of the History of Biology* 12: 83–112.
Murray, J.D. 2002. Temperature-Dependent Sex Determination (TSD): Crocodilian Survivor. In *Mathematical Biology I: An Introduction*, ed. J.D. Murray. New York, NY: Springer.
Nussbaum, Martha. 2001/1986. *Fragility of Goodness*. Cambridge: Cambridge University Press.
Nussbaum, Martha, and Juha Sihvola (eds.). 2002. *The Sleep of Reason—Erotic Experience and Sexual Ethics in Ancient Greek and Rome*. Chicago, London: The University of Chicago Press.
Partenie, Catalin. 2009. Introduction. In *Plato's Myth*, ed. Catalin Partenie, 1–26. Cambridge: Cambridge University Press.
Sampson, Kristin. 2004. Identity and Gender in Plato. In *Feminist Reflections on the History of Philosophy*, ed. Lilli Alanen and Charlotte Witt. Dodrecht, Boston, London: Kluwer.
Scott, Gary Alan, and William A. Welton. 2008. *Erotic wisdom—Philosophy and Intermediacy in Plato's Symposium*. Albany, NY: State University of New York Press.
Sheffield, Frisbee C.C. 2006. *Ethics of Desire*. Oxford: Oxford University Press.

Sihvola, Juha. 2006. Aristotle. In *Sex from Plato to Paglia—A Philosophical Encyclopedia*, vol. 1, 56–61. Westort, London: Greenwood Press.

Skinner, Marilyn B. 2013. *Sexuality in Greek and Roman Culture*. Malden, MA: Blackwell.

Tuominen, Miira. (forthcoming). Plato's *Symposium*: Erôs of the Individual in Diotima's Speech, unpublished manuscript.

Vlastos, Gregory. 1973. *Platonic Studies*, 1–34. Princeton: University Press.

CHAPTER 3

Semen, Zeus, and the Birth of Cosmos: Gender in Stoic Cosmogony and Cosmology

The Stoic sources sometimes use erotic images to illustrate their cosmological principles. According to the Christian thinker Origen (c. 185–c. 253 CE), the Stoic Chrysippus (c. 280–c. 206 BCE referred to a painting from Samos depicting an erotic act between Zeus and Hera (Origen *Cels.* 4.48). Also, Dio Chrysostom (ca. 40–ca. 120 CE) describes the lovemaking between the two Greek gods in his account of the origin of the cosmos (SVF 2.622). Stoic cosmogony and cosmology, in other words, their theories of the birth and nature of the cosmos, include elements of both myth and biology. They also use apparently gendered language in their metaphysics when they talk about rational seeds (*spermatikoi logoi*) that come to the world the same way as "semen passes through the genitals."

In Stoic scholarship, David E. Hahm has claimed that these theories are based on a "biological myth" (1977), and Kathy L. Gaca proposes a reading according to which the Stoics understood the entire cosmos as having a sexual origin (2003). In this chapter, I will scrutinize the position of gender and sexuality in Stoic materialistic metaphysics and theory of the first principles, paying attention both to the mythical and biological underpinnings of this theory. I will first analyze which metaphysical concepts might explain what gender and sexuality are. Then I will move on to discuss the sexual images in Stoic cosmology and scrutinize what exactly they are supposed to illustrate, and how we should interpret them.

I claim that the descriptions of mythical lovemaking between the gods should be understood in terms of analogy, not as a claim that gender was an actual aspect of the first principles. In Stoic epistemology, analogy

© The Author(s) 2018
M. Grahn-Wilder, *Gender and Sexuality in Stoic Philosophy*,
https://doi.org/10.1007/978-3-319-53694-1_3

is a way of expanding the field of knowledge from the familiar to the unknown. According to my reading, the familiarity of sexual reproduction motivated the use of sexual analogies in explaining the mysterious birth of the universe. Thus, I critically discuss both Hahm's and Gaca's readings, which treat the sexual images as literal statements of the Stoic account of the creation of the cosmos.

However, I claim that the sexual analogy is not very effective in casting light on the Stoic principles. Even if the Stoic sources refer to gender and sexuality in several of their major cosmological arguments, this part of their theory leaves the metaphysical status of gender unclear. Yet we can see that gendered assumption operate differently in the Stoics compared to their predecessors: for example, nothing in my material suggests that the main principles of Stoic cosmology, the active and the passive, should be read in a gendered way even if these concepts often receive a gendered interpretation, as in Aristotle's biology.

3.1 Gender and the Two Principles

Before turning to the Stoic descriptions of the birth of the cosmos and the particular question concerning the metaphysical status of gender, it is important to understand the general framework of their metaphysics. The primary doctrine is materialism: according to the Stoics, the world consists solely of material substance which nevertheless divides into two principles *(arkhai)*: "that which acts and that which is acted upon" (DL VII: 134). The passive principle, that which is acted upon, is understood as "pure" matter or "matter proper." Pure matter is like the bronze of which a statue is made—it is the material of the object, but it alone cannot explain how the object came to be. (Sextus M IX: 75–76) In Stoic metaphysics, pure matter is without qualities, completely passive, and subject to change that it is not capable of invoking. (cf. L&S 44 C–E) However, the idea of "pure matter" is purely hypothetical. We never encounter "pure matter" as such, since in reality matter is always intertwined with the active principle.

Thus formulated, the Stoic theory might appear similar to the Aristotelian distinction between form and matter (cf. Sect. 2.2). It is important to stress, however, that there are major differences between these two positions. Unlike Aristotle, the Stoics did not conceptualize the different aspects of the material world as a combination of *hylê* and *eidos*. In Aristotelian hylomorphism, it is claimed that forms only exist in matter, and likewise, matter is always formed in some way. In contrast to Aristotle, the Stoics did not discern separate entities (each one a combination of matter and form), but emphasized the continuum of matter in innumerable different manifestations, with different kinds of tensions (*tonos*) or soul functions (see e.g., Alexander in L&S 47 L). Alternatively, one could say that seen through the lenses of Stoic metaphysics, the world appears as one enormous whole consisting of different fields of energy, rather than a collection of solid and distinct objects, each of them consisting of matter and form. Thus, the Stoic view emphasizes the continuity—matter that is formed in one way now, and later serves as a constitutive element of some other material object. Thus the Stoic position is reminiscent of the Heraclitean notion of the world as in a continuous state of flux.

The Stoics considered body and soul to be so closely intertwined that even though it is possible to make a conceptual distinction between them (as they did), in reality, it is more or less impossible to separate them. They conceived of the cosmos as a *total blend* (*krâsis*) of these two principles, matter and soul. If you pour water and wine into one glass you get a new mixture in which the two original ingredients are completely blended. Similarly, the material world is a blend of the two principles, and even if it is possible in theory to discern them, in reality it is not.

The Stoics also explained the shaping activity in the material world through their notion of reason (*logos*). In fact, *logos* gives rise to all the particular things we encounter in the world. Stoic metaphysics understands also reason as material: it has different functions than pure matter, but is not of a different substance. This is a crucial point in Stoic metaphysics, in which the connection between reason and matter has a foundational position and forms the basis of the solution to numerous particular metaphysical problems. For example, the materiality of reason explains how it can act upon pure matter, because according to the Stoics, only the corporeal can act upon the corporeal (L&S 45 A–C).[1]

In this respect, for the Stoics there were no such things as "pure bodily phenomena." Consequently, a study on gender must pay particular attention to the specific way in which body and soul are mixed and how gender is conceived of as affecting this mixture. This is also crucial for

---

[1] Cf. Annas (1992: 37–56).

assessing the different statuses of gender in the Aristotelian and Stoic frameworks since feminist readers have often argued that Aristotelian hylomorphism is an inherently gendered theory.[2] Thus, one important task for a feminist inquiry into Stoic metaphysics is to analyze whether their theory gives the main principles ("pure matter," tension, soul, or reason) a gendered interpretation. A further question is to ask how would their metaphysics explain what gender is, and why this type of difference exists among living creatures. The Stoic concept of matter can obviously not provide a solution to either of the problems because everything in the cosmos consists of matter. Nothing in my sources supports a reading that they would have considered the hypothetical notion of pure matter as "feminine," or tension that creates differences in matter as "masculine." However, even if *logos* is usually used in a gender-neutral way in Stoic sources, especially in the context of Stoic cosmology there are certain interesting passages that explicitly adopt a gendered approach, in particular, in their discussion on the origin and formation of the cosmos. Thus, one might well ask if, given that the notions of matter and tension alone were not sufficient to understand the status of gender in the Stoic framework, the notion of *logos* could offer a solution.

3.2   Fire and Sperm: Generation in a Material World

Calcidius introduces gendered vocabulary on a cosmic scale in his discussion of the Stoic first principles. He presents the theory by comparing reason to semen and matter to the (presumably male) genitalia, and claims that the universal reason passes through the universal body, "just like seed *(semen)* through the genital organs *(per membra genitalia)*" (L&S 44 E).[3] Calcidius' analogy makes it clear that matter and reason are interconnected, and that a combination of both is needed for

---

[2] Cf. e.g., Charlotte Witt (1993: 121).

[3] Calcidius, who was 4th century Christian translator and commentator of Plato's *Timaeus*, most plausbily means the male genitalia here. Even if we assumed that the Stoics supported a *dual-seed theory*—I will return later to the question of whether or not they did—this theory only states that both man and woman *produce* seed, but this is still different from claiming that women actually *emit* it, at least as distinctly as a man does. Robert Mayhew similarly distinguishes between *producing* or *contributing* and *emitting* semen in the context of Aristotle's embryology (2004: 32). In Sects. 2.2 and 2.3, I introduced the Ancient dual-seed theory, according to which both the male and the female produce semen and the fetus is formed as a mixture of the two.

giving rise to new life. Taken a little further, it would seem that it makes reason dependent on matter, but not vice versa, as there can be male genitalia without semen, but no semen without male genitalia. This is also the order Calcidius' account suggests: first there is the matter (the genital), and then through it reason (semen) comes into world. Also other sources use expressions such as "passing through" in describing how reason came into the world. Alexander of Aphrodisias (late 2nd and early 3rd century CE), for example, claims that according to the Stoic theory of four elements, fire and air "pass as wholes through the other pair, earth and water." (L&S 48 C).

The analogy between *logos* and *sperma* occurs frequently in Stoic sources. Indeed, the Stoics commonly refer to the rational principle using the term *spermatikoi logoi*, "seminal reason," which is implanted into the passive matter (cf. L&S 46 A). The sources often specifically connect *spermatikoi logoi* to fire. In Stoic theory, fire is understood as the primary element, out of which everything else is born and into which everything disappears between the cycles of the world. Aetius (ca. 100 CE) states that for the Stoics, god was intelligent and a "designing fire" which "encompasses all the seminal principles." (Aetius I.7.33, SVF 2.1027; L&S 46 A) Aristocles (1st century CE) puts forward a similar notion: "But the primary fire is as it were a sperm which possesses the principles (*logoi*) of all things and the causes of past, present, and future events." (L&S 46 G) Both Aetius and Aristocles draw an analogy between fire and sperm in that both are active and generating. The theory of elements is further connected to the distinction between activity and passivity, since the Stoics understand fire and air as active elements (in that they sustain), whereas water and earth are passive (they are sustained).[4] Given that, as we saw in Chap. 2, Ancient myths and biological theories frequently connected fire, Sun, and heat to male gender, it is worthwhile to investigate whether this idea was also adapted into the Stoic theory.

Thus, the sources present sperm as analogical to reason, god, and fire. In Stoic metaphysics, all of these refer to the very same principle: the rational activity that gives rise to motion and change (cf. L&S 47 D–G). These analogies make a connection between the fiery element (or its corresponding quality, heat) and sperm, and presume that heat

---

[4] Stobaeus (ca. 5th c. CE) also mentions that air and fire are weightless (L&S 50 J).

has the ability to cause generation and thus to create life.[5] In connecting the warm element, activity, and sperm the Stoics seem to come close to Aristotle's embryology, although he explains the sperm's life-giving capacity in terms of *pneuma*, not fire (*GA* 737a20; cf. Sect. 2.2).

However, thus presented, there seems to be an apparent discrepancy in the Stoic theory. Aristocles claims that fire includes the *logos* of all things, past, present, and future, and compares this to sperm which then supposedly includes the *logos* of a (future) human being. But what does the sperm conceive when it gives rise to the material world in general, and human life in particular? Did Aristocles presuppose that there was a counterpart for both fire and sperm, like matter is to form in Aristotle's metaphysics, or female is to male in his biology? Or could it be that the only thing that is presupposed is "space," and that a female's role corresponds to this, as in Ancient preformationist theory? Thus, we will have to investigate more carefully how fire could create anything by and from itself. Certain early Stoic fragments address this problem by presenting explicitly sexual interpretations of the first creation.

3.3 On the Sexual Encounter Between Zeus and Hera—A Biological Myth?

Chrysippus connects Zeus, reason, semen, and matter in the following allegory: in an erotic painting portraying Hera performing a sexual act—apparently fellatio—with Zeus (Origen *Cels.* 4.48; Theophilius *Ad Autol.* 3.8 = SVF 2.885, cf. DL VII: 187–188).[6] According to Origen, Chrysippus discussed this painting to illustrate how "matter receives the generative principles of God, and contains them in itself for the ordering of the universe" (*Cels.* 4.48). So understood, the allegory seems to present Zeus' semen as the origin of the whole cosmos, and Hera as the matter. But how exactly should we interpret this illustration? In particular: how should we understand the relationship between Zeus and Hera?

According to Kathy Gaca, the sexual encounter between Zeus and Hera demonstrates how reason is mixed with matter. She seems to take

---

[5] Cicero (106–43 BCE) explicitly connects fire to the power of reproduction (L&S 47 C, 4) On the primary role of fire, see also Stobaeus (L&S 47 A). Cf. Long & Sedley 1987: 286.

[6] Cf. interpretation of this myth in Gaca (2003: 69) and Mansfeld (1979: 180).

Hera to represent something like the Aristotelian material cause in the process of cosmic generation, and takes quite literally the idea that the Stoics' cosmos originates sexually. According to her, the transformation from fire to wet semen takes place in Zeus' orgasm (Gaca 2003: 69–70.) She claims: "Without Zeus's sexual arousal, there is no transformation of reason from limitless mind to rational semen, and without the receptive body of Hera, no shaping of cosmos can happen." (Gaca 2003: 70).[7]

Gaca is right in drawing attention to this interesting problem concerning the roles of semen and sexual activity as building blocks of the Stoic explanation of the cosmos, as well as to the problem of how the different elements are created from the original fire. However, her reading seems to confuse the discussion on the erotic painting from Samos with other allegories that explicitly refer to *sexual intercourse* between Zeus and Hera. Since generation is the very topic of the discussion here, it is important to pay close attention to the details of these mythical stories: one depicts the erotic act between the gods as fellatio, another as copulation. Gaca's reading of Hera's "taking seed into her receptive body" suggests that the goddess is taking the seed into her womb—which in this particular case she is not. Indeed, the sexual image of fellatio seems an odd choice to explain birth of any kind. Moreover, Gaca's account does not specify exactly how we should read the story of Zeus and Hera: even though she uses the term "allegorize," she still seems to take it quite literally as suggesting that the early Stoics believed that the cosmos actually had a sexual origin.

Furthermore, the role of Hera seems ambiguous. On the one hand, Gaca pays attention to the connection between Hera and matter, but on the other she refers to Hera's "receptive body" that shapes the seed. She does not specify whether or not she takes these views to present two different aspects of the same theory of the female role in a generation. As we have seen, it is far from evident that they are: Aristotle's embryology discusses the female as the material cause, whereas Ancient preformationist theory only ascribes to her a receptive role. Both roles are essentially passive, but yet they are remarkably different. However, Gaca's interpretation points to yet another and less passive role we could assign Hera. Gaca formulates an interesting hypothesis when she mentions Zeus'

---

[7]Cf. J. Mansfeld, who connects the notion of *ekpyrosis*, the conflagration to which all things return, with orgasm, also mentioning the erotic image of Hera fellating Zeus (1979: 180).

sexual arousal as the starting point of the birth of the cosmos, but does not elaborate on this. If we take this notion further, Hera's role could be plausibly understood as the stimulating principle that, like an erotic muse, assists Zeus to ejaculate his creation. Seen in this light, she would also play a more active role in the creation of the cosmos than just serving as a "receptive body." Even if this reading does not exactly make her an equal partner in the creation either, at least her role would be significant in stimulating and giving rise to the process (like the fig coagulating milk, as in the analogy frequently used in Aristotle's embryology). Nevertheless, the end result would still be a birth without a woman, as in the ideal expressed in Pausanias' speech in Plato's *Symposium*—particularly if we understand the sexual act between the gods as fellatio.

However, other Stoic passages draw a different picture of the sexual connection between the gods. Diogenes Laertius presents the following Stoic view: Zeus (also called "god," "reason," and "fate") turns the entire substance (*tên pasan ousian*) into water. Then, "just as sperm (*sperma*) is enveloped in the seminal fluid (*gonê*)" he proceeds to create the four elements. (DL VII: 135; L&S 46 B) Dio Chrysostom gives the following account of the creation of the cosmos: Zeus, remembering Aphrodite, changes himself into fiery air, and makes love to Hera. Zeus' sperm (*sperma*) is the forming and shaping (*to platton kai dêmiourgoun*) *pneuma* in the seminal fluid (*gonê*) that he emits. Having made the substance wet, he then molds the things around him. (SVF 2.622) This image, unlike the other ones mentioned above, expressly presents the sexual act of Zeus and Hera as an intercourse. This allegory seems to reflect the cosmogonic theory presented in the previous section: fire has the foundational role and water (in Zeus' semen that makes everything wet) follow. Dio Chrysostom also applies other central Stoic metaphysical terminology in describing Zeus as *pneuma*, "resembling living beings consisting of body and soul." It is remarkable, however, that the passage does not present Zeus as the only or first god, who alone created the cosmos: on the contrary, he "remembers Aphrodite" in the process of creation and has intercourse with Hera. Thus there were other (female) gods involved in and preceding this very first creation.[8]

---

[8] Origen criticizes the discrepancy between discussing Zeus on the one hand as "the God," and on the other hand as someone "who is the son Kronos and Rhea, and the husband of Hera, and brother of Poseidon," etc. (Origen, *Cels.* 6.42) For how could Zeus be "the God" when there were all these other gods and goddesses, as well, some of which existed before him, as apparently his parents did?

David E. Hahm calls Dio Chrysostom's account "an allegorized myth" which presents the formation of the four elements. He reads Hera's role in this passage as similar to air through which the god, being fire, passes through into water (Hahm 1977: 61). He claims: "In biological terms Zeus's seminal emission supplies both the creative power and the matter out of which the cosmos is made. Hera, the female, has the function as inducing the emission of seed, but contributes nothing to the offspring." (ibid. 61–62) Hahm thus identifies sperm with both aspects of the material world as understood in Stoic metaphysics: the active, creative power on the one hand, and "matter proper" on the other. In his view, the female (Hera) would not be identified with matter as in Aristotle or Origen, but with air. Consequently, the female is not identified even with a material cause in the generation of the cosmos, but only as a means through which the masculine semen comes to shape the world. Nevertheless, Hahm also claims that in giving sperm the constitutional role in their cosmology, the Stoics adapted Aristotle's biological notion of generation but turned it into a cosmological explanation. He states further that the use of Aristotelian embryology in cosmology would be an original Stoic philosophical innovation because, as Hahm points out, Aristotle himself did not use embryological analogies to explain the origin of the cosmos.[9] According to Hahm, both Aristotle and the Stoics understand sperm as a mixture of *pneuma* and water, and "view the generative constituent of the semen either as this *pneuma* or, alternatively, as heat." In Hahm's reading, the Stoic cosmology is built on a biological and sexual foundation. The biggest difference he sees between the Aristotelian and the Stoic position is in the role assigned to the female: whereas in Aristotle, the female is a genuine cause in generation, the one supplying matter, the Stoics deny her even this role in their insistence that the "generative agent" is the male semen (ibid. 62–66).

A serious problem in Hahm's reading, as I see it, is that it does not explain how exactly the comparison to Aristotle helps us to comprehend the Stoic cosmological theory. He admits that the above sexual analogy depicts the role of the female differently from Aristotle by not discussing

---

[9] For Aristotle, the cosmos was eternal and thus there was no need for him to discuss its origin—with or without sexual analogies. As discussed in Chap. 2, one of the very few places where the science of living nature and the investigation of heavens meet is in his explanation of sperm as analogical to the essence of the stars.

her as a material cause. However, if Hera's role is understood as air, this would seem to bring the Stoic view closer to preformationism—which, as we have seen, is incompatible with Aristotelian embryology. Thus presented, the Stoic cosmogony would seem to come close to Plato's *Timaeus* where the Mother is compared to empty space (*Tim.* 37c; 50d–51a).[10] In line with Ancient preformationism, one could argue that the male sperm does not need a (substantial) female counterpart in order to generate new life, only a space (the womb). Similarly, in the context of cosmology, the idea would be that reason or fire only needed a space in which the entire cosmos could be created.

Indeed, we encountered above certain Stoic formulations indicating that fire alone gives rise to everything else and that other elements derive from it. This view is compressed by Stobaeus, claiming to report the early Stoic view of Chrysippus and Zeno, according to which "the first change" occurs from fire into air, and the second from air into water, and the third from water into earth (L&S 47 A). Thus, fire gives rise to other things and does not need a counterpart upon which to act because the other elements are born from it. In the framework of Stoic materialist metaphysics, we also have to remember that everything is understood as material, fire included. The Aristotelian model does not seem to do a good job, however, illustrating the Stoic cosmological notion of how the elements are created from the primary fire.

Further, I have emphasized above the difference in the relationship between form and matter in Aristotelian/Stoic metaphysics, and this is another reason why I do not find the Aristotelian embryological model as helpful for understanding the Stoic cosmological principals. I also do not find support from my sources for a reading suggesting that the Stoics would have actually based their cosmological theory on Aristotle's biology, as Hahm claims. Thus, I do not think that there is enough evidence to conclude that the Stoics conceived of the cosmos as solely, or even for the most part, the result of (masculine) sexual activity. I believe that the whole picture, in Stoicism, is more complicated than the passages discussed above or Gaca's or Hahm's readings would suggest. Rather than giving insight into the alleged genderedness of the first principles, the above erotic images raise the question of the role of analogies

---

[10]Cf. *Symposium* when the character of Pausanias speaks of a noble birth at which no woman is needed (*Symp.* 181 b–c).

in Stoic philosophical argumentation in general, and of the choice of using gendered/sexual images in presentations of their metaphysical doctrines.

3.4 Sexual Analogies in Stoic Cosmology

Let us examine how exactly the gendered/sexual terminology operates in Stoic metaphysics. Calcidius expresses the Stoic view, stating that reason enters the world "just like seed through the genital organs." Diogenes Laertius describes how god functions in the material world "just as sperm is enveloped in the seminal fluid." Aristocles describes fire "as it were a sperm." Thus, none of these passages explain or even purports to explain what semen, genitals, and gender are: they all rather refer to them as analogous to some other thing (reason, god, fire) they wish to explain. I have referred to the importance of analogy in Aristotle's scientific method, and it was also an essential aspect of Stoic epistemology. In fact, it was one of the main channels through which we, according to the Stoics, can derive knowledge from empirical facts. For example, they claimed to have knowledge about the center of the Earth by virtue of an analogy with small globes (DL 7.53, L&S 39D).[11] The reasoning was that it is difficult to directly obtain any evidence of the planet Earth (and it was particularly difficult in Antiquity given the level of technical equipment), whereas small globes are easy to grasp and to investigate. If we accept the premise that the Earth is also a globe, only on a very great scale, then the information we can obtain about small globes will give us further insight into the Earth. In the cases discussed above, the analogy is between sperm/genitals and certain metaphysical principles. Thus, the gendered elements of the arguments are supposedly something with which we are already familiar, and which help us to understand something that is unknown to us.

Even though the above analogies between the generation of the world and inseminating sperm refer to physical gender, gender in itself is left unexplained. On the contrary, the notions used in the doctrines on

---

[11] According to Diogenes Laertius, in Stoic epistemology, the main ways of obtaining knowledge include direct contact (*periptôsis*), analogy (*analogia*), resemblance (*hoimotês*), composition (*synthêsis*), transposition (*metathesis*) and contrariety (*enantiosis*) (DL VII: 52). On the role of analogy in Stoic epistemology and philosophical argumentation, see Miira Tuominen (2007: 240–250).

reason, god, and fire discussed above already *presuppose* gender. It seems that the Stoics expected gender to play such a major role in how people generally understand generation that they considered sexual analogies intuitive for explaining their metaphysical doctrines of the origin of the cosmos or the elements. That new life is created through copulation and subsequent pregnancy and childbirth is something that people have empirical evidence of, and thus this seems a plausible analogy to explain the birth of the cosmos—something of which no person can have any personal experience.

For the early Stoics, the sexual image might possibly provide an (admittedly not very detailed or theoretically well-founded) illustration of how the rational seeds are carried to the next cycle of the world, and the order of the creation of the elements. On the other hand, the model of two parents who give birth to a new person seems to face serious difficulties in its capacity to explain other central aspects of Stoic metaphysics. The main problem, as I see it, is linked to the relationship between "pure" matter and reason. As I stated at the beginning of this chapter, the Stoics considered matter to be *thoroughly* rational, and rational matter to be a continuum—everything in the entire world consists of rational matter. They also, as noted, understood matter and reason as a total blend (*krâsis*), it being impossible to separate one from the other. This seems to be quite different from the idea of a male fertilizing a female, with both of them functioning as separate causes in the process. Thus, the Stoic view does not appear to be analogous with a model according to which two different individuals with their respective reproductive functions give birth to a new person.

Neither Gaca or Hahm pay any particular attention to the kind of sexual act we are supposed to imagine taking place between Zeus and Hera. As I pointed out, fellatio has obvious defects in explaining conception. Yet the analogy with fellatio avoids the above-mentioned problem—it does not have to suppose that Hera gave anything substantial of herself to the thing that was created. Nevertheless, it functions quite badly from the everyday perspective, which does not support the idea that something new (other than sexual pleasure) is being produced as a result of the sexual act in question. Yet one could speculate whether the oral aspect could be understood as relating to speech and reason—both of which the Stoics express through the notion of *logos*. One could thus assume that the analogy to fellatio might have had a certain plausibility for the early Stoics if one reads Hera's role as to provide sexual stimulation, and not with just any part of her body but specifically with her mouth, which is connected to language and rationality.

A deeper underlying question concerns the distinction between activity and passivity. As indicated above, the Stoics divided principles into the active (air, fire) and the passive (water, earth). At first glance this might seem reminiscent of Aristotle's position discussed above, which gives a foundational role to the distinction between activity and passivity and (at least in his biology) connects this distinction to gender difference, presenting males as essentially active and females as essentially passive. Thus, if we assume (as Hahm did) that the Stoic position was an interpretation of Aristotle's embryology on a cosmological scale, then it would seem plausible to suggest that the roles of Zeus and Hera should be understood as corresponding to the active and passive elements. However, if Hera was identified with air, this would also make her active rather than passive. I also do not find support from the sources that the Stoics would have understood activity and passivity in gendered terms. I emphasized above that for the Stoics, pure matter is a purely hypothetical concept, and thus the "passive" matter is always intertwined with the active *logos*.

I have proposed a more plausible reading according to which the Stoics used gendered language in their cosmology in order to provide useful analogies for explaining a certain cosmological principle, not in order to claim that a certain cosmological principle was gendered as such. Given that gender appears in these analogies as the element with which the reader/listener is already supposed to be familiar with (like the roundness of a small globe as opposed to the roundness of planet Earth), this does not seem to support the claim that Stoic cosmology as such was particularly gendered, or that the Stoics themselves believed that the cosmos really had a sexual origin.

Still, it is worth emphasizing that the Stoic analogies are by no means gender-neutral, and they do not give equal importance to the male and the female as explanatory causes. They clearly encompass elements from earlier Ancient mythological, medical, biological, and philosophical sources. This tradition supports the choice of Zeus, the male, as the personification of reason and heat rather than Hera, who is assigned the role of matter or air—something through which the rational seed comes into the world—or in the most optimistic reading, of an erotic muse who helps the artist to create his masterwork.

Finally, the story of Zeus and Hera is not connected to sexuality in humans so as to explain why things such as sexuality and gender exist. Furthermore, even if the chosen analogies reflect the traditional view of male dominance in connecting higher and more noble entities (reason, fire, god) to males and lower entities (earth, air) to females, it is still far from clear that the Stoics actually supported a hierarchy between genders as such. However, to understand how the Stoics understood gender in humans, we have to look at their metaphysical and physical discussions that are for the most parts separate from the cosmological problems discussed in this chapter.

Appendix

Diogenes Laertius, *Lives of Eminent Philosophers* (DL)

Diogenis Laertii Vitae philosophorum. Miroslav Marcovich (ed.). *Bibliotheca scriptorum Graecorum et Romanorum Teubneriana*. Vol. 1. Stuttgart-Lipsia: Teubner, 1999–2002.
Lives of Eminent Philosophers. R.D. Hicks (transl.). Cambridge and London: Harvard University Press, 1995.

The Hellenistic Philosophers. A.A. Long and D.N. Sedley (eds.). Cambridge: Cambridge University Press, 1987. (L&S)

Origen, *Contra Celsum* (*Cels.*)

Contra Celsum. Henry Chadwick (transl.). Cambridge and New York: Cambridge University Press, 1980.
Die Griechischen Christlichen Schriftsteller der ersten Jahrhunderte (GCS), GCS 2–3, Origenes Werke: Contra Celsum. Paul Koetschau (ed.). 1. Aufl. 1899.

Plato

Tim.   *Timaeus*
Symp. *Symposium*

Platonis Opera (Oxford Classical Texts):
Vol. 1, ed. E.A. Duke et al. 1995.
Vol. 2, ed. J. Burnet 1922.
Vol. 3, ed. J. Burnet 1922.
Vol. 4, ed. J. Burnet 1922.

Respublica. ed. S.R. Slings 2003.
Complete Works. John M. Cooper (ed.). D.S. Hutchinson (associate ed.). Indianapolis: Hackett Publishers, 1997.
The Symposium. Christopher Gill (transl.). London and New York: Penguin Books, 1999.

Sextus Empeiricus

M IX–X *Against the Physicists*

Sexti Empirici Opera. H. Mutschmann and J. Mau (eds.). In: *Bibliotheca scriptorum Graecorum et Romanorum.* Lipsiae: Teubner, 1962.

Stoicorum veterum fragmenta. Vol. I–III. H. von Arnim (ed.). Leipzig: Lipsiae, in aedibus B.G. Teubneri, 1903–24. (SVF)

REFERENCES

Annas, Julia. 1992. *Hellenistic Philosophy of Mind.* Berkeley, Los Angeles and London: University of California Press.
Gaca, Kathy. 2003. *The Making of Fornication—Eros, Ethics and Political Reform in Greek Philosophy and Early Christianity.* Berkley and Los Angeles: The University of California Press.
Hahm, David E. 1977. *The Origins of Stoic Cosmology.* Columbus: Ohio State University Press.
Mansfeld, J. 1979. Providence and Destruction of the Universe in Early Stoic Thought—With Some Remarks on the 'Mysteries of Philosophy'. In *Studies in Hellenistic Religions,* ed. M.J. Vermaseren. Leiden: Brill.
Mayhew, Robert. 2004. *The Female in Aristotle's Biology—Reason or Rationalization.* Chicago: The University of Chicago Press.
Tuominen, Miira. 2007. *Apprehension and Argument—Ancient Theories for Starting Points of Knowledge.* Dodrecth: Springer.
Witt, Charlotte. 1993. Form, Normativity, and Gender in Aristotle—A Feminist Perspective. In *Feminist Interpretations of Aristotle,* ed. Cynthia A. Freeland. University Park, PA: The Pennsylvania State University Press.

CHAPTER 4

The Metaphysical Insignificance of Gender

In their ethics and political theory, the Stoics frequently appeal to or clearly presume some metaphysical facts in order to support explicitly gender-related statements concerning the education of girls (Musonius), for example, or the status of women in the ideal republic (Zeno, Chrysippus). Given the immense importance of the metaphysical underpinnings of the ethico-political discussions, it is surprising, however, that there is hardly any systematic research on the Stoic metaphysics of gender. On the one hand, this lacuna in the existing scholarship can be seen as reflecting the original sources: only seldom do the Stoics explicitly discuss gender within their metaphysical theory of the human being. On the other hand, as I will show, this investigation is crucial for our understanding of the Stoic outlook on gender and sexuality on the whole. In this chapter, I will approach some central Stoic metaphysical doctrines on human soul and body from the point of view of gender, and analyze the metaphysical status of gender in the Stoic theory.

A central problem in this inquiry is to decide which Stoic metaphysical concepts can give an insight into gender. As I showed in the previous chapter, Stoic cosmology does not provide a sufficient solution since, as I suggested, the sexual and gendered language should be understood in an allegorical sense. In this chapter, I will first scrutinize how gender would fit into the Stoic metaphysical notion of four categories. I have not seen this specific research question having been posed before, but I will show that this theory indeed provides a fruitful framework for analyzing the metaphysical status of gender. The four categories, as I will show, also provide a strong argument for indifference to the particular gender a person has. This idea receives further support when I turn to investigate the Stoic notion of *pneuma*. I suggest that, according to the Stoics, having sexuality (which implies being gendered) is a generic feature of all humans, whereas being gendered as a man or a woman only modifies this feature. This, I claim, is a fundamental point in the Stoic theory.

My investigation of the reproductive soul capacity leads me to analyze Stoic notions of embryology. Even though the Stoics allude to embryological theories in several sources, unlike Aristotle they did not support any particular embryological model. However, the Ancient embryological debates form a useful backdrop against which many of the fragmented Stoic views become more comprehensible. The Stoic embryological fragments do not support any difference between male and female infants, but they suggest a striking difference between adult humans and embryos, the latter of which are viewed more or less like plants. Seneca (ca. 4 BCE–65 CE) seems to suggest that this holds even to newborn babies. The embryological arguments point further to the fundamental importance of rationality in Stoicism—and their lack of interest in creatures that they consider to fall outside of rationality. Yet, when it comes to adult humans, the Stoic metaphysical and physical discussions have a general tendency to support a view of commonness and similarity, rather than differences. The final section of this chapter analyzes reproduction as an area of adult life, which is connected to rational choices and striving for a way of life in accordance with nature.

4.1 The Stoic Theory of Categories: Gender and Substance

Where does the notion of gender fit in the Stoic metaphysics? The first potential solution lies in the Stoic idea of four categories. Stoic metaphysics classifies existing things (things that are something, *ti*) as incorporeal (such as void, place, and time), bodily, or neither (fictional entities). Bodily things are further divided into four categories: (1) the substance (*hypokeimenon* or *ousia*), (2) the qualified (*poion*), (3) the disposed (*pôs ekhon*), and (4) the relatively disposed (*pros tis pôs ekhon*) (See L&S 27 A–G). According to Plutarch, the Stoics "make each of us four"; thus, a person belongs to all four categories, each of them showing a different aspect of him or her (L&S 28 A). Thus, these four categories appear potentially useful in enhancing understanding of the kind of quality gender is. I discuss the categories one by one in this and the following two subsections.

The first metaphysical category is *the Substance*. Gender obviously has a corporeal reality and thus would seem to fit at least partly in this category. Genitals and other gender-related physical features are parts of the substance of a human being. However, gender cannot be straightforwardly situated in this first category because "having a body" is much more generic than "being a man or being a woman." After all, the former can be ascribed to *anything* that falls under the category of substance. This category, being the most general of the four, can only confirm the fact that human beings are material entities, but does not help us to analyze any more specific features.

However, it is difficult to draw a direct line between what the Stoics took as falling under the category of "substance" and what belonged to the second category of "the qualified." As noted above, Stoic material metaphysics does not support any dualistic view of matter and soul, and their conception of the relationship between the two (both being material) is best expressed through their notion of total blend (*krâsis*). Thus, I think it would not give an accurate picture of Stoic metaphysical outlook to understand the category of substance as "pure matter" on top of which some qualities can be attached. The level of "substance" also includes the idea that the body is intertwined with tension, *tonos*, of some kind.[1] The specific way in which this happens, however, would be explained by the second category.

Exactly how we should understand the demarcation between the first and the second categories is finally insignificant for the present inquiry. To whatever extent "substance" is understood as including aspects of the soul, or *tonos*, under the first category, we are still not able to grasp any differentiating principles between human beings, such as gender. Moreover, the investigation of gender clearly requires us to analyze not only the Stoic understanding of the physical body but also their theory of the soul. Thus, in order to gain a deeper insight into what gender is,

---

[1] Stephen Menn, in his discussion of the Stoic theory of categories, emphasizes the difference between Stoic and Platonic/Aristotelian ontology, pointing out that they support different views on corporealism and the relationship between material bodies and qualities. See Menn (1999: 217–221). On the categories and corporeality, see also David Sedley (2005).

we have to consider other, more differentiating qualities, which in Stoic theory fall under the remaining three categories.

4.2 Gender and the Qualified: Common and Individual Features

It is under the second category of *the Qualified* that a thing can really be understood as a "something," one kind of a thing rather than another. Of the four categories, this looks at the outset to be the most promising in grasping where gender fits in the Stoic theory, since *poion* functions as a differentiating principle that determines what a given thing is—that it is not just a heap of matter, but Socrates, a hedgehog or a wooden horse, for example.[2]

The category of the qualified divides further into two subcategories: the commonly qualified (*koinos poion*) and the individually qualified (*idios poion*). An often-repeated example of common qualities is that "Socrates is a human being." Individual qualities, then, express the aspects of Socrates that make him exactly Socrates, as opposed to any other human being. However, Stoic scholarship has thus far not posed the specific research question of how gender fits in the picture. Which of these qualities explain what it means that Socrates is a man, or that Hipparchia is a woman?[3]

Thus, we need a more careful analysis of where the gendered features actually situate in the Stoic theory, and what kinds of consequences do these have for the position of gender in the metaphysical theory on the whole. To get a clearer picture, let us analyze certain important passages on Stoic theory of the soul. The Stoics made a distinction between different

---

[2] Cf. Long and Sedley (1987: 177).

[3] When Long and Sedley discuss the Stoic theory of *pneuma*, they mention that the fact that "Socrates is a man" is due to the particular portion of *pneuma* he has. They do not enter an explicit discussion on gender in their account, however, and the double meaning of the word "man" is slightly confusing. They give the following examples of individual qualities: "for Socrates, 'man,' 'Greek,' 'prudent', 'snub-nosed', etc." (ibid.). In this context, they probably mean "man" in the significance of gender. Unfortunately, they do not problematize this division in their discussion of the categories, nor do they enter any lengthier or more systematic discussion of gender (Long and Sedley 1987: 174). In this chapter, I provide a detailed argument, based on an analysis of several relevant passages, for placing "to be a man" or "to be a woman" under individual qualities in the Stoic theories, and analyze what this means for the position of gender in Stoicism in general.

capacities or faculties of the soul. The commanding and reasoning part of the soul is called *hêgemonikon*, and this part is responsible for dealing with impressions and impulses. Aetius gives the following account of the relationship between *hêgemonikon* and other soul capacities:

> From the commanding faculty, there are seven parts of the soul which grow out and stretch out into the body like the tentacles of an octopus. Five of these are the senses, sight, smell, hearing, taste, and touch. Of the remainder, one is called seed (*sperma*), and this is the *pneuma* extending from the *hêgemonikon* to the genitals (*parastatón*). The other, which they also call utterance, is breath extending from the commanding faculty to the pharynx, tongue, and appropriate organs. (Aetius, L&S 53H; SVF 2.836; Long and Sedley's translation slightly modified)

Aetius mentions utterance which is connected to the mouth and the speaking organs. As I pointed out in the previous chapter, the Stoics connected speech and the use of language to rationality. Aetius thus lists eight basic functions of the (human) soul: in addition to the highest, commanding part (*hêgemonikon*), there are the five senses, speaking capacity, and *sperma*.

For our present discussion, it is important to scrutinize what the notion of *sperma* means in this context. It is unlikely that Aetius was thinking about *spermatikoi logoi* as rationality is a quality of the highest part of the human soul, and by virtue of it, other capacities are also rational. Thus, rational seeds could not be only one aspect of the soul (and it is not self-evident that *spermatikoi logoi* could be understood as a *capacity*, either). On the other hand, we have seen that the notion of *sperma* has strong connotations with Ancient theories of embryology, and that there was a debate whether it belonged exclusively to males (the Aristotelian view) or whether females also produced it (the Hippocratic/Galenic view).

It is interesting that the Aetius passage draws attention to the respective organs when discussing soul capacities. For me, this also seems to provide the clue for understanding the specific status of gender. This becomes even clearer in the following passage from Galen, reporting the view of Chrysippus.

> The soul is *pneuma* connate with us, extending as a continuum through the whole body as long as the free-flowing breath of life is present in the body. Now of the parts of the soul that have been assigned to the several

parts [of the body], that of them which extends to the trachea is the voice; that to the eyes, sight; that to the ears, hearing; that to the nostrils, smell; that to the tongue, taste; that to the entire flesh, touch; and that which extends to the testicles, possessing another such *logos*, is seminal. That part where all these meet is in the heart, being the governing part (*hêgemonikon*) of the soul. (Galen PHP 287-89 K, 170 de Lacy, transl. de Lacy)

This passage expresses basically the same idea as the Aetius passage above, situating reproduction among the other capacities of the rational soul, adding the interesting mentioning that the "testicles posses another such *logos*." The idea seems to be that this particular part of the soul, extended to the testicles, possesses the *logos* of a future human being.[4] All in all, the model supposes a connection between the soul capacities and the organs through which they function (like the capacity of seeing functions through the eyes), as well as between all of these and the commanding part of the soul.[5] On the basis of this model, I suggest that we should understand the notion of *sperma* as referring to the reproductive capacity, and that this capacity should be understood as an essential function of the human soul, which is common to all human beings in the same way as seeing, hearing, and speaking are. The notions of "genitals" and "testicles," then, refer to the corresponding physical organs.

However, one could ask whether the choice of the terms "sperm" and "testicles" indicates that the underlying model was that of a man, or whether Aetiues and Chrysippus thought (as Galen himself later explicitly argued) that women also possess testicles, or produced semen. They may only have mentioned the male alternative because it

---

[4] However, even though Aetius and Chrysippus position reproduction among the basic soul functions in the discussed passages, there also seem to have been different positions inside the Stoic school on this subject. Nemesius (fl. 4th cent. CE) mentions that the Stoic Panaetius (ca. 185–110 BCE) would have agreed on situating the vocal capacity among the soul's rational functions, but he would have made "the reproductive capacity (*to spermatikon*) a part *not* of soul (*ou tés psychés*) but of physique (*physeós*)" (Nemesius, L&S 53 I, my emphasis). Long and Sedley, however, count the idea that reproduction "gets a whole part of the soul to itself" as the "orthodox Stoic account," and thus Panaetius' position may have been an exceptional one (Long and Sedley 1987: 319–320).

[5] My reading receives further support from another passage where Galen writes (addressing Chrysippus): "For conceptions and basic grasps are activities of the soul, but its parts, as you yourself explain elsewhere, are the auditory *pneuma* and the visual *pneuma*, and again the vocal in addition to these and the reproductive, but above all the leading part of the soul (...)" (Galen, PHP 5.3.7; SVF 2.841; translation Inwood & Gerson).

was, in Ancient philosophical discourse, the norm to take a man (not a woman) to represent "a human being as such." This formulation hence leaves us to speculate as to whether or not they agreed that female reproductive capacity (whether identified as "female testicles," the uterus, menstrual blood, or any other equivalent reproductive part in females) should also be called "seminal" or as "possessing *logos*." Still, the whole view would be problematic if it did not include women because of the general scope of the theory: it is about common functions of the soul (not only in humans but also in many animals). Moreover, women and female animals obviously also possess a reproductive capacity, whether or not it is agreed that they possess testicles or produce semen.

I take the main point of the arguments of both Aetius and Chrysippus to be about the soul's functions, not about any particular organ. The above passages expressly discuss capacities of the soul, not the physical features, but it is said that each capacity extends to the corresponding physical organ; in the case of *sperma*, to the genitals. Therefore, whether the general capacity of generation happens through the male or the female reproductive organs and secretions seems unimportant. My reading thus accentuates the universal human capacities, and the implication is that the reproductive capacity requires corresponding physical features. Accordingly, gender difference could thus be seen as merely two different variations in the way this basic human capacity is qualified.[6]

It is not clear at the outset, however, whether or not the reproductive capacity really is similar to the other mentioned soul capacities. The reproductive capacity functions differently in males and females, whereas all the others function basically the same way in all individuals (there are not two different modes of, say, perception even though there, of course, is plenty of variation in how this capacity works in different

---

[6]Cf. Long and Sedley (1987: 319–320) and Julia Annas (1992: 61), who also list reproduction among the basic functions of the soul in Stoicism, although without going into more detail about how this affects the metaphysical status of gender. Kathy Gaca also seems to support the view according to which gender is one of the basic aspects of the human soul, even though she does not mention the metaphysical categories. With reference to the Chrysippus passage in Galen, she also points out that the Stoics counted sexuality among the eight (if we include the commanding faculty) basic human rational functions (Gaca 2003: 68).

individuals). To what extent, then, are they similar? One solution could be formulated on the basis of Julia Annas' account of the difference between common and individual qualities. She writes: "Some of the soul's powers belong to it the way qualities belong to a subject" (Annas 1992: 65). She calls "dispositional powers" the powers which can be distinguished in terms of location (e.g., sight in eyes). "However, some other powers ... differ only in their 'individual quality' (*idios poiotêtos*)" (ibid. 66). Hence, it seems that reproductive capacity is common to all animals, and (in humans and many other species) is "dispositional" in that it is located in the reproductive organs. The genitals, however, have (basically) two kinds of "individual qualities" (the male and the female) in which they typically differ. On this level, gender difference does not seem any more significant than differences in eye colors. One person can have green eyes and another brown ones but for both of them, these are physical organs through which the rational capacity of "seeing" operates. The color only brings individual variation among humans, but does not alter this fundamental capacity, which is common to everybody (who has functional organs of sight). In the same way, the male and female reproductive organs appear as just different variations in the way in which the rational capacity of reproduction operates in the human body. Consequently, that "Socrates or Hipparchia is a human being and, as such, gendered" appears to be a common quality, whereas for Hipparchia "to be a woman" or to Socrates "to be a man" fall under their respective individual qualities.

The idea that reproduction is counted among the rational functions of the human soul leads us to wonder about the nature and rationality of sexual lust. Aetius mentions "impressions, assents, perception and impulses" as functions of the commanding part (*hêgemonikon*). It seems, then, that the impulse to (at least) reproductive sexual activity would be considered, not as a "drive" or a force stemming from our animal nature, but as a matter of rational decision. Indeed, by placing reproduction under rational capacities, the Stoics imply that also the corresponding decisions fall under rational and moral deliberation: we might experience the impulse to reproduce as members of the human species, but as individuals we still (at least ideally) can make decisions as to the right time, right place, and right person in relation to which we use this capacity. The question remains, however, how nonreproductive sexual activity would fit this picture. I will return to this question when I analyze the role of sexuality in Stoic ethics in Chap. 10. Yet, these considerations point to the fact that sexual capacities also involve relations to other people: a question that leads us to the sphere of the remaining two metaphysical categories.

4.3 The Disposed and the Relatively Disposed: Gender and Relations

The third of the Stoic categories is *the Disposed*. Whereas the second category qualified the substance, the third category further differentiates between individual entities. The standard examples of the kinds of qualities falling under this category include "Socrates as sitting" and "Socrates as blushing."[7] These entail a qualitative change, which is internal to the qualified subject: something changes in Socrates when he sits down or blushes, but these changes are not persistent enough to characterize him as a person.[8]

However, it is sometimes difficult to demarcate the third category clearly from the second. It would be tempting to think that the third category denotes qualities that are more temporary than those in the second (*poion*). For example, one could say that to have sexuality falls under the second category, whereas to be sexually aroused falls under the third. Still, there are cases in which it is difficult to decide whether the qualities are persistent enough to fall under the second category, or whether they should be placed in the third. For example, there are certain individual characteristics that the Stoics take to be long-lasting and only painstakingly changed, but which nevertheless can (and in philosophical education indeed must) be changed such as vices and emotional responses. However, as noted, to be gendered as such seems to be too persistent to fall into this category, as

---

[7] David Sedley emphasizes "mental states or psychic qualities," I think somewhat too strongly, in his account of the categories. He understands the category of quality as a soul of some kind and describes it as "psychic qualities which characterize you, both as a human being an as the unique individual you are." Similarly, he describes the category of the disposed as "further dispositions of those qualities, which represent your individual mental states" (Sedley 2005: 410). For instance, the standard example of the third category, "Socrates as sitting," does not seem to imply any particular "mental state," and I take this category to include many bodily states, as well.

[8] For a more detailed account of how the theory of four categories was developed in the Stoic school, and in particular how and why the third category was introduced into the theory, see Stephen Menn (1999: 215–247). See also Long and Sedley (1987: 177).

does sexuality as such, whereas the different modifications of sexuality (such as experience of sexual lust) would count as examples of the "(nonrelatively) disposed." Also, many aspects of our experiences of being gendered change as we grow, as do the gendered roles and identities. These types of changes will also be produced by the Stoic philosophical education, as I will demonstrate in Part II.

The fourth Stoic category is *the Relatively Disposed*. According to the neo-Platonic thinker Simplicius (6th cent. CE), this signifies the aspects an object has only in relation to something else, in other words, aspects that can change due to a change in the thing it is in relation to, without internal changes occurring in the object itself. For example, "to be a father" or "to be the man on the right" are only possible in relation to external conditions. According to Simplicius: "Hence without any internal change a father could cease to be a father on the death of his son, and the man on the right could cease to be the man on the right if his neighbor changed position" (L&S 29 C). In modern philosophical terminology, this would be called a "Cambridge change." (Yet it would be intuitive to state that even after the death of the son, the father can still be called "a father" in a relevant sense.)

Gender is clearly relevant in this category in that it is often in relation to other people that our roles as men and women become discernible: as a mother, a wife, a daughter, a sister, a lover, and so on. As I will show in Part III, Stoic ethics and political theory attach great importance to close human bonds such as family relations. However, as a metaphysical category, "the relatively disposed" does not explain what gender is—on the contrary, it assumes gender in cases such as "to be a father" and "to be a wife." In line with Simplicius' above demonstration, it is clear that one can cease to be a wife (if one is divorced or widowed), but would still remain a woman—even if, as we will see later, the different roles are crucial for what gender, according to the Stoics, fundamentally is. Yet, even if this category points to the context of human bonding, which has to be scrutinized in more detail in order to make sense of gender, it does not suffice to answer the metaphysical problem of what gender is.

4.4 Reproduction and Rational Capacities: The Stoic Theory of Pneuma

On the basis of the above discussion, I am now in a position to conclude that the Stoic theory of four categories connects gender with universal soul capacities as well as those physical features that correspond to those capacities. I have suggested that the second category, "the qualified," is the most plausible in terms of understanding gender in the Stoic metaphysical framework, whereby its different aspects fall into two different subcategories: the commonly and the individually qualified. I have proposed a reading according to which "to be gendered" belongs to the common qualities, but the specific gender one has belongs to the individual qualities. The categories of the "disposed" and the "relatively disposed" help to further qualify particular aspects of gender. I have also pointed out that the sexual capacity is of a different kind than the other listed soul capacities. Unlike the other capacities, gender generally differentiates people into two main groups (there are not, say, two different modes of sight such that one group of people are nearsighted and the other group is farsighted). Gender makes exactly this kind of demarcation in animals that reproduce sexually. Further, it is not quite as intuitive to imagine an undifferentiated gender, as we can think of the abstraction of "sight" in general, without thinking about a specific person or any particular kinds of eyes—brown or green, for example. Does Stoic theory, then, suggest an entirely new way of thinking about gender? Or is gender, in this respect, radically different from other common human capacities?

To solve this problem, let us next scrutinize how the Stoics understood human beings, body and soul, through their notion of *pneuma*. As described in the previous chapter, Stoic cosmology derives from two basic principles: the active and the passive aspects of matter. Similarly, when it comes to the human body, two principles are at stake: body as matter and body as soul. Here again, the soul is not to be understood as a separate substance, different from matter. On the contrary, the Stoics see the material soul as thoroughly intertwined with the material body. This mixture is explained through the Stoic notion of *pneuma* (which is related to the above-mentioned concept of tension, *tonos*).

Pneuma has an important function in Stoic metaphysics, since the concept is used to explain how rational activity forms and qualifies "pure" matter. *Pneuma* brings matter together and makes the material object what it is: in virtue of its *pneuma*, a stone is a hard and solid object, a pine tree is a living and growing organism, and a horse is a perceiving and moving animal. In what could be called Stoic philosophical anthropology, or philosophical inquiry into the human being, *pneuma* explains why the human body is not only a material entity but also a living and sensing whole, capable of complicated physical, psychic, and intellectual functions. According to the Stoics, the finer the *pneuma*, the higher the creature is situated in the natural hierarchy of things. By virtue of its very fine *pneuma*, the human being is the nearest of all living creatures to the universal *logos*: the human soul is rational and thus closely connected to the rational principle governing the whole *cosmos*. The Stoic explanation of *pneuma*, once again, leads us back to the Ancient element theory. According to Alexander, of the four elements, water and earth "lack tension" (they are *atonón*; L&S 48 C). Tension, then, comes to the body through *pneuma*, which according to the Stoics consists of the fire and air. These active elements are taken to consist of fine parts, whereas the passive elements, water and earth, consist of thick parts.[9]

However, the notion of *pneuma* did not alone suffice to explain human rationality, and therefore, the Stoics developed more nuanced, special terminology. As Sextus points out, the Stoics "say that soul has two meanings, that which sustains the whole compound, and in particular, the commanding faculty" (L&S 55 F). In humans, *pneuma* signifies soul in a general sense—the soul that sustains the body. It is spread all around the body and intertwined with it as inseparably as wine mixed with water. As we saw above, also Aristotle used *pneuma* as an explanation of what makes a body living and connected it to heat.[10] Also, the Stoics connected *pneuma* to body heat, and further to the element theory (see, e.g., Cicero, *On the Nature of Gods* II-23, 18). It is worth pointing out, however, that the Stoic metaphysical discussions of *pneuma* and warmth do not differentiate between men and women. Thus, if the Stoics partook in the Ancient discussion about the natural hotness or coldness of men and women, their arguments do not feature in the surviving sources. This an interesting observation in its own right,

---

[9] Cf. e.g. Galen's *On sustaining causes* (I.1–2.4; L&S 55 F).

[10] It is worth emphasizing that the concept of *pneuma* has a much more specific and foundational role in Stoic theory than in Aristotle, and the Stoics placed emphasis on the continuum of matter and the total mixture (*krásis*) between soul and body. Cf. my discussion in Chap. 3.

given that the dispute over the connection between temperature and gender prevailed throughout Antiquity, from Hippocrates to Galen and beyond.[11]

The Stoics also discussed the soul in a more specific sense. *Psychê* signifies a soul, and as we saw, they used the term *hêgemonikon* to refer to the rational center of the soul. The Stoics take the soul in the broad sense (as *pneuma*) to be spread throughout the human body, whereas they claim that the commanding faculty is situated in the heart. Thus, the material entities we humans are by no means make our bodies into heaps of nonliving material or "pure matter": the human body is a living, sensing, and rational unity. This view is, of course, connected to the general Stoic notion of *krâsis*: matter and the active principle, reason, are totally blended, not only in humans but in the entire cosmos. The human body is blended with the soul all the way. Yet, in a specific sense, the soul (understood as the commanding faculty, *hêgemonikon*) is that which controls its other functions, just as the octopus is in control of its tentacles.[12]

Thus, rationality of the commanding faculty of the human soul explains why the Stoics could call other capacities of the soul rational. To take sight as an example, sense data received by the human eye are not just an unstructured mishmash of shapes and colors, but are immediately perceived as "something" that can be expressed in verbal form (in Stoic terms, as a *lekton*). According to the Stoics, an animal reacts more or less automatically to impulses it receives through its senses: for example, a scorpion reacts by sticking, a dog by barking, and a rabbit by running (cf. Annas 1992: 57–61). Human beings, in contrast, also articulate thoughts that accompany their perceptions, as in "I am thirsty, I need something to drink."

It is precisely this Stoic notion of *pneuma* and the total blending of the human body and soul that give support to the idea that reproduction is also *rational* capacity in humans. The choice to include reproduction in the list of rational human capacities is consistent with the Stoic metaphysical conception of the human being. It is logical for the Stoics

---

[11] However, I return in Chap. 6 to the Ancient theory of physiognomy, which Seneca and certain other Stoics seem to have sympathized and which alludes to the different elemental constitutions of men and women. Yet, the Stoics remarks on physiognomy are usually not connected to any detailed metaphysical discussion.

[12] For a more detailed understanding of the Stoic philosophy of mind, see, e.g., Annas (1992: 37–120), Cooper (1999); Graver (2007), Knuuttila (2004), Sihvola and Knuuttila (1998), Sorabji (2000).

to claim that the reproductive capacity is rational given their belief that the rational human soul is spread throughout the human body. There is no reason why they should have considered the genitals an exception—particularly as these organs are connected to the production of new rational members of the human species. Moreover, as I demonstrate in detail later in this work, they did not consider sexuality to be something unworthy or ethically susceptible, which fits in with the idea that both the reproductive capacity and the accompanying impulses (closely connected to sexuality, although sexuality arguably encompasses more) in Stoic metaphysics is discussed neutrally along with other human functions, without any connotations of being less important or belonging to some "lower" or more animal-like aspects of the soul.

It is, indeed, important to emphasize that the Stoics, unlike Plato, did not distinguish different levels of the soul, but rather defended the view of a unified soul. This is significant from the perspective of sexuality, given that the difference between the models of Plato and the Stoics implies that sexual lust has a different role in their respective views. Plato explicitly situates sexuality on the lowest level of the soul, among appetites and thus as something that admittedly belongs to the human soul, but which should be subordinated to reason (see, e.g., *Rep.* 599a). Likewise, Aristotle understood reproduction as a function of the vegetative soul which is the most common soul function of all living beings: plants, animals, and humans. The Stoics obviously could not agree with either of these views, given that they did not accept the idea of a divided soul at all. However, the Stoic way of demarcating the human soul by its rationality becomes problematic in the context of embryology. The Stoic notions on embryology open up another perspective to the connections between *pneuma*, body and gender, and raise the question concerning the differences between plants, animals, and humans.

4.5 Stoic Notions of Embryology

The Stoic philosopher Hierocles (ca. 150 CE) states at the beginning of *Elements of Ethics* that the starting point of an ethical inquiry should concern the first things *oikeion*—things that are familiar to one or "one's own."[13] He adds that he finds it "no worse to begin further back and

---

[13] I return to the central Stoic notion of *oikeiôsis* in Sect. 8.2.

consider what the generation (*genêsis*) of a living thing is like" (Hierocles I.1, transl. Ilaria Ramelli). The Stoic sources lack a coherent causal explanation of gender dimorphism or sexuality as exists in Plato's philosophical myths and Ancient embryology. The few remaining Stoic passages that discuss embryology are not entirely compatible with each other, and they do not include any explicit argument concerning when, how, and why an infant assumes a gender. Nevertheless, to make sense of these partly fragmentary arguments, it is interesting to analyze the passages on embryology found in the sources.

Hierocles gives the following description of one Stoic account of the development of the embryo:

> If the seed (*to sperma*) falls into the womb (*eis hysteran*) at the right time and is received by the receptacle (*tou angeiou*) in good health, it no longer stays still as before but is set in motion and begins its own activities (*tôn idion ergôn*). It draws matter from the pregnated body, and fashions the embryo in accordance with inescapable patterns, up to the point when it reaches its goal and makes its product ready to be born. Yet throughout all this time—I mean the time from conception to birth—it remains [in the form of] physique (*physis*), i.e., breath (*pneuma*), having changed from seed and moving methodically from beginning to end (Hierocles 1.5-33, 4.38-53; L&S 53B; Long & Sedley's translation slightly modified).

Hierocles continues by explaining how the fetus is first "considerably distant from soul (*psykhê*)," but becomes finer the more it develops, and once born, it has been hardened and becomes "adequate for the environment" and "changes into soul" (*pros autou metabalein ... eis psykhên*). There are several important remarks to be made on this account. To begin with, Hierocles suggests that the embryo exists rather like a plant. The Stoics explain the life of a plant through the notion of physique (*physis*) and claim that in animals, reproduction belongs to the soul.[14] Throughout its development, the *pneuma* of the embryo gets finer, up to the moment of birth, which is when the infant becomes solid

---

[14] Long and Sedley take this to indicate that the Stoics wanted to emphasize the self-directing functions of animals as opposed to "automatic" growth in plants (Long and Sedley 1987: 320). This position comes close to Aristotle's embryology, according to which the embryo only possesses the nutritive soul (although the Stoics did not use this notion), and thus is capable of growth but no self-governed movement.

and receives a soul. After this, it is considered an animal, rather than some plant-like being (as Hierocles states, "whatever issues forth from the womb is at once an animal"). It follows that an embryo lacks both impulse and sensation, and consequently also self-perception, which are Hierocles' criteria for demarcating an animal from a nonanimal. He states explicitly, however, that as soon as an animal is born, it immediately starts to perceive itself (Hierocles 1.35; L&S 53B, transl. Long & Sedley).

Given the above-discussed Stoic idea that the specific human soul assigns to the human body the functions of senses, language, and reproduction, the human embryo does not fulfill the criteria of being a human in the full sense of the word. The idea that breathing is a function of human *pneuma* might also be relevant to the distinction: an infant starts to breathe on its own only after it is born (plants, in contrast, do not breathe). Given the central role of *pneuma* and breathing in Stoic theory, this might have supported their decision not to call an embryo human, or even animal.[15]

The idea that the Stoics did not consider an embryo fully human receives support in a later, highly interesting passage from Seneca. Even though the passage is not primarily concerned with embryology, it makes a remarkable point about fetal development.

> If someone were to say that the fetus lurking in its mother's womb with *its sex still undefined*, soft, incomplete, and unformed, was already in possession of something good, then he would be blatantly in error. But there is an awfully small difference between the one who is just receiving the gift of life and the one who is lurking like a lump in its mother's innards. As far as understanding what is good and bad is concerned, both are equally mature, and an infant no more capable of the good than is a tree or some speechless animal. (Seneca, *Letter* 124, 8, transl. Inwood, my emphasis)

Here Seneca indicates that the fetus cannot be properly called a human being because it lacks the demarcating quality of being human, namely reason. Strikingly, he includes also the newborn infant in this consideration. According to this account, an embryo or child cannot achieve the goal of good human life, which requires the active use of reason.

Furthermore, Seneca assumes that the embryo is not only plant-like but also undetermined by its gender. This remark leads us to wonder

---

[15] Cf. Long and Sedley 1987: 320, Annas (1992: 54).

when might a person receive a gender, according to Seneca? At the moment of birth, an infant already has genitals, which therefore must have developed beforehand. Seneca might have assumed that gender differentiation happens only at a very late stage of pregnancy. On the other hand, his point seems to give support to the above-mentioned Stoic idea of the minor importance of gender difference, thus implying the metaphysically equally important status of both genders. Gender differentiation also seems irrelevant to Seneca's main argument concerning the good life, which appears to be a common goal for all humans, regardless of gender. As Seneca's passage indicates, however, to understand the higher goals of human beings, we have to investigate the Stoic arguments concerning good life—in other words, theories that concern adults and children older than merely newborns. I will return to this question in Chap. 8 where I discuss children's capacities and the goal of good life in Stoic philosophical education.

Seneca's passage mentions the womb but without taking stances to the Ancient debate of its role in fertilization and the formation of the embryo. However, it is interesting to notice that the above-quoted Hierocles passage points to a view where the womb is presented merely as a passive "space." Hierocles calls it not only *hystera* but as *angeion*, which is derived from *angos* and signifies a hollow container. Further, his account assigns to the sperm the activity that causes the development of the fetus (he describes how the seed "no longer stays still" but "begins its own activities"). Accordingly, the seed is understood as the "core" of the fetus and the future human being (it "fashions the embryo in accordance with inescapable patterns"). Like Galen, Hierocles also ascribes to seed the specific capacity of "drawing matter from the pregnated body"—in other words, the womb includes material for the development of the fetus, but it is a capacity of the seed to draw this material from the womb to become part of the fetus (cf. Sect. 2.3).[16]

---

[16]A further interesting aspect in Hierocles' view concerns the importance attached to the moment and mode of fertilization. Hierocles mentions in passing the "right time" and the "good health" (or condition) in which the seed must come into the uterus so that the fertilization will succeed. This idea seems to have been somewhat common in Antiquity, and Plutarch, for example, emphasizes the importance of getting the time of fertilization right for the entire development of the embryo. Other conditions should also be favorable: Plutarch warns men against conceiving children while drunk, for example (*Moralia* I: 1.B.2–1.D.3).

In Hierocles, this view is simply mentioned in passing, but we saw earlier how this view can be defended in a more detailed embryological theory. Thus, the above-quoted passage from Hierocles appears to support a version of preformationism. Our sources suggest that at least certain other Stoics, too, would have favored this view. According to Galen, the Stoic Posidonius (c.135–51 BCE) would have admired Plato "for all he said about the forming of babies still unborn in the womb" (Posidonius, fragment 31B; Galen PHP v. 466–8). If Posidonius admired the view presented in *Timaeus*, this would indicate an embryological theory according to which the womb has, at best, a protective function. It is interesting that Hierocles and Posidonius seem thus to endorse a version of embryology that is older than Aristotle's, and which is the Aristotelian biology refutes. As noted in Chap. 2, Aristotle, and later Galen in particular, gave a more active role to the female than the preformationist theory does. However, Hierocles' language also suggests that the development of the embryo is somewhat predetermined: he refers to "inescapable patterns" and how the seed/embryo changes "methodically from beginning to end." Thus, it seems that at least some aspects of its development do not depend solely on the qualities of the semen or the womb, and that there are some metaphysical principles at play.[17]

However, the Stoics did not seem to have a uniform view on the topic. Diogenes Laertius reports that the Stoics understood seed as a mixture of the parts of the soul in the same proposition as they occur in the parents. Further, he suggests that Chrysippus would have defined seed as *pneuma* and compared it to seeds sown on the ground, whereas the Stoic Sphaerus would have claimed that it stems from the entire body

---

[17] Gretchen Reydams-Schils comments on Hierocles' embryological views and claims that he "is ambiguous: he distinguishes between seed and matter (*hylē*), and although the activated seed draws matter from the pregnant body, the womb plays a role in activating the male seed" (2005: 124). I claim that in the light of Ancient embryological theories, Hierocles' remarks are not ambiguous in themselves. They are compatible with Ancient preformationism, which does not treat the womb as completely passive, either: womb still plays a protective and nurturing role in the process. It was not uncommon for the Ancient embryologies to discuss "the formative movements" of the womb even if they assign the male seed a more substantial role in the process. Hierocles (and possibly Posidonius) thus assigns seed a fundamental role in generation, as did Plato's *Timaeus* and Aristotle.

and, furthermore, that the seed of females (*théleias*) was infertile (*agonos*) because it was without tension (*atonon*), scanty (*oligon*), and watery (*hydatôdes*) (DL VII: 158–159).[18]

Diogenes' report implies that some Stoic thinkers were also in favor of a view of procreation as a "mixture" where both parents play a significant role. This idea is in contrast with preformationism, and by giving an apparently equal role to both parents, it also comes close to Galen's position, which defended the notion of female sperm. Diogenes indicates that at least some Stoics, too, would have supported a theory of female sperm. However, he adds, somewhat ambiguously, that female sperm was considered infertile. This remark is puzzling, since it calls the female secretion *semen* even if he presumes that nothing could grow out of it. Why was it not rather called ejaculation, which is connected to pleasure rather than fertility, as Aristotle suggested? On the other hand, the notion of female sperm also seems incompatible with the notion of a female as nothing but a hollow container (a view that seems to be at the bottom of Hierocles' account).

Thus, there seem to have many different Stoic accounts on embryology, and none of these accounts seem original or nyanced as such. However, even if the Stoics did not have a philosophically sophisticated theory on the topic, the scattered remarks in the sources point to other relevant questions such as when the fetus or child becomes fully human. This question, however, has to be addressed in the context of Stoic views on children, character development, and education (cf. Chap. 8). Furthermore, even if the notions on embryology discussed in this section assign different roles to the female and the male in fertilization, following from my discussion in the previous sections, these differences would exist only on the level of the physical reproductive organs, not on the level of soul functions which, as I have shown, are the same for men and women. Clearly, the Stoics were not too interested in developing a coherent

---

[18] In late Stoicism, we find yet a different formulation of the male and female roles in generation. Marcus Aurelius claims that an embryo was formed from the sperm of the father and the blood of the mother (*to spermation ho pater mou synelekse kai to aimation té meter*). (*Meditations* V: 4). Even if Galen was Marcus Aurelius' doctor, the idea of describing fertilization through the seed on the one hand and blood on the other sounds very much like the Aristotelian position, even though it is ambiguous whether the role of the mother is here to be understood as only giving matter or whether blood is a similar and equally important factor in generation as sperm.

theory of differences that exist on the level of the organs. The embryological remarks are also distinct from the discussion of reproduction as a goal of life—in other words, an area in which adults can use their other rational capacities such as deliberation.

4.6 From Genital Difference to Good Life

The Stoic view of the unity of the human soul is probably one reason why many influential Stoic thinkers such as Chrysippus placed reproduction among its rational capacities. Still, this raises some further questions. Does this idea involve the expression of an accompanying thought in the form of a *lekton*, something like "I feel that I am now in the right state, in the right situation and in relation to the right person to use my reproductive capacities"? Further, does the idea of the rationality of reproductive capacities imply an ethical norm that, because they are rational capacities, in order to live rationally one *should* use them? Or even that one should use this capacity *in order to* reproduce, not for pleasure only?

At least some Roman Stoics indeed seem to understand this metaphysical idea not only as descriptive but also normative, in other words implying what types of choices we, as rational beings, should make to live our lives well. Musonius Rufus (ca. 30–100 CE) appeals to metaphysical facts and empirical observation of the human bodies to support his argument of commonness of virtue:

> (W)omen have received from the gods the same reasoning power (*logon*) as men—the power which we employ with each other and according to which we consider whether each action is good or bad, and honorable or shameful. Likewise, the female has also the same senses as the male: seeing, hearing, ability to smell, and the rest. Likewise, too, each has the same parts of the body, and neither one has more than the other. In addition, a desire (*oreksis*) for virtue and affinity for it (*oikeiôsis*) belong by nature not only to men but also to women (...) (Musonius Rufus, Lecture 3 in King 2011, p.28, transl. Cynthia King; Stob. 2.31.126).

Musonius thus draws attention to the above-discussed metaphysical idea of men and women's similar capacities. His position is line with the idea of eight soul faculties. Like the early Stoics, Musonius lists the senses, reasoning, and language the basic functions of human soul, and explicitly argues for the common rationality of men and women.

Musonius goes so far in his emphasis on the similarity between men and women that he claims that they have *the same* body parts. However, it was probably not his intention to claim there was no difference between the sexes on the genital level, just that both have genitals that are similar in function. This goes together with the above-discussed distinction between having a gender and being of a specific gender. This view is also similar to Galen, who claimed that males and females have all the same generative parts, only in females, they are on the inside, and in males, they are on the outside (cf. Sect. 2.3; Galen *On Semen* II.5.48).

Musonius' argumentation crosses the line between physics and ethics, and uses observations of the physical bodies and genitals to support his arguments concerning good human life. In another lecture, he points to genital difference in order to defend the naturalness of marriage and procreation. He asks rhetorically:

> Why else did the creator of humankind first cut our species into two and then make for it two sets of genitals, one female, one male? Why else did he then implant in each a strong desire (*epithymian iskhyran*) for companionship (*homilias*) and union (*koinônias*) with the other and mix into both a strong longing (*pothon iskhyron*) for the other, the male for the female and the female for the male? (Musonius Rufus, Lecture 14: 2 in King 2011, p. 59, transl. Cynthia King; Stob. 4.22a20)

Now, Musonius explicitly appeals to the "two sets of genitals", and takes this observation to provide evidence for the naturalness of reproduction. Playing with the double meaning of the verb *syneinai*, Musonius concludes that it is natural for a man–woman couple both to copulate (*syneinai*) and to live together (*syneinai*). He also gives a teleological explanation of gender: gender differentiation is *for* the purposes of mutual association, partnership, and reproduction. Here, he also alludes to a desire, not only for reproduction but also for companionship that he claims to be natural, and similar in men and women. He repeats an idea expressed both in Plato's *Symposium* and Aristotle's biology by connecting reproduction with the desire to make the species eternal (Musonius Rufus, Lecture 14: 2 in King 2011).[19]

---

[19] Musonius' rhetoric, mentioning the "creator" who "cut our species into two," further resembles Aristophanes' myth, as well as Plato's *Timaeus*.

There is a similar line of reasoning in *De Finibus*, where Cicero claims that parental love for children is evident when we observe the shapes, structures, and parts of our bodies. He also takes these empirical observations to be a proof that reproduction is a natural goal of humans. He further claims that the naturalness of the love for one's own offspring is the starting point for a feeling of affiliation with other human beings. By appealing to the notion of common humanity, so that no person should consider another one a stranger, Cicero points to the ideal of cosmopolitan ethics where one realizes the ethical worth of all humans (to be discussed in detail in Chap. 14) (*De Fin.* 3.62-8).

Thus, both Musonius and Cicero use empirical notions of human bodies, including genitals, in support of their ethical claims of human sociability, and of marriage and family life—topics to which I return in Part III. Both of them connect gender to the teleological goal of a good human life, which is social and involves participation in politics as well as marriage and starting a family. On this point, the Stoic position differs remarkably from the Aristotelian one. As noted, Aristotle considered the studies of nature and politics two separate spheres of inquiry, and he did not base his political views on the results of his zoological works (although he uses the term "nature" in a normative sense also in his ethical and political works). In Musonius and Cicero, in contrast, nature and social life coincide, and they explicitly draw ethical and political conclusions from their observations of the human body.

At this point, it is important to point out that the reading I have proposed in this chapter supports the idea that the Stoics defended a view of common, rational humanity. Stoic cosmopolitanism, to be explored in Chap. 14, draws far-reaching ethical consequences of these theoretical foundations. I have claimed that general tendency in Stoic metaphysical texts is rather to minimize than to maximize the difference between the genders, and that gender difference should be understood in Stoicism merely as two different modes of qualifying the reproductive capacity in individual humans. Thus, like brown and green eyes are different variations of the physical organs that correspond to the capacity of seeing, so also gender difference appears merely as a matter of variations in the physique that corresponds to the general reproductive capacity. This reading has important consequences. If indeed "to be a man" is a similar individual quality in Socrates as whiteness is, this would give strong support to the idea that men and women are essentially similar as human beings, as dark- and light-skinned or green- and brown-eyed people are, and whatever differences there are on the physical level, they do not affect what is really essential and valuable in us as humans.

Appendix

Aurelius, Marcus

Tôn Eis Heauton (Meditations)

Marcus Antonius Imperator Ad Se Ipsum. Jan Hendrik Leopold (ed.). Leipzig: B. G. Teubneri, 1908.
Marcus Aurelius. C.R. Haines (transl.). Cambridge, MA: Harvard University Press, 2014.

Cicero, Marcus Tullius

De Finibus bonorum et malorum (De Fin)
On the Nature of the Gods

De Finibus Bonorum et Malorum. H. Rackham (transl.). Cambridge and London: Harvard University Press, 1951.
On the Nature of the Gods. H. Rackham (transl.). Cambridge, MA: Harvard University Press, 1931.

Diogenes Laertius, *Lives of Eminent Philosophers* (DL)

Diogenis Laertii Vitae philosophorum. Miroslav Marcovich (ed.). *Bibliotheca scriptorum Graecorum et Romanorum Teubneriana.* Vol. 1. Stuttgart-Lipsia: Teubner, 1999–2002.
Lives of Eminent Philosophers. R.D. Hicks (transl.). Cambridge and London: Harvard University Press, 1995.

Galen

De Placitis Hippocratis et Platonis (PHP)
De Semine

Claudii Galeni Opera Omnia. C.G. Kühn (ed.). C. Cnobloch, Leipzig, 1821, 1833, 1964–5.
On the Doctrines of Hipporcates and Plato. Philipp de Lacy (ed. and transl.). Berlin: Akademie Verlag, 1978.
On Semen. Philipp de Lacy (ed. and transl.). Berlin: Akademie Verlag, 1992.

Hellenistic Philosophy—Introductory Readings. Brad Inwood and L.P. Gerson (transl.). Indianapolis and Cambridge: Hackett Publishing Company, 1997.

The Hellenistic Philosophers. A.A. Long and D.N. Sedley (eds.). Cambridge: Cambridge University Press, 1987. (L&S)

Hierocles

Éthikê stoikheiôsis (Elements of Ethics)

Hierocles the Stoic, Elements of Ethics, Fragments and Excerpts. Ilaria Ramelli (ed.). David Konstan (transl.). Leiden and Boston: Brill, 2009.

Musonius Rufus

Musonii Rufi Reliquiae. O. Hense (ed.). Leipzig: Kessinger, 1905.
Musonius Rufus: Lectures & Sayings. William B. Irvine (ed.). Cynthia King (transl.). CreateSpace, 2011.

Plato

Tim. Timaeus
Rep. Republic
Symp. Symposium

Platonis Opera (Oxford Classical Texts):
Vol. 1, ed. E.A. Duke et al. 1995.
Vol. 2, ed. J. Burnet 1922.
Vol. 3, ed. J. Burnet 1922.
Vol. 4, ed. J. Burnet 1922.
Respublica. ed. S.R. Slings 2003.

Complete Works. John M. Cooper (ed.). D.S. Hutchinson (associate ed.). Indianapolis: Hackett Publishers, 1997.
Plato in Twelve Volumes, Vol. 5–6, The Republic. Paul Shorey (transl.). London: Heinemann, 1969.
The Symposium. Christopher Gill (transl.). London and New York: Penguin Books, 1999.

Plutarch

Moralia. Frank Cole Babbitt (transl.). Cambridge, MA and London: Harvard University Press and W. Heinemann, 1967–1984.

Posidonius Rhodius

Fragments

Posidonius 1. The Fragments. L. Edelstein and I.G. Kidd (eds.). Cambridge: Cambridge University Press, 1972.
Posidonius 3. The Translation of the Fragments. I.G. Kidd (transl.). Cambridge: Cambridge University Press, 1999.

Seneca

Epistles. Vol. I–VI. Richard M. Gummere (transl.). Cambridge and London: Harvard University Press, 1917–1925.
Selected Philosophical Letters. Brad Inwood (transl.). Oxford: Oxford University Press, 2007.

REFERENCES

Annas, Julia. 1992. *Hellenistic Philosophy of Mind.* Berkeley, Los Angeles and London: University of California Press.
Cooper, John M. 1999. *Reason and Emotion.* Princeton: Princeton University Press.
Gaca, Kathy. 2003. *The Making of Fornication—Eros, Ethics and Political Reform in Greek Philosophy and Early Christianity.* Berkley, Los Angeles: The University of California Press.
Graver, Margaret. 2007. *Stoicism and Emotion.* Chicago: Chicago University Press.
Knuuttila, Simo. 2004. *Emotions in Ancient and Medieval Philosophy.* Oxford: Clarendon Press.
Knuuttila, Simo, and Sihvola, Juha. 1998. How the Philosophical Analysis of Emotions Was Introduced. In *The Emotions in Hellenistic Philosophy*, ed. Juha Sihvola and Troels Engberg-Pedersen. Dordrecht, Boston and London: Kluwer Academic Publishers.
Menn, Stephen. 1999. The Stoic Theory of Categories. In *Oxford Studies in Ancient Philosophy.* Oxford: Oxford University Press.
Reydams-Schils, Gretchen. 2005. *The Roman Stoic—Self, Responsibility, and Affection.* Chicago, London: The University of Chicago Press.
Sedley, David. 2005. Hellenistic Physics and Metaphysics. In *The Cambridge History of Hellenistic Philosophy*, 355–411. Cambridge: Cambridge University Press.
Sorabji, Richard. 2000. *Emotion and Peace of Mind—From Stoic Agitation to Christian Temptation.* Oxford: Oxford University Press.

CHAPTER 5

Perfumed Men and Bearded Philosophers—The Stoics on Signs of Gender

"Who is this who smells like a woman?" This question was posed, or so the story goes, by the Stoic Zeno, annoyed by a man who was wearing perfume (DL VII: 23).[1] Indeed, the Stoics as well as other Ancient philosophers paid a great deal of attention to smells, hairs, clothes, and adornments. All of these have to do with one's physical appearance, and all of them function as "signs of gender" as they have a role in constituting and demarcating femininity and masculinity. As opposed to the metaphysical questions concerning the "essence" of gender, we are now investigating signs that are expressed on the surface of the body, and that are embedded in cultural and social meanings.

Furthermore, cosmetics and embellishment of one's looks do not only involve our material bodies but also our choices and actions concerning our bodies. These choices are often discussed in a gendered framework. As Zeno's question indicates, Ancient thinkers tend to consider beautification and attachment to one's physical appearance a *womanish*

---

[1] According to Diogenes Laertius, the question, "Who is it who is smelling of perfume (*merymismenos*) here?" was also asked of the Cyrenaic philosopher Aristippus (c. 435—356 BCE), who replied: "It is poor me and the even poorer king of Persia." When these two anecdotes are compared, Zeno's attitude to perfume and 'to smelling like a woman' seems to be much more negative than Aristippus'. This is not very surprising, however, given that Aristippus' Cyrenaic School supported a strong version of hedonism connecting happiness solely to enjoyment of the flesh, which is almost as far as you can get from the Stoic position. (DL II: 76).

© The Author(s) 2018
M. Grahn-Wilder, *Gender and Sexuality in Stoic Philosophy*,
https://doi.org/10.1007/978-3-319-53694-1_5

characteristic, and as such, a harmful one. In Ancient sources, the image of the effeminate and self-adorning man is frequently contrasted with that of a bearded and stern philosopher. Although the Ancient philosophical discussion on physical signs of gender has been largely overlooked in the secondary literature, I will demonstrate in this chapter that it should not be dismissed as philosophically irrelevant. On the contrary, the philosophical significance is evident in the extensive discussions dedicated to these issues in the original sources, and also in the application of central philosophical terminology.

The discussion on bodily looks is further connected to the Stoic view of human nature and theory of *indifferent* and *preferable* things. Reference to a beautiful (*kalos*) body leads to the philosophical question of what makes a soul beautiful and good (*kalos kagathos*). However, particularly Roman Stoics often discuss physical looks and body hairs in ways where they clearly make a difference. Epictetus (c.55–135 CE), for example, declares that he would rather die than shave his beard. In this chapter, I will analyze the seeming paradox between indifference to and acceptance of physical signs as constituting a philosopher. To see how a Roman Stoic thinker can both share the early Stoic view of metaphysical insignificance of gender but yet assign great importance to physical signs in men and women, we have to consider the roles of choice and nature in Stoic philosophy, as well as notions of femininity and masculinity in Ancient philosophical discourses.

5.1 Hair, *Prohairesis*, and Human Flourishing

Ancient thinkers typically discuss outer, bodily beauty in relation or contrast to inner beauty. In Xenophon's *Oeconomicus*, the character of Ischomachus reveals that one of the secrets to his happy and well-organized marriage is that he had taught his wife not to beautify herself. He tells of an incident when his wife had rouged her cheeks with alkanet, powdered her face with lead and worn high heels, on account of which he gave her a philosophical lecture. Ischomachus reasons that as a cow is the most attractive of all beings for a bull, and a mare for a stallion, so is the plain human body for another human. Thus, he concludes, make-up is fraudulent and inappropriate in marriage, which requires the two spouses to be honest with each other. His wife promises never to use make-up again and announces that from now on, she wants to *be* beautiful rather than to *look* beautiful (*Oec.* X: 1–10).

Also, the Platonic tradition emphasizes that a beautiful body does not equal to a beautiful soul. In *Alcibiades I*, Socrates and Alcibiades agree that the person is different from the instruments he or she uses, such as words, money, and clothes. This leads the character of Socrates to formulate the famous Platonic doctrine that the body is something a person uses, something belonging to him or her, but different from the true self. In order to become good and beautiful (*kalos kagathos*), therefore, Alcibiades should apply the precept "Take care of yourself" (*epimeleia heautou*) to his soul, not his body (*Alcibiades I* 131b). The Stoic Epictetus condenses this idea in *Discourses*:

> But consider what Socrates says to that most beautiful and attractive of all men, Alcibiades: "Endeavor to make yourself beautiful." What is he trying to tell him? "Curl your locks, and shave your legs?" Heaven forbid! Rather, "Adorn your choice (*kosmei syn tén prohairesin*); throw away your wrong judgments." How, then, are you to deal with your body? Leave it to nature. (*Disc.* III.i.42–43, Hard's translation slightly modified; cf. *Alcibiades I* 131 d)

Here Epictetus connects the juxtaposition between outer and inner beauty to his central philosophical concepts of nature and choice (*prohairesis*). Both concepts have a fundamental position in the Stoic discussions on beautification. It is also noteworthy that Epictetus does not here express a negative view of beauty as such, since he also describes the philosophical activity itself in terms of adornment. The reader cannot help to associate to the Platonic ideal of ascending forms of loving beauty, as expressed in *Symposium*.

In his teaching of Stoic philosophy, Epictetus also gives his own students advice on what to do (or rather, not to do) with their hair. Book III in *Discourses* reports an encounter between the Stoic philosopher and a young student of rhetoric "who had his hair arranged in a rather elaborate fashion and was in general richly dressed" (*Disc.* III.i.1, transl. Hard). The student's hair provokes Epictetus (as Ischomachus was provoked by his wife's make-up) to philosophize on the natural beauty in animals. What makes a dog, horse, or a nightingale beautiful, he reasons, depends on their special nature, and thus each of them is beautiful in a different manner. He infers that the same applies to humans, too. The specific nature of human beings that makes them beautiful lies in their rational virtues: justice, temperance, and self-control. Finally, Epictetus advises his student to adorn and beautify (*kosmeó kai kallópizó*) himself, but to leave his hair "to him who fashioned it as he pleased" (*Disc.* III.i.26). Like Plato, Epictetus insists that, in the end, the challenge is to recognize what really is essential for oneself as a human, and what is only a superfluous decoration. He concludes: "(F)or you yourself are not your flesh and hair, but your choice (*prohairesis*). If you take care to have this beautiful, then you will be beautiful" (*Disc.* III.i.40, transl. Hard).

Prohairesis is a key philosophical term in Epictetus' thinking. In a nutshell, it signifies the human soul's capacity to make a free choice in relation to impressions. More precisely, when an impression comes to our mind, by virtue of our *prohairesis*, it is in our power either to accept or reject it. We are always able to control our *prohairesis*, unlike the things in the world outside of us. Indeed, we constantly apply this natural ability of ours, but more often than not, we fail to use it correctly. Thus, the story of Epictetus and the extravagant student connects with a central topic in Stoic philosophical lectures: the ideal of choosing and rejecting impressions in a rational way.

It is notable that Epictetus' interlocutor is a student of *rhetoric*, which the Ancient philosophers typically define as an art of persuasion through skillful arrangements of words and beautiful expressions, regardless of the philosophical content.[2] In another passage, Epictetus compares beautification of expression to the work of a hairdresser and distinguishes this from the faculty of moral deliberation (*Disc.* III.xxiii.15). Clearly, the student of rhetoric exemplifies a person who only pays attention to the outer appearance, aims at pleasing others, and consequently, has set inappropriate goals for life. If he wanted to become a real student of *philosophy*, he should shift his attention from his hair to his *prohairesis*—from the surface to his innate capacity to moral deliberation and making a free choice.[3]

---

[2] Plato used similar arguments concerning the difference between rhetoric and philosophy in *Gorgias*.

[3] The rhetoric student in Epictetus' example also resembles the Peripatetic thinker Theophrastus' (c. 371–287 BCE) description of the 'obsequious man' (*areskos*), who is characterized by his exaggerated attention to his outer appearance as he constantly has haircuts, changes his clothes, and uses body oils. (*Characters*, V.5). Aristotle, too, discusses a person who is *areskos* as the exaggerated extreme that exceeds the ideal medium of friendliness: a person who tries too hard to please (*EN* 1108a25–30; 1126b11–13; cf. Diggle's commentary on *Characters*, p. 222).

Seneca connects the juxtaposition between internal beauty and fancy hairstyles to a philosophical discussion of nature and human goals. Like Xenophon and Epictetus, he supports his argument with an analogy to animals: if true human beauty really depended on bodily factors, humans would always lose in comparison to animals, as they lose to rabbits in speed and to "cattle and beasts" in strength. Seneca writes:

> Why do you cultivate physical beauty? Whatever you do, you will be outdone in attractiveness by dumb animals. Why do you pour enormous effort into doing your hair? Whether you have it flowing in the Parthian style or bound up in the German mode or in disarray as the Scythians wear it, still, any horse's mane will be thicker and the mane on a lions' neck will be more beautiful. (*Letter* 124: 22, transl. Inwood)

Given the common Ancient idea of a hierarchic nature, it seems rather extraordinary that a philosopher should place animals above humans as Seneca here does. He clearly wants to stress the point that there is only one way in which humans can be better than animals, and this is through virtue and rationality.[4] In all bodily aspects—strength, speed, and looks—there are animals that will outdo humans. Thus, humans should not even try to compete in these respects because they are bound to lose—which, in effect, would position them below lower species, which is against the hierarchic order of nature. The above passage emphasizes that the specific nature of humans lies exactly and exclusively in their rational capacities (also connected to the capacity of speech, which allegedly the "dumb animals" lack). Therefore, it is this nature that people should cultivate instead of hairs and looks, which are a part of nature that humans share with animals.

Seneca's view of human body sounds thus rather pessimistic: the body is vulnerable, feeble, and not even particularly attractive. He expresses this pessimism clearly in his consolation letter to the Roman lady Marcia:

---

[4]According to the Neoplatonic philosopher Porphyry, however, humans outdo animals also in vices. He says of humans: "(M)any of them surpass the most terrible wild beasts in cruelty, anger, and rapine, being murderous of their children and their parents (…)" (*On Abstinence from Animal Food* 3.19.3; transl. Taylor).

> What is man? A body weak and fragile, naked, in its natural state defenseless, dependent upon another's help, and exposed to all the affronts of Fortune; when it has practiced well its muscles, it then becomes the food of every wild beast, of everyone the prey; a fabric of weak and unstable elements, attractive only in its outer features, unable to bear cold, heat, and toil (…). (Seneca, *To Marcia on Consolation*, xi. 3, transl. Basore)

This view has an interesting implication from the perspective of gender. It would seem to follow that the physical differences between men and women (something he does not here even mention even if he is addressing a woman) are unimportant, given the general weakness and fragility of the human condition. Indeed, he presents this bodily fragility as the common lot of all human beings, something that connects rather than distinguishes them. If men (in many cases) happened to be slightly bigger or physically stronger than women, it seems to follow that this is only a difference in degree, but not in kind. A minor difference like this would clearly not suffice to make men more enduring or long-lasting than women (not to mention in any way *morally* superior). Thus, whatever the bodily differences, according to Seneca, men and women are both characterized by fragility. Again, as in the context of Stoic metaphysics, the emphasis is on common human characteristics rather than differentiating features.

Thus, we can now see how Stoic (as well as other Ancient) views on bodily beauty tend to reflect philosophical theories of nature: the positioning of the human being on the top of the hierarchic order of nature, and the idea of a specific human nature (as opposed to animal nature). According to Epictetus and Seneca, as well as their predecessors Xenophon and Plato, the human body, hair, and looks although natural are different from true human nature. In other words, they presume a difference between *nature as given*, something we already are, and *nature as a goal*, something that expresses our distinctively human ideals.

5.2 On Hairy Bodies and the Works of Nature

Discussing the problem of whether human virtues arise naturally, Alexander of Aphrodisias draws attention to the philosophical problem of nature:

Now if we had this ability receptive of the virtues from nature in such a way that we just got it as we advanced and became completed, as we walk and grow teeth and grow a beard, and other things that happen to us in accordance with nature—if so, the virtues would still not be up to us, just as none of these things are. (Alexander, Fat XXVII, 197.25–198.26, transl. Julia Annas, as in Annas 1993: 147)[5]

This passage captures the idea that in one sense, nature is something that "makes things happen to us," such as a beard growing on a man or teeth coming through in a child. This is not our own choice and cannot be changed through deliberation. It is the aspect of the Ancient philosophical view on nature that Julia Annas calls "mere nature," in other words nature as "the inescapable aspects of ourselves" (cf. Annas 1993: 135–220).

Virtue is obviously nothing like this because not many people (hardly any according to the Stoics) ever become virtuous. Further, even though it is possible to become virtuous, this would not just naturally happen to us in the same way hairs grow on our body. The Stoics emphasize that the process of becoming virtuous requires effort, education, dedication, and constant practice. On the other hand, we do not acquire virtues *against* nature, either. On the contrary, the Stoics call the life of the sage *kata physin*—living in harmony or in accordance with nature. Thus, this is the other sense in which the Ancient philosophers used the concept of nature—on the normative level to express the ideal form of life for humans (and other living beings).[6]

Epictetus makes a distinction between "chief works of nature" (*ta erga physeôs*) and "its by-products" (*parerga autês*). Again, body hairs serve as a case-in-point of things that fall under the second category. Yet, even by-products can have an important natural function. Epictetus poses a critical rhetorical question through the mouth of an imagined opponent, who suspects that nothing "could be more useless than the hairs on the chin," and gives the following expressly gendered reply: the body hairs serve the function of distinguishing between male (*arren*) and female (*thêly*). In Epictetus' words: "Does not nature thus let us

---

[5] Alexander of Aphrodisias was appointed chair in Aristotelian philosophy in Athens in 198–209 CE and was thus slightly later than Marcus Aurelius.

[6] On the goal of living in accordance with nature, and the assimilation of nature and virtue in Stoicism, see, e.g., DL VII: 86–89; Stobaeus II.7.6e (L&S 63A).

straightaway cry aloud, even at a distance, 'I am a man (*anêr eimi*), approach and address me accordingly, inquire no further, see the signs (*idou ta symbola*)!'" (*Disc.* I.xvi.10–14, Hard's translation slightly modified). Epictetus anticipates that his interlocutor will be unsatisfied with this answer and would wish that the "genders were undistinguished (*adiakriton*)," indicating that the opponent was leaning toward an ideal of gender neutrality, or crossing over the traditional gender norms. Epictetus answers this possible counterargument by declaring: "But how beautiful this sign is, how becoming and dignified! How much finer than a cock's comb, and more majestic than a lion's mane! Therefore, we ought to preserve the signs conferred by god, we ought not to throw them away, nor, as far as it is up to us (*eph' heautois*), confound the genders (*ta genê*) that have been thus distinguished (*diêrêmena*)" (*Disc.* I.xvi.10–14, Hard's translation slightly modified).

Epictetus idea is thus that even though physical signs of gender might be mere by-products of nature, they still belong to natural order of things, and thus are useful and worth respecting. This goes well with the general Stoic view that nature is good and does not produce anything bad or useless. As we saw in the previous chapter, the Stoics considered nature as inherently rational, and thus even its by-products serve a rational function of some kind. Epictetus applies this Stoic principle to physical signs of gender and claims that their natural function is to physically manifest gender dimorphism. Their usefulness lies in the fact that a person's gender can be recognized "from afar," and thus, the distinction between men and women can easily be made.

Epictetus thus takes beard to function as a physical sign of a man, and the lack of beard together with softer voice as signs of women. In another passage, he claims that hairiness belongs to the nature (*physis*) of man and hairlessness to the nature of woman, and thus seems to indicate that men and women had at least to a certain extent different natures. In his typically exaggerated manner, he calls a woman with plenty of hair (*trikhas pollas*) "a freak" (*teras*) who should be "exhibited in Rome among other freaks" (*Disc.* III.i.27).[7] However, even though body hairs

---

[7] It is interesting to pay attention to Epictetus' choice of the term *teras* ("a monster, a freak, a deviation"), which is the same term Aristotle used for the female gender in his biology. I discussed this term and how it should be read in the Aristotelian context in Sect. 2.2.

fall under the category of *nature as given*, since the hairs naturally grow on our bodies, Epictetus also discusses them as a matter of choice and deliberation. Pointing back to the distinction between things that are inside and outside of our power, he states that we should not confuse gender distinction *as far as it is up to us*. Thus, when we do make choices concerning our body hairs, these choices should reflect the natural order that has produced them for a specific purpose.

The relationship between nature and our choices concerning nature is at stake also in Musonius Rufus' lecture on cutting hair. Like Epictetus, he discusses hairs on the head and on the man's cheeks as works of nature. He claims that Zeno had advised letting the hair grow naturally, and cutting it only if it gets too disturbing: too heavy or hindering one's movements. Musonius urges people to use reason as to when to remove hair or to let it grow: when cutting hair one should only remove what is excessive. Moreover, a man should not remove his facial hair in order to look like a beardless boy, or act like a woman who does her hair in order to look more beautiful. He adds that some men try to please either boys or women by going in for an androgynous look, which is something "real men would never tolerate" (Musonius Rufus, in Cynthia King: 21, p. 81; Stob. 8.6.24).[8]

Both Musonius' negative remarks on androgynous men and Epictetus' advices for the embellished rhetoric student take facial hairs as signs of being a "real man." This image is contrasted with that of a beardless, smooth man, which alludes to the image of a *kinaidos* that frequently occurs in Ancient sources.[9] *Kinaidos* could be translated as "toy-boy," and the connotations of the term are usually negative. Indeed, when the rhetoric student defends his choice of shaving his body hairs by saying that women adore smooth men (*tois leiois*), Epictetus'

---

[8] A similar ideal of nature occurs in the anecdote on the Cynic Diogenes (c. 412–323 BCE), who is reported to have said to an effeminate young man (*neaniskon thélynomenon*): "Are you not ashamed for taking worse care of yourself than nature does? Nature made you a man but you try to make yourself a woman" (DL VI: 46, 65). Also, this anecdote builds on the juxtaposition between nature (as given) and the choices we make on our bodies, and expresses a negative attitude on blurring signs of gender. Thus, the Stoic position on nature at least to some parts reminds the Cynic ideal of living in accordance with nature. I compare the Stoic and Cynic standpoints in Chaps. 11 and 12.

[9] On further discussion on the term *kinaidos* in Antiquity, see David Halperin (2002: 29–34).

counterattack is to ask: "If women liked toy-boys (*kinaidoi*), would you also become one?" In his view, the student has set wrong goals for his life if he aims at pleasing "uninhibited women" (*hai gynaikes hai akolastoi*) (*Disc.* III.i.32).[10] The image of *kinaidos* is clearly associated with uncontrolled sexuality as well as confusion of traditional sexual roles, whether expressed between a man and a woman or in a pederastic relationship between two men.

Accordingly, the beard resonates with the Ancient ideals of masculinity and masculine sexuality. This ideal is often expressed in "leonine" terms, as does Epictetus in the above-quoted passage when he calls the beard "more majestic than a lion's mane." Maud W. Gleason points out that lions are often mentioned in the context of Ancient (Roman) beauty ideals for men, expressing the ideal of sexual activity (1995: 74; cf. 62–67).[11] Michel Foucault points out the importance of the beard as a sign of maturity in Ancient texts (Greek and Roman). He connects this to his analysis of Ancient sexual ethics as a system in which the major concern was the question of taking an active versus a passive role (or being the "lover," *erastês*, or the "beloved," *erastos*) in an erotic relationship between an older and a younger man. Beard, according to Foucault, shows that a man is mature and thus too old to play the passive role (Foucault 1982/1997: 229).[12]

---

[10]Cf. Diogenes the Cynic, who refused to answer the question of a "decorously attired young man" unless he lifted his dress to reveal whether he was a man or a woman (DL VI: 46, 65). As an example of the inhuman treatment of slaves, Seneca mentions having to serve wine dressed like a girl. He clearly assumes that this treatment was inhumane both from the perspective of gender and age: even if the slave already exhibits physical signs of a man, he is kept smooth and hairless in order to sexually satisfy his master (*Letter* 47, 6–8). In another context, Seneca compares Epicurean philosophy to a man in a dress (*De Vita Beata* 13). I will return to the topic of slavery as well as the (gendered) rivalry between the Stoics and the Epicureans in Sect. 9.1 and 10.2.

[11]When Aristotle lists the characteristics and virtues of animals, he refers to the lion as a "noble, brave, *andreia*, and high-bred, *eugenê*" animal (*HA* I.1.488b15–25). Also, Diogenes the Cynic allegedly said to a man who was boasting of having a lion's skin: "Do not disgrace the hero's clothing" (DL VI: 45). It is interesting to remark, however, that Seneca seems to take a slightly different stance than Epictetus when it comes to the respective beauty in bearded men and hairy lions, since in the passage quoted earlier in this chapter, he claims that no man was (physically) so beautiful as to compete against "the majestic lion's mane" (*Letter* 124).

[12]Also, Marilyn Skinner, in her discussion on Ancient pederasty, points out that the adolescent became "objects of open admiration from the time of the appearance of secondary sex characteristics at puberty until the growth of the full beard, and approximate range of

Thus, even though Epictetus and Musonius appeal to nature in their praise of men's hairy cheeks, one can clearly see how their arguments reflect socially and culturally coded ideals of masculinity. In these discussions, body hairs do not simply fall under the category of "nature as given." They are connected to choices and thus also elements of "nature as a goal" seem to be at stake. This, however, seems perplexing in the light of the argument that I have defended in the earlier chapters, namely, the idea of metaphysical insignificance of gender. If gender indeed was metaphysically insignificant, as my reading suggests, why then would a Stoic thinker give any importance to physical signs of gender, such as hairs?

Even more problematic seems to be the transition from mere bodily differences to the ethically relevant realm of behavior when Epictetus expressly suggests that a man should be approached and talked to "as a man." When Plato mentions hairiness in *Republic*, he does so in order to show the *insignificance* of this characteristic. According to his famous argument, the same way hairiness is irrelevant for a person's abilities to work as a cobbler, gender is irrelevant for person's abilities to rule (*Rep.* 454 c). However, Epictetus now seems to see hairiness as something much more significant than Plato. In order to scrutinize more closely the seeming contradiction between the significance and insignificance of the physical sign of gender, let us consider a particular philosophical debate in Ancient sources that is highly illuminating: the question of the philosopher's beard.

5.3 The Philosopher's Beard

The image of the bearded philosopher is a famous one. The Ancient thinkers also debated whether or not a beard was to be taken as a sign of a philosopher. This raises questions related to indifference, body and gender. Why should a philosopher be concerned about anything as seemingly irrelevant as hairs growing on the chin? Furthermore, if a beard did make a philosopher, where would philosophizing women stand?

---

fifteen or sixteen to eighteen" (2013: 14). It is worthwhile to remember, however, that pederasty was unlikely to play a similar pedagogical role in the thinking Hellenistic and Roman philosophers as it did in the Classic thinkers like Plato.

(There may have been a few bearded women, but Epictetus at least, in his own words, would rather see them in a freak show than doing philosophy on the *stoa poikile*.)

Arrian tells an odd story about Epictetus' relationship with his beard. The context is a discussion about an athlete who had chosen to die rather than to allow his genitals to be amputated. When Epictetus is asked whether the man had died "as an athlete or as a philosopher," he replies: he died "as a man" (*anêr*). He adds, however, that this was not just any man, but a man who had been successful in the Olympic Games and for whom this had been a way of life. Epictetus' point is that the man acted in accordance with his own character (*prosôpon*), whereas someone with a different disposition would have rather had "his very head cut off, if he could have lived without it." The discussion continues with a radical proposal from the interlocutor: "Come now, Epictetus, shave off your beard!" Epictetus replies: "If I am a philosopher, I answer, I will not shave it off—'Then I will have you beheaded'—If it will do you any good, behead me" (*Disc.* I.ii.25–30, transl. Hard).[13]

Was Epictetus really, as it seems, more attached to his beard than to his head and consequently his life? He might have answered in a Socratic vein that a life without philosophy was not worth living, and that this is why he did not want to lose his sign of being a philosopher. And not being just any philosopher but precisely a *Stoic* one, since the Stoics seem to have enjoyed a reputation of being a particularly manly school of philosophy in their time—contrary to that of the (allegedly) more effeminate school of Epicureanism (to be discussed in Sect. 9.1).

The image of a "manly Stoic" is humorously displayed in the Roman rhetorician Lucian's (c. 120–190 CE) dialogue *Hermotimus*, where the protagonist declares that he finds Stoicism to be the best of all the philosophy schools largely because of their manly (*arrenôpous*) looks, expressed in their dignified walk, thoughtful countenance and short haircuts (Lucian, *Hermotimus* 18).[14] Hermotimus' interlocutor Lycinus remains (for good reasons) dissatisfied with his answer and wonders how one

---

[13] Cf. Galen's discussion of an athlete whom he advised not to have his testicles amputated since this would have negative effects on his strength (see Sect. 2.3).

[14] In Lucian's satire *Philosophies for Sale*, it is the Cynic philosopher who is portrayed as manly (*andrikos*) as he is dressed in a raggedy sleeveless shirt that he calls his "lion skin." The contrary image is personified in the Cyrenaic philosopher, dressed in a purple cloak and reeking of myrrh (Lucian, *Philosophies for Sale*, 8–12).

should discern the qualities of the philosopher's soul on the basis of his physical appearance. The signs of a true philosopher should be evident in his words (*logos*) and his action, not his looks. Lycinus points out that at the gates of the ideal city, no man would be refused entry if he were virtuous, even if he came there naked (ibid. 18–23). The Stoic Zeno would have certainly agreed, as we shall see at the end of this chapter. It seems that Epictetus refers to a similar image of a masculine Stoic philosopher as portrayed in Lucian's play. Yet, this leaves us to wonder why an outer image would play such a big role in his conception of a philosopher.

In another passage, Epictetus expresses the opposite idea and ridicules people who think they could become philosophers just by letting their beards grow and dressing in a cloak, just as one does not become a musician by buying a cithara and a plectrum. He proclaims: "See how I eat, how I drink, how I sleep, how I bear and forbear (*apekhomai*), how I assist others (*synergô*), how I make use of my desires and aversions (*orekseis khrômai*) (…)" (*Disc.* IV.viii.20, transl. Hard.). Here, Epictetus emphasizes the same idea as Lycinus in his critical counterarguments in *Hermotimus*: a virtuous character should be expressed in virtuous action. In this passage, remarkably different from the one where he refuses to get a shave, Epictetus admits that even though beard commonly functions as a sign of a philosopher, not every bearded man is like Socrates. But does he allow that Socrates might have been Socrates even without the beard?

Maud W. Gleason draws attention to Epictetus' refusal to shave his beard, claiming that he was "sliding dizzyingly between a constructionist and an essentialist view of masculinity," confusing "the natural and the cultural appearance," and thus "masculine integrity appears as both a natural phenomenon and a cultural construct" (1995: 73). In her view, Epictetus contradicts himself in giving gendered signs a different status in different passages, treating them as natural, on the one hand, and cultural, on the other hand.

Also, Gretchen Reydams-Schils discusses this problem and suggests that, in Stoic thinking, beards have more to do with being a man than being a philosopher, and that a philosopher refusing to shave his beard is afraid of losing his manliness, not of ceasing to be a philosopher. She claims: "(T)he beard is, after all, a divinely bestowed sign of masculinity and, as such, a necessary, if not sufficient, condition for dignified manliness. It may not make the philosopher—nor may any other outer trappings, for that matter (...)—but insofar as he is a man, the philosopher does not do without it" (2005: 46).

I think Reydams-Schils is right in drawing attention to the fact that a beard also stands for being a man, and that for a philosopher who refuses to shave this might be an issue, as well. Furthermore, I would like to add that, as stated above, beard also stands for adulthood, and thus keeping the beard might also refer to age and to the fact that he is past adolescence and in a position, as a man, to take care of his civic duties and his household. In line with Foucault, we could also emphasize the importance of maturity in male sexual roles in Antiquity. Yet even if beards were taken to stand for manliness, philosophers, and maturity (in both social and sexual sense), how would Reydams-Schils' proposal solve the problem of the apparent discrepancy between beards as insignificant and significant? What would it mean if a male philosopher "could not do without" his beard, as she claims, or that beard is a "necessary if not sufficient" condition for manliness? Or was Epictetus really contradicting himself, as Gleason suggested?

I would first like to point out that when Epictetus ridicules the idea that someone would become a philosopher just by letting his beard grow and dressing in a cloak, he clearly does not take beard to be a sufficient condition for being a philosopher (*Disc.* IV.viii. 20). Here, Epictetus emphasizes living and acting like a philosopher, not just looking like one. However, I do not think that Epictetus would take beard to be a necessary condition for being a philosopher, either. Reydams-Schils treats beards in her reading in a similar way as Epictetus discussed the athlete's genitals in the example discussed above: the athlete would rather die than have his genitals amputated, and by so doing he would die as a man. This is misleading, however, since if we read the above-discussed passage carefully, this is not what Epictetus is implying.

I claim, against Reydams-Schils' position, that a beard does not constitute manliness, any more than it constitutes being a philosopher (or maturity, for that matter). I also disagree with Gleason who states that Epictetus would be "ambiguous, confused, and inconsistent." On the contrary, I suggest that he could consistently consider a beard both as something natural and as something "chosen." In seeking a solution, one should once again pay careful attention to Alexander's above-mentioned distinction between "things that happen to us in accordance with nature" and things that are up to us. This is also a distinction Epictetus frequently makes when differentiating things within our control (*eph' hêmin*), from those beyond it (*ouk eph 'hêmin*). As noted above, Alexander explicitly placed body hairs in the former category. According to the well-known Stoic notion, all things that are not up to us are indifferent (*adiaphora*) and do not contribute anything to virtue. Whether or not hair grows on the chin is not up to us and therefore falls outside the sphere of ethically relevant things.

However, we can still use deliberation and choice in deciding what to do with things that, as such, are indifferent and outside the sphere of virtue, such as hairs. We can decide to let them grow or to shave them off (in this way, a beard is different from some of Epictetus' other examples of gendered signs, such as the high-pitched voice of females, which is not as easily changed). It is also worth noting that the Stoics had different ways of talking about indifferent things: one way is to discuss things that are completely indifferent, such as whether the number of hairs on the head is odd or even, for instance, since in this case we do not (hopefully, I would add) use deliberation and choice (cf. DL VII: 104; Stob. 7; SVF 3.118). In my view, however, at least in the Roman culture of Epictetus' time, a beard carried enough social meaning and symbolic value that a person could legitimately use deliberation and choice in deciding what to do about it. Thus, when Epictetus is asked whether he would shave his beard, he refuses because this is not something he would *choose* to do. He is a man and a philosopher, and he wants to maintain these signs *as long as it is up to him*. Even though the beard as such is insignificant, it might still be one of the things the Stoics refer to as preferable (*ta proêgmena*) or as having selective value (*aksian eklektikên*; cf. Stob. 7). For the Stoics, preferable things were not actually good and did not contribute to virtue, but there were still rational reasons for pursuing them. Stoic examples of preferable things concerning the body (which, according to Stobaeus, are also *kata physin*, in accordance with nature) include health, property, and strength (DL VII: 104–107; Stob, 7a; SVF 3.140). Accordingly, dispreferred things concerning the body are the opposites (e.g., illness). Finally, there are things concerning the body that are so insignificant for what is really important in humans that they should not affect our preferences in any way whatsoever. Examples of this type of insignificance are "pale or dark skins and the brightness of eyes" (Stob. 7 b; SVF 3.136).

The notion of preferable things is connected to the notion of "selective value." Even if a thing is indifferent, it can, according to the Stoics, still have more or less selective value. Things with much value are to be preferred, and likewise, things lacking in value are to be dispreferred (Stob. 7b; SVF 3.133). In Stobaeus' example, having pale or dark skin is among the things that are to be neither preferred nor dispreferred (and thus, this has no selective value). However, I have argued that the beard carries enough social and symbolic meanings, standing for being both a philosopher and a (mature) man, that we can consider having a beard as something with a certain amount of selective value.[15] Even if, admittedly, a beard is likely not to have very much selective value, it is still not quite as meaningless as whether the number of hairs is odd or even. Thus, Epictetus could legitimately choose to keep his beard and still admit that a beard, as such, is indifferent.

There is no reason to suspect that Epictetus would have jumped off a cliff if he had been shaved by force. If his interlocutor had threatened to shave him, Epictetus would probably have given the same response as when the interlocutor said he would cut off his head: "If it will do you any good, take it off." After all, the interlocutor's first line suggests that Epictetus *himself* should shave his beard (*age oun, Epiktête, diaksyrêsai*). If losing his beard was something that just befell a philosopher, as shipwreck befalls a sailor, then I think there are good reasons to assume that the Stoic philosopher would take this as calmly as any misfortune in life and go on practicing his philosophy. After all, eventual death is indifferent to the Stoic, and thus, he does not have to be afraid of shipwrecks or of being beheaded any more than of being shaved. He may prefer to keep his beard as long as it is up to him, both because he is a philosopher and because he is an adult man, but this does not require acceptance of the problematic supposition that having beard is a necessary or a sufficient condition for being a philosopher, man, or adult.

---

[15] Nancy Sherman also pays attention to the social expectations concerning the body, and that certain care of the body such as fitness is also a social duty as well as a sign of self-respect and other-regard (2005: 32). This line of thinking could be easily applied to the specific question concerning body hairs, and thus, the man and his beard should be understood within a complex framework of social expectations, evaluations, and (self-)representations that legitimately can have "selective value" in the Stoic theory.

5.4 Gendered Signs and Effeminate Vanity—Early and Roman Stoics Compared

The idea of "selective value" of body hairs and Epictetus' appeal to "respecting the signs" of gender sound quite distant to the early Stoic discussions. In Zeno's ideal state, men and women would wear similar clothes, which should not entirely cover any part of their bodies. Men and women are discussed equally as citizens of the utopian society, and no physical differences between them are mentioned in this context (DL VII: 32–24). This leads us to wonder whether the importance of culturally coded gendered signs changed from early to Roman Stoicism. Do social and cultural signs of gender receive a special status in late Stoicism?

Let me elaborate on this a little. I think the difference between the early and later Stoics is understandable if we consider the differences in their focus on political philosophy. The early Stoic utopias, which in many ways are reminiscent of Plato's *Republic* and the Cynics, should, I claim, be understood as thought experiments on what a virtuous society of sages would be like (I elaborate on this argument in more detail in Chap. 12). These early utopias were not real-life political proposals for how contemporary society should be changed, but attempts to imagine an entirely wise community. Thus, the conventions or cultural norms of the existing societies did not have to play any role in the imaginative ideal society of the early Stoics, particularly given their very pessimistic view of existing cultures, which they blamed for the morally and cognitively corrupt state in which virtually all normal people live. The Roman Stoics, in contrast, did not formulate social utopias, but tried to encourage people to live well even if they lived in a thoroughly corrupted society. One should not retreat into a philosophical life outside of society, but try to become virtuous in the life one is already leading and to fulfill the accompanying social obligations. In other words, the choice between a philosophical life and "ordinary life" was not mutually exclusive for the Roman Stoics: those leading a philosophical life have to cope with social surroundings that are far from being wise by Stoic standards.

The Roman Stoics guide their students in the difficult tasks of practicing philosophy and striving toward good life as citizens with social roles and obligations. Thus, the teacher has to meet his pupils as both a philosopher and Roman. As a philosopher, he leads them toward a life of indifference, totally free from any outer burdens. However, as a Roman, a teacher like Epictetus would not be ignorant of the habits and customs of his society. Gender roles (made visible through bodily signs such as clothes and beards) were admittedly an important aspect of that culture. Moreover, Roman Stoics were rather reactionary in maintaining that people should not oppose their cultural norms or standards. In order to attain peace of mind, one should change oneself on the inside, not the world on the outside. I claim that the importance of social obligations and public life in Roman Stoicism opens up one perspective that sheds light on why the later Stoics did not follow the founders of their school in arguing for insignificance of gendered signs such as clothing.

The Stoics did not discuss the problem of what the ideal of a bearded philosopher would mean to philosophizing women. Of course, it would be ridiculous to claim that women would need beards in order to practice philosophy. Epictetus would, presumably, have encouraged a woman to follow her nature and to keep her natural gendered signs (in the sense that they have similar "selective value" as beards). However, as far as the contents and goals of philosophy are concerned, I claim that the Stoics would have agreed that they were the same for men and women (I will defend this argument in more detail in Chap. 9).

Interestingly, both the early and the Roman Stoics apparently agreed in their critical views on beautification and cosmetics. I have quoted Zeno's disapproving attitude to a young man wearing perfume and Epictetus' and Musonius' criticism of young men attempting to become smooth and pleasing. As all of these examples are of a man adorning himself, it might seem that the Stoic criticism is directed exactly toward men, rather than women, who pay too much attention to their looks (and who want to take up the role of a *kinaidos*). However, I suggest that the Stoics would not approve of women who beautified themselves, either. I imagine they were critical of make-up and perfume in general, being signs of vanity even more than of femininity. Thus, the Stoics would have agreed with Ischomachus who criticized his wife for wearing make-up and high heels. Epictetus also demonstrates a disapproving attitude to beautification in *Encheiridion* when he mentions that right after they have turned fourteen years old, girls are being called "ladies" (*kyriai*) by men. When women notice that there is nothing else for them to do but to sleep with men (*synkoimôntai*), they start to beautify themselves. With a paternalistic tone, he then advises the men to honor women for nothing but appearing orderly (*kosmiai*) and modest (*aidêmones*)—and making sure that women, too, understand this (Epictetus, *Ench.* 40). Here, Epictetus does clearly not consider beautification to be any more in accordance with the nature of women than in the case of men. Indeed, if young women do not have other expectations for future but to become lovers of men, and bodily beauty is what helps the women to achieve their goal, then beautification appears only as a logical choice. An optimistic reading would be that it was good if young women had something else to look forward to in their lives than sleeping with men—and that it was good if men appreciated also other qualities in them than their looks (even though the ideals of "orderly and modest" appearance might not sound like particularly appealing from the present-day perspective, and of course, this ideal, too, is formulated exclusively from the male perspective).

That beautification is considered vanity in both men and women has an interesting implication: namely, if paying a lot of attention to one's hair, looks, and bodily odors is perceived as "womanish" or "effeminate," the ideal for women, too, is to get rid of some of these characteristics. Moreover, being womanish does not directly follow from and is not restricted to the female gender (whether this is defined biologically, socially, or as a combination of both). This idea will receive further support in the context of Stoic physiognomics, which I explore in the next chapter.

Appendix

Aristotle

HA   History of Animals

The Complete Works of Aristotle. The Revised Oxford Translation. Jonathan Barnes (revised). Princeton, NJ: Princeton University Press, 1984.
Historia animalium. A.L. Peck (ed. and transl.). 3 vols. Cambridge, MA: Harvard University Press and London: Heinemann, 1965.

Epictetus

Discourses (Disc.)
Encheiridion (Ench.)

Discourses and Selected Writings. Christopher Gill (ed.). Robin Hard (transl.). London: J.M. Dent & Vermont, Tuttle/Everyman, 1995.

Discourses, Books I–IV. W.A. Oldfather (transl.). Cambridge and London: Harvard University Press, 2000.

Diogenes Laertius, *Lives of Eminent Philosophers* (DL)

Diogenis Laertii Vitae philosophorum. Miroslav Marcovich (ed.). *Bibliotheca scriptorum Graecorum et Romanorum Teubneriana.* Vol. 1. Stuttgart-Lipsia: Teubner, 1999–2002.
Lives of Eminent Philosophers. R.D. Hicks (transl.). Cambridge and London: Harvard University Press, 1995.

The Hellenistic Philosophers. A.A. Long and D.N. Sedley (eds.). Cambridge: Cambridge University Press, 1987. (L&S)

Lucianus Samosatensis

Hermotimus
Philosophies for Sale

Lucian in Eight Volumes. A.M. Harmon (transl.). Cambridge, MA and London: Harvard University Press and W. Heinemann, 1959–1972.

Musonius Rufus

Musonii Rufi Reliquiae. O. Hense (ed.). Leipzig: Kessinger, 1905.
Musonius Rufus: Lectures & Sayings. William B. Irvine (ed.). Cynthia King (transl.). CreateSpace, 2011

Plato

Alcibiades I
Gorgias
Rep.   Republic

Platonis Opera (Oxford Classical Texts)
Vol. 1, ed. E.A. Duke et al. 1995.
Vol. 2, ed. J. Burnet 1922.
Vol. 3, ed. J. Burnet 1922.
Vol. 4, ed. J. Burnet 1922.
Respublica. ed. S.R. Slings 2003.

Complete Works.. John M. Cooper (ed.). D.S. Hutchinson (associate ed.). Indianapolis: Hackett Publishers, 1997.

The Dialogues of Plato. Vol. 2: *Republic, Gorgias, Parmenides*. Oxford: Clarendon Press, 1953.
Plato in Twelve Volumes. Vol. 5–6, The Republic. Paul Shorey (transl.). Heinemann, London, 1969.

Porphyry

On Abstinence from Killing Animals. Gilliam Clark (transl.). Ithaca: Cornell University Press, 2000.

Seneca, Lucius Annaeus

Ad Marciam
De Vita Beata
Epistulae

Opera Philosophica. Louis Delatte (ed.). Olm, Hildesheim, 1981.
Moral Essays. Vol. I. John W. Basore (transl.). Cambridge and London: Harvard University Press, 1928.
Moral Essays. Vol. 2. John W. Basore (transl.). Cambridge and London: Harvard University Press, 1932.
Epistles. Vol. I–VI. Richard M. Gummere (transl.). Cambridge and London: Harvard University Press, 1917–1925.
Selected Philosophical Letters. Brad Inwood (transl.). Oxford: Oxford University Press, 2007.

Stoicorum veterum fragmenta. Vol. I–III. H. von Arnim (ed.). Leipzig: Lipsiae, in aedibus B.G. Teubneri, 1903–24. (SVF)

Stobaeus

Anth.   Anthology

Anthologium, Ioannis Stobaeus. Otto Hense and Curtius Wachsmuth (eds.). Weidman: Berolini, 1884–1909.

Theophrastus

Characters. James Diffle (ed. and transl.). Cambridge: Cambridge University Press.

Xenophon

Oec. *Oeconomicus*

Oeconomicus—A Social and Historical Commentary. Sarah B. Pomeroy (transl.). Oxford: Clarendon University Press, 1994.

REFERENCES

Annas, Julia. 1993. *The Morality of Happiness*. Oxford: Oxford University Press.
Foucault, Michel. 1982/1997. Technologies of the Self. In *The Essential Works of Foucault, volume 1: Ethics, Subjectivity, Truth*, ed. Paul Rabinow, trans. Robert Hurley et al., 223–251. London: Penguin. (TS).
Gleason, Maud W. 1995. *Making Men—Sophists and Self-Presentation in Ancient Rome*. Princeton: Princeton University Press.
Halperin, David. 2002. Forgetting Foucault: Acts, Identities, and the History of Sexuality. In *The Sleep of Reason—Erotic Experience and Sexual Ethics in Ancient Greek and Rome*, ed. Martha Nussbaum and Juha Sihvola, 21–54. Chicago and London: The University of Chicago Press.
Reydams-Schils, Gretchen. 2005. *The Roman Stoic—Self, Responsibility, and Affection*. Chicago and London: The University of Chicago Press.
Sherman, Nancy. 2005. *Stoic Warriors—The Ancient Philosophy Behind the Military Mind*. Oxford: Oxford University Press.
Skinner, Marilyn B. 2013. *Sexuality in Greek and Roman Culture*. Malden, MA: Blackwell.

CHAPTER 6

Fiery and Cold Natures—Stoic Physiognomics of Gender

According to the Skeptic thinker Sextus Empiricus, the Ancient science of physiognomy treats the body as a "picture of the soul" (*PH* I.xiv.85). Indeed, physiognomy (*physiognômonia*) draws connections between physical features and characteristics of the soul, presuming that the inner character is displayed in the outer appearance among both animals and humans.[1] The theory also often connects the shape of the body, physical appearance, facial expressions, and gestures to assumptions on gender. Thus, in conclusion of my discussion on beauty, the body and physical signs of gender, I now consider the connection between the body, gender, and characteristics in Ancient physiognomics.

At least certain Stoic thinkers seemed to sympathize with physiognomic ideas. Zeno, for example, portrays a young man, the beauty of whose soul is displayed in his perfectly harmonious face and body. Seneca also alludes to physiognomic ideas and the connection between climate and disposition in *De Ira* and in some of his letters. Galen, in turn, praises the Stoic Posidonius for having attached his discussion of

---

[1] On the historical background of physiognomics, and the development of the discipline in Hippocrates', pseudo-Aristotle's, Polemo's, and Peripatetic treatises, see Tamsyn S. Barton (1994: 100–109). Barton points out that physiognomics rely on the ideas that one can learn about humans from animals, and that the stars, the climate, and/or bodily humors influence people's bodies and characters. It was also often assumed that climate caused certain proportions in the humors, which further caused certain dispositions (Barton 1994: 95–98). Cf. Marke Ahonen (2014: 623–624).

emotions to the discussion on physiognomy. He gives the following overview of Posidonius' views:

> (A)ll broad-chested and warmer creatures and humans are more spirited by nature, the broad-hipped and colder, more cowardly. And environment contributes to considerable differences in human character with regard to cowardice, daring, love of pleasure, or toil; the grounds for this are that the emotional movements of the soul follow always the physical state, which is altered in no small degree from the temperature in the environment. For he [Posidonius] makes the point too that even the blood in animals differs in warmth and coldness, thickness and thinness, and in a considerable number of other different ways, a topic which Aristotle developed at length. (Posidonius, fragment 169 F; Galen, *De Placitid Hippocratis et Platonis*, 459–465, transl. De Lacy)

The point about variation in the temperature of the blood of different animals, which further affects their characteristics (warmer creatures are naturally braver), sounds very much like Aristotle's position in his biology. The end of the quoted passage explicitly states that Posidonius discussed many topics that Aristotle had developed in length. Thus, as we can see, physiognomy is closely connected to the theory of elements and natural temperatures discussed in Chap. 2.

Brad Inwood assigns physiognomy a strong role in Stoicism in claiming that the Stoics "consistently held to the tradition of physiognomy, which maintained that character traits could in many cases be read from physical appearance" (1997: 60). I do not think the evidence in Stoic sources supports quite as strong a statement as Inwood makes, but I agree with him that at least when it comes to Zeno, Seneca, and Posidonius, physiognomic ideas are clearly integrated into Stoic theory.

The physiognomic theory is interesting from the point of view of gender because it connects the investigation of the physical body to the discussion of dispositions, assuming an immediate connection between these two areas. Even if there is no uniform physiognomic theory of the exact nature of this connection, it raises the question concerning the nature and origins of gendered character features. Indeed, to point out differences between the sexes and ethnic groups was one of the standard applications of the art of physiognomy. Physiognomy also tends to discuss characteristics as "male" or "female," or "masculine" or "feminine." Traditionally, male and female characteristics were considered polar opposites, and male characteristics were categorically considered to be on the higher level (as is evident, e.g., in Aristotle's biology). However, as

Maud Gleason points out, a female could have masculine characteristics (and vice versa), and thus, male and female characteristics are not determined by one's biological sex (Gleason 1995: 60). The central question of this chapter concerns the relationship between feminine and masculine characteristics and the physical male and female gender.

6.1 Beautiful Souls in Beautiful Bodies

One reason why the Stoic authors discuss the outer appearance of the physical body is to draw an analogy with the soul. As stated above, analogy was one of the main ways of deriving knowledge in Stoic epistemology (cf. Chap. 3). The Stoics frequently compared mental disturbances with physical illnesses, and accordingly happiness with health. In addition to the analogy with health, the sources sometimes describe a harmonious mind as analogical to a beautiful body. According to Stobaeus, for example, the beauty of the body and the beauty of the soul are analogous in that both have the right proportions (Stobaeus, *Anthology* 2, 7.5b4; SVF 3.278, 1.563).

Seneca raises the question of whether a virtuous person also necessarily looks beautiful, and as a case in point, he describes his apparently old and ugly-looking friend Claranus, who despite his physical shortcomings had an outstandingly virtuous character. Seneca declares that he appreciated his friend's virtuousness so much that he was able to forgive him his physical deficiencies: "I certainly began to look at my friend Claranus in a new way: I think he is attractive and as straight in body as he is in mind" (*Letter* 66: 2). Seneca also explicitly includes physical beauty (or the lack of it) among the accidental characteristics that also exist among sages, but which do not affect their virtue and are thus unimportant for their reciprocal equality (ibid: 24). The last remark is significant in the context of gender, too, even though Seneca does not discuss gender at this point: here, again, we can see that the Stoic thinkers tend to emphasize that the only thing that matters is virtue and it is this, not physical qualities that make the sages each other equals.

Seneca seems to assume, however, that his friend Claranus was somewhat exceptional in being both ugly and virtuous. It seems indeed that at least some Stoic thinkers accepted the idea that physical qualities (more often than not) correspond with moral character. Diogenes Laertius reports that Zeno was of the opinion that "a man's character (*éthos*) can be known from his looks (*eidos*)," and that Cleanthes could recognize that a man's character was soft (*malakos*) on the basis of his sneeze (DL VII: 173).² Diogenes Laertius also points out that Zeno, Chrysippus, and Apollodorus (2nd century BCE) would have written that sages fall in love with young men whose appearances express a natural inclination to virtue (DL VII: 129).

Here, beauty of the soul and beauty of the body are not only used as being analogical to each other, but the argument assumes an actual link between the physical looks and mental characteristics. The idea of a connection between outer and inner excellence is also clearly stressed in Clement's (c. 150–215 CE) report on Zeno's position on beauty. According to Clement, Zeno would have described "a beautiful and properly loveable" (*kalê tina kai axieraston*) young man through the following features: his facial expression is calm, his eyes are neither closed nor wide open, the limbs of his body are not too relaxed, his movements do not indicate licentiousness (*tois akolastois*), and so on. He expresses modesty and manliness (*appernôpia*), and stays away from the perfume and wool stores and avoids effeminate beautification (Clement, *Paidagogos* III, 11, 74; SVF 1246).

Again, we see a Stoic thinker present a juxtaposition between a self-adorning, effeminate man, and idealized manliness. Yet again, the warning image of the *kinaidos* is lurking in the background.³ I suggested in Chap. 5 that the main target of Stoic criticism in passages such as these are wrong goals (such as looks) and bad characteristics (such as vanity). It is made clear that one does not achieve a beautiful appearance by going to the perfumer's or the wool shop. Nevertheless, the physical appearance seems to be relevant also for the ideal masculinity. Zeno

---

²In Malcolm Schofield's reading, the mentioning of the sneezing young man signifies that Cleanthes "was able to spot a passive homosexual by his sneeze" (1991: 31). Although the term *malakos* can also signify "delicate," "gentle," and "effeminate," I think Schofield is reading too much into this term. Besides, because of the enormous difference between Ancient conceptions of erotics and our present-day categories of sexual identity, I find it safer to avoid using the terms "homo/heterosexuality" in an Ancient context (cf. David Halperin 2002: 3). Possibly, however, despite his inexact choice of terms, Schofield was thinking about the role of the *erômenos*, the younger man in a pederastic relationship. Marke Ahonen reads this passage as suggesting that Cleanthes recognizes a *kinaidos* (the term is mentioned earlier in the same passage) (2014: 629). Cf. my discussion of *kindaidos* in Sect. 5.2.

³Maud W. Gleason reads this passage as suggesting that the young man should avoid giving signals of being sexually available (1995: 71).

seems to indicate that if one's inner character is beautiful, this would reflect on the surface of the body and facial expressions. In the previous chapter, we learnt that the Stoics advised a person to focus on his or her source of true human beauty: the reason. Now, Clement's passage seems to suggest that virtue would even affect the body.

Malcolm Schofield reads Clement's passage as "one of our best pieces of evidence for Stoic physiognomics" and claims that Zeno "is urging young men to aim for a particular sort of physical bearing" (1991: 115, 117).[4] Unfortunately, Schofield does not elaborate more on this claim. However, I think he might well be right that Zeno actually was urging young men to strive not only for virtue but also for certain physical looks. This would be in line with the interpretation I give in Chap. 5: that our physical appearance is not only something we are born with but can also be something to "aim for"—something about which we can legitimately deliberate as to what to choose and what to avoid (as in the case of the beard). However, one has to set one's goals carefully since, as noted above, the Stoics recognized many dangers connected to physical beauty, including signs of vanity or extravagance. These dangers are also clearly expressed in Clement's report on Zeno. Moreover, in the same way, as cosmetics are dispreferred, there are other physical things that can be legitimately preferred.[5] For example, a calm facial expression is often described as characteristic of a stabile mind, and having a beard as characteristics of a philosophizing man. But how would the Stoics explain the link between looks and characteristics? Does a certain look actually follow from a mental state, as some of the above-discussed passages seem to suggest?

That the Stoics sometimes expressed sympathy with physiognomics fits together with their metaphysical notion of a "total mixture" of the body and the soul, as discussed in Chap. 4. The belief that the soul is of bodily substance, and that the material soul and the material body are totally blended, gives a certain plausibility to the idea that the soul could be displayed in the body. However, it should be emphasized that the Stoics were by no means material reductionists and did not hold that

---

[4] Marke Ahonen suggests that this passage could be read not as a physiognomic analysis of how a virtuous person looks like but a piece of advise for young people (2014: 629).

[5] Similarly, Seneca declares that he has deliberately accustomed himself to living without using perfume and bathing too often (*Ep.* CVIII 15).

phenomena of the material body determined the material phenomena of the soul. Similarly, even if they sometimes allude to physiognomics, it does not imply that the opposite was the case: that the material phenomena of the soul dictated the material body. Nor does it follow that the Stoics generally believed that it was possible to draw reliable conclusions about a person's soul on the basis of his or her body (this, of course, is also the point of Seneca's discussion of his friend Claranus who was both good and ugly). A question to be explored in more detail is how well physiognomics fits into the Stoic way of thinking on the connection between the body, gender, and character.

6.2 Seneca on the Elements and Gendered Characteristics

As noted above, Ancient physiognomy rests on the idea that the inner and the outer forms of a person (or animal) are interconnected, and that the appearance of one's body can give some reliable insight into one's character. From another perspective, one could say that this tradition supposes that the character has a physiological foundation. From this arises the specific question concerning the role of gender: did the Stoics think that men and women had different bodily constitutions in terms of elements? If so, did this lead them to consider them as typically having different characteristics? These questions provide a fruitful starting point for approaching Seneca's *De Ira* which alludes both to physiognomics, element theory, and gender.

Seneca claims that different climates have different mixtures of elements, and this further causes differences both in regions, animals, and characters. Accordingly, the qualities of the elements (hot, cold, moist, and dry) can be used both of places and people: we can talk about hot places and hot-natured men, for example. Seneca states further that these two frequently go together: the climate of one's place of birth often influences one's character. Seneca claims that a person's character is determined by the element (such as moist, cold, or hot) that is dominant in his or her elemental constitution (*De Ira* I.11.3; II.19.1–3; III.2.1; III.7).[6]

---

[6] I also find evidence for this view in Cicero who claims that there is a connection between the climate and the state of the soul (Cicero, *On the Nature of the Gods* 2:42; Inwood & Gerson II.23). He also mentions that the food one eats has an influence on one's mental acuity (ibid.: 43).

Did Seneca, then, suppose that men and women typically have different elemental constitutions, as Aristotle and Galen did when they claimed that men were naturally more fiery and women naturally colder? Even if Seneca does not present any explicit argument on this subject, he, too, alludes to the idea that men and women have different constitutions, temperatures, and consequently, at least to a certain degree, dispositions. The first context in which Seneca alludes to this idea is his discussion of the four elements and their respective qualities in human characters. He claims that those whose constitution is by nature hottest are most prone to anger, whereas those with a cold constitution are timid (*timidos*). He also claims that in those with a dominant proportion of moisture in their constitution, "anger grows up gradually"—and that this is the case in women and children. Furthermore, Seneca claims that anger in women and children is not quite as destructive (as anger in men, that is) and comes out in a lighter form. Seneca gives a physical explanation for this, referring to the earlier Stoic view that anger is "aroused in the breast by the boiling of the blood about the heart."[7] Moist natures do not have enough heat to create powerful anger. Thus, the theoretical background of Seneca's conception of anger lies in both the Stoic theory of emotions as psycho-physical states and the Ancient element theory. In this context, Seneca groups together women and children as belonging to the same character type and categorizes them among those with a moist constitution (ibid. II.19.1–5). He clearly assumes that men and women, because of their different elemental constitutions, either always or in most cases have different dispositions, which makes them prone to a different set of emotional responses, such as different ways of experiencing and expressing anger.

Another context in which Seneca assumes a difference between men's and women's constitutions is when he compares a mind prone to anger with a sick body that is overly sensitive and reacts violently to the slightest touch. After presenting this analogy, he states that anger is a womanish and childish weakness (*ira muliebre maxime ac puerile vitium est*). At this point, Novatus, the text's inscribed "interlocutor" (to whom the treatise is addressed and whose anticipated opposition Seneca often uses as a rhetorical tool), protests: "But surely men get angry, too." Seneca confirms this and states that there are also womanish and childish

---

[7] Cf. Aristotle *De An.* I.4.

natures among men (*viris quoque puerilia ac muliebria ingenia sunt*) (I.20.3).[8]

This remark, however, seems to be inconsistent with the previous example, in which Seneca claims that hot natures are more prone to anger and indirectly indicates (in line with Aristotle) that men are naturally warmer than women: now, he is implying that women are more prone to anger than men because of their overly sensitive souls, comparable to sick bodies. However, this does not mean that he was necessarily drawing two different types of connections between anger and gender. The first statement referring to the anger of "fiery types of people" could be understood as reflecting Seneca's views on natural constitutions. Thus, the idea would be that men react with anger more powerfully than women due to their respectively more fiery constitution. On the other hand, the second statement that anger is a womanish weakness should be understood in the context of the notion of "womanish characters." This, however, is not necessarily connected to the physical gender in that the Ancient thinkers frequently admit that men may also have a womanish character. Thus, in the second case, "womanish" stands for a certain sort of weakness and unwanted character trait, and probably also for lack of self-control. People who allow themselves to give in to the impulse of anger are not in control of their emotions, which is not fitting for those who are supposed to be free and in charge of themselves. In other words, giving in to anger is not in line with the Stoic ideal of "manliness," closely connected to self-control. Further, I refer above to a tendency in Stoic texts to connect certain harmful characteristics such as vanity with the notion of femininity, and that to get rid of these characteristics is common both to men and women.

Hence, my reading of Seneca's *De Ira* gives support to Maud Gleason's argument that biological gender and gendered characteristics are not necessarily related in physiognomics. Indeed, even if the Ancient physiognomic discourse labels traits of character as "manly" and "womanish," the development of these characteristics is a more

---

[8] In another passage, Seneca advises us to forgive a child because of his/her age and a woman because of her gender (*feminam sexum*) (III.24.3). Here, the context is different, however, and the notion of forgiving women because of their gender is one of many examples Seneca gives of situations in which one should not give in to anger even though there is a strong impulse to do so. This is one of many contexts where the notion of "gender" only implies women: Seneca does not ask us to forgive men because of their gender.

complex process than a simple reference to biological sex would allow. This complexity is also indicated by Cicero, who claims to be referring to Chrysippus in his discussion on natural differences among people. Cicero first describes the drastic variations between different places and climates, and how the qualities of these areas are reflected in the dispositions of the people: "At Athens the atmosphere is rarefied, resulting in the Attics' reputedly sharp wits." However, he continues: "Yet neither will that rarefied atmosphere bring it about whether someone attends Zeno's lectures or those of Arcesilaus or of Theophrastus" (Cicero, *On Fate* 7–8; L&S 55Q, translation Long & Sedley). Thus, even if climate can explain certain differences between people, the question remains, why there still are so many differences between the individuals even within the same area: why does someone decide to study Academic Skepticism while another feels inclined to practice Peripatetic philosophy? According to Cicero, the atmosphere will not bring about these types differences. Attending a philosophical lecture does, after all, require a certain choice and deliberation, not just blindly following the calling of one's elemental constitution. All in all, despite certain tendencies of sympathizing physiognomics, this is also where the Stoics generally place the philosophical weight. Stoicism strongly emphasizes the importance of choice and character development, which presumes that our characters are not fixed by their elemental constitutions, but flexible and moldable through philosophical practice. Therefore, also the question of gendered characteristics has to be posed in the context of education and habituation.

Appendix

Aristotle

De An.   De Anima

De anima. W.D. Ross (ed.). Oxford: Clarendon Press, 1956.

Cicero, Marcus Tullius

De Fato
De Natura Deorum

De natura deorum. O. Plasberg and W. Ax (eds.). Leipzig: Teubner, 1933.

On fate & The Consolation of philosophy. R.W. Sharples. (ed. and transl.). Warminster: Aris and Phillips, 1991.
On the Nature of the Gods. H. Rackham (transl.). Cambridge, MA: Harvard University Press, 1931.

Clement of Alexandria

Paidagogos

Clemens Alexandrinus 1, Protrepticus und Paedagogus. Otto Stählin (ed.). Leipzig: Hinrich, 1936.

Diogenes Laertius (DL)

Diogenis Laertii Vitae philosophorum. Miroslav Marcovich (ed.). *Bibliotheca scriptorum Graecorum et Romanorum Teubneriana.* Vol. 1. Stuttgart-Lipsia: Teubner, 1999–2002.
Lives of Eminent Philosophers. R.D. Hicks (transl.). Cambridge and London: Harvard University Press, 1995.

Galen

De Placitis Hippocratis et Platonis (PHP)
De Semine

Claudii Galeni Opera Omnia. C.G. Kühn (ed.). C. Cnobloch, Leipzig, 1821, 1833, 1964–5.
On the Doctrines of Hipporcates and Plato. Philipp de Lacy (ed. and transl.). Berlin: Akademie Verlag, 1978.

The Hellenistic Philosophers. A.A. Long and D.N. Sedley (eds.). Cambridge: Cambridge University Press, 1987. (L&S)

Hellenistic Philosophy—Introductory Readings. Brad Inwood and L.P. Gerson (transl.). Indianapolis and Cambridge: Hackett Publishing Company, 1997.

Seneca, Lucius Annaeus

De Ira (On Anger).
Epistulae

Opera Philosophica. Louis Delatte (ed.). Olm, Hildesheim, 1981.
Moral Essays. Vol. I. John W. Basore (transl.). Cambridge and London: Harvard University Press, 1928.

Moral Essays. Vol. 2. John W. Basore (transl.). Cambridge and London: Harvard University Press, 1932.
Epistles. Vol. I–VI. Richard M. Gummere (transl.). Cambridge and London: Harvard University Press, 1917–1925.
Selected Philosophical Letters. Brad Inwood (transl.). Oxford: Oxford University Press, 2007.
17 Letters. C.D.N. Costa (transl.). Warminster: Aris and Phillips, 1988.

Sextus Empeiricus

PH I–III Outlines of Pyrrhonism

Sexti Empirici Opera. H. Mutschmann and J. Mau (eds.). In: *Bibliotheca scriptorum Graecorum et Romanorum.* Lipsiae: Teubner, 1962.
Sextus Empiricus, *Outlines of Scepticism.* Julia Annas and Jonathan Barnes (eds.). Cambridge: Cambridge University Press, 1994.

Stobaeus

Anth. Anthology

Anthologium, Ioannis Stobaeus. Otto Hense and Curtius Wachsmuth (eds.). Weidman: Berolini, 1884–1909.

Stoicorum veterum fragmenta. Vol. I–III. H. von Arnim (ed.). Leipzig: Lipsiae, in aedibus B.G. Teubneri, 1903–24. (SVF)

References

Ahonen, Marke. 2014. Ancient Physiognomy. In *Sourcebook for the History of the Philosophy of Mind—Philosophical Psychology from Plato to Kant*, ed. Simo Knuuttila and Juha Sihvola, 623–632. Dordrecht, Heidelberg, New York, and London: Springer.
Barton, Tamsyn S. 1994. *Power and Knowledge: Astrology, Physiognomics, and Medicine under the Roman Empire.* The University of Michigan Press.
Gleason, Maud W. 1995. *Making Men—Sophists and Self-Presentation in Ancient Rome.* Princeton: Princeton University Press.
Halperin, David. 2002. *How to Do the History of Homosexuality.* Chicago: The University of Chicago Press.
Inwood, Brad. 1997. "Why Do Fools Fall in Love?". In *Aristotle and After*, ed. Richard Sorabji, Bulletin of the Institute of Classical Studies, Supplement 68.
Schofield, Malcolm. 1991. *The Stoic Idea of the City.* Cambridge: Cambridge University Press.

PART II

Character: Education of Gender and Therapy of Sexuality

CHAPTER 7

Gender, Character, and Education from Classic to Hellenistic Thought

7.1 Character as a Philosophical Problem

In Ancient philosophy, as still today, the notion of gender is often connected to assumptions on a person's character and capacities, and concepts such as reason, emotion, courage, compassion, care, severity, and sensitivity frequently receive gendered interpretations. In the context of physiognomy, we already saw that Ancient thinkers labeled certain dispositions feminine and others masculine. Also, Ancient philosophical discussions on education contain numerous remarks on gendered characteristics. Typical examples are that the tendency to weep is called effeminate, or that manliness is connected to courage and self-control. The very term *andreia* seemingly limits courage to men (*anêr* is the Greek term for "a man"—a similar etymological observation can be made of the Latin term *virtus* that stems from the term *vir*, signifying a man).

Since the notion of "character" plays a crucial role in this part of my study, let me elaborate a little more on it. In referring to the concept, I tend to translate the Greek terms *êthos* or *kharaktêra*, or the Latin equivalent *mores*, although my discussion is not limited to these terms. Aristotle's *Poetics* offers a useful point of departure for understanding the philosophical importance of characters. In Aristotle's definition, character is something that is reflected in a person's behavior, choices, and avoidances, as well as in speech, which in the context of poetics refers to the kinds of lines that a playwright lets a personage utter in the play. In tragedies, characters are of an uttermost importance because they reveal to the spectator what kind of action can be expected from a personage, and what kind of destiny he or she is liable to face. In a nutshell, Aristotle's idea is that, say, Medea's furious, desperate, and hard-tempered character explains why she is able to perform extreme and violent actions such as killing her children. In Aristotle's words, a tragedy expresses general truths concerning character inside of a particular story: it is not explicitly about *akrasia* (weakness of will), it is about Medea, but yet it can, by telling the story of a particular person, such as Medea, reveal what *akrasia* is all about. (*Poet.* 1451b7–10).[1] Thus, the character is closely linked to emotional responses, deliberation, decision-making processes, and action. Aristotle also suggests that gender is relevant for characters since according to him, a good tragedian would not attribute characteristics such as courage (*andreia*) to a woman (*Poet.* 1450a15–b14; 1454a16–29).

Even if Aristotle's discussion of character in *Poetics* is limited to tragedies, it gives a valuable insight into the philosophical problems that are at stake. In the first place, "character" refers to a certain way of being human. One's character is reflected in one's responses to things encountered in the world. To use examples derived from Ancient texts: a timid person is scared of evil-looking masks, whereas a courageous person is not afraid even in peril on the sea. Some might get frustrated about the book they are reading, whereas others remain calm even when their family members are murdered. Some react to bad news by crying, while others, such as the Stoic sage, do not react at all—even if they might tremble or become pale because of a certain physical reflex. All of these examples illustrate differences in character and in that sensibility with which we react to different circumstances, which emotions we experience, and how strongly we express them.

A deeper philosophical problem concerns the origin and nature of character: whether it is considered to be inborn or acquired through education, or even a mixture of both. As I argue in this part of my work, Ancient philosophers from Plato to the Stoics commonly conceived of characters as flexible and educable, and they even considered character modification an integral part of philosophical education. Indeed, both Classic and Hellenistic thinkers claimed that education should produce character virtues. This has further implications for the philosophical

---

[1] Cf. Euripides, *Medea*. The Stoic philosopher and playwright Seneca later reiterated his version of this classic play.

theories of happiness, since in Antiquity, happiness was commanly understood as living virtuously. In what follows, I will discuss character, education, and happiness from the point of view of gender in Plato and Aristotle. This discussion forms a backdrop for my analysis of Stoic theories in Chaps. 8 and 9, where I will show that the Stoics formulated a position of girls' educability and female happiness that was radical in its own time—and radically different from the earlier positions of both Plato and Aristotle. Yet the Stoics also adapt many philosophical concepts and topics from their predecessors.

7.2 Equal Education and Gendered Characteristics—Critical Assessments on Plato's Republic

In Plato's *Republic*, the character of Socrates famously proposes that women, too, could and should become guardians, in other words, the philosopher-rulers of the ideal state, and that they should receive the same education as the male guardians. Since this idea is widely discussed in Ancient scholarship, I will limit my discussion to the specific problem concerning the relationship between character, education, and gender in this dialogue. Even if Plato's main argument on female guardians is well known, scholars have paid less attention to the connection between gender and character. However, a careful scrutiny of dispositions, gender, and education will not only help in painting a comprehensive picture of the role of women in Plato's *Republic*, it will also serve as a background against which to analyze the same problem in Stoicism, since several sources explicitly refer to Plato's *Republic* when explicating the Stoic views. I focus here on *Republic*, which provides the most comprehensive philosophical discussion on gender, but in the last section, I briefly comment on Plato's arguments for equal virtue and rationality in *Meno*.[2]

---

[2] In this chapter, I scrutinize arguments on education, character, and gender with reference to both Plato and the interlocutors in the dialogues with whose mouth the arguments are presented (in most cases, that of Socrates). In this context, I take no stance in the scholarly discussion concerning the extent to which we can identify arguments presented in these dialogues as "Plato's arguments": entering into this debate would take me too far outside of the scope of this work. Thus, my focus is on analyzing arguments concerning gender, education, and character that are to be found in *Republic* (as well as *Meno*). I also do not read *Republic* as a political program, and I think that the reader of the work needs to keep in mind that the underlying philosophical question in the dialogue concerns justice,

7.2.1 Educability of Men and Women

Socrates illustrates his idea of equal education for ruling-class men and women through a comparison to dogs—an analogy repeatedly used in *Republic*, and reiterated later by the Stoic Musonius Rufus. Socrates states that male and female dogs are used to the same extent for purposes such as hunting and shepherding: the sex of the dog is not considered relevant for their training or use. (*Rep.* 451d–e). The dog analogy supports the conclusion that no difference should be made between men's and women's education and tasks either.

Underlying is thus a presumption that there is no intrinsic difference between men and women—at least not a difference that would affect their capacities of ruling the state. In order to defend this standpoint, Socrates draws an analogy to bald and long-haired cobblers. The argument is that if all cobblers were bald it would not prevent long-haired people from becoming cobblers given that the difference is obviously utterly irrelevant to their work (cf. my discussion on the insignificance of hairs in Chap. 5). Similarly, if a man and a woman both have the "mind of a physician" and thus the same nature (*tên autên physin ekhein*), then both of them are qualified as physicians (*Rep.* 454d). Socrates goes then on to demonstrate that since the only difference between men and women is that the female bears and the male begets (*to men thêly tiktein, to de arren okheueiv*), gender is not relevant for becoming a philosopher (*Rep.* 454d–e).

Socrates' defense of this position is somewhat strange, however.[3] When Socrates asks his interlocutors whether they know any activity in which men were not superior to women, excluding cake baking, cookery, weaving and other traditional female duties, Glaucon answers that men generally seem to be more capable than women. After having thus referred to the traditional male and female spheres of life with their accompanying duties as well as to the hierarchy between them, Socrates makes a rather surprising

---

a manifestation of which the ideal society is imagined to be. I will later propose a reading of the Stoic utopias as thought experiments. One could propose a similar approach to Plato, too. On the scholarly debate concerning problems of interpretation in Plato, see, e.g., Michael Frede (1992).

[3] For a more detailed analysis of Socrates' argument and its defects, see Julia Annas (1996: 4–5).

argumentative move and asserts that there are no separate political duties for men and women in the republic. One's gender does not determine one's natural talents with regard to certain professions, and in a just state, people should have professions that best suit their natural endowments (*Rep.* 455a–456a).[4] Socrates concludes: "The women and the men, then, have the same nature (*physis*) in respect to the guardianship of the state, save in so far as the one is weaker, the other stronger." (*Rep.* 456a, transl. Shorey) It remains unclear, however, what relevance the references to women's weakness and baking talents have to the main argument, and what exactly Socrates meas when he adds that women should be assigned "lighter jobs."

From the point of view of this research, it is interesting to remark that inherent in the discussion is the presumption that gender roles are at least partly a matter of custom and cultural construction, rather than "nature." When Socrates proposes that women should participate in all the same activities as men, including doing gymnastics naked, the idea provokes a good deal of resistance and amusement among the interlocutors. Socrates points out, however, that what would at first glance seem funny and out of place for most people would soon become commonplace when they became used to the sight of naked women doing sports. (*Rep.* 452b-e; 457b) Thus, gendered expectations can change when people become accustomed to new ways of displaying gender. Furthermore, the educational program of *Republic* would also radically change the traditional gender roles of a Greek *polis*.

7.2.2 The Seed and the Soil—On the Origin of Gendered Characteristics

Socrates uses an agricultural analogy in *Republic* to illustrate how the surrounding society partakes in the development of individual characteristics.[5] He compares the character of the philosopher-ruler to a rare seed that needs the right soil and climate for growing into a full flourish. (*Rep.* 497b) But how exactly should one understand the impact of the seed on the one hand, and of the soil on the other in this analogy?

---

[4] Plato presents the principle of distribution of work in *Rep.* 370a.

[5] As I showed in Chap. 2, the agricultural analogy was widely used in Ancient embryology for illustrating generation. This analogy was also common in the philosophy of education and it appears in several Stoic texts. I analyze this analogy and Plato's philosophy of education in more details in Grahn–Wilder (2018).

Is the philosophical endowment inherent in the person ("the seed"), or produced by the surrounding sociocultural setting ("the soil")?

The discussion seems to build on an assumption that becoming a philosopher requires an inborn disposition, as a rose will only grow from a rose seed.[6] The republic also actively attempts to produce philosophically endowed individuals through the controlled process of eugenics. Indeed, Plato attaches a great deal of importance to genetic factors, assuming that natural talents are inherited at least to certain likelihood. Thus, even though the dialogue makes it clear that being born into a particular social class does not determine what one can become, it is also assumed that the child's capacities have a tendency to reflect those of the parents.

On the other hand, the dialogue places considerable emphasis on the circumstances in which the person lives and grows up. Obviously, the whole point of the long and demanding process of education is to create this perfect "soil" for philosophical development. Thus, the idea is that characteristics (for which Plato uses the concepts of both *physis* and *êthos*) may be inborn, but they are also subject to social, cultural and educational influences. One might wonder, however, how we should understand the exact relationship between these two factors, genetics and habituation, and whether gender had any impact whatsoever on the dispositions of the infant.

One aspect in *Republic* that someone trying to read it through feminist eyes might find disturbing concerns the repeated disdainful comments on women. I have mentioned the "weakness argument" claiming that women are generally weaker than men. The dialogue also makes several other remarks on women, such as that they are fond of everything colorful, prone to lamenting, and easily carried away by diverse emotions and lust (*Rep.* 557c; 549d–e; 431c). All of these remarks concern characteristics that are both considered as typical of women, and incompatible with the virtuous character of a philosopher-ruler.

Scholars who read *Republic* as a feminist work have attempted to defend Plato on this point in different ways. Susan B. Levin and Gregory Vlastos explain that these negative comments are based on empirical observations of women living in a society that was far from ideal and, therefore, their bad characteristics are attributable to the corrupt culture

---

[6] This is also implicit in the famous "gold analogy", which presents the philosopher-rulers as being born with a "piece of gold" in their souls (*Rep.* 415a–c).

in which they grew up. Thus, the disdain is directed not toward the female gender as such, but at its contingent members in the empirical world. (Levin 1996: 14; Vlastos 1994: 17) Even though the dialogue does not explicitly answer the question of whether "womanish characteristics" are innate or learned, it seems plausible to suggest, in line with Vlastos and Levin, that Plato indeed assumed that there were no significant differences in the *inborn* characteristics of men and women. However, I would use partly different arguments in defending this reading.

First, Plato clearly assumed that there were more or less balanced numbers of men and women in the ruling class: for example, the eugenic practices imply that there are enough guardian women to ensure procreation. Second, the early education of guardians explicitly aims at molding their characters, including their emotional lives and their "taste" in what they find detestable or pleasant. Plato explicitly argues that education should be similar for girls and boys, and would aim to produce similar characters among both (cf. the analogy to the training of dogs). The educational ideal in *Republic* thus seems to be based on the assumption that, to a great extent, gender differences are attributable to differences in education. This is also what I take to be at the core of Levin's and Vlastos' positions. Third and most importantly, the ability to rule is a disposition of the soul and not of the body, and thus the souls and not the bodies of men and women are decisive in terms of whether or not they can become rulers. *Republic* does not in any way support the view that the soul is gendered. Thus, it seems that in this dialogue Plato was arguing for women's equal rational capacities. However, there is still more to be said of the evaluation of gendered characteristics in the dialogue. We still have to scrutinize the role of gender in the ideal outcome of the educational program, and whether the ideal is to get rid of gender difference altogether.

7.2.3 *Philosophers, Lovers, and the End of Gender Dimorphism?*

Plato describes happiness as perfect harmony of the soul that prevails when reason governs both the willing and the lusting parts (*thymos* and *epithymia*). This implies, among other things, that sexual lust should be subordinated to reason. Indeed, the long description of the soul of a tyrant in Book IX emphasizes the excess of appetites and, in particular, giving in to sexual lust as well as other vicious pleasures (cf. e.g. *Rep.* 587b). However, this reason-governed ideal does not lead Plato to assert, as the Stoics did later, that the sage should be entirely free from emotions (these thinkers had a very different conception of emotions, as we shall see). Plato claims that a person should keep her lusts and pleasures under control—not that there was anything wrong in having emotions as such.

Furthermore, Plato describes the virtuous person as a *good lover*, and erotic undertones are detectible.[7] However, "good lover" is described as a person who does not strive for sexual pleasure, defined as the most intense of all enjoyments that could take one even to the verge of madness (*Rep.* 403a). In the same manner as a lover of music admires a well-composed song, the good lover admires a young boy's beauty and goodness—these qualities being expressed in both his physical appearance and his character (*Rep.* 403a–c; 490b; cf. my discussion on outer and inner beauty in Chap. 5).[8] In this context, the text only mentions an erotic relationship between an older and a younger man, which gives further support to my reading in Chap. 2 that male–male and male–female sexual relations are treated differently because of the reproductive function of the latter and the pedagogical role of the former. Plato gives no example of attractive women causing problems for self-control, nor he does mention whether women, too, are capable of experiencing love in its highest form. Thus, it remains ambiguous, whether a woman, too, could be either the subject or the object of the ideal and virtuous love relation.

In addition to the exclusively male perspective in his description of ideal love, there are other passages in *Republic* that seem to indicate that an ideal ruler is *a man*—regardless of his or her physical gender. In a passage of *Timaeus* that reiterates the main arguments of *Republic*, it is explicitly stated that in a good republic, women are educated to resemble men as far as possible in their *characters* (18c). This, I claim, is the implicit ideal of the educational program of the *Republic*.

When Plato sets out his plan for the good education of the ruling class, he states that a man should not imitate a woman—"young or old, wrangling with her husband, defying heavens, loudly boasting fortunate in her own conceit, or involved in misfortune and possessed by grief

---

[7] Cf. also the connection between erotic love and wisdom in *Symposium* discussed in Sect. 2.1.

[8] On this topic, see also Gabriel Richardson Lear (2006: 105–120).

and lamentation–still less a woman that is sick, in love (*erôsan*) or giving birth" (*Rep.* 395d–e, Shorey's translation slightly modified). Since the education is the same for all guardians, it follows that women are not allowed to imitate (these types of) women, either. Furthermore, according to Socrates' description, proper objects of imitation should be "courageous (*andreious*), sober, pious, free (*eleutherous*) men" (*Rep.* 395c.) Of course, presenting a list like this in the masculine form was the norm in the Ancient literature. Yet, it is clear that there is only one ideal in Plato's *Republic*, and striving toward it seems to remove all the differences between men and women–except the unavoidable physical differences. As I see it, the ideal person is imagined to be a man, and the dialogue assumes that this ideal is also attainable for women. Yet, the implication is that they in some sense must start to resemble this manly ideal.

According to Julia Annas, Plato's arguments in *Republic* are irrelevant to present-day feminism because he had purely utilitarian motives for including women in the ruling class—he was not in the least interested in whether or not this would actually benefit them (Annas 1996: 4; cf. 1981: 181). I agree, and I also think that implicit in Annas' comment is something of what we should take as decisive for using the term "feminism" in a relevant sense. For a theory or a political program to be feminist, it should *aim* at gender equality, and not just produce it as an arbitrary by-product. Moreover, it should be borne in mind that whatever is stated about women in *Republic* concerns only a scant minority: the reforms would do nothing for the members of the other classes. The idea of creating hierarchic differences between women would clearly be incompatible with any plausible notion of feminism. For these reasons, I disagree with Vlastos' and Levin's readings of *Republic* as a feminist work. I return to this argument in Sect. 11.1.

7.2.4 Beyond the Republic—On Uniformity of Virtue and Female Happiness

With regard to Plato, it must, of course, be emphasized that *Republic* is by no means his only work that discusses philosophical education and characters. I have here focused on *Republic* because, first, its lengthy arguments on gender, and second, because certain central Stoic arguments explicitly build on *Republic* (unlike, say, the *Laws*, which would open a wide field of research on gender in its own right).

However, it is important to remember that many other dialogues develop the idea of character-education in largely different ways than the *Republic*. For example, the idea of a pedagogical function of pederastic relationships between the lover and the beloved (*erastês* and *erômenos*) is prominent in *Symposium*, and the above-mentioned notion in *Republic* of a philosopher as a good lover could allude to this. It is also worth noting that not all of Plato's works connect philosophical education to political aims in the way *Republic* does, and that other dialogues argue for equal virtues in men and women from a different angle. I will here shortly analyze the argument from *Meno*, which seems to come close to the position later defended by the Stoics.

When Socrates asks for a definition of virtue, Meno replies by giving the following list: the virtue of man consists in taking good care of public affairs and in treating his friends well and his enemies badly; the virtue of the woman consists in taking good care of the household and in obeying her husband; similarly, there are specific virtues for a girl, a boy, an older man, a slave, and a freeborn man. (*Meno* 71e) This answer would be in line with the Ancient art of economics (*oikonomikê*), to be discussed in Sect. 11.2, which builds on the idea of separate spheres of life and duties for the different members of the Greek household, *oikos*. Socrates, however, does not accept this traditional way of reasoning and wonders whether, if virtue were different in man and woman, this would also apply to health and strength. Meno admits that health and strength are no different in man and woman, and finally he has to agree with Socrates that virtue is the same in both, as well. (*Meno* 71e–73c) This argument draws no connection between virtue, educability, and "class-membership." This becomes even clearer later in the dialogue when Socrates asks the slave-boy to solve the geometrical problem of reduplicating the area of a square. The intended conclusion is that any human being can infer the right conclusions even on matters on which he or she received no teaching, as the slave-boy obviously was uneducated in geometry. This would seem to indicate that all humans have similar souls and inborn capacities. This reading would also give further support to the reading I propose above that in Plato's view, bodies are gendered but the soul is not.

A similar argument occurs also in *Gorgias* when Socrates defends his doctrine that happiness consists of education and justice, and claims: "The men and women who are righteous and good are also happy, as I maintain, and the unjust and evil are miserable." (*Gorgias* 470e, B. Jowett's transl. slightly modified) Also, this argument presumes that virtue was the same for men and women, and implies that women, too, become happy and virtuous when correctly educated. These dialogues do unfortunately not elaborate further on the connection between gender and education, however. Yet it is noteworthy that the arguments in *Meno* and *Gorgias* indicate that happiness is valuable in itself in the individual, not only in the state. This remark is relevant for my discussions on the drastically different views on female virtue and happiness in Aristotle and later in the Stoic philosophy.

7.3 Aristotle on the Education of Young Men: Habituation of Character and Political Goals

There are certain interesting similarities between the approaches on education in Plato's *Republic* and Aristotle's ethical and political works. Both connect education with political life: they exclusively discuss the education of those who, in their adult lives, will exercise political power. Both also make a distinction between education of character and intellectual education and claim that the latter builds on the former. Not only are these similarities between Plato and Aristotle, they also represent differences between them and the Stoics. Moreover, they all carry important implications for the role of gender: whether both men and women are supposed to participate in political life (in Plato they are, in Aristotle they are not), and whether both are supposed to have exactly the same potential in terms of achieving the highest possible form of life and becoming happy.

One major difference between Plato and Aristotle concerns gender as a selective criterion of those who should receive the highest philosophical education. As noted, Plato did not regard gender as a criterion in this respect. At no point does Aristotle explicitly claim that it should be, but as I argue, he *de facto* restricts his educational plan to boys and men. Aristotle's political philosophy has often been accused of being antifeminist.[9] In this chapter, I will show that the focus on the education of citizens who will in the future exercise political power also carries important implications for Aristotle's views on women's virtues. Although Aristotle's

---

[9] Yet, the target of the feminist critique has primarily been *Politics* and, to a lesser extent, *Nicomachean ethics*. On feminist readings of Aristotle, cf. Cynthia A. Freeland (ed.) (1998), Michael Slote (2011).

notorious remark on the female deliberative soul as *akyron* has provoked a vast amount of scholarly debate, the feminist scholars have paid less attention to analyzing Aristotelian philosophy from the perspective of happiness. As I will show, his view does not allow the conception of autonomous happiness in women, and it unavoidably subordinates the female happiness to that of the man. Against this background, the Stoic views on gender and happiness appear all the more radical.

7.3.1   Aristotle on Childhood and Habituation

In *Nicomachean ethics*, Aristotle gives education a remarkable role in human life. He makes a distinction between intellectual virtues and virtues of character asserting that even though humans have natural capacities for both, they can only be actualized through education (*EN* II.1). Thus, without education, people could not become virtuous (and consequently happy, which is connected to having virtues), actualize their cognitive skills, or practice reasoning and syllogism, which in Aristotle's view constitutes the basis of scientific thinking. Thus, it is highly relevant to ask whether women, too, are supposed to be educated: what is at stake is nothing less than the fulfillment of the highest human capacities, and consequently utmost happiness.

Aristotle considers human beings to be naturally capable of receiving knowledge. According to him, a person can be called 'knowing' in two senses, first in the sense of the *first potentiality*, as when we say that a human is capable of learning how to speak, and second in the sense of *first actuality* (or *second potentiality*) when the person starts to use these cognitive skills, as when the child actually learns to speak. (*De An.* 417a1–417b16) In as much as Aristotle considered rationality a demarcating feature of all humans, it would seem that the process of actualizing inborn cognitive skills was common for both boys and girls. Clearly, girls, as well as boys, learn how to speak, and women, as well as men, use language in an apparently rational way.

However, Aristotle does not mention gender in the context of intellectual development. Further, intellectual development is not a separate process and is closely linked to the education of character. In *Parts of Animals* and *Metaphysics*, Aristotle lists skills in logical thinking as a criterion for a person to be considered well educated: an educated person can distinguish a sound argument from an unsound one, and knows when to accept an argument and when to require further proof.

(*PA* 639a15; *Met.* 1006a7) He remarks in *EN*, however, that not everybody accepts sound reasoning, but the soul of the student has to be prepared through habituation "for enjoy and hating properly." In line with the agricultural analogy, Aristotle compares this to preparing the soil for sawing. (*EN* 1179b25) Thus, intellectual education builds on successful education of character.

According to Aristotle, virtues (*éthos*) develop from customs or habits (*ethos*), and modification of the student's character through habituation (*ethismos*) plays a crucial role in education. The goal is to modify our emotional responses and reactions in different situations, so that they will be in accordance with the ideal of virtue.[10] Moreover, habituation modifies our whole way of seeing the world and acting upon what we see. Through it, virtues become, as it were, "second nature."

Like Plato, Aristotle advocates starting the habituation of character at an early age and accentuates that this plays a foundational role for the child's whole future development, since it is difficult to change bad habits rooted in childhood (*EN* 1103b23–25; 1105a3). After modification of character, Aristotelian education apparently focuses on the student's deliberation (*boulesis*), and gradually incorporates rational skills.[11] In this context, it is worth pointing out Aristotle's remark in *Politics* that a child's soul has a deliberative part (*bouleutikon*), although it does not yet function properly, but in a woman, it "lacks authority" (it is *akyron*). (*Pol.* 1260a13) This clause seems to speak against the inclusion of women in the highest form of education, as one of the required soul capacities does not function properly in them. Aristotle does not explicitly draw the conclusion that this was a reason for excluding women from education, however. The question remains, then, whether it follows from Aristotle's other premises, or could we stretch his arguments so as to accommodate girls and women as well?

---

[10] Nancy Sherman emphasizes that habituation is much about learning the right kinds of emotional responses. According to her, emotions should be understood as intentional and cognitive in Aristotle's theory. Thus, they are not merely something we passively "feel," but rather "selective responses to articulated features of our environment." (Sherman 1998: 240) This aspect is important also for my discussion in this chapter.

[11] M.F. Burnyeat claims that Aristotelian moral education must start from the character because we first have to learn to *act* in a noble and just way before we can learn to reason *why* it is the right action to take. (Burnyeat 1998: 208–209). This reminds the idea in *An. Post.* II.19, in which Aristotle claims that points of departure are better known to us than proofs.

7.3.2 Gender, Virtue, and the Politics of Education

Aristotle was an objectivist not only about knowledge but also about the good life. The purpose of ethics, then, is to help people to achieve happiness (*eudaimonia*), understood as the naturally highest goal of human life. Moral education is indispensable in this process: even if human beings naturally have the capacity (*dynamis*) to become good, it must be cultivated and put into practice. Just as one does not become a good lyre player without ever playing the lyre, one does not become virtuous without practicing virtue (*EN* 1103b7–20).

In *EN*, Aristotle classifies the philosophical inquiry of *eudaimonia* under political science, which he calls the most important of all sciences as it deals with those skills that are useful in a city–state (*politeia*). Politics also encompasses the skills of economics (or good household management, *oikonomikê*), rhetoric, and the art of warfare. In accordance with Plato in *Republic*, Aristotle points out that individuals and the political community share the same goal, but in a city–state this can be seen more clearly and on a wider scale. Even though admitting that individual happiness is valuable, he considers the well-being of an entire city–state to be more important and divine. The happiness of the city–state is also the goal he sets for his philosophical inquiry in *EN*. On this basis, it would seem that education is closely intertwined with activities, such as economics and warfare, which were traditionally connected to the social roles and obligations of freeborn male citizens in an Athenian *polis*. Indeed, the art of economics includes taking care not only of money and material property, but also the humans that belong to the household, such as one's wife and slaves. In *Politics* Aristotle explicitly classifies the power of the husband over his wife as the third aspect of economics (*oikonomikê*), the other two being the master's power over his slaves and the father's power over his children (*Pol.* 1259a37; cf. *Econ.* 1343b1–20; I will return to economics in Sect. 11.2).

Also the virtues Aristotle discusses in *EN* are expressly social and closely connected to his contemporary political world. He writes at length about the virtue of *andreia*, for instance, and takes courage in war as a paradigmatic example (e.g., *EN* 1115a35). Some examples are expressly gender-specific, such as "fearing violence towards one's wife and children" (*EN* 1115a20–23), others just generally stem from an exclusively manly sphere in a Greek *polis*. He uses the exercising of political power as an example of the highest virtue, justice, which he refers to as a virtue of which both rulers and citizens are capable (*EN* 1130a1–5). Similarly, he illustrates generousness through the right way of dealing with money in *EN* Book IV. All these examples inhibit the inclusion of women in the "everybody" whose happiness *EN* is concerned about: women did not own or deal with property in a Greek *polis*, nor did they carry out military duties or function as the heads of their households. Aristotle claims that a person becomes virtuous by acting virtuously, but several of his examples of virtues are such that, in his time, women would not have had access to the necessary resources to perform corresponding virtuous acts in a society in which they are excluded from political, economic, and military life.

However, given that Aristotle also discusses virtues on a general level, the above-listed examples do not necessarily imply that women could not be courageous or just. Even though he does not discuss examples of female virtue in *EN*, there is as yet no apparent reason why he could not admit that women, too, could be just, courageous, generous, and so on in their own spheres of life. This would, more or less, be Xenophon's solution in *Oeconomicus*, in which the wife and the husband are equally responsible for maintaining the household, and the husband's responsibility for earning money is presented as equal to the wife's responsibility for making a good use of the property and household goods (*Oec.* VII). As I show later, also the Stoic Musonius Rufus used exactly these kinds of examples in defending female *andreia* and justice: to be able to defend one's offspring, to be just in the division of household duties, and so on.

Aristotle could be plausibly seen as supporting this kind of position, as well, since he states in *Politics* that women may have virtues too, but those of temperance, justice, and courage are different from the corresponding virtues in men (*Pol.* 1260a20).[12] Similarly, the work *Economics* (which probably was not one of his original works even though it is included in the Aristotelian corpus) includes a claim very similar to Xenophon's that men and women are (naturally) distinguished from each other in that they have opposite dispositions and separate spheres of life with their corresponding duties and virtues. This line of thinking

---

[12] In *Poetics* Aristotle states explicitly that, at least among the characters of a tragedy, it is not fitting for a woman to have *andreia* (*Poet.* 1454a22). Interestingly, this statement implies that he did not think it was *de facto* impossible for a woman to be courageous, but at least in a tragedy, braveness was just not a proper characteristic for a woman. On the connection between *Poetics* and Aristotle's ethics, see Cynthia Freeland (1996).

would affirm that women, too, have virtues which nevertheless are different from those of men. However, the production of virtues is of concern in both *EN* and *Politics*, and these works were focused precisely on the education of freeborn men who exercise virtues in relation to their social, gender-related roles and to their property, including their children, slaves, and wives. This also provides a clue to the question concerning female happiness.

7.3.3 Female Virtue and Happiness

Happiness, according to Aristotle, is one of the most divine things. However, it does not become a person's lot by divine gift as it is based on "virtue, learning and practice." The Aristotelian understanding of happiness can also be defined as the functioning of the soul in accordance with virtue. He states that everybody "who has not become incapable of virtue," will be able to attain it through learning and practice (*EN* 1099b12–20). Aristotle claims that an animal or a child cannot be happy in the proper sense of the word—the former because it lacks the necessary rational capacities for *eudaimonia*, the latter because these capacities have not yet developed. Thus, according to him, when we say a child is happy we are actually referring to the child's inborn potential for happiness and our aspirations for the person's future, not to the state of "being a child" (*EN* 1099b30–35). Could, then, Aristotle's theory allow that a slave or a woman could attain virtue through learning or practice, or be able to function in accordance with virtue?

At least to some extent, Aristotle seems to be aware of this problem. In *Politics* Book I he wonders whether a slave is only suitable for physical labor, his good thus being connected to serving his master, or whether he could also have virtues such as justice and courage. Aristotle sees difficulties in both possibilities: if a slave had virtues, how would he differ from the freeborn? Here, the Stoics—as well we who read Aristotle today—would immediately reply that the correct solution is precisely that they *do not* differ from each other, as both are humans in equal measure. However, Aristotle asserts that some humans are naturally slaves, and that there is a definite difference between slaves and free men (*Pol.* 1260b2; cf. *Econ.* 1344a20cc). On the other hand, he admits that it would be weird if slaves did not have any virtues in that they are humans and as such, rational. After making this remark he asks the same question about women and children: do they have virtues? (*Pol.* 1259b18–32).

As Aristotle remarks, women form half of the population and, therefore, their happiness is relevant for the entire society. This is particularly relevant for Aristotle's notion that it is the happiness of the whole that really matters. In this context, he also mentions that women, too, should receive some sort of education. (*Pol.* 1260b12–15) However, even though he refers to the education of women and children "in accordance with the polity of the state," it is obvious that he does not here mean the same education as outlined in *Nicomachean Ethics* and *Politics* which is described as "useful or necessary for freeborn citizens." (*Pol.* 1337b7) Thus, it is clear that women must have virtues of some kind (because they, too, should be good), but that they differ, at least in part, from the male-related virtues. Aristotle further states that virtues are needed not only for ruling well, but also for obeying well. He also points out, however, that some people naturally rule, whereas others naturally obey, and his argumentation builds on the premise that women, slaves, and children belong to the second category of people. (*Pol.* 1259b35–1260a5) Given the importance of this premise in Aristotle's argumentation, it is perplexing that he does not seem to provide his reader with any particularly good reasons for accepting it. Or why should one accept the even more problematic presumption of "natural slaves"?

Aristotle's argumentation for this point is far from convincing. He claims that the idea that some people should naturally rule is based on "knowledge of the soul" (*Pol.* 1260a4). Once again, however, it should be noted that even though he states in his biology that males are naturally superior (*GA* 732a5–10), his works on natural philosophy and metaphysics do not give support to the idea that women should obey in a society or that there were natural slaves. On the contrary, the view of the soul in these works rather seems to support the opposite view that all humans have an equally rational soul (cf. Sect. 2.2). Now in *Politics*, he claims that the human souls are divided into a ruling and an obeying part and that these two parts have their respective virtues. This far his reasoning follows Plato, who also defends his ideal of a hierarchic republic with reference to the corresponding hierarchic structure of the soul. However, Aristotle goes on to make his notorious assertion: "A slave does not have a deliberative part (*bouletikon*) of the soul at all. A woman has it, but it is without authority (*akyron*), while the child has it, but in an undeveloped form." (*Pol.* 1260a7, H. Rackham's transl. slightly modified).

The point of the whole statement is, in itself, confusing enough. For example, what difference is there really between the notions that a slave does not have a deliberative part at all, and that a woman does but it is without authority? If the point is that a slave cannot deliberate because of a deficiency and a woman because of an imperfection, it seems weird. If she cannot use her deliberative part, why should we assume that she has is in the first place—it would be like claiming that humans have the capacity to fly, only they are unable to use it. A more plausible reading would thus be that a slave could not deliberate at all, whereas a woman could to some extent but less perfectly than a man.

However, the picture is still perplexing. For example, how should we understand the position of female slaves? Are they demarcated by the lack or by the "lack of authority"? Aristotle would probably answer that "to be a slave" corresponds to the characteristic "not to have a deliberative part," and thus this is decisive in the case of female slaves. This interpretation has an interesting implication, however. Aristotle's model builds on a distinction between four different states in the development of the soul: fully developed (adult, freeborn man), the deliberative part lacking authority (woman), the undeveloped deliberative part (child, i.e., a boy), and the deliberative part completely lacking (slave). It follows from this distinction that, among slaves, men, women, and children are on the same level: all of them are characterized by the same lack, whereas among the freeborn they differ crucially.

Further, Aristotle claims that a father's relationship with his children is analogical to a king's with his subjects, whereas the husband's relationship with his wife is analogical to the aristocratic model of rulers and citizens. The master's relationship with his slaves is a relation of ownership. Thus, in Aristotle's view, a freeborn man divides himself between these three roles: master, husband, and father, whereas slaves and women only have one social role each: as servants or wives. (Cf. *Pol.* 1259a37 ff.) The political implication of this distinction is that it justifies the radically different social statuses and separate spheres of life among men, women, and slaves, as well as the hierarchic relationship between them. This hierarchy also provides the basis for Aristotle's utterly paternalist solution to how women, slaves, and children can partake in virtue. He states that the ruler (a man) should be perfectly virtuous because he must be "the constructor" (*arkhitektôn*) in the society in the same manner as reason is the constructing part of the soul. He claims that children and slaves can only have virtues in relation to their master, which is to say that the father is the cause of a child's virtue and the master of the slave's

(*Pol.* 1260a30–b5). Similarly, the freeborn men are also responsible for the virtue in women.[13]

Finally, Aristotle's reasons for excluding girls and women from education are the same as Plato's (in *Rep.*) reasons for including them in it: both thinkers connect education with politics. According to both, only individuals who as adults will participate in political life and exercise political power should be educated. Both thinkers also build on an analogy between the soul and the society, but the implications with regard to gender are different: Plato compares rulers with reason to support his view that women, too, can rule, whereas Aristotle compares the status of men in the society and in the family with the status of reason in the soul. Plato favors a hierarchic society, but the hierarchy should prevail between different classes of people, not between men and women (at least as far as the ruling class is concerned). Aristotle, in contrast, sees the relationship between the genders as hierarchic, and considers it worth maintaining as such since men are "naturally better suited to rule" (*Pol.* 1259b1).

For Aristotle, then, the virtue of women comes finally from their men on the one hand, and from their functioning in their own, limited sphere of life on the other. The source of woman's happiness, then, is not inside but outside of herself, in a virtuous man, who is the head of the household of which she is a part. As we shall see, the Stoics took a remarkably different course in their discussion of happiness, virtue, and the goals of education.

Appendix

Aristotle

An.Post.	*Posterior Analytics*
De An.	*De Anima*
Econ.	*Economics*
EN	*Nicomachean Ethics*
GA	*Generation of Animals*
Met.	*Metaphysics*
PA	*Parts of the Animals*
Poet.	*Poetics*
Pol.	*Politics*

---

[13] I agree here with Marguerite Deslauriers, who argues that women have to "borrow *phronêsis*" of free men in order to be virtuous. (Deslauriers 2003: 229).

Aristotle in 23 Volumes. Vol. 21. H. Rackham (transl.). Cambridge, MA and London: Harvard University Press and William Heinemann Ltd., 1944.
The Complete Works of Aristotle. The Revised Oxford Translation. Jonathan Barnes (revised). Princeton, NJ: Princeton University Press, 1984.
De anima. W.D. Ross (ed.). Oxford: Clarendon Press, 1956.
Generation of animals. A.L. Peck (transl.). Cambridge, MA and London: Harvard University Press and W. Heinemann, 1979.
Parts of animals. A.L. Peck (transl.). Cambridge, MA and London: Harvard University Press and W. Heinemann, 1983.
Historia animalium. A.L. Peck (ed. and transl.). 3 vols. Cambridge, MA and London: Harvard University Press and Heinemann, 1965.
Metaphysics. W.D. Ross (ed.). Oxford: Clarendon Press, 1924.
Metaphysics, Oeconomica, Magna Moralia. C.G. Armstrong and H. Tredinnick (ed. and transl.). Cambridge, MA and London: Harvard University Press and Heinemann, 1996.

Plato

Gorg.   *Gorgias*
Meno
Rep.   *Republic*
Symp.   *Symposium*

Platonis Opera (Oxford Classical Texts):
Vol. 1, ed. E.A. Duke et al. 1995.
Vol. 2, ed. J. Burnet 1922.
Vol. 3, ed. J. Burnet 1922.
Vol. 4, ed. J. Burnet 1922.
Respublica, ed. S.R. Slings 2003.

Complete Works. John M. Cooper (ed.). D.S. Hutchinson (associate ed.). Indianapolis: Hackett Publishers, 1997.
The Dialogues of Plato, Vol. 2: Republic, Gorgias, Parmenides. Oxford: Clarendon Press, 1953.
Plato in Twelve Volumes, Vol. 5–6, The Republic. Paul Shorey (transl.). London: Heinemann, 1969.
The Symposium. Christopher Gill (transl.). London and New York: Penguin Books, 1999.

Xenophon

Oec. Oeconomicus

Oeconomicus—A Social and Historical Commentary. Sarah B. Pomeroy (transl.). Oxford: Clarendon University Press, 1994.

References

Annas, Julia. 1981. An Introduction to Plato's *Republic*. New York and Oxford: Oxford University Press.
Annas, Julia. 1996. Plato's *Republic* and Feminism. In *Feminism and Ancient Philosophy*, ed. Julie K. Ward. New York and London: Routledge.
Burnyeat, M.F. 1998. Aristotle on Learning to Be Good. In *Aristotle's Ethics—Critical Essays*, ed. Nancy Sherman, 205–230. Lanham, MD: Rowman & Littlefield.
Deslauriers, Marguerite. 2003. The Virtues of Women and Slaves. In *Oxford Studies in Ancient Philosophy*, vol. XXV, Winter, 213–231. Oxford: Oxford University Press.
Frede, Michael. 1992. Plato's Arguments and the Dialogue Form. In *Oxford Studies in Ancient Philosophy*, supplementary volume. Oxford: Clarendon Press.
Freeland, Cynthia. 1996. Aristotle's *Poetics* in Relation to the Ethical Treatises. In *Philosophical Issues in Aristotle's Development*, ed. William Wians, 327–345. Oxford: Rowman and Littlefield.
Freeland, Cynthia (ed.). 1998. *Re-reading the Canon: A Series Devoted to Feminist Interpretations of Major Philosophers: Aristotle*, 138–167. University Park: Pennsylvania State University Press.
Grahn-Wilder, Malin. 2018. Roots of Character and Flowers of Virtue: Childhood in Plato's *Republic*. In *Childhood in History: Perceptions of Children in the Ancient and Medieval Worlds*, eds. Reidar Aasgaard, Cornelia Horn and Oana Maria Cojocaru. New York: Routledge.
Levin, Susan B. 1996. Women's Nature and Role in the Ideal Polis. In *Feminism and Ancient Philosophy*, ed. Julie K. Ward. New York: Routledge.
Richardson Lear, Gabriel. 2006. Plato on Learning to Love Beauty. In *The Blackwell Guide to Plato's* Republic, ed. Gerasimos Santas. Malden, Oxford and Victoria: Blackwell.
Sherman, Nancy. 1998. The Habituation of Character. In *Aristotle's Ethics—Critical Essays*, ed. Nancy Sherman, 231–260. Lanham, MD: Rowman & Littlefield.
Slote, Michael. 2011. *The Impossibility of Perfection: Aristotle, Feminism, and the Complexities of Ethics*. New York: Oxford University Press.
Vlastos, Gregory. 1994. Was Plato a Feminist? In *Feminist Interpretations of Plato*, ed. Nancy Tuana. University Park, PA: The Pennsylvania State University Press.

CHAPTER 8

The Stoics on Equal Educability of Girls and Boys, and the Origin of Gendered Characteristics

"The doctrine of the philosophers encourages a woman to be happy and to rely on herself," states the Roman Stoic thinker Musonius Rufus (Lecture 3: 7, transl. Cynthia King, in King 2011, p. 30). Musonius considers education (*paideia*) to be vital for good human life, and defends his proposal of equal education by appealing to female happiness. This position sounds strikingly different from Plato's and Aristotle's views discussed in the previous chapter: neither one of them were interested in women's happiness as such, nor did they propose educating women for their own sake. Musonius, by contrast, points out that since women comprise very nearly half of the population, it is of the utmost importance for the happiness of the whole humankind whether women can attain education and accordingly study those things that help her to strive for happiness.

As I discuss the specific question of gender and education in this chapter, I argue that Stoic sources provide the premises on which to construct a strong case for the equal education of girls and boys. Musonius presents this argument explicitly, as well as his argument for female happiness, but as I will show, this position should be considered genuinely Stoic. To demonstrate this, I will analyze notions on children and their capacities that were generally accepted in the Stoic school. In this context, we will see that the Stoics have a strong tendency to emphasize the "common ground" in all children. They demarcate childhood as a phase of its own, different from the subsequent phases of adolescence, maturity, and old age, and not differentiated on a gendered basis—they did not discuss "girlhood" as opposed to "boyhood," although they tended to follow the conventional, gendered manner of referring to "a boy" rather than "a child," or "a man" rather than "a human."

However, the question remains as to how, if the Stoics emphasized the sameness of human capacities in their metaphysics and their views on childhood, they could conceive of gender difference at all. If the Stoics did not discuss certain gendered tendencies in children (e.g., they do not suggest that girls cry more than boys), what is the source of such tendencies they explicitly point out in adults (e.g., the often repeated claim that women cry more than men)? Further, if all children are so much alike, but categorically so different from adults, how should we understand that the Stoics sometimes adopt the common tendency in Ancient literature to group children and women together?[1]

To address these problems, we will have to consider the Stoics' generally pessimistic view on culture. Building on Martha Nussbaum's remarks on the social construction of characters and Michel Foucault's reading of Stoicism as a critical practice of the self, my reading suggests that the Stoics conceived of many observed characteristics and emotional responses as culturally constructed, and that this also plausibly applied to many of the characteristics they labeled as gendered. As a result, the Stoic philosophy itself appears to have certain transformative potential, treating gendered characteristics as mere cultural artifacts that are subject to change in the philosophical process.[2]

---

[1] For example, Seneca groups women and children together in *De Ira* (cf. Chap. 6). In *Discourses*, Epictetus asks scornfully: "Do the tears of poor foolish women make you effeminate (*apothemlunei klainonta gynaia môra*)? And will you never cease to be a little child?" (*Disc.* III.xxiv.53; transl. Hard) Here, as in many other remarks certain tendencies in children are compared to tendencies in women or effeminate men (here, however, Epictetus talks about *gynaia môra*, which could indicate that he did not take all women to be prone to weeping). Grouping women and children together could be understood in the Stoic context as signifying that neither of them can realize their full rational potentiality as both are uneducated, *amathés*.

[2] Thomas Wallgren draws evidence from Socrates, Foucault, and Wittgenstein in his discussion on "transformative philosophy" by which he means a form of philosophy that is rooted in the problems individuals encounter in their daily lives. He also analyzes the Ancient notion of care of the self which finally can expand to encompass care of others. Cf. Wallgren 2006. Stoicism would certainly provide fruitful material for this type of philosophical research.

8.1 Musonius on Why Girls Should Be Educated

Musonius begins his defense of equal education with an analogy to the training of dogs—an argument that is familiar from Plato's *Republic* (451b; cf. Sect. 7.2). Musonius repeats Socrates' and Glaucon's statement that it is the intended use of dogs (e.g., for hunting) that determines the way they are trained, not the secondary fact of whether they are male or female. Musonius asks why this should be different in the case of humans. He states: "As if it were not necessary for both a man and a woman alike to have the same virtues, or as if it were possible to achieve the same virtues not through the same lessons, but through different ones!" (Lecture 4: 1, transl. King, in King 2011: 31) Musonius thus attempts to demonstrate two separate points: first, that virtue is the same in men and women, and second, that to become virtuous, they should be educated in exactly the same manner.[3]

Both Plato and Musonius use the dog analogy to argue for the second point. However, it is noteworthy that there is a significant, underlying difference in their ways of using this analogy. Plato uses it to illustrate his idea that if a dog is naturally suited to hunting, then there should be no distinction between the male and the female. The presumption is, however, that not all dogs are suited for hunting. In contrast, in Musonius the analogy builds on the presumption that they essentially are. Musonius' point is that all humans have one highest goal, and education is required in order to reach it. Given that his point is about the commonality of human nature, his argument (unlike Plato's) encompasses all women, not only a selected few.

The first claim that same virtues indeed do belong to both men and women is a radical one with which Musonius' contemporary reader was most likely not immediately to agree. As we saw above, Plato had previously presented arguments in defense of this position in *Meno* (without drawing any conclusions concerning education), whereas Aristotle partly denies it in *Politics*, and according to my reading, in *Nicomachean Ethics*.

---

[3]In this chapter, I focus on analyzing the arguments Musonius provides for the equal education of girls and boys. For further information on Musonius, see Nussbaum (2002). Some of the texts dealing with gender and sexuality are also either entirely or partly translated by Martha Nussbaum in an appendix to this article. Cynthia King (2011) provides new translations of Musonius' text, which are the ones I use for the direct quotations in this section. For the original source, see Stobaeus 2.31.123.

Musonius clearly sees a need to use powerful rhetoric strategies for convincing his reader on this point.

Musonius embarks on a common-sense argument which builds on the four cardinal virtues: of course, we wish women, too, and not only men to be self-controlled (*sôphrosynê*), just (*dikaiosynê*) and to have practical reason or "good sense" (*phronein*)—(Lecture 4: 2, p. 31). Musonius puts the most effort into convincing his listener that also the fourth cardinal virtue, courage (*andreia*) equally applies to both men and women. As noted above, for example, in *Poetics* Aristotle did not consider it proper for women to possess *andreia* (*Poet.* 1454a16–29). However, in line with Socrates in Plato's *Meno*, Musonius wants to show that all of the virtues were the same for men and women. He defends his claim of female *andreia* with a twofold argument: first, that *andreia* is also necessary in women and second, that it is an empirical fact that women and female animals have it. Musonius justifies the first half of his argument in claiming that a woman needs to be courageous "so that she is overcome neither by pain nor by fear": thus, nobody can ever force a courageous woman to do anything shameful. In support of the second half of his argument, he appeals to evidence of female bravery: female birds who defend their chicks, as well as the courageous Amazons. From this, he draws a remarkable conclusion: "So, if some women lack courage, it is from lack of practice rather than from courage not being an innate quality." (Lecture 4: 3, transl. King, in King 2011: 32) Thus, he explains possible differences in male and female characteristics by differences in cultural habituation.

Having argued that men and women have the same virtues, Musonius returns to his earlier claim that attaining the same goal implies having the same education. In the case of teaching somebody how to play a musical instrument such as the flute or cithara, the teaching would not differ depending on the gender of the musician. (Lecture 4: 4) This argument is similar to the dog analogy.[4] Nevertheless, Musonius anticipates another potential counterargument that his still unconvinced opponent might make: "What? Do you advise men to learn spinning along with women and women to pursue gymnastics along with men?!"

---

[4] I have already noted the importance of analogy in Stoic philosophical argumentation. Musonius also uses multiple analogies in order to appeal to something the reader already accepts and on the basis of which she or he can be led to accept the more controversial part of the argument. On Musonius' rhetoric, see also Nussbaum (2002).

(Lecture 4: 5, transl. King, p. 32) Despite his earlier arguments for similarity in men and women, he now replies that he, for the most part, would maintain the traditional division of labor even if it sometimes could be reasonable that a man took over tasks that are considered more suitable for women and vice versa. In part III, I shall return to the Stoic discussions on the gendered division of labor as well as the compromising tendencies in late Stoicism that make them reluctant to support any kinds of real-life social reforms. In the present context, it is worth noting that even if Musonius here defends an idea of gendered division of labor, unlike in Xenophon, his idea is not based on a presumption of a categorical difference between the genders. In Xenophon's *Oeconomicus* the division of labor and spheres of life between men and women is presented as definite and God-given (*Oec.* VII). Musonius rather uses an argument that is similar to Plato's in *Republic*: he takes natural endowments and individual capacities, not gender as such, as the basis for dividing labor. However, in line with the traditional ways of thinking of his time, he claims that in most cases the physical capacities of men and women support a division that assigns lighter duties such as "spinning and inside work" to women and harder physical labor and outdoor work to men.[5] Musonius points out, however, that men sometimes undertake lighter jobs that are considered women's work, and likewise women can perform heavier jobs that are considered suitable for men, if this is in accordance with the condition of the body and the circumstances.[6] However, when

---

[5] This reminds the "weakness-argument" in Plato's *Republic* discussed in Sect. 7.2; yet these arguments are not identical. I will return to this discussion in Sect. 13.5.

[6] Musonius also remarks that he does not suggest that women should possess professional skills in logic, but adds that he does not admire these competences much in men, either. (Lecture 4, in King 2011) This remark is peculiar and seems to refer rather to sophism or rhetoric than to logic proper. The Stoics generally include logic as one of the three areas of philosophy, together with ethics and physics. They were famous for developing propositional and modal logic, and they gave logic an important position in their philosophy: some even called it a virtue (*areté*; DL VII: 92). Stoics generally claimed that a sage, being infallible, would necessarily think logically. They compared the division between the three parts of philosophy to a garden, in which physics corresponds to the soil, ethics to the useful fruits, and logic to the protecting fence. This analogy illustrates the protective and restrictive functions of logic: all philosophical activity must take place within the prescribed limits because no rational activity is possible without the requirement of sound reasoning. On Stoic logic, see, e.g., DL VII: 55–83; Barnes et al. (2005: 77–176); Bobzien (2003).

it comes to the most important matters, in other words, "philosophy proper," both women and men have the same capacities for practicing it, and thus should receive the same education in it. In another treatise, Musonius elaborates further on his argument that philosophy leads to full human flourishing, and that, therefore, women should also receive education in it. "For women no less than men are pleased by noble and just action, and reject the opposite. Since this is the way things are, why on earth would it be appropriate (*prosékoi*) for men to inquire and examine how one should live well—which is what it is to do philosophy—and women not?" (Lecture 3: 1–2, in King 2011, p. 28).[7]

Musonius' proposal of equal education is appealing, but his approach is less than satisfactory in terms of understanding the underlying conception of the human soul and educability. What exactly are the underlying capacities and features of the soul by virtue of which girls and boys, or women and men could become virtuous and rational? Did the Stoics assume any difference at all between the boys' and girls' soul capacities? Could their theory even allow that such differences exist? Musonius' text is rhetorical rather than philosophical in the sense that it clearly aims at convincing the reader on the matter of girls' education, and he does not explicate the theoretical background for his claims. Thus, in seeking answers to these questions we need to scrutinize the Stoic philosophy of childhood and the child's capacities in order to see how these general Stoic views make his practically and rhetorically oriented arguments more comprehensible.

8.2   Inborn Capacities, Cultural Impact, and the Question Concerning Gendered Characteristics

The Stoics make two quite striking and, at the first sight, contradictory claims on children: first, that children perceive the world correctly in some sense, and second, that children do not have reason (*logos*). From the Stoic perspective, how could a nonrational being have correct conceptions of the world? Further, the remark on the nonrationality of

---

[7] Although Musonius does not specify who should be responsible for educating children, one could speculate that because he considered education such an important issue, he might also have supported the education of women for the reason that educated and intelligent mothers would make better role models and educators for their children.

children seems to be in contrast with Musonius' educational ideal, which presumes rationality as a distinctive human feature that girls and boys possess in equal measure.[8]

In the following, I analyze the role of gender in the Stoic views on childhood, and show how the above-mentioned views on children (the epistemological correctness, reason-based educability, and children's irrationality) go together. I divide my discussion here into three subsections: the first one investigates the Stoic claim of the irrationality of children and the consequent idea of their moral irresponsibility; the second approaches Stoic views on childhood in positive terms rather than through privation, and analyzes children's natural tendencies, and finally, I scrutinize the cultural impact on the development of gendered characteristics. Even if the Stoics do not often explicitly discuss gender in the context of children and education, as I will show, they provide us with arguments that are crucial for comprehending their views on men's and women's capacities, rationality and educability.

8.2.1 Nonrationality and Moral Irresponsibility—Stoic Views on Children

According to the doxographer Aetius, the Stoics claimed that children could only be called rational at around the age of seven: "Reason, for which we are called rational, is said to be completed from our preconceptions during our first seven years." (Aetius 4.11.1–4; L&S 39E; SVF 2.83) According to Diogenes Laertius, on the other hand, the Stoics considered reason to be fully developed only at the age of fourteen: "An animal's utterance is air that has been struck by an impulse, but that of a man is articulated and issues from thought as Diogenes [of Bablylon] says, and is perfected at the age of fourteen." (DL VII: 55–56; L&S 33 H) Galen refers to Posidonius' notion that the rational faculty "achieves strength and fitness about the age of 14, when now it is

---

[8] In this chapter, the Stoic views are placed into the context of philosophy of childhood, which in recent philosophical scholarship has been established as a field of its own and distinguished from philosophy of education. The main problems in this field, and in this part of my discussion on Stoicism, concern philosophical views on children, childhood as a specific phase of life and children's capacities, for example. Cf. Matthews and Mullin (2015). On a reading of philosophy of childhood in Plato, see Grahn-Wilder (2018).

appropriate for it to control and rule (...)." (Posidonius fragment 31D; Galen, *PHP* v.466–8, transl. De Lacy) Thus, there were apparently different views inside the Stoic school concerning the age at which a person could be called fully rational (yet the number seven seems to carry an important meaning).

The three passages also emphasize different aspects of the Stoic view of rationality. Aetius connects the development of reason to the technical Stoic concept of "preconceptions" (*prolêpsis, praesumptio*), to which I return in the next section. Diogenes' remark points to the interconnectedness of language and reason which occurs even on the level of terminology in that the Greek term *logos* signifies both, whereas Galen draws attention to the commanding role of rationality. All three sources assume that the child does not immediately make active use of reason, and that this capacity is "completed" or "perfected" only after a certain period of time.[9]

The claim of irrationality seems to indicate that the Stoics did not consider children to be fully human either, given that they define a human being in terms of rationality. In Sect. 4.5, I quoted a Stoic description of the embryo as more of a plant-like being—a view that was apparently rather common in Ancient embryological theories. However, even if the children in a sense fall outside of the technical definition of a human being, the argument is not that children are nonrational in the same sense as plants or animals are, because as members of human species they have the potential of one day becoming fully

---

[9] Not only is the assertion of the nonrationality of children unlikely to convince any contemporary readers, it also seems to cause certain problems in other parts of Stoic theory. The child's capacity to learn and make use of language seems particularly problematic in the light of Stoic premises positing that the use of language is a rational skill. One could defend the Stoic position by pointing out that they meant "rationality" in a very specific sense: to be rational means to have full rationality and the ability to act as an agent of rationality who makes independent use of rational skills such as inference, not just repeats rational activities. The same could be said about language skills: a rational language user not only repeats some rationally formed utterances like a trained parrot but also makes use of internal speech, inferences, combinations, and signs (Sextus Empiricus makes a similar point in *Against the Professors* 8.275–6; L&S 53T). However, this definition would not only leave some adults outside of rationality (e.g., people suffering from certain forms of brain damage), it also apparently includes, rather than excludes, children above a certain age that is clearly much younger than 7 or 14 years. In defense of their position, the Stoics might claim that children have a slowly developing capacity to use rationality, but are called nonrational until it is fully developed.

rational. Presumably, this is precisely what early education aims at: that when grown up, children will be able to make full use of their rational capacities.

Given that a child is only on the way to becoming rational and hence fully human, the Stoics tended to describe childhood as a state of imperfection. Cicero articulates this straightforwardly: "Therefore Chrysippus did well to prove by appeal to analogies that all things are better in perfect and mature specimens – for instance, in horse than in foal, in dog than in pup, in man than in a child." (Cicero, *On the Nature of the Gods* 2.37–9, L&S 54 H) Epictetus, too, defines childhood through privation, but he focuses more on the amount of teaching they have received and alludes to the idea that children, too, can have knowledge similarly to adults: "What is a child? Ignorance (*agnoia*). What is a child? Lack of education (*amathia*). For where a child does know (*oiden*), it is no way inferior to us." (*Disc.* II.i.16–17). I return below to Stoic arguments of what "knowledge" might signify in the case of children.

Seneca discusses childhood in his letters as a separate phase of life, significantly different from youth, adulthood, and old age that follow. He writes:

> Each period of life has its own constitution, one for the baby, and another for the boy, <another for the youth> and another for the old man. They are all related appropriately to that constitution in which they exist. A baby has no teeth - it is attached to this constitution, which is its own. Teeth emerge - it is attached to this constitution. (*Letter 121*, 15, transl. Inwood)

Seneca continues by drawing an analogy to plants which have one constitution as tender shoots, and another when they are ripe and fully grown. He makes it clear that one's natural constitution develops and changes naturally through one's growth. It is notable, however, that Seneca does not indicate that there was a different constitution for boys and girls or for men and women.[10] As was standard among the Ancient authors,

---

[10]To understand the concept of "constitution," it is helpful to look at Brad Inwood's analysis of the concept (in his part of his joint-article with Pierluigi Donini, referring to Cicero's *De Fin.* III and Seneca's *Letter* 121). He defines "constitution" as the "person, the compound of body and soul which constitutes the identifiable individual." He also compares this to the more modern concept of the "self." (Inwood and Donini 2005: 679–680).

Seneca uses the masculine form as a "universal genus," but the point of his use of the terms "boy" and "man" is clearly to emphasize the temporal aspect of these phases, not the gendered significance of the terms. Seneca illustrates his idea further by writing:

> A baby, a boy, a teenager, an old man: these are different stages of life. Yet I am the same human as was also a baby and a boy and a teenager. Thus, although everyone has one different constitution after another, the attachment to one's own constitution is the same. (*Letter 121*: 16, transl. Inwood)

The fact of having to go through the stages of childhood, adolescence, and maturity (sometimes old age is also mentioned separately), to grow and develop from one to the other while still remaining the same person is something all humans share. Gender, in contrast, does not appear to be a similarly relevant factor. In their discussions of natural constitutions, the Stoics do not divide human beings into two groups on the basis of gender in the same way as they divide them into three (or sometimes four) groups on the basis of age.

The Stoic demarcation of childhood as a phase of its own, characterized by irrationality, has several other important consequences. First, the Stoics did not consider children to be moral agents in the full sense of the word. Seneca illustrates this by describing how children strike their parents in the face or pull their mothers' hair, or walk around naked—in other words, behave in ways he surely would find unacceptable in adults. (Seneca, *De Constantia*, xi.2) Stoic sources abound with similar descriptions of children's "silliness": playing gladiators, or being scared of evil-looking masks (an example used both by Seneca and Epictetus; *Letter 24*: 13, *Disc.* II.i.15). Often these descriptions serve the purpose of pointing out the foolishness of adults, who are blamed for doing what children do: first playing a rhetorician and then at the next moment a philosopher, or being afraid of imagined horrors (cf. Epictetus *Ench.* 29:3).

Second, the idea of children's nonrationality seems to imply that children do not have emotions either, in the technical sense in which the term "emotion" is used in Stoicism. Indeed, Galen states explicitly that most Stoics were of this opinion (Posidonius fragment 159; Galen, PHP v.431) According to the Stoic definition, an emotion always includes a cognitive element asserting that a certain, in itself ethically neutral things is good or bad. According to the Stoics, this assertion is always false.[11] When a child cries or strikes its parent in the face, these responses would, in the Stoic view, not count as emotions proper, but rather as natural reactions to outer impulses that are in accordance with the child's own specific constitution—something like when a threatened hedgehog raises its prickles or when a satisfied dog wags its tail. Because children are still beyond reason, they do not make false cognitive assertions about the good or bad nature of the events they react to (and of course, according to the Stoics, they are right in not doing so).

The Stoic tendency to discuss childhood as a phase of its own without differentiating between "girlhood" and "boyhood" could be seen as supporting Musonius' appeal for equal education, and as being in line with Stoic metaphysics, in the context of which gender is not treated as an essential feature of a human being. However, this section focused strongly on how the Stoics conceived of childhood in terms of deficiency: as a state of imperfection, irrationality, moral irresponsibility, lack of education, and even a lack of proper emotions. I now turn to the more positive content of childhood in Stoicism, and see whether these views give more insight into the role of gender in the Stoic notion of children. I then return to the apparent paradox between the ideas of children's irrationality on the one hand, and their epistemological correctness on the other. I show that, in the end, the Stoic conception of childhood indeed coherently adopts these two claims.

8.2.2 Oikeiôsis and the Theory of Preconceptions: Arguments for Equal Educability of Girls and Boys

Seneca illustrates children's self-awareness and natural impulses by way of comparison with animals. Above I referred to his concept of natural constitution of different phases of life. Likewise, in his view, humans as well as all animal species, have their own special constitutions. According to him, as soon as an animal is born it is aware of its own constitution and it knows to avoid harmful things, just as newborn chicks naturally run from raptors. Animals do not acquire this awareness through experience or training (and certainly not through theoretical demonstration),

---

[11] I do not enter into a more detailed discussion of Stoic theory of emotions, which is a wide subject in its own right. On scholarship on this topic, see e.g. Graver (2007), Knuuttila (2004), Knuuttila and Sihvola (1998), Nussbaum (1994), Sorabji (2000).

but they seem to be already born with it. The same goes for children, who also have the inclination to do what is natural for them even if they are able neither to contemplate it nor to articulate it rationally. Seneca gives the example of a child who despite difficulties and occasionally even pain practices standing up and walking: children are naturally impelled to strive for an upright position and to walk on two feet, as this is part of the human constitution (*Letter 121*: 5–6, 19–20).

In this Seneca captures the central Stoic notion of *oikeiôsis*. The term is difficult to translate and thus I, like many scholars (e.g., Striker 1996), only transliterate it here. In Stoic scholarship, it has been translated as "appropriation" (Long & Sedley 1987; Reydams-Schils 2005), "familiarization" (Annas 1993), "congeniality" (Inwood and Gerson 1988) and "affiliation" (Inwood and Donini 2005), for example.[12] The connotation, in a nutshell, is "to make something one's own". Through the notion of *oikeiôsis* the Stoics conveyed their idea that in accordance with their specific natures, animals and humans find some things harmful and avoid them, and similarly, find other things beneficial and strive for them. The Stoics also used it with reference to the natural inclination in humans to other-regard: non-egoistically motivated concern for and the protection of others arise from the natural striving for self-preservation.[13] Thus, children start with animal-like self-preservation impulses, toward which as they grow up they gradually start to develop a rational attitude, and to use deliberation in matters of choice and avoidance. Virtue and other-concern thus develop, as it were, out of natural tendencies.[14]

Further, the Stoics suggest even more strongly that the child, in a sense, perceives the world correctly: "The starting points of nature are uncorrupted" (DL VII: 89).[15] The lack of emotions, in Stoic definition of the term, would surely have counted as one instance where the children are generally more correct than adults. The idea of uncorruptedness also goes to moral knowledge: even if the Stoics generally considered

---

[12] For a more detailed discussion on Stoic views on *oikeiôsis*, see Julia Annas (1993: 159–187); Gretchen Reydams-Schils (2005: 53–82); Inwood and Donini (2005: 677–682).

[13] Cf. Diogenes Laertius (VII:85).

[14] This argument is closely connected to the Stoic idea that the natural impulses to love and take care of one's offspring lead to genuine other-concern. The Stoics defend this position partly with physiological observations of male and female bodies which, according to them, provide a proof of naturalness of procreation (cf. Sect. 4.6). This idea culminates in Stoic cosmopolitan ethics, to be analyzed in Chaps. 13 and 14.

[15] On the so-called Stoic cradle argument, see Jacques Brunschwig 1986.

children to be free from moral responsibility, they seem to have considered that the child still has the starting points to virtue. For example, Seneca mentioned in *Letter 124* quoted above that virtue is present in a child "in the form of a seed." The Stoic theory of preconceptions helps to expand on this remark. At the beginning of this section, I mentioned Aetius' claim that *reason is completed from preconceptions* during the first 7 years of life (Aetius 4.11.1–4, L&S 39E, SVF 2.83). This gives a clue to the Stoic view on children's inborn features. Moreover, the theory of preconceptions provides further, and I think particularly powerful, arguments in favor of the equal educability of girls and boys.

Epictetus claims that preconceptions are inborn, and that humans are born with certain natural criteria (*to kritérion*) or standards (*kanón*) for measuring the things they encounter in the world.[16] For example, they all have preconceptions of noble conduct, holiness, and happiness; of their duties toward other human beings; of things appropriate and inappropriate for a good human life; and of the predetermined world and their own freedom in it. The last point refers to the fundamental Stoic idea of freedom of choice in terms of attitudes and how people let things occur to them.[17] Epictetus claims that people do not acquire these ideas through proof or demonstration, as they acquire the concepts of an equilateral triangle or a musical interval (*Disc.* II.xi.2–3).

The Stoics thus claim that people really can gain genuine knowledge of the world and of ethical good and bad, and that everyone already possesses all the necessary equipment. This, of course, does not alter their view that humans continually make epistemological and moral misjudgments. In relation to ethical misjudgments, Epictetus claims that conflicts, inner as well as interpersonal, arise from the inability to apply preconceptions correctly to different situations. Education (*paideuesthai*), on the other hand, means "learning to fit natural preconceptions to particular entities in agreement with nature, and further, making

---

[16] Seneca's version of this is that humans are not actually born with these conceptions, but with an innate ability to receive them (*Letter* 120: 4) There was apparently some disagreement within the Stoic school over the right way of understanding preconceptions—a discussion I do not enter into here. For the present purpose, it is sufficient to consider the crucial role of preconceptions in the Stoic view of education. In my discussion on the theory of preconceptions, I concentrate on the view of the Roman Stoics, leaving aside the possible differences between earlier and later thinkers in this regard.

[17] On the notion of freedom and how it fits in with Stoic metaphysical determinism, see Bobzien (1998), Striker (1996).

the distinction that some things are in our power and others are not" (*Disc.* I.xxii.1–10; L&S 40 S).[18]

In this context, Epictetus also states that preconceptions are *common to all human beings*. This I take to be a general Stoic position, expressed also in the above passage quoted from Aetius, according to whom human rationality develops from preconceptions, and it serves further as a crucial premise in my argument that the Stoics believed that literally everyone had all the necessary capacities for being educated in and practicing philosophy. Thus, again there is evidence that the Stoic theory of soul generally tends to emphasize the common ground in all humans rather than differences. Education, consequently, should be based on this common ground. Although Musonius did not specify the common nature of girls and boys, or the actual content of childhood education, I have shown how other sources can be used to elucidate his view. Musonius' argument for equal education for girls and boys follows from these general Stoic views: they give strong support to the idea of similarity in all humans, and there is no evidence that the Stoics saw any relevant differences between the genders when it came to educability.

8.2.3 Gendered Characteristics and Cultural Corruption

In her article "Therapeutic Arguments and Structures of Desire," Martha Nussbaum discusses the roles of biological determinism and social constructivism in explaining emotions and desires. According to the former view, such phenomena as emotions and desires derive from an underlying biological cause, whereas the latter presents them as products of the complex sociocultural context in which they are experienced and expressed. Martha Nussbaum explores the idea that the Stoics could be considered social constructivists in relation to "our basic emotion categories such as fear, anger, love," as well as "the basic sexual categories into which erotic agents are divided." She continues by stating:

> Stoics may even hold this position about gender itself; at any rate, it is clear that they treat gender as a morally irrelevant attribute on par with national origin, and as one that would be minimized in the ideal city, by a scheme of unisex clothing, and by the continual teaching that our real

---

[18] Cf. Cicero's "natural light argument", according to which bad cultural influence dims our "natural light" (*Tusc.Disp.* III.i.2).

identity is that of rational personhood, which is, it would seem, not gendered. (Nussbaum 1996: 196–197)

Unfortunately, Nussbaum neither elaborates further on her argument nor specifies on exactly what grounds one should take it to be "clear" that the Stoics "treat gender as a morally irrelevant attribute on par with national origin." I have presented several arguments (derived from Stoic metaphysics and views on childhood) for accepting Nussbaum's claim that gender, for the Stoics, was a morally irrelevant attribute and was not, on a profound level, related to rational personhood. However, is this enough to draw the conclusion that they were social constructivists with regard to gender?

First of all, it has to be kept in mind that the Stoics did discuss the physical and inborn aspects of the human character, and they also explicitly mentioned gender in this context. As I showed in Chap. 6, the available evidence does not unquestionably support an interpretation suggesting that the person with her entire emotional life was purely a "social artifact." We have seen that the Stoics sometimes approved of physiognomic doctrines positing a connection between physical constitution and character. In this respect gender is on par with national origin, as Nussbaum remarks, but both of them are considered, at least to some extent, relevant rather than irrelevant for the character. Further, according to Plutarch, Chrysippus also believed that character was, at least partly, inborn, because some children resemble their parents not only in looks but also in temperament and disposition. (Plutarch, *On Stoic Self-Contradictions* 1053D; SVF 2. 806; L&S 53 C) Some Stoics discussed the influence of both *natural* and *sociocultural* factors on the human character. Stobaeus, for example, reports that the Stoics would have both accentuated inborn capacities and agreed with the proverb: "Practice (*meletê*) over a long time turns into second nature" (Stob. 11 m; SVF 3. 366) This goes against the idea that Stoic, on the whole, considered characters as purely cultural constructions. Yet, the exact relationship between inborn and acquired characteristics remains diffused in the sources.

However, as I have argued before, even if the Stoics sometimes express sympathy for physiognomic ideas and refer to certain dispositions as inborn, their main philosophical doctrines strongly emphasize the sociocultural environment. This is true even of Seneca, who claims that humans have certain inborn characteristics due to their elemental constitution, which he doubts could be altered (*De Ira* II.xx.2). Seneca sets out his position in stating that nature (i.e., the proportion of elements) is one, but not the only, reason why people have the characteristics they do. He lists other accidental causes that he believed affected a person's character just as much as nature does: illness, injury, toils, vigils, anxiety, yearnings, and love relations, for example, and concludes that the most powerful influence is the habit (ibid, xx.1).[19] Both Seneca and the above quote from Stobaeus remind the famous Aristotelian notion of "second nature" that is achieved through education and practice. It is habituation, not inborn features that finally makes us the kinds of persons we are. This is also where the Stoic philosophical therapy steps in as character-formation is one of its the most central goals.

Michel Foucault has analyzed Stoicism as a *practice of the self* which has an important critical function. He emphasizes that the Stoic education is fundamentally a process of *unlearning* and a critical reformation of the self. The criticism is directed toward one's childhood in general, as well as the nurses, teachers, and the traditional education, as all of these are listed as sources of our distorted views. Accordingly, the practices of the self invite us to actively get rid of characteristics, values, beliefs, habits, and fallacies of thinking that we have internalized in the culture and society we grew up in (Foucault 2005: 93–99).

Foucault is right in paying attention to the general Stoic tendency to blame bad cultural influence for all bad characteristics. In addition to the traditional education, the Stoics were particularly concerned about the influence of the masses (the *hoi polloi* to which Ancient thinkers often refer in their arguments). Seneca describes the corrupting effect of the company of "ordinary people" by stating: "One cause for our troubles is that we live by the example of others; we do not settle ourselves by reason but get swept away by custom." (Seneca, *Letter* 124, 6, transl. Inwood) Here, Seneca alludes to the mimetic nature of humans: we easily start to imitate the things that are commonly accepted among the people around us. Consequently, also many of our characteristics develop through the

---

[19] When Marcus Aurelius praises his parents and forefathers in *Meditations* Book I he was clearly thinking about the things he had learned from them rather than biological heredity, since he also praises his educators and several thinkers who obviously could only have influenced his character through education. He praises his father extensively in I.16, describing how he had acted correctly in different situations and thus exemplified a virtuous character in action (the list includes virtues such as modesty and justice, and other more specific features such as having given up all love-relations with young boys and never taking a bath at unusual times).

corrupting influence of our surrounding culture that provides us with bad role models whom we start to imitate in our own behavior.

This idea also has important implications with regard to the role of gendered characteristics. Given the Stoic mistrust of culture and ordinary education, it seems plausible that also many of the observed differences between men and women's characteristics would be attributed to cultural influence. Nussbaum's reading suggests that this might even apply to all gendered characteristics. Following from Musonius' views, one could state that if women seem often to be less competent in practical reasoning, this is due to lack of education and practice, and not to any essential female features. Thus, the Stoic theory could plausibly explain certain differences they point out in adults (e.g., that women have a stronger tendency to weep) by referring to cultural factors. When the Stoics sometimes group women and children together they probably are following traditional categorizations of their time, but a positive reading of this grouping would suggest that in the Stoic context this signifies that neither children nor women can realize their full rational potentiality as both are uneducated, *amathês*.

Following from Foucault's analysis of the critical function of Stoic philosophy, it seems plausible to suggest that the Stoic education would also entail unlearning certain culturally and socially constructed gendered characteristics. For example, we might have to get rid of the belief that women cannot do philosophy and (if we are women) get rid of the characteristics that stand in the way of leading a philosophical life; or (if we are men) get rid of those characteristics that make us feel uneasy about philosophizing women.

In this sense, the Stoic position could be seen as compatible with feminist arguments: in Stoicism, we find an argument that whatever the observed difference in the cognitive skills of men and women might have been in the days of the Stoics, this was attributable not to any inherent difference between the genders, but due to differences in education. Thus, inherent in the notion of equal educability is the radical notion that also women have the full potential to live a rational life, which at the time of the Stoics was generally denied them for cultural and political reasons.[20] On the other hand, as I shall show later, they failed to take this argument onto a political level that would have actually influenced

---

[20] I here agree with Martha Nussbaum, who writes that at least in the context of philosophical education / therapy the Hellenistic philosophers in general "appear to achieve an egalitarian result that would have been unachievable in the world around them." (1994: 12).

women's possibilities to be educated. However, the next task for this investigation is to look closer at what exactly was the Stoics' standpoint to culturally constructed femininity or masculinity, and the role gendered ideals play in the goal of good, Stoic education: in other words, in their ideals of wisdom and virtue.

Appendix

Aristotle

EN   Nicomachean Ethics
Poet.   Poetics
Pol.   Politics

Aristotle in 23 Volumes. Vol. 21. H. Rackham (transl.). Cambridge, MA and London: Harvard University Press and William Heinemann Ltd., 1944.
The Complete Works of Aristotle. The Revised Oxford Translation. Jonathan Barnes (revised). Princeton, NJ: Princeton University Press, 1984.

Cicero, Marcus Tullius

De Natura Deorum

De natura deorum. O. Plasberg and W. Ax (eds.). Leipzig: Teubner, 1933.
On the Nature of the Gods. H. Rackham (transl.). Cambridge, MA: Harvard University Press, 1931.

Diogenes Laertius, *Lives of Eminent Philosophers* (DL)

Diogenis Laertii Vitae philosophorum. Miroslav Marcovich (ed.). *Bibliotheca scriptorum Graecorum et Romanorum Teubneriana.* Vol. 1. Stuttgart-Lipsia: Teubner, 1999–2002.
Lives of Eminent Philosophers. R.D. Hicks (transl.). Cambridge and London: Harvard University Press, 1995.

Epictetus

Discourses (Disc.)
Encheiridion (Ench.)

Discourses and Selected Writings. Christopher Gill (ed.). Robin Hard (transl.). London: J.M. Dent & Vermont, Tuttle /Everyman, 1995.

Discourses. Books I–IV. W.A. Oldfather (transl.). Cambridge and London: Harvard University Press, 2000.

Galen

De Placitis Hippocratis et Platonis (PHP)
Claudii Galeni Opera Omnia. C.G. Kühn (ed.). C. Cnobloch, Leipzig, 1821, 1833, 1964–5.
On the Doctrines of Hipporcates and Plato. Philipp de Lacy (ed. and transl.). Berlin: Akademie Verlag, 1978.

The Hellenistic Philosophers. A.A. Long and D.N. Sedley (eds.). Cambridge: Cambridge University Press, 1987. (L&S)

Hellenistic Philosophy—Introductory Readings. Brad Inwood and L.P. Gerson (transl.). Indianapolis and Cambridge: Hackett Publishing Company, 1997.

Musonius Rufus

Musonii Rufi Reliquiae. O. Hense (ed.). Leipzig: Kessinger, 1905.
Musonius Rufus: Lectures & Sayings. William B. Irvine (ed.). Cynthia King (transl.). CreateSpace, 2011.

Plato

Meno
Rep. Republic

Platonis Opera (Oxford Classical Texts):
Vol. 1, ed. E.A. Duke et al. 1995.
Vol. 2, ed. J. Burnet 1922.
Vol. 3, ed. J. Burnet 1922.
Vol. 4, ed. J. Burnet 1922.
Respublica, ed. S.R. Slings 2003.

Complete Works. John M. Cooper (ed.). D.S. Hutchinson (associate ed.). Indianapolis: Hackett Publishers, 1997.

Plutarch

Moralia. Vol. 1. Frank Cole Babbitt (transl.). Cambridge, MA and London: Harvard University Press and William Heinemann Ltd., 1989/1927.

Moralia. Vol. 13. Frank Cole Babbitt (transl.). Cambridge, MA and London: Harvard University Press and William Heinemann Ltd., 1949–1976.

Posidonius Rhodius

Fragments

Posidonius 1. The Fragments. L. Edelstein and I.G. Kidd (eds.). Cambridge: Cambridge University Press, 1972.
Posidonius 3. The Translation of the Fragments. I.G. Kidd (transl.). Cambridge: Cambridge University Press, 1999.

Seneca, Lucius Annaeus

Ad Marciam
Epistulae

Opera Philosophica. Louis Delatte (ed.). Olm, Hildesheim, 1981.
Moral Essays. Vol. I. John W. Basore (transl.). Cambridge and London: Harvard University Press, 1928.
Moral Essays. Vol. 2. John W. Basore (transl.). Cambridge and London: Harvard University Press, 1932.
Epistles. Volumes I–VI. Richard M. Gummere (transl.). Cambridge and London: Harvard University Press, 1917–1925.
Selected Philosophical Letters. Brad Inwood (transl.). Oxford: Oxford University Press, 2007.

Sextus Empiricus

Sexti Empirici Opera. H. Mutschmann and J. Mau (eds.). *Bibliotheca scriptorum Graecorum et Romanorum.* Lipsiae: Teubner, 1962.
Sextus Empiricus. Works. R.G. Bury (transl.). Cambridge, MA: Harvard University Press, 2014.

Stoicorum veterum fragmenta. Vol. I–III. H. von Arnim (ed.). Leipzig: Lipsiae, in aedibus B.G. Teubneri, 1903–24. (SVF)

Xenophon

Oec.   Oeconomicus

Oeconomicus—A Social and Historical Commentary. Sarah B. Pomeroy (transl.). Oxford: Clarendon University Press, 1994.

References

Annas, Julia. 1993. *The Morality of Happiness*. Oxford: Oxford University Press.
Barnes, Jonathan, Susanne Bobzien, and Mario Mignucci. 2005. Logic. In *The Cambridge History of Hellenistic Philosophy*, ed. Keimpe Algra, et al., 77–176. Cambridge: Cambridge University Press.
Bobzien, Susanne. 1998. *Determinism and Freedom*. Oxford: Oxford University Press.
Bobzien, Susanne. 2003. Logic. In *The Cambridge Companion to the Stoics*, ed. Brad Inwood, 84–123. Cambridge: Cambridge University Press.
Brunschwig, Jacques. 1986. The Cradle Argument in Epicureanism and Stoicism. In *Norms of Nature*, ed. Malcolm Schofield, and Gisela Striker. Cambridge: Cambridge University Press.
Foucault, Michel. 2005. *The Hermeneutics of the Subject*. New York: Palgrave Macmillan. (HS).
Grahn-Wilder, Malin. 2018. Roots of Character and Flowers of Virtue: Childhood in Plato's Republic. In *Childhood in History: Perceptions of Children in the Ancient and Medieval Worlds*, ed. Reidar Aasgaard, Cornelia Horn and Oana Maria Cojocaru. New York: Routledge.
Graver, Margaret. 2007. *Stoicism and Emotion*. Chicago: Chicago University Press.
Inwood, Brad, and Pierluigi Donini. 2005. Stoic ethics. In *The Cambridge History of Hellenistic Philosophy*, ed. Keimpe Algra, et al., 675–738. Cambridge: Cambridge University Press.
Knuuttila, Simo. 2004. *Emotions in Ancient and Medieval Philosophy*. Oxford: Clarendon Press.
Knuuttila, Simo, and Sihvola, Juha. 1998. How the Philosophical Analysis of Emotions Was Introduced. In *The Emotions in Hellenistic Philosophy*, ed. Juha Sihvola and Troels Engberg-Pedersen. Dordrecht, Boston, and London: Kluwer Academic Publishers.
Matthews, Gareth, and Amy Mullin. 2015. The Philosophy of Childhood. In *The Stanford Encyclopedia of Philosophy*, ed. Edward N. Zalta, Spring 2015 edition. http://plato.stanford.edu/archives/spr2015/entries/childhood/. Visited 8 Dec 2015.
Nussbaum, Martha. 1994. *The Therapy of Desire: Theory and Practice in Hellenistic Ethics*. Princeton: Princeton University Press.
Nussbaum, Martha. 1996. Therapeutic Arguments and Structures of Desire. In *Feminism and Ancient Philosophy*, ed. Julie K. Ward, 195–216. New York and London: Routledge.
Nussbaum, Martha. 2002. The Incomplete Feminism of Musonius Rufus. In *The Sleep of Reason—Erotic Experience and Sexual Ethics in Ancient Greek and Rome*, ed. Martha Nussbaum and Juha Sihvola, 283–326. Chicago and London: The University of Chicago Press.

Reydams-Schils, Gretchen. 2005. *The Roman Stoic—Self, Responsibility, and Affection*. Chicago and London: The University of Chicago Press.
Sorabji, Richard. 2000. *Emotion and Peace of Mind—From Stoic Agitation to Christian Temptation*. Oxford: Oxford University Press.
Striker, Gisela. 1996. *Essays on Hellenistic Epistemology and Ethics*. Cambridge: Cambridge University Press.
Wallgren, Thomas. 2006. *Transformative philosophy—Socrates, Wittgenstein, and the Democratic Spirit of Philosophy*. Lanham, MD: Lexington Books.

CHAPTER 9

To Become Properly Manly—Gender, Happiness, and the Figure of the Sage

It has been a common criticism among feminist scholars in the history of philosophy that the allegedly gender-neutral ideals of rationality have served to underrate emotions and other features such as imagination and care traditionally associated with women. Thus, the philosophical ideal—even when presented as "universal" or "gender-neutral"—has been a manly one that has explicitly or implicitly excluded women and everything "womanish." Marcia L. Homiak summarizes this discussion by stating that "the feminist criticism of rational ideals" highlights that these ideals "ignore the role of emotions and of the nonuniversalizable particularity of human life"—in other words, areas traditionally connected to women. Homiak concludes: "Hence, the rational ideal suggests that the concerns most typical of women's lives are irrelevant to the best human life and to the reasoning about what to do." (Homiak 2002: 80–81) According to Genevieve Lloyd, feminist readings of past philosophers tend to question dichotomies, such as reason–emotion and soul–body, and to emphasize notions such as "collective" rather than "individual," and "care" rather than "justice." She suggests that a related task is to question the idealized type of philosopher (Lloyd 2002: 1–25).

However, this feminist critique should be discussed critically in its own right. To begin with, we should not accept at face value that to have emotions is a feminine feature, and accordingly that rationality is masculine, or that they were straightforwardly labeled this way by past thinkers, and that the problem could thus be identified in the rationalist ideal as such. As I will show, even though the Stoics unquestionably favored

© The Author(s) 2018
M. Grahn-Wilder, *Gender and Sexuality in Stoic Philosophy*,
https://doi.org/10.1007/978-3-319-53694-1_9

181

rationality over emotions (for reasons to be specified in this chapter), a straightforward juxtaposition between reason as something masculine and emotions as something feminine does not quite fit the picture of Stoicism, according to which all ordinary human beings are both essentially rational and thoroughly emotional. Also, the Stoics' cognitivist view of emotions makes a straightforward opposition between reason and emotion problematic. Admittedly, however, as I showed above, at least some of the Stoics seemed to assume that men and women were prone to at least partly different kinds of emotional responses. Yet, I have shown that both in their metaphysics and views on childhood and education, the Stoics argued for rationality being the same in both men and women.

Even if we accept the idea that emotionality and rationality as such belong equally to men and women, it is still relevant to pose the feminist question concerning the Stoic philosophical ideal. I discussed earlier the Stoics' reputation of being a particularly "manly" (*arrenôpous*) school of philosophy, characterized by the image of a bearded philosopher (cf. Chap. 5). Both in Stoic and other original sources, this manly image is straightforwardly contrasted with that of (allegedly) effeminate Epicureanism. Further, even if the Stoic endorsement of beards as signs of being a philosopher did not, as such, occlude women, it still presents the rationalist ideal in a manly form. Thus, the task of this chapter is to critically examine the Stoic philosophical ideal of becoming a sage. Is this ideal a manly one? If it is, what does this mean for women who wish to practice Stoicism and to proceed to its highest stage? Or did the Stoics implicitly aim at undoing gender differentiation altogether, as I claimed earlier was the implication of Plato's ideal in *Republic* (cf. Chap. 7)?

It is also relevant to ask whether the Stoics idealized men exclusively in their philosophical discourse and to analyze the female exemplifications and idealizations found in Stoic sources. It is an integral part of the Stoic philosophical style to argue from exempla. Even though the cases-in-point and "role models" discussed in Stoicism are mostly men, the sources contain also a range of female exempla such as Medea, Hipparchia, Lucretia, Cloelia, and even the Amazons. Through these cases of either historical or fictive women, mentioned in the texts for philosophical purposes, I bring a new perspective to my investigation of Stoic views on female virtue and character.

I show that the Stoic ideal indeed applies terms of manliness and masculinity in presenting their philosophical ideal. In Roman Stoic sources, the very term for virtue explicitly draws this connection (the Latin term *virtus* derives from *vir*, signifying a man).[1] However, through evidence drawn particularly from Cicero, I also propose an alternative and more optimistic reading according to which women could strive for the Stoic philosophical ideal without any obligation to, as far as possible, resemble men. Furthermore, referring to Homiak's and Lloyd's criticisms, it turns out to be far from clear that the Stoics were one-sidedly in favor of justice over care, or of the individual over the collective, or that whatever they had to say of justice, individuals or rationality would unquestionably favor men. By contrast, in Stoic philosophy these topics do not often occur as straightforward dichotomies, but as topics more intricately interwoven with each other.

9.1 Manly Stoics, Effeminate Epicureans

At the beginning of the second book of *On Firmness*, Seneca addresses his correspondent Serenus with the following words:

> I might say with good reasons, Serenus, that there is as great a difference between the Stoics and the other schools of philosophy as there is between males and females, since while each set contributes equally to human society, the one class is born to obey, the other to command. (*De Constantia Sapientis*, II.1.1, translation Basore)

After this perplexing opening, however, Seneca does not elaborate further on the analogy between genders and schools of philosophy. Nevertheless, his point becomes clear: among the different schools, Stoicism is the one that deserves to be assigned masculine attributes such as "manly" and "heroic." Some other schools, in contrast, attempt to prettify their doctrines—in the same manner as women prettify their faces, we are led to believe. As we saw above in Chap. 5, both the Stoics and other Ancient thinkers frequently criticized makeup, cosmetics, and beautification as fraudulent and philosophically irrelevant. Also in Seneca's juxtaposition, Stoicism appears as the stern and

---

[1] On the masculine connotation of the term *virtus*, see Gordon (2012): 114–115.

severe alternative, as opposed to the soft and pleasing type of philosophy offered by the rival schools—presumably Epicureanism.[2]

Indeed, the very ideals of philosophy, and the rivalry between the Stoics and their main opponents, the Epicureans, are often expressed in explicitly gendered terms. In her research on gendered images of Epicureanism, Pamela Gordon claims that the opponents "sometimes use Epicurus as the converse of their own presentation, particularly in regard to their masculinity" (Gordon 2012: 10). She shows that in particular during the Roman era, the manly virtue (*virtus*) was frequently juxtaposed with pleasure (*voluptas*, in Greek *hêdonê*). Pleasure is further commonly presented as effeminate and womanish. Gordon further compares this dichotomy to the one between soul and the body: pleasure is associated both with the feminine and the body, and presented as a lesser goal of philosophy than the masculine doctrines of the mind (Gordon 2012: 112–115).

In Chap. 5 we saw that the masculine ideal is made clear in the physical descriptions of the philosopher. As Gordon points out, this ideal is also expressed in the terminology itself: the Latin texts sometimes remind the reader of the etymology of the term *virtus*, stemming from the word man, *vir* (cf., e.g., Cicero *Tusc.Disp.* 2.43; Gordon 2012: 114–118). Furthermore, the sources refer to masculinity and femininity as character traits and modes of behavior. Indeed, some Stoic sources include several negative remarks on female characters. For example, Marcus Aurelius provides the following list of bad dispositions: "A dark character (*melan êthos*), a female character (*thêly êthos*), a stubborn character (*periskelês êthos*) (…)" (IV: 28). Women are also criticized for their feminine tendency to mourn and weep. and their typical ways of experiencing anger (cf., e.g., Seneca *Ad Marciam* xi:1; *De Ira* I.12). Seneca suggests that lamenting (particularly in a loud, strong, or long-lasting way) is typical

---

[2] One might also wonder whether the Stoics really thought that their rival schools had an equally necessary role in human society as the female gender. The human population would probably not do very well without women (at least if generation is considered one of the natural goals of the human species, as the Ancient thinkers commonly thought), but could it *mutatis mutandis* do without, say, the Epicureans? Given the important role of dialogue with opposing doctrines in the Hellenistic philosophical style, it would be plausible to claim that a philosophical school needs rivals in order to survive, because it needs opposing views against which it can clarify its own position. Yet no particular school (e.g., the Epicureans) is needed for this purpose, just as no particular woman is needed for the maintenance of the human kind (it is the female gender, in general, not one particular individual that is needed for this purpose).

of women, although he admits that men are not free from sorrow, either (*Ad Marciam* i.1.; *Ad Helviam* iii.2; xvi.1). The sources also typically ascribe these types of "effeminate" behaviors to the Epicureans: for example, Cicero describes the Epicurean as a person who would cry out as a woman and not be able to endure pain (*Tusc.Disp.* 2.46).

I already analyzed the (physical) presentations and images ascribed to the Stoic school. Now the crucial task is to scrutinize what the masculine image means to the ideal of philosophy itself. Is the Stoic ideal of a sage, by default, understood as a man? Do happiness and wisdom require extirpation of everything "feminine"? Or are the remarks of masculinity and femininity merely connected to the philosophers' self-presentation, rivalry with other schools, and attack on traditional cultural norms?

9.2 The Sage, Apatheia, and the Feminine

The figure of the sage is a personification of the Stoic views of virtue and a naturally good human life. The Stoics describe the sage as a person who has achieved complete peace of mind (*ataraxia*) and thus happiness (*eudaimonia*): a person who is undisturbed and calm. The sage does neither make any epistemological misjudgments or logical fallacies, nor erroneously believe that things that are inherently neutral and morally insignificant would have any real value. As a result, the sage has achieved the state of emotionlessness (*apatheia*). As their happiness lies entirely in the mind, sages are also free and autonomous (*autonomos*), not enslaved to any external conditions or occurrences.[3] Thus, the Stoic sage is also characterized by perfect self-control and self-sufficiency. According to the Stoics, outer circumstances do not affect the person's possibilities of becoming and remaining happy in any way whatsoever.[4]

In my reading, I would like to emphasize that being a sage means not only acquiring an inner state of tranquility but also developing a character that is capable of ethically correct judgment and functioning—a character that always produces the right reactions and actions. In this sense, I see the Stoic ideal as active and directed toward not only one's own

---

[3] The Stoics often juxtapose inner and outer forms of slavery: even one who serves as a slave can have a free mind, and on the contrary many people are apparently free but have enslaved themselves with their wants, fears, and aspirations. It is clear that for the Stoics, the second form of slavery was worse because it was considered self-imposed. Cf. Sect. 10.2.

[4] On the Stoic description of the sage, cf., e.g., Seneca's *Letter 66*.

inner contemplations but also outwards, toward others and the world that always serves as the raw material for the exercise of virtue. Seneca conveys this idea by comparing the sage to a skillful sculptor, Phidias serving as his case-in-point, who always creates the most beautiful artwork out of whatever material happens to be available. Whether Phidias had ivory, bronze, marble, or any cheap material, he would turn it into the best possible statue that could be made of this substance. *Mutatis mutandis*, a sage can make the best out of his life, whatever the circumstances: whether poor or wealthy, sick or healthy. (Seneca, *Letter 85*, 40) Thus formulated, the ideal does not seem to favor one gender more than the other. By contrast, it seems plausible that a sage would also make the best out of life whether as a man or as a woman, whether these were understood as bodily conditions or social roles. From the perspective of the majority of women in Seneca's times, this might have sounded like good news: their subordinate position in a contingent society did not imply that they were subordinate in relation to the highest goal of human life, or that the unwise customs of their times would alienate them from true wisdom (of course, one might add, this is not to say that they would not have had good reason to wish to change such oppressive conditions).[5]

What, then, about the role of feminine features in the character of the sage? It is often stated in modern feminist discourse that true equality requires the acceptance of the feminine style as equally important and valuable as the masculine style.[6] At least at the outset, the Stoic ideal does not seem to accommodate a variety of different styles of philosophizing and fulfilling one's highest human nature. The Stoic idea was clearly that even if the paths leading to wisdom are various, wisdom itself is the same for everybody. Also, the sage is described as being one, uniform person. According to the Stoics, virtue is always the same, and the virtuous person is constant and coherent, but vices, on the other hand,

---

[5] Thus, the Stoic position on happiness differs radically from Aristotle's view of the good life as requiring certain outer conditions and a social standing. Hence, luck plays a considerable role in the Aristotelian view of happiness: if one happens to be born a female, a slave or poor, one is not in a position to attain the highest human happiness. The Stoic notion of happiness, in contrast, eliminates the role of luck altogether, and is certainly very distant from the view presented in Aristophanes' speech in Plato's *Symposium* where life appears to be a constant search for the "right one." Cf. Sect. 2.1 and 7.3.

[6] On the notion of style in feminist phenomenology, see Sara Heinämaa (2003).

are numerous and individual, and the vicious person possesses not one but many conflicting sets of characteristics. Seneca gives a vivid description of the idea that the virtuous character is uniform, whereas the vices are various:

> There isn't anybody who doesn't change his advice and his wishes every day. First, he wants a wife, then a mistress; first he wants to be king; then he behaves in such a way that no slave could be more fawning (…). We change roles frequently and put on a mask opposite to the one we just removed. (*Letter 120*, 20–22, transl. Inwood)

As noted, the Stoics considered playing various roles and "changing masks" appropriate for a child, but unacceptable in an adult (cf. Epictetus *Ench.* 29: 3–7). A man who first wants a wife and then a mistress is unable to lead a stable adult life as he splits himself between different roles (husband, lover, and so on) but never does anything seriously enough to develop his virtues in any of the particular social roles he has.[7]

Thus, as the ideal is formulated in terms of sameness, there do not seem to be two different ways of being a sage, a female, and a male variant: there is one and only one ideal that applies to everybody. Furthermore, we have seen that the Stoic philosophical practice would also transform some characteristics that they labeled "feminine," such as vanity or certain typically "female" emotions. However, this is not enough to support the claim that the Stoics considered emotions in general feminine, or that they rejected them precisely because of their connection to the feminine (this, basically, would be one of the main feminist charges discussed above). This line of thinking would be problematic in the context of Stoicism because they use the term "emotion" in a specific and technical sense. As mentioned previously, each emotion always includes a false cognitive element (stating that an external present or future thing

---

[7] In the Stoic texts, masks are connected to the pleasing and fraudulent philosophies (such as, allegedly, Epicureanism), but also to the character of *kinaidos*, a "toy boy." Origen, for example, states that male prostitutes "hired themselves out to those who desired them outside the city and wore masks," and mentions that this was said by Chrysippus in his "Introduction to the Subject of Good and Evil." In the same context, Origen also talks about "doubtful" men (i.e., eunuchs since their sex is doubtful) serving as prostitutes (*Cels.* 4.63). Cf. my discussion of *kinaidos* in. Sect. 5.2.

is good or bad in itself), and it is expressly because of this cognitive falsity that the Stoics rejected emotions. Further, they claimed that basically all humans make these cognitive mistakes: men as well as women. The sources include at least as many descriptions of emotional men as of emotional women. Achieving the Stoic philosophical ideal required getting rid of emotions that are typical of women, but also those considered typical of men.

Indeed, particularly, the Roman Stoic thinkers criticized certain elements of their contemporary world that unquestionably belonged to the traditionally "manly" sphere of life: war, violence, and the misuse of political power. Seneca, for example, criticizes the violent entertainment offered by gladiator games: just being at a spectacle where people take pleasure in the uttermost cruelty is so corrupting to the soul that even Socrates probably would not remain virtuous there (*Epistle* 7, 2–6).[8] In *De Ira*, Seneca paints grotesque pictures for his reader depicting the cruelty and brutality inflicted in the name of war or political power. In Stoic theory, all of these immoral acts are understood as effects of certain underlying characteristics. Thus, even if the Stoics advocated a certain type of manliness and the discarding of effeminate characteristics, it should be remembered that this version of manliness is significantly different from the "usual" manliness of the time. They would also have been critical of many characteristics that go along with this traditional masculinity. Further, the Stoic ideal of "manliness" is something that men also must achieve, not something they as (biological) men already are. The same ideal holds to women, as well. However, the question still remains, whether women who wanted to practice Stoicism only had male role models to look up to.

9.3 Female Idealizations and Exemplifications

The Platonist thinker Plutarch dedicated an entire work, known to us as "On the Virtue of Women" (*Mulierum virtutes*), to his female friend Clea in order to provide her with concrete cases of female virtue. His explicit aim was to illustrate that the virtue of man and the virtue of

---

[8] This is a strong claim from a Stoic given that Socrates was often presented as the only possible real-life candidate to be considered a sage in the Stoic sense, and because there was a dispute within the school over whether a sage could ever lose his virtue (cf. DL VII: 127).

woman are the same. By the same token, he also wanted to give Clea "consolation drawn from philosophy," after the death of Leontis, "that most excellent woman," and thus the work has the function of promoting therapeutic philosophy to a woman. In fulfilling this task, Plutarch dedicates a total of 27 chapters to cases of virtuous women, both as groups (such as Trojans, Persians, and Celts) and as individuals (such as Pieria, Camma, and Timocleia).

The Stoic corpus also includes an interesting consolation letter that explicitly takes up the question of philosophical female role models: Seneca's letter to the Roman lady Marcia. Seneca anticipates an objection he expects his female correspondent to raise against him: "You forget that you are giving comfort to a woman; the examples you cite are of men" (*Ad Marciam* xvi: 1, transl. Basore). Here, Seneca pays attention to a feature of Stoic philosophy that we can observe in the existing sources: the exemplifications and idealizations used in Stoic philosophical argumentation are mostly men. This is not too surprising in its own right, however, given that de facto all the known Stoic authors were men, and when they addressed an identifiable audience, in most cases it consisted of men.[9] In any case, we certainly lack a similar kind of near hagiography of exemplary females as Plutarch's treatise is.

As for Stoic idealizations, Socrates is often mentioned as a philosopher par excellence—he was almost the only candidate who might, on Stoic premises, have been considered a sage; Heracles is another, somewhat strange (but surely masculine) example. Given the Stoics' emphasis on idealizations and role models in philosophical education, the question Seneca puts in the mouth of Marcia is an important one. The Stoics often advised their followers to have an ideal character in mind when attempting to transform oneself.[10] Should the women, then, also try to be like Socrates?

---

[9] Michel Foucault also points out that the way of life proposed by Hellenistic and Roman schools of philosophy was primarily intended to freeborn men (see "Introduction" to *History of Sexuality*, volume 2: The Use of Pleasure). In terms of the historical reality of the Ancient era, it is true that most of the people who had the opportunity to dedicate their life to a study of philosophy were men. It is another question, however, whether the philosophical arguments themselves include, or could include women, as well.

[10] For example, Epictetus recommends his students to lay down for themselves a character (*kharaktêra*) and a type (*typos*) for how they wish to behave in public. (*Ench.* 33).

The present-day feminist-oriented scholarship, too, has criticized the Stoics for the lack of female exempla in their texts, and for the strange, unflattering ways in which females are put forward as exemplary characters. Gretchen Reydams-Schils claims with reference to Cicero's *Tusc. Disp.*: "(T)he only examples of tough women are old ones, who are able to do without food (2.40), and Spartan women, who are subjected to the same kind of drills as are the men (2.36)" (2005: 120). In the same spirit, Martha Nussbaum remarks on the absence of the woman's voice and first-person perspective in Musonius' texts: "In *Should Daughters and Sons*, the only women named are the Amazons and the murderous Eriphyle – despite the fact that Roman life provided a rich range of cases of female excellence (...)" (2002: 312). As noted above, Musonius mentions the Amazons as a positive example to show that women, too, can be courageous (*andrizesthai*) and, it seems, act "manly": thus they are praised not so much for being women as for their "manliness." It is indeed noteworthy that even if Musonius explicitly argues for equal rationality in men and women, he does not give any examples of intelligent women. The same could be said about Epictetus, who not only advocates compassion for the murderous Medea, but also praises her for "acting in great spirit" (*megalophyôs*) (*Disc.* II.xvii.19).[11] All this raises the question whether women can only attract Stoic admiration through manly (and even violent) acts.

Instead of joining Reydams-Schils and Nussbaum in criticizing Stoic texts for lacking content that, at the time, would have been considered exceptional and controversial, I will highlight the positive female examples that Seneca portrays for Marcia. What is particularly interesting in this letter is that here a Stoic philosopher expressly offers philosophical therapy to his female correspondent. To bring her consolation in her sorrow of having lost her son, he both presents philosophical arguments of the equal male and female capacities and depicts several interesting cases of female excellence.

Seneca presents cases of notable historical women, such as Lucretia and the Roman heroine Cloelia "who braved both the enemy and the river"—she escaped the Etruscans by swimming across the Tiber (*Ad Marciam* Xv:2, transl. Basore). Referring to Marcia's personal situation,

---

[11] However, in his discussion on marriage Epictetus portrays the Cynic female philosopher Hipparchia in a favorable light (*Disc.* III.xxxii.76). Cf. Sect. 13.2.

he cites examples of Roman women and cultural icons who also had experienced a loss of a loved one: Cornelia, the daughter of Scipio and mother of the Gracchi ("twelve births did she recall by as many deaths," xvi: 3), and another Cornelia, the wife of Livius Drustus, whose son was murdered (ibid. xvi: 4). He dedicates a particularly long discussion to Julia Augusta, to whom Seneca refers to as "an intimate friend" of his correspondent.[12]

The case of Julia Augusta is particularly interesting in that it highlights how women could benefit from philosophical therapy. After losing her son Julia had visited the philosopher Areus, (apparently referring to the Stoic philosopher Arius Didymus, 1st century BCE-CE), a friend of her husband. Areus proceeded to cure Julia of her sorrow through rational argumentation. For example, he reminded her of the precepts of the good life he expected her to accept: that she should do nothing that she would wish undone or done otherwise (ibid. iv.4.4). He asked her to keep the good memories of her son alive and not to become unapproachable to her friends. If she were only to think about her son's death, and thus forget about all the good things he had done for her and others, she would seek "the most perverse renown (*perversissimam gloriam*): to be considered the most unhappy." Areus reminded Julia of the importance of living for those family members that were still alive, and that she should show the strength of her character at the very moment of hardship: "A quiet sea and a favoring wind do not show the skill of a pilot either" (ibid. iv.4–5, transl. Basore). By these remarks, Seneca connects his letter to central content of Stoic therapy of emotions.

The letter makes it clear that Seneca believed in women's capacities for philosophical thinking. According to him, Julia Augusta had confessed later that Areus' philosophical lessons had been very beneficial for her. Seneca also makes it clear that he told Marcia about Julia because of the similarity in their situations, hence implying that the philosophical precepts should help her, as well. Seneca is thus consciously taking the role of a philosopher who transmits philosophical therapy to its female receiver, delivering his message through philosophical doctrines, storytelling, and female exempla.

---

[12] Julia Augusta is better known as Livia Drusilla (58 BCE–29 CE), the wife of Roman emperor Augustus. I will here only analyze Seneca's philosophical arguments without entering the historical background of his cases-in-point.

It is remarkable that in the process, Seneca both argues for women's capacities to virtue and pays attention their own freedom and agency in the therapeutic process. He writes:

> But who has asserted that Nature has dealt grudgingly with women's natures and has narrowly restricted their virtues? Believe me, they have just as much force, just as much capacity (*facultas*), if they choose to (*libeat*), for virtue (*par ad honesta*); they are just as able to endure suffering and toil when they are accustomed to it (*si consuevere*). (*Ad Marciam*, xvi.1–2, Basore's transl. slightly modified)

These lines echo Musonius' claim that if women possess less courage or practical reason, this is not because they lack any natural ability, but because they lack practice. Seneca, too, argues that women have exactly the same natural capacities for virtue and overcoming hardship (and thus striving for happiness) as men but adds: "if they choose to" and "when they are accustomed to it." The natural capacities must be activated, which requires both habituation and will. Women must thus be willing to use their highest capacities, and they must choose to aim at the goal of rationality and happiness. This is also something he wishes to demonstrate by quoting the example of Julia: finally, she was responsible to choose whether she wanted to become "the most unhappy of women" or alternatively to take the attitude of a skilled sailor in a storm and decide to endure her hardships bravely.

Seneca's consolation letter to Marcia gives further support to my previous argument that, for the Stoics, women had exactly the same potential as men to achieve the ideals of Stoic philosophy.[13] A woman is an independent agent of her own happiness, which is thus not a reflection of the more profound happiness of her husband (cf. my reading of Aristotle in Sect. 7.3). This letter serves also as a counterexample against the claim that Stoic philosophy, on the whole, did not include any positive role models for philosophizing women to look up to.

---

[13] The same point could also be made of Seneca's consolation letter to his mother Helvia.

9.4 Genders and Personae

Even if the philosophical ideal of wisdom is the same for all, the route leading to it is not. Consequently, philosophical education and therapy should start from the person in question, with all his or her individual peculiarities, strengths, and weaknesses. Seneca points out that not every person is hit on the same spot—in other words, all of us have our own personal problem areas (*De Ira* III: 10). Presumably, therefore, a good Stoic educator and therapist would pay attention to the student's gender, too, whenever this was relevant for their educational or therapeutic needs. This, after all, is what we see Seneca do in his consolation letter to Marcia.

In conclusion of the discussion on Stoic philosophical ideals and the character of the sage, let us return to the notion of sameness and the role of femininity. The Stoics claim that there is only one ideal character and only one mode of being a sage. Wisdom is thus characterized by "sameness"— as opposed to individual and various vices. The rationalist ideal is also frequently presented in terms endorsing masculinity. Should we, then, conclude that this ideal implies demolishing gender difference altogether, as I claim is the case in Plato's *Republic*?

I suggest that a more plausible reading would be that a sage necessarily has features that are not necessary for being a sage; and that some of them can be gendered. Thus, a sage may be short or tall, light- or dark-skinned, a man or a woman, but none of these features are in any way relevant to being a sage. In other words, the definition of a sage does not take account of individualizing features as far as they do not influence wisdom and virtue. Furthermore, it does obviously not follow from being a sage that a person would not have any of these other individual features. Thus, even if sages were the "same" as far as rationality is concerned, they would still also be individuals with their various personal features, as far as these features do not stand in the way of virtue.

This reading is also consistent with my argument that in Stoic metaphysics, to be of a specific gender should be understood as an individual quality, *idios poion*, whereas to be gendered is a common quality, *koinos poion* (cf. Sect. 4.2). To see how this view fits into the Stoic views on wisdom and character features, let us consider the following passage from Cicero, explaining the Stoic Panaetius' distinction of four personae. I will here discuss the first two personae, and return to the remaining two in the context of social roles in Part III. The first role is universal, arising from our shared rational nature, and the second one individual, reflecting our bodily and mental differences. Cicero writes: "(E)ach person should firmly hold on to those characteristics of his which are not vicious but peculiar to himself. For we must so act that we do nothing in opposition to human nature in general, and yet, while keeping that secure, follow our own nature." (Cicero, *On Duties* 1.107, 110, 114–117, L&S 66E, transl. Long & Sedley) He stresses both universal and individual features; both rationality and our idiosyncratic characteristics. In order to understand the role of the latter in our personal pursuit of philosophy, we, first of all, have to know ourselves, both our strengths and weaknesses. Thus, we can see how this discussion falls under the general Socratic framework of following the precept "know thyself" (*gnôthi sauton*). Because of individual differences, not everybody has the same concerns: some should work on their anger, others on the excessive experience of grief and yet others on the weakness of their will. The same idea occurs also in Seneca, who points out that a doctor does not order the same treatment for each and every patient either, but pays careful attention to their individual bodily conditions (*De Ira* I.16.). In accordance with the medical analogy, the same, then, should apply to philosophy, that should be approached with similar sensitivity to individual differences.

This reading is also more promising from a female point of view: on the basis of Cicero's/Panaetius' and Seneca's arguments one could conclude that a person who practices Stoicism does not have to get rid of (at least all of) his or her gendered features. After all, Cicero expressly states that one should maintain those characteristics which are peculiar to oneself, as long as they do not stand in the way of virtue. (Cicero, *On Duties* 1.107,110,114–17, L&S 66E)

Thus, I suggest a reading positing that gender in Stoic philosophy, while involving certain physical differences, is also portrayed as a certain kind of role in which the wise person lives. The implication is that a sage can be and remain a sage in any social roles. Furthermore, the Stoics accentuate that one must live virtuously exactly within one's own sphere of life and take care of one's social duties, some of which may be gender-related (a topic I shall return to in Part III). Thus, it seems plausible that the sage would also consider his or her gender to be one of those many roles he or she has assumed. Gender would thus appear as a role that in some way does influence life, yet not the fact whether or not one is a sage. For example, a female sage would have realized the Stoic idea that her duty as a virtuous person is to live as well as possible in whatever inborn or acquired roles she has, and her personal goal is to live as well as possible in all of her different spheres of life. Some of her roles might be gender-specific, such as being a wife, mother, or a sister. However, her being is no way reduced to any of these accidental roles.

This kind of reading would also fit Marcus Aurelius when he reminds himself: "Let the god inside you be the guard (*prostatēs*) for this living creature who is male (*zóou arrenos*), and an old (*presbutou*) and political (*politikou*) and Roman and a ruler (*arkhontos*)." (*Ta Eis Heautou* III.5). Being male, old, political, Roman, and ruler—all of these are roles Marcus lives in, yet his person cannot be reduced to any one or even the sum of them. In fact, after the quoted passage Marcus, being the Roman emperor, strikingly concludes that, in the end, he is a citizen of the whole cosmos and thus his role as a Roman citizen (and ruler) is only an accidental and conventional one. As a citizen of the cosmos, he is not defined by any of his other accidental roles, such as being a male. However, we might still want to add that the social roles of a female, a slave, and the Roman emperor were significantly different in the time of Marcus Aurelius. Yet, it is encouraging to think that there is a fundamental cosmic equality even between people living in unequal societies and that social roles are not determined by the universal order of nature.

In this chapter, I have scrutinized gender in the Stoic philosophical ideal. I concluded that despite the apparently masculine image of the Stoic sage, the rational ideal is open to all genders and does not require "women to resemble men." Furthermore, I have claimed that Stoicism would also mold several traits of masculinity and femininity, as they were traditionally understood, and that they conceived of gendered characteristics for the most part as products of sociocultural influence. The question remains, however, how sexuality as a specific and central area of (adult) human life fits this picture. We have seen that both men and women could be sages—but would they, as sages, cease to be sexually active? Or is sexual agency yet another role that people can choose to live in? In the next chapter, I will move on to scrutinize, how the Stoic philosophical therapy would mold people's sexual conduct.

Appendix

Cicero, Marcus Tullius

De Officiis
Tusc.Disp.   Tusculanae Disputationes

De officiis. M. Winterbottom (ed.). Oxford: Clarendon Press, 1994.
Tusculanae Disputationes. M. Pohlenz (ed.). Leipzig: Teubner, 1918.
Tusculan Disputations. J.E. King (transl.). Harvard, MA: Harvard University Press, 1960.

Diogenes Laertius

Lives of Eminent Philosophers (DL)

Diogenis Laertii Vitae philosophorum. Miroslav Marcovich (ed.). *Bibliotheca scriptorum Graecorum et Romanorum Teubneriana.* Vol. 1. Stuttgart-Lipsia: Teubner, 1999–2002.
Lives of Eminent Philosophers. R.D. Hicks (transl.). Cambridge and London: Harvard University Press, 1995.

Epictetus

Discourses (Disc.)
Encheiridion (Ench.)

Discourses and Selected Writings. Christopher Gill (ed.). Robin Hard (transl.). London: J.M. Dent & Vermont, Tuttle/Everyman, 1995.
Discourses. Books I–IV. W.A. Oldfather (transl.). Cambridge and London: Harvard University Press, 2000.

Origen

Cels.   Contra Celsum

Contra Celsum. Henry Chadwick (transl.). Cambridge and New York: Cambridge University Press, 1980.
Die Griechischen Christlichen Schriftsteller der ersten Jahrhunderte (GCS), GCS 2–3, Origenes Werke: Contra Celsum. Paul Koetschau (ed.). 1. Aufl. 1899.

Seneca, Lucius Annaeus

Ad Helviam
Ad Marciam

De Constantia Sapientis (On Firmness)
Epistulae

Opera Philosophica. Louis Delatte (ed.). Olm, Hildesheim, 1981.
Moral Essays. Vol. I. John W. Basore (transl.). Cambridge and London: Harvard University Press, 1928.
Moral Essays. Vol. 2. John W. Basore (transl.). Cambridge and London: Harvard University Press, 1932.
Epistles. Vol. I–VI. Richard M. Gummere (transl.). Cambridge and London: Harvard University Press, 1917–1925.
Selected Philosophical Letters. Brad Inwood (transl.). Oxford: Oxford University Press, 2007.

Plato

Rep. Republic

Plato in Twelve Volumes, Vol. 5–6, The Republic. Paul Shorey (transl.). London: Heinemann, 1969.

Plutarch

Mulierum virtutes (Bravery of Women)

Moralia. Vol. 3. Frank Cole Babbitt (transl.). Cambridge, MA and London: Harvard University Press and William Heinemann Ltd., 1949–1976.

References

Foucault, Michel. 1990. *History of Sexuality, volume 2: The Use of Pleasure*, trans. Robert Hurely. New York: Vintage Books. (UP)
Gordon, Pamela. 2012. *The Invention and Gendering of Epicurus*. Ann Arbor: University of Michigan Press.
Homiak, Marcia L. 2002. Feminism and Aristotle's Rational Ideal. In *Feminism and History of Philosophy*, ed. Genevieve Lloyd, 80–102. Oxford: Oxford University Press.
Lloyd, Genevieve. 2002. LeDoeuff and History of Philosophy. In *Feminism and History of Philosophy*, ed. Genevieve Lloyd, 27–39. Oxford: Oxford University Press.
Heinämaa, Sara. 2003. *Toward a Phenomenology of Sexual Being*. Oxford: Rowman & Littlefield.
Nussbaum, Martha. 2002. The Incomplete Feminism of Musonius Rufus. In *The Sleep of Reason—Erotic Experience and Sexual Ethics in Ancient Greek*

and Rome, ed. Martha Nussbaum and Juha Sihvola, 283–326. Chicago and London: The University of Chicago Press.

Reydams-Schils, Gretchen. 2005. *The Roman Stoic—Self, Responsibility, and Affection*. Chicago and London: The University of Chicago Press.

CHAPTER 10

How to Take "Certain Spasms" Calmly—Sexuality in Stoic Philosophical Therapy

Even if the Stoics categorize sexual impulses as indifferent (*adiaphoron*) in their metaphysics, they still consider sexuality a significant topic in their philosophy of life. Sexuality features strongly in Stoic texts as an important sphere of life in which self-control, emotions, correctness of impressions, and virtuous human relationships are at stake. Complementing philosophical theory, the Stoics also proposed concrete exercises through which to put the philosophical therapy into practice. My aim in this chapter is to analyze the special role assigned to sexuality in Stoic ethics in general, and in the context of their philosophical exercises in particular.

In this chapter, I discuss both sexuality (*aphrodisia*), including specific sexual acts such as lovemaking (*synousia*), and the more general concept of erotic love (*erôs*), which does not necessarily involve sexual acts (although they are not excluded). Many sources indicate that an erotic love is about more than merely sexual relations.[1] However, even though this difference is an important one on the terminological level, when it comes to the content of Stoic sexual ethics, it seems less relevant. From the ethical perspective, what is crucial is the character of the erotic subject. In other words, the philosophical focus is on sexual thoughts, emotions,

[1] Cf. Gretchen Reydams-Schils, who writes: "*Eros* is not reducible to sex (*aphrodisia*)," and claims that both Plato and Musonius "limits (limits, not eliminates) in favor of the former" (2005: 151). For reasons to be specified in this chapter, however, I will suggest that Plato and Musonius present two significantly different standpoints on sexuality.

© The Author(s) 2018
M. Grahn-Wilder, *Gender and Sexuality in Stoic Philosophy*,
https://doi.org/10.1007/978-3-319-53694-1_10

and impulses, rather than the acts as such. The main goal, as I will show, is to make the person a well-functioning moral agent with control over any impulses, and who remains virtuous also in his or her erotic relations. Further, I will show that the key notion in the Stoic discussion on excessive forms of erotic lust is their juxtaposition between freedom and self-inflicted slavery. Also, the philosophical notions of friendship form one important context for the Stoic discussion on erotic relations. Friendship generally holds a high status in Ancient philosophy, and the fact that erotic love is discussed in the context of friendship gives further support to the argument that sexuality, as such, was not considered incompatible with philosophical life.

10.1 Making Friends Through Erotic Love

Stobaeus provides the following list of different types of friendships, counting "erotic friendship" as one of them:

> Friendship is a partnership in life (*philian d'einai koinōnian biou*). Harmony is an agreement in beliefs concerning matters in life. On friendships, acquaintance is friendship of those known to one another; intimacy is the friendship of people grown accustomed to one another; comradeship is friendship by choice, for example, with those of the same age group; hospitality is friendship with strangers. There is also a kin friendship of kinsmen, and ***an erotic friendship*** (*erōtikē*) ***from erotic love*** (*erōtos*). (Stob. 5l, transl. Pomeroy, my emphasis)

Friendship as such, of course, is ranked highly in Ancient philosophical discussions of the good life, and the Stoics also count it among the things that are preferable and have a high selective value. Friendship is thus compatible with happiness even if not constitutive of it, given that happiness is an entirely internal matter. The fact that Stobaeus counts erotic love as a form of friendship indicates that the Stoics had a fairly positive picture of it. However, the remark about erotic friendship should not be understood as applying to all erotic relations, but only those that are noble and virtuous. Stobaeus further demonstrates this by describing the Stoic notion of a virtuous person who always acts in the right way. He states that such a person acts "sensibly and dialectically, and convivially and erotically (*erōtikōs*)" (Stob. 5b9). He makes a distinction between two different types of erotic lovers (*erōtikon*): the orderly person (*spoudaion*), who masters the erotic virtue (*tê erôtikê*) and aims at friendship, and the vicious one who might even be mad with erotic love (*erôtomanê*). Like the other virtues, *erôtikê* is about behaving and acting in the appropriate manner, which Stobaeus compares to other modes of virtuous behavior, such as knowing how to conduct oneself at the drinking party (*symposia*). Likewise, when it comes to "the hunt for young men of natural ability," one ought to know how to lead the youngsters toward virtue and master the knowledge of loving beautifully (*epistêmê tou kalôs eran*). Stobaeus summarizes the Stoic position as follows:

> Hence they also say that the person who has good sense will fall in love (*phasin erasthêsesthai ton noun ekhonta*). To love (*eran*) by itself is merely indifferent (*adiaphora*), since it sometimes occurs in the case of the worthless (*peri phaulous*) as well. But erotic love (*erôta*) is not an appetite (*epithymia*) nor is it directed at any worthless thing (*phaulon pragmatos*); rather it is an inclination to form an attachment arising from the impression of beauty (*epibolên philopoias dia kallous emphasin*). (Stob. 5b9; Pomeroy's translation slightly modified)

Stobaeus here repeats the idea I already discussed in the context of Stoic metaphysics: that *erôs* in general is, in itself, indifferent (*adiaphora*). Consequently, erotic love is considered ethically neutral, and thus, I claim, it is not occluded from the lives of sages, since also "a person who has good sense" may fall in love. I have argued that for the Stoics, sexuality is not detached from rationality, and also Stobaeus here points out that erotic love is not an appetite (cf. Chap. 4).[2] Accordingly, sexual impulses should not be understood as either rational or irrational per se: what is relevant are the emotions and beliefs (*doxa*) attached to these impulses. However, according to Stobaeus, the Stoics classify erotic desire in its *excessive form* as an appetite, which is further defined as "a desire disobedient to reason." This type of excessive or violent form of love is compared to other disturbances of mind such as "anger and its species

---

[2] Thus, there seems to be a remarkable difference between Plato, Aristotle and the Stoics in their treatments of sexual impulses. As the Stoics have no notion of a "lower" part of the soul, they cannot attach sexuality to any "lower-level" soul functions. The reasoning concerning sexual impulses can be more or less sound, but sexuality in such is not anything "lower" or foreign to reason.

(temper, rage, wrath, rancor, cases of ire, and such," and cravings for pleasure or wealth (Stob. 10b; SVF 3.394).

Stobaeus makes a distinction between good and bad (or "orderly," *spoudaios*, and "worthless," *phaulos*) form of erotic love, and states that the good *erôs* aims at friendship. The above passage is less explicit on aims of the "bad *erôs*," but presumably the answer would lie in the (purely) sexual nature of these relations. Diogenes Laertius indicates this kind of an answer when he, too, states that the virtuous person will fall in love, but adds that the aim of such love is friendship, *not copulation* (DL VII: 130). Thus, even though a good erotic relationship might include sexual acts, the virtuous lover would not establish such a relationship with the aim of sexual pleasure for its own sake. The passage also suggests in terms reminiscent of Plato's *Symposium* that "an impression of beauty" gives rise to the erotic friendship—we are left to imagine that this friendship will ascend from love of physical beauty to more noble philosophical love. Yet, again we can notice the Stoic disdain toward pleasure as such, as well as those types of acts (and forms of philosophy) that set pleasure as their primary goal.

Brad Inwood (1997) claims that the distinction between good and bad *erôs* in Stoicism was inspired by Pausanias' speech in Plato's *Symposium*. As noted in Sect. 2.1, Pausanias distinguished between good and bad forms of erotic love and explained them with reference to their respective mythical origins in the heavenly and the common Aphrodite. Inwood states: "It is Pausanias' theory, taken at face value, which I claim is the most appropriate backdrop for and explanations of *erôs* in Stoic thought" (1997: 57). Inwood does not elaborate on what he means by "face value" or on what exactly he takes to be the relevant similarities between Pausanias and the Stoics. Neither does he give any textual evidence showing that the Stoics really were inspired by Pausanias' speech, or even aware of it. Furthermore, as I hope that my analysis in the following subsections will demonstrate, the Stoic views on good and bad erotic love are much more nuanced than Pausanias' position. In Stoicism, the discussion of different types of *erôs* relates ultimately to moral characters, and therefore, a straightforward juxtaposition between "a common" and "a heavenly" type provides too simplistic a model.

However, Inwood's reading points to an important question concerning the gender of the subjects and objects of a virtuous erotic relationship. Pausanias' view is strikingly gendered and posits pederastic relations hierarchically higher than male–female relationships. Was this also the Stoic position? The above passage from Stobaeus mentions "the hunt for young men of natural ability," and Diogenes Laertius states that a sage would fall in love with *young men*. However, not all of the examples are from male–male relationships, and Diogenes also mentions that a Stoic named Thrasonides did not touch his beloved because *she* detested him. Diogenes Laertius gives this example just before remarking: "Thus, love is directed at friendship" (DL VII: 130). Ignoring the case of Thrasonides, who was expressly in love with a woman, Inwood comments on the Diogenes Laertius passage by stating: "By and large, it seems, the young people in question [i.e. the young people a Stoic sage will fall in love with] will be men—i.e. the assumed form of *erôs* is homosexual."[3] However, after this remark, he admits that there is no textual evidence that would suggest that the "noble *erôs*" could not similarly apply to women, as well. Inwood concludes: "(T)he official Stoic theory did not make much fuss over the issue of homosexual versus heterosexual love, for philosophical purposes." (1997: 59).

I agree with Inwood's conclusion, since, as I see it, it follows from the doctrine of *adiaphora* that the gender of the sexual partner is a matter of indifference. Indeed, the sources do not give any clear indication that the Stoic arguments could not apply similarly to both men and women. The general principle of Stoic ethics is that the moral evaluation is directed toward the person's character, not toward the act itself. A good erotic subject would be able to do the right choices, behave in the right way, and build the right kind of a relationship with his or her partner. This is what matters, not one's gender, or the gender of the beloved one. Thus, what is at stake in the Stoic distinction between good and bad *erôs* is not simply a hierarchic preference of one type of erotic relation over another, or classifying certain types of sexual acts as good and other ones as bad.[4] Clearly, their view is also ethically neutral about sexuality as such—it is not sexuality in itself that is considered morally susceptible, but the

---

[3] A.W. Price claims that, like Plato, the early Stoics preferred pederastic relationships for pedagogic purposes (with the exception of the utopias which, in Prince's words, "feature educational equality between the sexes" in both Plato and the Stoics). (2002: 170–199).

[4] However, this attitude somewhat changes when we get to the Roman Stoics who often prefer male–female relations and sometimes even express harsh criticism against same-sex relationships. For example, Musonius Rufus' lecture about sexual matters states that neither adultery nor "relationships in which males relate to males" should be tolerated because they are "contrary to nature." In Cynthia King 2011: 55–56.

main question concerns what kind of an erotic and moral agent a person makes of him or herself.

Michel Foucault famously claims that it was only in Christianity that sexuality started to appear as a moral problem in its own right; in other words, that the mere fact of having sexuality was seen as morally susceptible. According to Foucault, Ancient ethics treated sexuality as an ethical issue similar to food or drink.[5] The above passage from Stobaeus lends support to Foucault's reading: erotic love is compared to appropriate behavior while drinking and attending a symposium (Stob. 5b9). However, I agree with Martha Nussbaum both in her support of Foucault to the point that food, drink, and sex appear as morally relevant topics in Stoicism as far as they can affect one's moral agency and in her criticism of him for not taking account of the interpersonal aspect of sexual relations. As she points out, sexuality, unlike food and drink, involves an intimate relationship with another person, and this makes it ethically more relevant and complex area of philosophical inquiry than whether or not to have another drink at a symposium (Nussbaum 2002: 57–58). The Stoics, too, were obviously aware of this difference in that they discuss relations with other people much more extensively than food and drink. Furthermore, sexuality deserves special kind of moral attention since the Stoic philosophers seem to think that there was something in sexuality that makes it easy to slip from the virtuous erotic love to vicious, pleasure-seeking lust. As philosophical therapists, the Stoics are concerned about this genuine danger.

10.2 Sexuality and Inner Freedom

Stoic texts frequently use sexuality as a cautionary example of a situation in which the risk of allowing oneself to be carried away with wrong impressions and overwhelmed by emotions is particularly high. Thus, the problem with erotic love is the same as with any particularly strong emotions that arise even in people with strong self-control. Epictetus comments:

> I should like to be near one of these philosophers when he is making love (*synousiazonti*), that I might see how he exerts himself, and what words he

---

[5] Foucault elaborates on this view in particular in the chapter "Dietetics" in *History of Sexuality, Volume 2: The Use of Pleasure*.

utters, whether he remembers his own name and the arguments that he hears or delivers or reads." (*Disc.* IV.i.143–144, Hard's translation slightly modified)[6]

Epictetus' criticism is directed to philosophers who defend in public ideas that go against the way they act and behave in private. He also assumes that, at the moment of lovemaking, a philosopher will easily fall into the trap of forgetting firmly held principles. Lovemaking takes place in the most intimate sphere of human life, but for a Stoic philosopher, this is no excuse for going against those philosophical principles one supports in public. On the contrary, a real Stoic would be able to recite the doctrines anytime and anywhere, having internalized them so that they are an integral part of the self, and would not act any differently even in his or her own bedroom. Epictetus continues by asking: "And what has this to do with freedom (*eleutherian*)?" (*Disc.* IV.i.144). His point is that a man who cannot control his impressions, passions, and finally even his words and actions cannot properly be called free. A person can, of course, still be free in the political sense of not being a slave, but could still fall victim to another form of slavery—to one's own opinions and uncontrolled emotions. This is the level of freedom on which the Stoics focus.

It is important to note, however, that even if the Stoics seldom discuss freedom in a political sense, their notion of "freedom" relates to two different types of discussions within the Stoic philosophy. On the one hand, Epictetus asks what it is in us that is genuinely free, i.e., under our own control (*eph' hêmin*) and does not come from the outside, beyond our own power (*ouk eph' hêmin*). His answer is that nobody can compel us to accept or reject impressions that come into our mind and let the world appear to us in a certain way. Here, we can encounter something naturally free (*eleutheron physei*) inside of us (*Disc.* III.xxii.43).

---

[6]A similar idea is expressed in Galen's report of Chrysippus: "For that reason we can hear utterances of this sort in the case of persons in love (*epi tôn erôtôn*) and persons with other violent desires (...)."(*PHP* 4.6.23–29, De Lacy's translation slightly modified). Here, as in Epictetus, the philosopher expresses a concern that at the moment of lovemaking, one might not be able to control one's speech which, as stated earlier in this work, is closely connected to rationality.

On the other hand, "freedom" can be used in the normative sense, indicating that only the sage is actually free. Even if all people *de facto* freely accept and reject impressions, they do it in a way that leads them to make themselves dependent on outer things. Only the sage knows how to do it correctly and to use impulses (which are always free in the sense of *eph' hêmin*) in such a way that he or she can be called "free" in the full sense of the term. Sexuality, then, always involves using one's freedom in the first sense but, more often than not, endangers one's freedom in the second sense.

Thus, even if the Stoics do not refer to sexuality as "evil" or "sinful," they still consider it to be inherently dangerous in terms of giving in to fallacious impressions and emotions, and letting oneself be carried away. Passions enslave us in that they make the state of our mind dependent on something that is beyond our control, as the object of our desire inevitably is. It is finally not up to us to make the other person respond to our affection. The explicit aim of Stoic therapy, on the other hand, is: "Neither to fail to get what we aim at (*oregomenon*), nor to fall into what we would avoid" (*Disc.* III.xii.4, transl. Hard). In the end, emotions endanger our freedom because when we are under their spell, we cannot stop them whenever we wish. According to the Stoics, once an emotion is awoken, it has the tendency to intensify and finally take over from reason. The Stoics compare emotions to a runaway horse, a rolling cylinder, or feet running downhill. Once an outer impulse has started a cylinder on a downhill path, its own mass keeps it moving; once a horse runs wild, it will only calm down after having exhausted its energy (cf. L&S 65 J; Posidonius fragment 166 E). This is what happens when we accept erroneous impressions: they give rise to impulses, the power of which easily carries us away—even if this makes us go against our reason. The Stoic view is that once you are on the slippery slope of emotions, it is difficult not to go all the way down.

10.3 Philosophical Exercises on Sexuality 1: Impressions

Stoicism expressly promoted a therapeutic philosophy of life that aims at curing the human soul in the same way as a medical doctor cures physical illnesses. The analogy between philosophy and medicine is repeated numerous times in the philosophy schools of the Hellenistic and Roman era, and the Stoics, too, frequently define their philosophical activity as a *therapeia*.[7] The therapeutic goal also implies that philosophy cannot be only a theoretical system, but it has to provide its audience with concrete tools for putting the philosophical doctrines into practice. The Stoics propose practical philosophical exercises that are often referred to as asceticism, although it should be borne in mind that the Greek term *askêsis* signifies training and exercising, and thus does not have the connotations of extreme severity and bodily endurance often associated with the term. I will here use the terms "philosophical exercise" and "philosophical practice," signifying both exercises of impressions and bodily ascetics.[8]

Epictetus' *Encheiridion* sets out the general precept that one should not pay too much attention to the body, and that just like drinking and eating, copulating (he uses the term *okheuein*, which usually denotes the mating of animals) should not occupy too much of human life. By contrast, it should be done "in passing," allowing one's full attention to be devoted to the mind (*Ench.* 41). He typically describes one's "attention to the mind" as a type of vigilance. In other passages, he compares the process of receiving, accepting, and rejecting impressions with the work of a night watchman, who performs an identity check before letting anyone enter (*Disc.* III.xv). It is with the same watchful attitude we should check the impressions we receive. This is also (and especially) true in a stimulating activity such as lovemaking, when our inner guard is easily breached. Similarly, Marcus Aurelius refers to being prepared at any moment to give a truthful answer if someone were to ask: "What are you thinking right now?" At any given moment, his answer should immediately show that his thoughts are "worthy of a social animal (*zóou koinônikou*)" and demonstrate that he is free of pleasure as well as of fantasies of enjoyment (*apolaustikón phantasmatón*) (*Meditations* III: 4).

---

[7] On the idea of therapeutic philosophy, see also Cicero, *Tusc.Disp.* III 6. On the different philosophical therapies in the Hellenistic and Roman era, see Martha Nussbaum 1994. Also Michel Foucault (1982/1997; 2005) and Pierre Hadot (1995) have emphasized the therapeutic aspect of Stoic philosophy.

[8] Michel Foucault discusses Stoic philosophical exercises through the concept of technologies of the self (*technique de soi*), whereas Pierre Hadot refers to spiritual exercises (*exercices spirituels*). Cf. Foucault (1982/1997; 2005); Hadot (1995).

The Stoic philosophical exercises of impressions precisely aim at gaining control of one's mental activities and strengthening the inner guard. Marcus Aurelius proposes an exercise in which the object of thought is decomposed into its constituent parts, which are then further analyzed and defined. He asks what a delicious fish dinner consists of, and answers: a dead animal carcass. In the same way, he describes making love as "nerves rubbed against each other, followed by a certain spasm and secretion" (ibid. VI: 13). The philosophical idea behind this meditation is to clarify for oneself the difference between the object (fish, lovemaking) and the ideas, values, and wishes we, without even noticing, attach to them ("good," "a thing that I want," "a thing significantly increasing my happiness"). For the Stoics, of course, all external things are utterly irrelevant for real happiness. Marcus also suggests that the value of these kinds of philosophical exercises is that one will be able to see the role and value of each thing in the entire cosmos. Referring to the Stoic ideal of cosmopolitanism (to be discussed in Chap. 14), he asks us to consider what role and value would the thing have for human beings who are just inhabitants of the greater city. From a cosmological point of view, sexual pleasure seems like a feeble and ephemeral goal (ibid. III: 11).

However, from the point of view of the individual, particularly the present-day reader, the ideal of lovemaking "done in passing" might not sound too appealing. Why, after all, should our pleasant impressions be stripped of their pleasant content? Moreover, the epistemological mistake in question might not appear to us so dangerous—why could I not go on enjoying my fish dinners and my sexual life, and if I do enjoy them, why can't I go on thinking about them as something good? Could I not at least think of them as something good *for me*, while admitting that they are not good in any universal sense?

The core of the Stoic answer is somewhat familiar from earlier parts of this book. First, unlike the Epicureans, the Stoics would not think that people's feelings provided any reliable criterion for what was actually good and natural. The Stoic *kritérion* or *kanón* for measuring things was reason, not feeling. Second, the genuine mistake they warn against is that if one accepts that externals could really do something good for us, we would cease being autonomous in relation to happiness. If I really need a good fish dinner or enjoyable lovemaking for making my life complete, fulfilling these wishes is not altogether up to me. Moreover, they make me crave and seek them when they are not available, which takes away my focus of being happy right here and now. This is exactly why the Stoic ideal appears to be the direct opposite to Aristophanes' description of the human lot in Plato's *Symposium* (cf. Sect. 2.1).

However, I do not think that we need to draw the conclusion that the Stoic sage would directly despise sexuality, or that the erotic experience would not arouse any sensation whatsoever. Erotic friendship, after all, seems to be a highly valued goal in Stoicism, and perhaps as best this relationship can be seen as mutually beneficial for both partners. Although *apathés*, the sage is still not like a stone or a statue, but feels things and is moved, only in a different way than ordinary fools. In contrast, as I stated above, I see no reason why the Stoics could not accept that the sage, too, has certain physical and mental sensations, which are experienced as positive, and that sexual acts could have "selective value" which makes them worthwhile choosing. Of course, a Stoic would not feel pleasure as defined in their technical vocabulary on emotions, according to which it signifies an emotion that includes a false judgment of something present and external as inherently good. Yet, in this way, the Stoic sage could combine the ideals of making friends and making love, and maintain both his or her sexual relations and peace of mind.

Despite their noncompromising stance on emotions and the insignificance of externals, I claim that certain aspects of the Stoic response are not quite as far from present-day intuitions as it may seem at first glance. First, the Stoics make no normative claims such that I should not eat fish or have a sexual partner, or that if I did, I should not have positive sensations about it. Instead of norms, their ethics is based on the conception of virtue, and thus, it emphasizes the urgency of strengthening virtuous sexual agency. Second, another aspect of the exercises discussed above that I think further bridges the gap between the Stoics and present-day intuitions is the role of moral authority. When Marcus and Epictetus state that one should, even at the moment of lovemaking, be able to reveal what one is thinking, this does not mean opening one's most private thoughts to a moral authority who analyzes and judges their value. What they suggest is rather a thought experiment that helps people to be aware of their state of mind and level of self-control. As Foucault argues, the point of the Stoic exercises is not to confess the content of one's mind that is considered to be ethically problematic.[9] Rather than

---

[9] On the technique of confession in Christianity and a comparison between Christian confession and Ancient philosophical exercises, see Foucault (1982/1997: 224, 234–248; 2005: 363–365) and Hadot (1995: 126–144).

confession, the internal analysis of one's sexual impressions is connected to the presence of *logos* in everyone. The Stoic philosophical therapist aims to help others in fulfilling their rational natures and thus achieving happiness.

10.4 Philosophical Exercises on Sexuality 2: Abstinence

Virtuous ethical agency does not come about only in one's mind but also in action. Likewise, sexual agency is not only about having the right principles about sexual ethics but also, significantly, about acting virtuously in real-life sexual encounters. In order to promote this idea, Stoic thinkers devise philosophical exercises that focus on actions and choices, rather than on impression. One of these kinds of exercises is the Stoic recommendation of abstinence from sexual activity.

In particular, the Roman Stoic thinkers frequently warn against the dangers related to sexuality. Seneca refers to abstinence (*venus*) as a sign of willpower—other similar examples include refraining from laughter or drinking wine, or getting accustomed to having little sleep (*De Ira* 2.12.3–4).[10] Musonius argues that a person giving in to lust and pleasure turns out more animal-like than human-like, and thus, one should engage in sexual activity only for the purpose of procreation.[11] Epictetus' recommendation is to remain "pure" (*kathareuteon*) in terms of sexuality (*peri aphrodisia*) as far as possible before marriage. He also urges his reader: "And if you indulge, let it be lawful. But do not therefore become aggravating nor frequently boast that you yourself do not indulge" (*Encheiridion*, 33, Hard's translation slightly modified). Thus, Epictetus makes it clear that the main point in the exercise of abstinence is the reinforcement of one's own virtuous development, which requires self-control—it is not to moralize to others about their sexual conduct or to present oneself as sublime. Yet even if the Stoics are not laying down any absolute moral laws, the ideal seems very stern and strict—and as unattractive as Seneca's recommendation of never laughing.

---

[10] On the notion of the will in Stoicism, see Brad Inwood and Pierluigi Donini (2005: 132—156); Michael Frede (2011: 31–48).

[11] See Musonius Rufus' lecture *About Sexual Matters* in Cynthia King 2011: 55–56.

Seneca is aware that the path he is proposing is hard and not immediately appealing. In his letter to Lucilius, he clearly assumes that his correspondent would intuitively be inclined to support the position that emotions and erotic love should have a place in good life.[12] Seneca demonstrates his position by referring to Panaetius' account of love. When a youngster had asked the Stoic philosopher whether the wise man would choose to become a lover (*amaturus*), Panaetius gave him the following answer:

> We shall see later about the wise man. But you and I, who are yet far removed from wisdom, should not trust ourselves to fall into a state that is disordered, uncontrolled, enslaved to another, contemptible to itself. (...) An easily-won love hurts as much as one which is difficult to win; we are captured by that which is compliant, and we struggle with that which is hard. Therefore, knowing our weakness, let us remain quiet. (Seneca, *Epistle* 116.4–5; Gummere's translation slightly modified)

Here again is the Stoic philosopher warning against love on the grounds of the excessive nature of emotions and the challenges it causes to self-control. For ordinary people, both good and bad luck in love are detrimental to happiness, and as a result, they lose their autonomy, freedom, and peace of mind in the above-discussed sense, referring to the normative ideal of using one's impressions in accordance with nature and thus avoiding enslavement to disturbing beliefs and emotions. Seneca anticipates Lucilius' reaction in a rhetorical counterargument: the Stoic ideal is too difficult to attain, it is inhuman ("we are just small human beings, *homunicones*, unable to deny ourselves anything"), and emotions should have a place in human life ("we shall desire, *concupiscemus*, but moderately;" ibid. 6–7). Seneca's reply is that the Stoic ideal seems difficult to attain only because people refuse to believe in their own power and rational capacities, and grow attached to their own vices. Seneca thus suggests that though changing one's habits is difficult, it is still easier than changing one's conception of oneself.

---

[12] As Martha Nussbaum argues, the Stoics seemed to assume that the Aristotelian ideal of moderation was intuitively appealing for most people, and it is exactly these ordinary/Aristotelian intuitions the Stoic philosopher attempts to overrule. Cf. Nussbaum 1994: 402–438.

It is also important to notice that for the Stoics, abstinence is not the end but a means to the end: to the invaluable goal of being the autonomous agent of one's own actions, capable of deliberation, and making a free choice. In this respect, abstinence appears as only one among many concrete bodily exercises through which Stoicism can be practiced. This is also evident in Seneca's *Epistle* CVIII where he describes different ways in which philosophy has changed his daily routines, including grooming (he gave up using perfume and bathing too often) and diet (he was a vegetarian for a while and avoided extravagant dishes), as well as other customs (he started to sleep on a hard mattress).[13] Seneca also tells Lucilius how practicing philosophy affected his sexual life (*Epistle* CVIII: 17–22). Apparently, he once practiced total abstinence, but then gave it up: "I have observed a limit which is indeed next door to abstinence; perhaps it is even a little more difficult, because it is easier for the will to cut off certain things utterly than to use them with restraint" (ibid. 16). The choice between total abstinence and practicing moderation in sexual life appears as ethically insignificant—the author only sees one as a more difficult route than the other.

Seneca's letter makes it clear that he does not give his correspondent personal information about his sex life or bathing habits in order to lay down norms for how one should act. He emphasizes that a teacher should guide his student to live well, and not reduce philosophy into mere study of words. For this reason, Seneca describes the path that he followed himself. Nevertheless, his main point is to demonstrate that in order to become a philosopher, one has to pay careful attention also to the details of one's everyday life. He is thus not suggesting that his personal route to philosophical life is that which everybody else should follow (*Epistle* CVIII: 23).

There is yet another argument for abstinence that can be constructed from Stoic views on friendship discussed above. Stobaeus states that according to the Stoics, there is only friendship among the wise. The "worthless ones" (*phauloi*) are too "unreliable and unstable and in possession of contradictory beliefs" to be capable of friendship: they only build superficial ties dictated by need and opinion (Stob. 11 m; SVF 3.630).

---

[13] Cf. Marcus Aurelius' *Letter* 39 to Fronto, in which he describes in detail the entire course of his day from waking up and washing his mouth with honey water through dining and bathing in the afternoon until night when he writes down an account of his day in a letter to his teacher and his beloved one.

If the Stoics thought that ordinary people cannot be friends in the true sense of the word, then it is plausible that they also considered that there was no virtuous, friendship-building erotic love among them either. Since only the sage can build truly affectionate and loving bonds with other people, a Stoic would probably consider it a safer choice for an ordinary person to restrain from erotic love altogether.

Whether the Stoic philosopher would recommend abstinence on the basis of their theory of emotions, their ideal of autonomous agency, or their views of true friendship, I do not think that we should read them as positing that there was something ideal in not being sexually active. I have suggested that we should understand abstinence as another philosophical exercise that a Stoic philosopher-therapist recommends as a concrete way of making their philosophy a lived practice. It would clearly be a bad strategy in the rehabilitation of alcoholics to send them into a bar and ask them only to drink water—for a start, it would be safer to keep them out of places serving alcohol altogether. *Mutatis mutandis* with emotions: people at the beginning of Stoic therapeutic treatment are likely to suffer, depending on the diagnosis, from emotions that make them vulnerable to the turbulences of the world around them. First, it would be safer not to be exposed to anything that potentially brings about big emotional challenges. This is also the strategy Epictetus recommends in philosophical *askêsis*—in order to get rid of a bad habit, one should train exactly the opposite characteristics. He sums that one should pay particular attention in practicing those things that one experiences as difficult (*Disc.* III.xii.7–8). Thus, in the framework of Stoic philosophical therapy, abstinence appears as one way to test whether one really masters one's sexual impulses. However, the sage, having accomplished full mastery of impulses, would exercise his or her freedom also for building virtuous, erotic friendships whenever this would seem to be in accordance with *logos*.

Appendix

Aurelius, Marcus

Tôn Eis Heauton (Meditations)

Marcus Antonius Imperator Ad Se Ipsum. Jan Hendrik Leopold (ed.). Leipzig: B. G. Teubneri, 1908.

Marcus Aurelius. C.R. Haines (transl.). Cambridge, MA: Harvard University Press, 2014.

Diogenes Laertius, *Lives of Eminent Philosophers* (DL)

Diogenis Laertii Vitae philosophorum. Miroslav Marcovich (ed.). *Bibliotheca scriptorum Graecorum et Romanorum Teubneriana.* Vol. 1. Stuttgart-Lipsia: Teubner, 1999–2002.
Lives of Eminent Philosophers. R.D. Hicks (transl.). Cambridge and London: Harvard University Press, 1995.

Epictetus

Discourses (Disc.)
Encheiridion (Ench.)

Discourses and Selected Writings. Christopher Gill (ed.). Robin Hard (transl.). London: J.M. Dent & Vermont, Tuttle/Everyman, 1995.
Discourses, Books I–IV. W.A. Oldfather (transl.). Cambridge and London: Harvard University Press, 2000.

Fronto, Marcus Cornelius

Epistulae

The Correspondence of Marcus Cornelius Fronto with Marcus Aurelius Antonius, Lucius Verus, Antonius Pius and various Friends. C.R. Haines (ed.). Cambridge, MA and London: Harvard University Press and Heinemann, 1982.

Galen

De Placitis Hippocratis et Platonis (PHP)

Claudii Galeni Opera Omnia. C.G. Kühn (ed.). C. Cnobloch, Leipzig, 1821, 1833, 1964–1965.
On the Doctrines of Hipporcates and Plato. Philipp de Lacy (ed. and transl.). Berlin: Akademie Verlag, 1978.

The Hellenistic Philosophers. A.A. Long and D.N. Sedley (eds.). Cambridge: Cambridge University Press, 1987. (L&S)

Musonius Rufus

Musonii Rufi Reliquiae. O. Hense (ed.). Leipzig: Kessinger, 1905.
Musonius Rufus: Lectures & Sayings. William B. Irvine (ed.). Cynthia King (transl.). CreateSpace, 2011.

Plato

Symp. Symposium

Complete Works. John M. Cooper (ed.). D.S. Hutchinson (associate ed.). Indianapolis: Hackett Publishers, 1997.
The Symposium. Christopher Gill (transl.). London and New York: Penguin Books, 1999.

Seneca

Epistles. Vol. I–VI. Richard M. Gummere (transl.). Cambridge and London: Harvard University Press, 1917–1925.
Selected Philosophical Letters. Brad Inwood (transl.). Oxford: Oxford University Press, 2007.

Stobaeus

Anthologium, Ioannis Stobaeus. Otto Hense and Curtius Wachsmuth (eds.). Weidman: Berolini, 1884–1909.
Arius Didymus: Epitome of Stoic Ethics. Arthur J. Pomeroy (ed. and transl.). Atlanta, GA: Scholars Press, 1999.

Stoicorum veterum fragmenta. Vol. I–III. H. von Arnim (ed.). Leipzig: Lipsiae, in aedibus B.G. Teubneri, 1903–1924. (SVF)

REFERENCES

Foucault, Michel. 1982/1997. Technologies of the Self. In *The Essential Works of Foucault, Volume 1: Ethics, Subjectivity, Truth*, ed. Paul Rabinow, trans. Robert Hurley et al, 223–251. London: Penguin.
Foucault, Michel. 1990. *History of Sexuality, Volume 2: The Use of Pleasure*, trans. Robert Hurely. New York: Vintage Books.
Foucault, Michel. 2005. *The Hermeneutics of the Subject*. New York: Palgrave Macmillan.
Frede, Michael. 2011. *A Free Will: Origins of the Notion in Ancient Thought*, ed. A.A. Long. Berkley, Los Angeles and London: University of California Press.
Hadot, Pierre. 1995. *Philosophy as a Way of Life: Spiritual Exercises from Socrates to Foucault*. Oxford and Malden: Blackwell.
Inwood, Brad. 1997. Why Do Fools Fall in Love? In *Aristotle and After*, ed. Richard Sorabji, Supplement 68. Bulletin of the Institute of Classical Studies.
Inwood, Brad, and Pierluigi Donini. 2005. Stoic ethics. In *The Cambridge History of Hellenistic Philosophy*, ed. Keimpe Algra, et al., 675–738. Cambridge: Cambridge University Press.

Nussbaum, Martha. 1994. *The Therapy of Desire: Theory and Practice in Hellenistic Ethics*. Princeton: Princeton University Press.
Nussbaum, Martha. 2002. Erós and Ethical Norms: Philosopher Respond to a Cultural Dilemma. In *The Sleep of Reason: Erotic Experience and Sexual Ethics in Ancient Greek and Rome*, ed. Martha Nussbaum, and Sihvola Juha, 55–94. Chicago and London: The University of Chicago Press.
Price, A.W. 2002. Plato, Zeno, and the Object of Love. In *The Sleep of Reason: Erotic Experience and Sexual Ethics in Ancient Greek and Rome*, ed. Martha Nussbaum, and Sihvola Juha, 170–199. Chicago and London: The University of Chicago Press.
Reydams-Schils, Gretchen. 2005. *The Roman Stoic—Self, Responsibility, and Affection*. Chicago and London: The University of Chicago Press.

PART III

Community: Marriage, Family, and Human Bonding

CHAPTER 11

Gender, Politics, and Economics: From Plato's Utopianism to Cynic Radicalism

11.1 Marriage and Private Ownership from Plato to the Cynics

"Of the many admirable themes contained in philosophy, that which deals with marriage deserves no less serious attention than any other." Thus writes the Platonic thinker Plutarch in *Conjugalia Praecepta*, an essay providing philosophical precepts for newly married couples. A similar statement is to be found in the Stoic Hierocles' treatise *On Marriage* where he claims that "a discussion of marriage is most necessary" (Stob. *Anth.* 4.67.21). From Plato to the Hellenistic and Roman thinkers, family and marriage are a reoccurring topic of philosophical reflection.

The Ancient philosophical discussions on marriage and family are also, alongside the embryological theories, the most extensive context where gender is explicitly discussed in the available sources. A more general discussion of economics and private property forms an indispensable background for the philosophical views on marriage and family.

In this chapter, I will first discuss Plato's famous proposal of replacing traditional marriage with a form of polygamy. This ideal is related to his proposal of reorganizing the structures of economy and ownership in the republic: in Socrates' words, the ruling class would "have nothing in private possession but their bodies" and hold everything else in common. Thus, monogamy is understood as just another form of private property (*Rep.* 464c–e). The early Stoics Zeno and Chrysippus also promoted a polygamous ideal, and scholars such as Malcolm Schofield have compared the early Stoics and Plato on this point (1991). Therefore, it is relevant to enter Plato's *Republic* one more time, this time looking at marriage and the family on the one hand and the status of gender on the other. I am particularly interested in analyzing whether or not the Stoics can be seen as adapting the same idea as expressed in Plato's *Republic*.

The second subchapter provides a compact overview of the Ancient art of economics as expressed in Xenophon's *Oeconomicus* and the Pseudo-Aristotelian work *Economics*. The Ancient art of economics includes taking care not only of money and material property but also the humans that belong to the household, such as one's wife and slaves. Plato, the Cynics, and the early Stoics can all be seen as, in their own ways, attacking this line of thinking. However, as I will show later in this work, the economic idea of men and women's separate spheres of life with their distinct duties can be traced also in later Stoic discussions on marriage.

The last subchapter presents the Cynic upheaval of the economic and monogamous ideal. The Cynic philosophers are famous for their scorn of private property and traditional monogamy. The Cynic school had a huge impact on Stoic thinking—such that the Cynics could be considered the predecessors of Stoic philosophers. Zeno, the founder of Stoicism, was a pupil of the Cynic Crates (c. 360–280 BCE). Even some later Stoic thinkers such as Epictetus praised Cynicism. Even if the Stoics were careful about encouraging anybody to go against laws and customs, the Cynic philosophers articulate certain important philosophical standpoints that affect the Stoic views.[1]

11.1.1 End of Monogamy and (Other Forms of) Private Ownership in Plato's Republic

Socrates formulates the ideal of polygamy by stating: "For if a right education makes them [i.e. the rulers] reasonable men, they will easily discover (…) that to the possession of women and marriage and the procreation of children applies the proverb that the good things of friends

---

[1] Cynic treatises have not survived, and we have to rely on Ancient doxographers and other authors. Whether or not these give a reliable account of the Cynic doctrines is impossible to ascertain from the available textual evidence. On the sources on Cynic philosophy as well as the historical background, see John Moles 2000: 415–423.

are common *(koina)*" (*Rep.* 423e–424a). Later, he reiterates this proposition as follows: "(T)hese women shall be common to all these men and none shall cohabit with any privately; and (...) the children shall be common and no parent shall know its own offspring nor any child its parent." (*Rep.* 457c, Shorey's transl. slightly modified).

Some scholars read the notion of "common ownership" as bringing emancipation to women in that they cease to be private wives of men, grouped together with their other property.[2] For example, Susan Moller Okin emphasizes the connection between gender inequality and monogamy where the husband keeps his spouse as a "private wife"—that is, as she puts it, "an important subsection of property" (Okin 1977: 349). She points out that women's lives are not restricted to the sphere of the home in Plato's ideal state, and in ceasing to be private wives, women can share the public space with men. Okin accentuates the controversial nature of Plato's proposition contrasted with the values and traditions in Greek culture at the time. In the Ancient Greece society, the wives did certainly not have the same opportunities as their husbands to develop their intellectual capacities, or to make free decisions concerning their own sexual lives (Okin 1977: 347–351).

Okin is right in pointing out that Plato's proposal was bold in the context of the traditional Greek *polis* in putting an end to institutional marriage. Indeed, Okin's argument could be stretched a little further: I would add that Plato's line of thinking was radical in that it did not take the private household *(oikos)* as a field in which a man should exercise his power and his skills over his wife and family. When it comes to the ruling class of the ideal society, Plato would do away altogether with the idea of a private household with its private property, and thereby with the idea that the wife belongs to her husband's household. However, I do not think that Okin pays enough attention to the fact that Plato's proposal concerns only the elite section of the population. Presumably, traditional marriage would still prevail among the producing class.

---

[2] This reading is in line with the idea Friedrich Engels puts forward in his work *The Origin of the Family, Private Property, and the State* (1884). He discusses monogamy as one instance of private ownership that leads to the oppression of women. Cf. Kathy L. Gaca, who compares Plato and Engels (2003: 44–45). Read from this angle, Plato's proposal in *Republic* would at least seem to imply the end of relationships in which one person owns another as a wife.

Furthermore, it is questionable whether the idea of "common possession of women" promotes equality between men and women even within the ruling class. What is disturbing from the feminist point of view is that the ideal is formulated from an exclusively male perspective. Plato systematically puts men in the subject position as owners and women as possessed objects. The question arises, then, who are the intended subjects and objects, and whether the "common ownership" of wives could be understood as a symmetrical and reciprocal relationship between men and women. Would the wives also keep their husbands in common?

Already the Stoic Epictetus criticized Plato for being blurry on this point. He reports how the women of Rome had started to read Plato's *Republic* since it deals with the idea that women are held in common (*hoti koinas aksioi einai tas gynaikas*). However, according to Epictetus, Roman women optimistically misread Plato's *Republic* as abolishing monogamy, even though the marital reform only replaces one kind of marriage with another kind (Epictetus, *Fragments* 15; Stob. III, 6, 58). Epictetus thus suggests that the only difference would be that whereas in traditional marriage one single man owned one single woman, now the relation of ownership exists between men and women as groups. That marriage is understood as a form of ownership does not change, nor the fact that men are still in the position of owners and women in the position of possession. Even though Epictetus does not quite put it in this way, his argument could be taken to entail that the relationship between men and women remains asymmetric. Contemporary feminist philosopher Michèle LeDoeuff gives a similar critique of Plato's *Republic*. According to her, the "sexual commonality" among the guardians is still a form of marriage, and appropriation of female guardians as a group by the male guardians as a group. According to her, the dialogue leaves the question unanswered what would happen if women refused this type of appropriation, together with the form of marriage still existing among other classes (LeDoeuff 2003: 61–62).

Of course, as sympathetic readers, we might assume that Plato was simply using his familiar, culturally bound forms of expression, according to which he formulated his suggestion solely from the male perspective without necessarily putting too much philosophical content into it. This is also Susan Moller Okin's solution: she claims that Plato's formulation simply reflects the fact that women were owned by their men in the traditional form of marriage, and that his proposal could just as well have been put the other way around: that women keep men in common (Okin 1977: 349–350). Indeed, in the dialogue, Socrates explicitly states that everything he has said of men would also apply to women (*Rep.* 540c). However, if Plato was specifically aiming at building a political system that would respect gender equality, as Gregory Vlastos claims, one might expect him to have avoided asymmetric expressions of the above-mentioned kind (Vlastos 1994: 21–22). This is particularly relevant in Plato given that the search for terminological clarity and precise definitions, and criticism of customary ways of thinking, are defining characteristics of Socrates in his dialogues. However, that *Republic* is not a feminist work (as Vlastos claims it is) becomes particularly clear when we look at the details of the proposed marriage reformation.[3] This analysis shows that LeDoeuff's concern, indeed, is well founded.

11.1.2 Sexual Control and the Problem of Equality

According to Socrates, the benefits of the marriage reform are twofold. First, the abolition of private ownership ends jealousy and selfishness, as the guardians cannot "tear the republic apart" by calling different things, including wives and children, their own (*Rep.* 464d). Second, the common ownership of women is connected to the above-mentioned eugenic ideal of providing the state with as noble offspring as possible (cf. Sect. 7.2). A man and a woman should not marry in the traditional sense because in the ideal state, reproduction is a public rather than a private matter, and hence, polygamy in *Republic* has nothing to do with sexual freedom. On the contrary, it is interwoven with an extremely strict system of fraud, matchmaking, and eugenic calculation.

Interestingly, however, Gregory Vlastos takes this very control of the sexual lives of the ruling class as giving support to his argument that *Republic* stands for gender equality. He writes: "Among Plato's guardians the interdict on sexual intercourse outside of eugenic unions during the childbearing age is the same for men as it is for women. The liberty after that age is also the same for both. The double standard of sexual

---

[3] Gregory Vlastos maintains that "the decisive reason for the feminism of Book V" is Plato's "theory of political justice" (1994: 21–22). On the contrary view concerning the feminism of *Republic*, see Julia Annas (1996). According to her, Plato's "arguments are unacceptable to a feminist, and the proposals made in *Republic* V are irrelevant to the contemporary debate." (1996: 3).

morality is wiped out." (Vlastos 1994: 14). Thus, according to Vlastos, the limits on sexuality in *Republic* apply symmetrically to both men and women. In the same vein, Susan Moller Okin suggests that, against the backdrop of Plato's contemporary society, his proposal to apply the same standards of sexual ethics to men and women was astonishingly radical (Okin 1977: 353–354).

Even though Vlastos and Okin use the example of sexual ethics to support their reading of *Republic* as a feminist work, I take it as evidence of exactly the opposite: a serious problem in the allegedly equal status of men and women. For one thing, it is physically, psychologically, and temporally not the same thing to conceive or give birth to a child. When the matchmakers of the ideal republic decide which man should copulate with which woman, the situation is not symmetrical—both the man and the woman participate equally in the lovemaking, but it is the woman's lot to go through the pregnancy and child labor, after which the child will be taken away from her to be taken care of in the public nursing houses. The dialogue pays no attention to how these arrangements would emotionally affect the mother or the child.

Thus, the case of sexual control is far from being a convincing example of a situation that would be symmetric to men and women. However, this example also reveals that a plausible conception of equality requires more than making rules that are systematically and symmetrically applied to everybody. On the contrary, they must be sensitive to the relevant differences in the situations of the people concerned. Some groups of people have certain specific needs, the denial of which will inevitably put the members of the group in an unequal position. Thus, giving special attention to a specific group may constitute an act that creates equality rather than inequality: an obvious example is providing special assistance to people with handicaps. Likewise in the case of pregnancy and giving birth, women are in a special situation and have specific needs to which a just society should pay attention. Plato's *Republic* exercises totalitarian power over women's bodies, which are treated merely as vehicles for producing new members for the society without considering the women's willingness or physical well-being.[4] Thus, Plato's discussion on women is subordinated to the aim of outlining a society that reflects the hierarchic

---

[4] Martha Nussbaum's capabilities approach provides a detailed philosophical theory of what "producing equality" entails (Nussbaum 2000: 1–33).

ideal of both the society and the soul presented in the dialogue, and it is the interest of the society that dictates the position of women.[5] This is an essential aspect of Plato's ideal state that should be kept in mind when comparing it to the Stoic utopias or the Cynic upheaval of monogamy.

11.2 The Economics of the Free Man's Household: Wife, Property, Slaves, and Cattle

The Pseudo-Aristotelian work *Economics*[6] defines the art of economics (*oikonomikē*) as consisting of two component parts: (1) human beings and (2) goods and chattels. The wife is the first and most important token of the first category (*Econ.* 1343b1–20). In *Politics*, Aristotle classifies the power of the husband over his wife as one of the three aspects of economics, the other two being the master's power over his slaves and the father's power over his children (*Pol.* 1259a37; cf. *Econ.* 1343b1–20). Economics thus forms an indispensable framework for analyzing the position of women or slaves in Ancient social and political philosophy. As we saw above, the marital reform of Plato's *Republic* can be seen as an attack against the economic way of thinking which treats one's spouse and family as a part of the man's private property, even if also his own proposal leaves the women subordinated to the interests of the society.

In his classic work on the art of economics, *Oeconomicus*, Xenophon emphasizes the gendered division of labor as well as the complementary roles of the husband and the wife. In this work, Xenophon describes the different characteristics, physical differences, and the respectively distinct social roles of man and woman as God-given. Ischomachus, who in the dialogue is presented as an exemplary husband and manager of his household, claims that gods designed the physiological differences between men and women for the purpose of their different duties: they

---

[5] Here, my reading agrees with Julia Annas who suggests that Plato was not interested in gender equality in the first place (1996: 7–8).

[6] The work *Economics* is included in the Aristotelian corpus, although it is dubious whether the author was one of Aristotle's students. The question concerning the authenticity of the work is not relevant for my discussion here. My main aim is to draw attention to certain ideas expressed in Ancient economics which is useful for understanding both the Platonic and the Stoic positions on private households. However, for the sake of convenience, I refer to this work as "Aristotelian" or "Pseudo-Aristotelian" hereafter in this chapter.

created the male body for the purpose of outdoor labor, and the female for staying indoors and taking care of the household duties. Accordingly, the gods also ascribed certain different characteristics to the two genders, for example, making women naturally more timid and more loving toward babies. Because the separate roles of men and women are divine, people's duty is to fulfill them as well as possible. Indeed, going against them such as if the man takes his wife's occupation might invoke the wrath of the gods (*Oec.* VII: 18–31).

Although Xenophon presents the roles of men and women as definite, God-given, and separate, he also presents them as equally important for a well-functioning household and allows Ischomachus to say that, in the ideal case, the wife turns out to be even better than her husband and makes him her servant (*Oec.* VII: 42). It is the duty of the husband to bring income, and it is the duty of the wife to spend such income rationally—the roles are distinct but equally valuable for the *oikos*. Ischomachus refers to the property of the household as common to both the husband and wife. Comparing his wife to the queen bee, Ischomachus demonstrates the importance of her role as the supervisor inside the home, making sure that the products that are brought into the household are taken care of in the best possible manner (*Oec.* VII: 16–22). However, it remains within the power of the man to allow his wife to appear as his equal, or even to make him her servant. The art of economics is expressly for the man, and the woman is one of the objects to which this art is applied.

Also, the Pseudo-Aristotelian *Economics* makes a sharp distinction between the man's and the woman's duties in the household. The woman should take care of indoor duties, in other words, the private sphere of life, whereas the man should work outdoors, which corresponds to the public sphere. Thus, the division between private and public reflects the gender binary. The Pseudo-Aristotelian treatise also describes the relationship between the spouses in terms of strict hierarchy: the wife should obey her husband and let him be her lawmaker, and only when it comes to housekeeping is it fitting for a wife to know certain things her husband does not know. The man is the law of the family and the one the wife is expected to obey, and even to fear in appropriate measure (*Econ.* III.1–3; III.1.18–20).[7]

---

[7] Aristotle did not undervalue housekeeping as such, however, and compares nature to a good housekeeper, for example. For a discussion on this, see Mariska Leunissen (2010).

However, both Xenophon and the Pseudo-Aristotelian treatise make it clear that the wife is not a part of the man's property in the same sense as cattle and slaves are. The wife is also her husband's companion and has her own household responsibilities.[8] Furthermore, the wife needs to be able to take care of the household in her husband's absence. Therefore, one of the indispensable skills of a freeborn man is to train his wife to take the best possible care of her duties. These separate duties also shed more light on my previous argument in Sect. 7.3 that Aristotle's education aimed at producing good citizens who participate in political (*politikê*) and economic (*oikonomikê*) life, and thus by implication his proposals exclude girls and women. Whether or not he would have agreed with everything stated in the Pseudo-Aristotelian work *Economics* (or in Xenophon's work, for that matter), it is clear that also Aristotle had in mind a *polis* with separate spheres of lives and duties. These differences are based on an idea of social roles as "natural" (or God-given, as in Xenophon), or of a hierarchic difference between men and women (as well as between the head of the household and his property). In what follows, I will show how first the Cynics and later the Stoics questioned the whole idea of naturalness of hierarchies and social roles, including gender roles. However, the idea of separate spheres of life reoccurs in a somewhat different form in Roman Stoicism.

11.3 Cynic Upheavals of Gender and Family Roles

The Cynic philosophers open up a totally different perspective on household and family matters from those of Plato and Aristotle, juxtaposing the entire conventional field of *nomos*, habits and customs, against their conception of nature, *physis*. The Cynic attempt to live in accordance with *physis* involved powerful criticism of the values, beliefs, customs, and institutions of *nomos*, including sexual ethics and institutional matrimony. The stories told of Cynic philosophers provide vivid descriptions of a philosophical way of life that concretely puts philosophical doctrines into practice, including their views on sexual ethics.

---

[8] Aristotle even states that there is a natural friendship between husband and wife (*EN* 1162a16). This is a remarkable claim, given the high rank friendship receives in his conception of good life in *EN*. Cf. Juha Sihvola 2002: 214–215.

Diogenes Laertius' account of Cynicism includes several stories of how the Cynics favored simple living, free from institutions, customs, and property. When the Cynic Diogenes saw a boy cupping his hands to drink water, the philosopher noticed that he, too, could do without a cup and thus he could further minimize his material needs. He disapproved of any form of marriage and even recommended (as did Plato before him and the Stoics after him) that wives and children should be held in common (DL VI: 72).

Diogenes' pupil Crates also scorned traditional marriage and allegedly took his son to a brothel and stated that this was "a marriage to the father's taste" (DL VI: 89). Before he married Hipparchia, he showed his future wife his bare body and his simple property, and told her that she could only be his companion (*koinônos*) if she shared in his poverty. Hipparchia famously agreed and dressed herself in similar garments as her husband. That Hipparchia chose to marry Crates, even if both her father and Crates himself warned her of the hardships of the life she was about to choose, is another concrete example of how the Cynics despised traditional marriage: the philosophical union between Hipparchia and Crates was a completely different kind of a relationship than that between a husband and wife in the *oikos* of Xenophon's or Pseudo-Aristotle's treatises.[9]

Indeed, the Cynic upheaval of traditional norms challenges the very distinction between private and public spheres of life. Diogenes Laertius mentions that Diogenes the Cynic "performed in public both the works of Demeter and Aphrodisia"—in other words, performed the actions associated with the goddesses of agriculture and love (DL VI: 69). The public lovemaking of Crates and Hipparchia is a well-known illustration of the Cynic criticism of traditional sexual norms: what married couples usually do in the privacy of their home, the Cynics do in open, public space. This act could be seen as both performative and provocative, but it also illustrates the Cynic philosophical insight of *physis*. By making love in the public, the Cynic couple demonstrates that lovemaking as such is a natural act, and claiming that it is shameful is nothing but cultural artifice. Animals copulate without shame. Given that the Cynics' ideal of

---

[9] John Moles further suggests that the Cynic upheaval of traditional marriage would entail that "incest is permissible (as sanctioned by the 'natural' behavior of animals)"(2000: 430). The idea of "permissibility of incest" reoccurs in early Stoicism, and I shall discuss in Sect. 12.4 how we should understand this rather questionable-sounding idea.

life in accordance with nature idealized the simplicity of animal life, they strived for a way of living enabling them to satisfy their basic needs without cultural intervention. They saw sexual desire in humans as an appetite, similar to the sex drive in animals as well as to other bodily needs such as thirst or hunger. Diogenes the Cynic illustrates this in his comment on masturbation that he wished hunger could also be got rid of simply by rubbing the stomach (DL VI: 46).

The unconventional marriage between Hipparchia and Crates can be seen as an antithesis of the gender roles as understood in the context of Ancient economics. Diogenes Laertius' short biography of Hipparchia describes a debate between this famous female philosopher and an atheist named Theodorus. Hipparchia presents the following syllogism: "Any action which would not be called wrong if done by Theodorus, would not be called wrong if done by Hipparchia. Now Theodorus does no wrong when he strikes himself: therefore neither does Hipparchia do wrong when she strikes Theodorus" (DL VI: 97). As Theodorus is unable to answer this piece of sophism, he tries to rip off Hipparchia's cloak instead. Hipparchia refuses to respond "in the customary womanish fashion." Theodorus asks her: "Is this she/Who has left her shuttle by the loom?"[10] In response, Hipparchia asks whether her interlocutor thinks she has done badly by spending her time on education (*paideia*) rather than weaving. She thus consciously escapes a social order which leaves a woman uneducated, merely sitting by her loom, and juxtaposes philosophical education with traditional female duties.

A further important point to be emphasized is that Hipparchia *chose* (*eileto*, DL VI: 97) her husband and that she did so precisely because of his way of life, which she wanted to follow. As the story goes, "she fell in love with the doctrines (*logos*) and the way of life (*bios*) of Crates, and would not pay attention to any of her suitors, their wealth, their high birth or their beauty." (DL VI: 96, Hick's translation slightly modified). Here, too, the figure of Hipparchia personifies a woman who exercises her own rational deliberation and chooses to oppose traditional roles in order to follow a philosophical way of life. Her relationship with Crates is apparently equal: there are no different spheres of life or duties. Later, the Stoic Epictetus describes the relationship between Hipparchia and

---

[10] A reference to Euripides' play *Bacchae*, in which Agave says that she has left her "shuttle at the loom and gone on to greater things" (Euripides, *Bacchae*, 1235–6).

Crates as an exemplary although rare form of marriage that arose out of erotic love (*ex erôtos*) and was a relationship between two equals, Hipparchia being "another Crates"—an allusion to Aristotle's famous definition of friendship as "holding another person as another self" (*Disc.* III.xxxii.76; *EN* IX: 1166a31).[11]

The Cynics questioned not only the entire structure of a private *oikos* but also the importance of political life and citizenship. Allegedly, it was the Cynic Diogenes who first claimed to be a *kosmopolitês*—a citizen of the entire *kosmos* rather than of the particular *polis* in which he happened to be born (DL VI: 63). The Cynic philosopher of Lucian's play *Philosophies for Sale* says: "You see in me a citizen of the world" (*tou kosmou politên horâs*). The idea of cosmopolitanism becomes prominent in Stoicism—an idea to which I return in Chap. 14.

All the above-mentioned fundamental Cynic philosophical insights—cosmopolitanism, the juxtaposition between *physis* and *nomos*, and the questioning of the traditional *oikos*, division of labor, and sexual norms—continue in early Stoic political utopias. However, even if the Stoics, too, express their philosophical ideal as a life in accordance with nature (*kata physin*), for them it does not involve going against existing customs in the same way as the Cynics did. As I will show, the view on marriage also underwent several important changes within the Stoic school of philosophy.

Appendix

Aristotle

Econ. Economics
EN Nicomachean Ethics
Pol. Politics

The Complete Works of Aristotle. The Revised Oxford Translation. Jonathan Barnes (revised). Princeton, NJ: Princeton University Press, 1984.

---

[11] However, the sources on Cynicism also include elements of the Ancient tradition of despising femininity in both looks and character (cf. Chap. 5). In Diogenes Laertius' report, when Diogenes the Cynic saw women who had hanged themselves on a tree, he stated that he wished all trees would yield such fruits (DL VI: 53). He also makes fun of effeminate men and compares beautiful courtesans to poison and a woman in a sedan chair to a beast in a cage (DL VI: 51–66). Thus, the disapproving view on femininity, discussed above, is also evident in the Cynic view (or at least the stories told of it).

Diogenes Laertius

Lives of Eminent Philosophers (DL)

Diogenis Laertii Vitae philosophorum. Miroslav Marcovich (ed.). *Bibliotheca scriptorum Graecorum et Romanorum Teubneriana.* Vol. 1. Stuttgart-Lipsia: Teubner, 1999–2002.
Lives of Eminent Philosophers. R.D. Hicks (transl.). Cambridge and London: Harvard University Press, 1995.

Epictetus

Discourses (Disc.)
Encheiridion (Ench.)
Fragments

Discourses and Selected Writings. Christopher Gill (ed.). Robin Hard (transl.). London: J.M. Dent & Vermont, Tuttle/Everyman, 1995.
Discourses. Books I–IV. W.A. Oldfather (transl.). Cambridge and London: Harvard University Press, 2000.

Euripides

Bacchae

Fabulae, Volume III: Helena, Phoenissae, Orestes, Bacchae, Iphigenia Aulidensis, Rhesus. J. Diggle (ed.). Oxford: Oxford University Press, 1994.

Plato

Rep.   Republic

Platonis Opera (Oxford Classical Texts):
Vol. 1, ed. E.A. Duke et al. 1995.
Vol. 2, ed. J. Burnet 1922.
Vol. 3, ed. J. Burnet 1922.
Vol. 4, ed. J. Burnet 1922.
Respublica, ed. S.R. Slings 2003.

Complete Works. John M. Cooper (ed.). D.S. Hutchinson (associate ed.). Indianapolis: Hackett Publishers, 1997.

Plato in Twelve Volumes. Vol. 5–6, The Republic. Paul Shorey (transl.). London: Heinemann, 1969.

Plutarch

Conjugalia Praecepta

Moralia. Frank Cole Babbitt (transl.). Cambridge, MA and London: Harvard University Press and W. Heinemann, 1967–1984.

Stobaeus

Anth. Anthology

Anthologium, Ioannis Stobaeus. Otto Hense and Curtius Wachsmuth (eds.). Weidman: Berolini, 1884–1909.

Xenophon

Oec. Oeconomicus

Oeconomicus—A Social and Historical Commentary. Sarah B. Pomeroy (transl.). Oxford: Clarendon University Press, 1994.

REFERENCES

Annas, Julia. 1996. Plato's *Republic* and Feminism. In Julie K. Ward (ed.), *Feminism and Ancient Philosophy.* New York and London: Routledge.
Gaca, Kathy. 2003. *The Making of Fornication—Eros, Ethics and Political Reform in Greek Philosophy and Early Christianity.* Berkley and Los Angeles: The University of California Press.
Engels, Friedrich. 1963/884. *The Origin of the Family, Private Property, and the State.* New York: International Publishers.
LeDoeuff, Michèle. 2003. *The Sex of Knowing.* Kathryn Hamer & Lorraine Code (transl.). New York and London: Routledge.
Leunissen, Mariska. 2010. *Explanation and Teleology in Aristotle's Science of Nature.* Cambridge: Cambridge University Press.
Moles, John. 2000. The Cynics. In *The Cambridge History of Greek and Roman Political Thought*, ed. Christopher Rowe, and Malcolm Schofield, 415–434. Cambridge: Cambridge University Press.
Moller Okin, Susan. 1977. Philosopher Queens and Private Wives: Plato on Women and the Family. In *Philosophy & Public Affairs.* Vol. 6, no. 4, Summer, 345–369. Blackwell Publishing.

Nussbaum, Martha. 2000. *Women and Human Development—Capabilities Approach*. Cambridge: Cambridge University Press.
Schofield, Malcolm. 1991. *The Stoic Idea of the City*. Cambridge: Cambridge University Press.
Sihvola, Juha. 2002. Aristotle on Sex and Love. In Martha Nussbaum and Juha Sihvola (eds.). *The Sleep of Reason—Erotic Experience and Sexual Ethics in Ancient Greek and Rome*, 200–221. Chicago and London: The University of Chicago Press.
Vlastos, Gregory. 1994. Was Plato a Feminist? In *Feminist Interpretations of Plato*, ed. Nancy Tuana. University Park, PA: The Pennsylvania State University Press.

CHAPTER 12

"Holding Women in Common"—Gender in Early Stoic Utopias

The textual evidence of early Stoic political philosophy is both scant and scattered, as none of the original works of Zeno and Chrysippus have survived.[1] However, of the little that is known, a strikingly large portion has to do with sexual ethics and gender roles. The indications are that the early Stoic political utopia would have radically reorganized existing customs regulating sexual conduct and gender relations, in particular marriage and the traditional family.

I believe that the early Stoic utopias should be understood as idealizations of what a perfectly virtuous state or community would be like; as contra-factual arguments or "thought experiments" rather than actual suggestions that imply any kind of real political reform. These thought experiments challenge us to critically think about the rationale of many customary institutions, including traditional marriage. Thus, I disagree with readings that treat the Stoic utopias as actual political programs, directed toward the real-life society.

Here, I also question Elizabeth Asmis, according to whom "(t)he community of the wise is necessarily a part of the cosmopolis that includes all humans" (1996: 91). She seems to understand the Stoic utopian society as existing among the entire human race, and by implication in a world in which there is wickedness. This interpretation is problematic as far as

[1] For a doxographic study on the textual material on early Stoic philosophy and an attempt to reconstruct the historical background of this material, see Schofield (1991: 3–21).

constructing a coherent picture of the existing textual evidence. Further, I consider it highly implausible that Zeno and Chrysippus believed in the realization of a utopia, or intended it as a guideline for real-life political programs of how current societies should be changed and in what direction. As I understand them, Stoic utopias, cosmopolitanism, and political philosophy concerning the real society are separate discussions, even if they are all based on certain common Stoic premises such as the equal rationality of all humans and the corruption of existing customs. I will here analyze the role of gender and sexuality in the early Stoic political thought, and then turn to discuss Stoic real-life political philosophy and cosmopolitanism in Chaps. 13 and 14.

12.1 STOIC ABOLISHMENT OF MARRIAGE AND OTHER SOCIAL INSTITUTIONS

The utopia is the Stoic vision of a perfectly virtuous republic—one in which all citizens were sages, truly virtuous, and holding only the right beliefs. Diogenes Laertius reports that Zeno's state would have no sport arenas (*gymnasia*), courts (*dikasteria*), or temples (*hiera*), and thus apparently no institutionalized forms of religion or law. Men and women would wear similar clothes that do not entirely cover any part of the body. All the women would be held in common. (DL VII: 32–34). Diogenes describes the Stoic ideal as follows:

> It is also their doctrine that among the wise the women should be held in common (*koinas einai tas gynaikas dein para tois sofois*) with free choice of partners, as Zeno says in his *Republic* and Chrysippus in his treatise *On Government* (and not only they, but also Diogenes the Cynic and Plato). Under such circumstances, we shall feel paternal affection for all the children alike, and there will be an end of the jealousies arising from adultery. (DL VII: 131, translation R.D. Hicks)

Thus, monogamous marriage as a social, juridical, and economic institution would be demolished and replaced with a form of polygamy. The traditional family would also disappear and be replaced with "paternal affection for all children alike." The above also seems to indicate that sages of the utopian society would be free to choose their sexual partners.

If we now read the Stoic utopia as a thought experiment, as I have suggested, one of the main "results" of this thought experiment would be to show the contingency and moral insignificance of many of the existing customs and institutions. For example, if we take the "court house" to represent the institution of law, this institution would turn out to be unnecessary among sages—as all of them would be fully virtuous, they would not break the universal laws of reason and thus not need any conventional laws to guide them.[2] Likewise, the sages would not need to cover their bodies with clothes because they have nothing to be ashamed of. Thus, the thought experiment also shows that many institutions and conventions only have a rationale among fools, people who err in their rational judgments.[3]

Monogamy is thus abolished alongside other traditional institutions. In my reading, also this indicates that the Stoic utopia would leave all of the ethical decisions to the individual who, being a sage, would be able to do the best possible choice in all circumstances. Thus, I do not believe that polygamy was the main point as such, or that the ideal was to have sexual relations with many different people. Nor do I think the intention was to exclude the possibility that two sages might decide to have sexual relations only with each other if this was a decision stemming from free and rational deliberation and if they could do it without forming an inappropriate preferential attachment to only one person.

---

[2] Also, Katja Vogt suggests that one possible way of reading the statement that the ideal state had no temples is to understand it as conditional: "if people were genuinely pious, there would be no need to build temples" (2008: 33).

[3] Of the mentioned institutions, I find sport arenas the most difficult to understand. I can see how no courts or temples in a Stoic utopia would indicate that the corresponding institutions of conventional law and religion were not needed. The sages would obey the natural law and realize their divine nature by living by *logos*, which humans share with gods. Thus, according to my reading, the point is to show that the conventional institutions were radically different from the natural order (here, again, is the juxtaposition between *nomos* and *physis*), and that one does not become virtuous by obeying laws, any more than one becomes pious just by going to the temple. But why should there be no *gymnasia*? Why should the sages not take care of their health and bodily condition? One possible explanation could be that sport arenas here represent military education, in the same way as I take the court to represent the law institution and the temple to represent institutionalized religion. After all, this was one of the reasons why the guardians of Plato's *Republic* received sport education. Thus, the Stoics may not have been against sports as such (at least in its noncompetitive forms), but against educating people to become soldiers. This reading is necessarily speculative given the lack of original sources, but it would make sense of the passage and fit together with the general framework of early Stoic utopias.

Elizabeth Asmis claims that the early Stoics were only thinking about communities in virtue, which she takes to signify communities in non-sexual relations, and that it does not "follow from the community of women among the wise that men and women have sex freely with each other." She goes on to suggest that there would still be marriage even among the sages: "Instead of showing that wise men are exempt from the institutions of marriage, Zeno's claim that 'wise men have women in common' shows that women rank among the wise" (1996: 90).

Asmis' reading seems to present the early Stoics in a rather moderate light: as thinkers who favored life in accordance with laws and customs, and who therefore also appreciated traditional marriage. My reading, by contrast, is based on the idea that Stoic philosophy includes both sides: the radical and idealistic as well as the practical and realistic. I see these two as existing side by side so that the realistic approach does not diminish the radical nature of the utopian approach. I elaborate further on this argument below. Thus, I find it more plausible that the early Stoic utopias would indeed have abolished monogamy as a social institution and endorsed the free choice of sexual partners. This becomes even clearer when we compare the Stoic position with that of Plato or the Cynics, both of which expressly connected their polygamous ideal to a criticism of traditional marriage. However, it does not follow that the Stoics would have advocated free sexual relations or abolishment of monogamy in real life.

12.2 Platonic, Cynic, and Stoic Ideals of Polygamy Compared

As we have seen, Plato claims in *Republic* that the old proverb "the good things are common (*koina*) to friends" should apply to the possession (*ktêsis*) of women, and that in a good society, all men would possess all women in common (*tas gynaikas tautas tôn andrôn toutôn pantôn pasas einai koinas*; 457 c–d). Diogenes Laertius writes of Diogenes the Cynic as advocating that women should be held in common (*koinas einai dein tas gynaikas*; DL VI: 72). Now the same idea and terminology reappear in early Stoic thought.[4] Many scholars read the Stoic ideal of polygamy

---

[4] In the passage from DL VII: 131 quoted above, Diogenes Laertius mentions Plato and the Cynics as the predecessors of the Stoic view. Unfortunately, we lack the original sources that could prove this claim.

as a continuation of the marital reform in Plato's *Republic*. Malcolm Schofield points to the similarities between these two philosophies and states that in neither is the ideal society understood as "a male club" (1991: 45). Also, Elizabeth Asmis claims that there was "an underlying agreement" between the early Stoics and Plato's proposal in *Republic* "that men and women are equally fit to be philosopher rulers in a state that forms a single, sexually permissive family." (Asmis 1996: 68).[5]

First, as I demonstrated in Chap. 11, I find it absurd to call Plato's *kallipolis* "sexually permissive" since sexuality is strictly restricted to promote the goals of the republic. It also seems far-fetched to me to suggest that the state as a whole would form "a family": the guardians and the rest of the population seem to have hardly anything to do with each other, and thus even at best the unity associated with belonging to the same family would reach only a small, selected minority. Even the relations inside of this small elite group are highly regulated. For this reason, it is also a vexed question whether or not we should call Plato's ideal republic "a male club"—as we have seen, women's position would be made better only among the guardians, and also here, there seems to be an underlying ideal that women should resemble the men as far as possible. This ideal was expressed explicitly in *Timaeus* (18c; cf. Sect. 7.2).

Malcolm Schofield claims that both Plato and Zeno advocated the same kind of communistic ideal (1991: 26). According to Schofield: "Several of the provisions itemized in DL VII: 32–33, of course, are naturally interpreted as repeating elements in Plato's communist programme or as pushing it further than Plato himself had done" (1991: 25). In my view, however, it is an oversimplification to claim that Zeno's ideas "naturally" reiterated Plato's thinking or were even in any important sense similar to it. I wish to point out, first, that also the Cynics mentioned most of the elements of the Stoic utopia, whereas many do not arise in Plato. Although Schofield recognizes this, he still emphasizes the

---

[5] Cf. Brad Inwood, who draws a parallel between the Stoics and Plato's *Symposium* (cf. Chap. 10). Inwood claims that "the earliest Stoics all shared Plato's interest in developing a model for an ideally stable society governed in accordance with principles of unity, cohesion and virtue" (1997: 58). For reasons specified in this chapter, I tend to emphasize that the Stoics were utterly uninterested in thinking about questions concerning "governing" the utopian state, and that the philosophical questions at the bottom of Plato's and the Stoics' ideal societies are essentially different.

similarity, or even continuity, between Plato and Zeno more than that between the Cynics and the Stoics (e.g., 1991: 13; 46–56).[6] Whereas in my view, the question of actual influence among Ancient thinkers is speculative, particularly given that the sources do not provide any reliable answer, a philosophically more interesting concern is whether Zeno's/Chrysippus' ideals are compatible with Plato's. In other words, should one read the early Stoics as (re)interpreting an idea that Plato already formulated, or did they invent their own and original position? Or did they hold the same position as the Cynics?

One major difference between Plato's *Republic* and the Stoic utopia concerns the relationship between the structures of the society and the happiness of the individual. In the context of Plato's *Republic*, Socrates and his interlocutors discuss at length how the everyday lives of rulers should be arranged so as to ensure that they remain truthful to their duty, which is to ensure the best for the whole—not just for a few. The underlying idea is that if the entire republic is properly structured, both justice and happiness will prevail on all levels of society. Common ownership—including the "common ownership of wives"—is one example. From the childhood on, the guardians' lives are strongly regulated in Plato's *Republic*, and education as well as the eugenic system are designed to produce virtuous rulers and thereby to make the entire society flourish. This way of thinking, I claim, seems almost as far as one can get from the Stoics. Their utopia provides a thought experiment that encourages us to think how a perfectly virtuous society would look like. It is remarkable that the Stoic utopia was apparently not at all concerned with the question of what structures there would be in the perfect society—hardly any, we are led to believe. Since all of the members of the utopian society are autonomous and self-sufficient in terms of reason, they do not need any particular forms of external government. Consequently, in the Stoic utopia, there is also no need for external control of sexual conduct. The infallible Stoic sage does not need telling with whom to copulate, when, where, and for what purpose. Since the Stoics emphasize that anyone can become a sage, and this

---

[6]On the Cynic influence on the Stoic theses, see Katja Vogt (2008: 20–29). She also mentions, even if only in parenthesis, that even though Plato also argues for the community of women, this "by no means makes Zeno a follower of Plato" (2008: 27; cf. 33). I agree with this reading, for reasons I wish to demonstrate in this chapter.

is not determined by any physical factors, they do not need any eugenic policies in order to ensure "good offspring."

Thus, there is a striking difference between the central ideas of Plato's *Republic* and the early Stoic utopias. On the other hand, the Stoic position seems to come close to the Cynic suggestion of "holding women in common." As I argue in Sect. 11.3, the Cynic ideal of polygamy should be understood against the backdrop of their juxtaposition between *physis* and *nomos*, which leads to a general critique of cultural and political institutions, marriage included (cf. DL VI: 20–98). The Cynics do not need any institutionalized sexual codes, either, because they just follow nature, like animals do.

The critique of traditional education and ways of life is a prominent theme also in Stoicism, as well as the ideal of living in accordance with nature. Here the point, both for the Cynics and the early Stoics, is to criticize existing institutions, not to develop new forms of controlling marriages or sexual relations. The Stoic position also seems to follow the Cynic cosmopolitan ideal of replacing the traditional family with "paternal affection for all children alike" (DL VII: 131). According to the Stoic Epictetus, the Cynic philosopher makes all mankind his children and treats all men as his own sons and all women as his own daughters (*Disc.* III.xxii.81–82). This kind of a cosmopolitan ideal became also prominent in Stoicism.

Thus, the Stoic position seems to come close to the Cynics in terms of the philosophical thinking supporting the proposal of ending monogamy. Yet, the major difference between the Stoics and Cynics is, of course, that for the Stoics this proposal happens in the purely idealistic space of the utopia, whereas the Cynics carried their philosophy out in their very action and way of living.

12.3 Wives, Pork, and Theater Seats—Stoic Views on Women and Common Property

Epictetus criticized Plato's ideal of "holding women in common" by stating that he was really just replacing one form of marriage (and ownership) with another (Epictetus, *Fragments* 15; Stob. III, 6, 58; cf. Chap. 11). But would the Stoics themselves be safe from this criticism? What exactly would the position of women be in the utopian society—would they be equals to the men? Could the ideal be formulated the other way around that the women "hold the men in common?"

According to Malcolm Schofield's reading, the women would be equal to men in both ideal republics: "(W)e must conclude that Zeno's city was no more a male club than was Plato's." (1991: 45). He bases his argument about Stoicism mainly on two different kinds of evidence: Stoic views on human nature, on the one hand, and views on sexual conduct with either male or female partners, on the other hand (or what he discusses, I think inaccurately, under the terms "homo—vs. heterosexuality," 1991: 43–45). Schofield deals with the first step quite hastily, pointing out in a rather general manner: "There is even some reason to think that the school [i.e. the Stoics] explicitly rejected Aristotle's position, which makes women and slaves naturally inferior kinds of human beings" (1991: 43). I agree with this generalization, though Schofield does not provide a convincing argument to justify it. My analysis of Stoic metaphysics and philosophy of education above provided a detailed argument of how they, indeed, differ from Aristotle's position and emphasize the common nature in men and women.

However, I fail to see the relevance of Schofield's second premise to the current issue. He refers, for example, to the passage in Sextus Empiricus stating that Zeno would have given the advice: "Have sex with favorites no more and no less than with non-favorites; with girls no more and no less than with boys. Favorite or not, girl or boy, make no difference: what benefits and is fitting is the same" (*PH* III: 245). On the basis of this evidence, Schofield argues that the Stoics did not favor pederastic (or what he calls "homosexual") over male–female relations, and that "Zeno's city will have retained the advantages of the male club without its philosophically unjustifiable restriction to males" (1991: 46). It is also on this basis that Schofield formulates the premise that the Stoics treated men and women equally in their sexual ethics, which he in turn takes to support the claim that "Zeno's city was not a male-club." However, Schofield's reading of the Sextus passage is problematic. I read this passage as supporting the general Stoic idea that ethics (sexual ethics obviously included) is about *how* one does something, not *what* one does. I think that the main point of this passage is not so much to emphasize the gender of one's sexual partner, but to focus on "what benefits and is fitting"—in other words to act in concord with virtue.

Thus, although I agree with Schofield in his general claim that the Stoic utopia did not favor males over females, I disagree with his argumentation. Even the way he formulates his research problem on the role of gender in Stoicism is misleading. Schofield writes:

> We know that Zeno's republic like Plato's advocated that (i) women be held in common. But we have no explicit information as to whether Zeno like Plato proposed that (ii) they qualify for the same political responsibilities as men. It is easy to make the mistake of assuming that assent to (i) must go hand in hand with assent to (ii). But Plato argues the two points quite separately in *Rep.* V, on distinct grounds. (…) So we cannot infer Zeno's commitment to (ii) from his allegiance to (i). Is there any other evidence which might enable us to determine his attitude to (ii)? (Schofield 1991: 43)

The first problem with Schofield's perspective as I see it is that he relies too much on the analogy with Plato in his search for the Stoic position. I have argued above that the entire agenda of Plato's *Republic* is remarkably different from Stoic philosophy and does thus not seem to provide a helpful starting point for solving the problem in the context of Stoicism.

As to Schofield's clause (ii), that women qualify for the same political responsibilities as men, I argue in detail in Parts I and II of this book that the Stoics did indeed take women and men equally to have all the qualities needed for the good life and for becoming citizens of the utopian state. However, I find Schofield's formulation misleading in that the Stoics do not seem to be particularly interested in the question of "political responsibilities." This is particularly true in the context of a political utopia in which it is taken for granted that all citizens are sages—obviously, all of them individually will then know how to take care of their responsibilities in the best possible way. However, given that the society seems to have virtually no structures or institutions, such responsibilities should be understood as ethical rather than strictly political.

Yet another thing that should be taken into account is women's own perspective on the Stoic utopia, and their willingness to comply with the suggested arrangements. I raised this question earlier in the context of Plato, but it is obviously equally relevant in the context of Stoicism. It is striking that although Schofield explicitly discusses the position of women, he does not consider the formulation of his own clause (i), "keeping women in common." As in the context of Plato's

Republic, again men are placed in the subject position as those who own, and women in the object position as those who are owned. Thus, this formulation has to be discussed critically in its own right before it can be used as evidence of equality between the two genders.[7]

Indeed, there seems to be a reoccurring tendency in Stoicism to discuss the "ownership of women" in asymmetric terms. After the early Stoic utopias, this line of thinking is repeated by Roman Stoic Epictetus who compares women as common property to seats in the theater. The idea seems to be that theater is a public space, but all spectators (who hold a ticket, I should add) can legitimately claim their right to their own seats.[8] Even less appropriately, he also compares the common ownership of women to pork at the dinner table. His point is that even though the pig was slaughtered in order to provide dinner for all the guests equally, each person should nevertheless keep his hands and mind on his own portion (*Discourses*, II.iv.8–11, 235–237).

The analogies with a pork dinner and theater seats are apparently intended to illustrate the idea that women are common property in the universal order of nature, but in the praxis of everyday life, a man should keep only one wife and remain faithful to her. In other words, from the perspective of cosmos or *logos*, it is not the case that precisely one woman should belong to precisely one man—but once a man and a woman get married, they have certain obligations such as mutual respect and fidelity. Here, we can see how the Roman Stoics tend to discuss social customs and institution differently from the early Stoic utopias.

---

[7] Cf. Elizabeth Asmis, who claims that the early Stoic thinkers advocated women's "equality as sex objects," that is, "(a)ny woman is equal to any other woman or man as a sexual partner" (Asmis 1996: 69). Later, she claims that men and women should be understood equally as both sexual subjects and objects (ibid.: 92). However, like Schofield, she does not comment on the asymmetry of the Stoic formulation of "common ownership" and does not enter into a detailed discussion of why she believes that the Stoics considered sexual relations to be both symmetrical and reciprocal.

[8] The image of theater as common property also appears in Cicero's *De Finibus*: 3.62–68. Julia Annas makes an interesting point on the theater-seat analogy in pointing out that the seating arrangements were different in Greek and Roman theaters: "While the Greek theater was like a modern one as far as seating arrangements went, the Roman theatre was organized strictly on class lines: you could sit only in the part of the theatre assigned to people of your social standing. It thus comes to serve as an analogy for more restrictive implications of property-owning than it originally did." (Annas 1993: 308–309).

According to Epictetus as well as many other Roman Stoic thinkers, the existing society with its habits and customs is not virtuous or rational, but it is nevertheless good to partake in political life and to take care of one's social duties, even with regard to indifferent institution such as marriage. Yet, even if the analogy to pork and theater seats illustrates a slightly different point than the "common ownership of women" in the early Stoics, in both formulations men are presented as the possessors and women as the possession.

Reciprocity could, in a case like this, be taken as a necessary condition for equality: if the marital relationship is not reciprocally the same for men and women, it cannot be called equal. A relation of ownership would seem to be a paradigmatic example of a non-reciprocal relationship: a chair, a horse, or a slave does not own its master; nor does a theater seat own the spectator or a pork chop the one who is about to eat it. Thus, the question of reciprocity needs to be clarified before any statements can be made about the level of equality in early Stoic utopias (or Epictetus' idea of marriage, for that matter).

Even if the known sources only take the male perspective, and some of the analogies are far from admiring from a female perspective, I claim that the most plausible reading of the Stoic stance is that the relationship between men and women should indeed be understood as reciprocal. For one thing, this reading is consistent with the thought experiment that the utopia provides. If one takes for granted that utopia is a community of sages, then all of its members are sages. The sources state explicitly that there are women in the utopian society, which implies that these women are rational and virtuous, as well. The Stoics did not allow degrees of wisdom: one either is or is not a sage, and there is no way for one to more of a sage than another. Consequently, the male and female sages must be understood as being equally rational, and equally members of the utopian society. Furthermore, as I argue above, unlike Plato's *Republic*, the Stoic utopia has no rules governing sexual conduct, given that the perfectly functioning reason of the sage will guarantee the right decisions anyway—and perfect virtue needs no external moral authority. This, too, obviously applies equally both to males and females in as far as they are sages. Thus, it would be consistent for the Stoics to suggest that women hold men in common just as men hold women in common, which is to say that men and women are reciprocally free to choose their sexual partners. However, the Stoics also follow the custom, handed down from the Ancient tradition, of expressing their views exclusively from the male perspective.[9]

Finally, the idea of gender equality also follows from the Stoic ideals of reason and education discussed above. As I have argued in the earlier parts of this work, in the Stoic view, rationality is a common human feature that men and women possess in equal measure; gender is one of the individual human features (*idios poion*) and thus the real human good is not dependent on it; and girls and boys can be educated to the same degree. It is this, I claim, that finally shows why men and women of the Stoic utopia would be equals; thus, a comparison to Plato is irrelevant to the argument.

12.4 Marriage and Non-Marriage, Incest, and Virtue—Contradictory and Controversial Elements in Early Stoicism

To end the discussion on gender and sexuality in early Stoic political philosophy, I will comment on certain elements in the sources that, at least at first sight, might seem contradictory or controversial, or both. I focus first on the seeming contradiction that the Stoics were both for and against marriage, and second on the claim that they accepted incest.

I will begin with the first-mentioned (alleged) contradiction concerning whether or not the Stoic sage would marry. In addition to Zeno's suggestion that "women should be held in common," Diogenes Laertius presents the two following statements as Zeno's views: "the wise man *will not* marry," and "the wise man *will* marry and have children" (DL VII: 121, my emphasis). The first statement, "that the wise man will not marry" is compatible with the above-mentioned utopian view given that the Stoic ideal state would not recognize marriage in any traditional or institutional sense. Why, then, would Zeno also claim that the sage will marry?

Malcolm Schofield argues plausibly that this inconsistency is best explained if the claim "the sage will not marry" is taken as referring to the ideal state, and the claim "the sage will marry" as referring to the real circumstances in a society that is not (or, optimistically, not *yet*) perfect

---

[9] I agree here with Katja Vogt who claims that the formulation "to hold women in common" might just be the expression used to denote "any Zenonian claim on how sexual relations among unmarried partners are not shameful" (2008: 33).

and wise.[10] Accordingly, the claim that the sage will marry and have children should be understood in the context of the Hellenistic philosophical debate concerning the correct mode of life. A central question in this debate is whether or not one should lead a public and political life in order to live well.

This reading is also in line with my earlier suggestion that the Stoics discussed political philosophy on two levels, the ideal or utopian, and the "realistic," connected to the existing but corrupted societies. If one is to believe the testimony of Diogenes Laertius, already early Stoic thinkers such as Zeno discussed political philosophy on both of these levels. Zeno's idea, then, would be that only among other sages would a sage not marry, for the reasons specified above. But why should the sage want to marry among fools? Why would he not follow the Cynic example and despise institutionalized marriage while living in a corrupted society?

In addition to the radicalism of the utopias, Stoic philosophy also contains a strong tendency of conformism: it does not encourage acting against the existing political order, even if it was considered corrupt. Indeed, the Stoics were extremely pessimistic about the existing political orders and did not consider them rational or virtuous. Nevertheless, they advised people to live in accordance with the current circumstances rather than to oppose them, taking thus a radically different course than their Cynic predecessors.[11] Since the utopia is merely a thought experiment, not a political program, as I have suggested, also the ideal of polygamy remains purely

---

[10] Gretchen Reydams-Schils, however, seems to think that there is a real contradiction in early Stoic views on marriage: they were both against it and in favor of it. She is clearly dissatisfied with Malcolm Schofield's solution, but does not explicitly argue against it in order to show what she takes to be the problem with it. Moreover, she does not provide any alternative reading of how these two claims, that the Stoic sage both marries and does not marry, go together. For her, it remains a paradox (2005: 145).

[11] This reading strategy also sheds light on other elements of early Stoic political thought that do not seem to fit the utopian ideal. For example, according to Diogenes Laertius, Zeno would have stated: "The best form of government they hold to be a mixture of democracy, kingship, and aristocracy (or the rule of the best)" (DL VII: 131; the same idea is also to be found in Cicero's *De Re Publica* I.xxxv.55). It does not really make sense that a perfectly wise utopian society would have people in different social roles, particularly as rulers or kings who rule over others. Thus, the idea of a mix of governance modes seems to fit better in a discussion on the best form of government for the existing society (interestingly, this is also how Aristotle formulates his recommendation for aristocracy in *Politics* IV).

hypothetical. Therefore, the first alleged contradiction is resolved: Zeno could claim that the sage will and will not marry because the two statements should be understood in different contexts: the former in the context of the utopia, and the latter in the context of an existing society in which even the sage needs to conform with the prevailing institutions.

Then, there is allegation that the Stoics would have approved of incest. This raises serious ethical questions: could they have accepted sexual relations with one's family members or with under-aged children? How does this tie in with the above-discussed ideal of virtuous sexual agency?

First of all, it is important to take a critical look at the textual evidence. Our most important evidence on Zeno's and Chrysippus' views on incest stems from Skeptic sources. Sextus Empiricus claims that the following statement is a quotation from Chrysippus' *Republic*: "It seems good to me to organize these matters, too—as is the custom even now among many peoples, to no bad effect—so that the mother has children with the son and the father with the daughter and the brother with the sister born of the same mother" (*Ad. Math.* XI: 192). Sextus also claims that Zeno would have approved of incest in his utopian society (ibid. 190–191). Sextus gives the following account of (what he takes to be) Zeno's sexual ethics:

> At any rate Zeno, having put down the things which are recorded about Jocasta and Oedipus, says that it was not an awful thing for him to rub his mother. If he had helped her by rubbing her body with his hands when she was sick, there would have been nothing shameful; if, then, he stopped her suffering and cheered her up by rubbing her with another part, and creating children that were noble on their mother's side, what was shameful in that? (Sextus Empiricus, M XI: 192, transl. Annas & Barnes, cf. PH I.160; III.205-6)

A similar standpoint can be found in Diogenes Laertius' report on Chrysippus: "Again, in his *Republic* he permits marriage with mothers and daughters and sons. He says the same in his work *On Things for their own Sake not Desirable*, right at the outset. In the third book of his treatise *On Justice*, at about line 1000, he permits eating of the corpses of the dead" (DL VII: 188).

It should be kept in mind that Sextus Empiricus was a Skeptic and thus an opponent of the Stoics: provocative and exaggerated formulations of Stoic theses are to be expected from such a source. Diogenes Laertius was apparently not a great spokesman for the Stoics either, and he also mentions a Skeptic named Cassius as the source of his report. Thus, the way in which Stoic views on incest are presented stems from rival sources, and possibly, the point was to make the Stoic position appear absurd and thus worth rejecting.[12]

Further, it is important to note that the claim of permissibility of incest is usually made in conjunction with the other notorious notion that, according to the Stoics, the human corpse could legitimately be used as nutrition. Grouping incest and cannibalism together gives further support to the suggestion that one should approach the testimony regarding the Stoic views from a critical perspective.[13] The only connection between these two types of action is that they are liable to sound shocking to almost any listener. Nevertheless, it is a valid question whether approval of incest would fit into the framework of Stoic sexual ethics. Could the Stoics allow that sometimes the right decision for the sage to make was to have sexual intercourse with his mother? Or child?

The idea that there was no rule against incest would seem to be in line with the idea that Stoic sexual ethics was not a rule-based ethical system in the first place. I have defended the view that Stoic sexual ethics is fundamentally about virtuous action, which signifies the ability to make the right ethical choice in each and every situation (Cf. Chap. 10). Here, I agree with Julia Annas, who notes the juxtaposition between nature and cultural norms in early Stoicism and connects the acceptance of incest to the general

[12] On the possible hostility of the sources on early Stoic philosophy, cf. Schofield 1991: 3–21.

[13] Katja Vogt calls these controversial elements "disturbing theses" in early Stoicism (2008: 20–64). She groups them together with the marital reform and the abolishing of courthouses, as well as the critique of traditional education. In my reading, however, these claims are connected to different philosophical discussions, and therefore, I would not group them together. The Stoic critique of education in particular, I claim, should be understood in its own right, in the context of their views of character development and virtues. Further, since I have suggested a reading of the early Stoic utopias as thought experiments, it follows that there should not be anything disturbing in the idea that there were no courts, because this follows naturally from the idea that all the citizens were perfectly virtuous and there would thus be no evildoers. Vogt herself remarks later: "Theses such as 'education is useless' or 'temples need not be built' should be read in the context of thinking about what being educated and piety *really* are—these are facets for being wise." (2008: 23). I agree—but precisely for this reason I would not call these theses "disturbing" and in my reading, I do not group them together with the alleged approvals of incest and anthropophagy.

Stoic critique of existing cultures. According to her, since established moral codes are not based on nature, there is "no serious reason for the virtuous person not to break them in certain circumstances" (1993: 106). I take this also to be Vogt's solution when she suggests that the theses about incest and anthropophagy "illustrate how, for the Stoics, no type of action is generally forbidden" (2008: 23). Similarly, she interprets the suggestion of anthropophagy as implying that this act could be permitted if, in some highly unlikely situation, it happened to be the most appropriate thing to do (ibid. 34). For example, the film *Alive* from 1993 displays this kind of a scenario when a Uruguayan rugby team has a plane crash at the Andes Mountains, and they decide to eat the flesh of the dead ones to survive (the film is based on a true story on a plane crash from 1972). But could incest ever be this kind of a rational choice?

Elizabeth Asmis suggests that the acceptance of incest might come into question in certain very special (or, rather, hypothetical) circumstances such as when "a wise man and his daughter are the only two persons left on earth" (1996: 89). If one's own survival depended on eating a dead person or an amputated limb, or the survival of mankind required reproduction via one's own family members, the Stoics could count these as rational choices in these extreme situations. Note that none of the sources suggest that the Stoics advocated killing someone for nutrition. Similarly, the Stoic position on incest is still far from promoting it or displaying it in a positive light. I also find it unthinkable that Stoic sexual ethics would allow that virtuous sexuality could sometimes involve the sexual violation of another person. Virtuous action, by definition, requires taking the other person into account.[14] One could still speculate on whether the requirement to act virtuously toward another person also applied to children, given that the Stoics did not conceive of children as fully human in the first place. Yet, it would be absurd to suggest that they would exclude children from the sphere of ethics only because of their non-rationality. First of all, they were obviously aware of the fact that a child grows into a mature and rational human being. Second, as I illustrate in the next two chapters, the Stoics place great emphasis on love for one's children in their views on ethical growth and cosmopolitanism.

---

[14] Diogenes Laertius' anecdote about the Stoic Thrasonides, who never touched the woman he was in love with because she detested him, illustrates this point (DL VII: 130).

Appendix

Aristotle

Pol. Politics

The Complete Works of Aristotle. The Revised Oxford Translation. Jonathan Barnes (revised). Princeton, NJ: Princeton University Press, 1984.

Cicero, Marcus Tullius

De Finibus bonorum et malorum (De Fin)

De Finibus Bonorum et Malorum. H. Rackham (transl.). Cambridge and London: Harvard University Press, 1951.
De re publica. Oxford Latin Texts. J.G.F. Powell (ed.). Oxford: Clarendon Press, 2006.

Diogenes Laertius

Lives of Eminent Philosophers (DL)

Diogenis Laertii Vitae philosophorum. Miroslav Marcovich (ed.). Bibliotheca scriptorum Graecorum et Romanorum Teubneriana. Vol. 1. Stuttgart-Lipsia: Teubner, 1999–2002.
Lives of Eminent Philosophers. R.D. Hicks (transl.). Cambridge and London: Harvard University Press, 1995.

Epictetus

Discourses (Disc.)
Encheiridion (Ench.)

Discourses and Selected Writings. Christopher Gill (ed.). Robin Hard (transl.). London: J.M. Dent & Vermont, Tuttle/Everyman, 1995.
Discourses, Books I–IV. W.A. Oldfather (transl.). Cambridge and London: Harvard University Press, 2000.

Plato

Rep. Republic
Tim. Timaeus

Platonis Opera (Oxford Classical Texts):

Vol. 1, ed. E.A. Duke et al. 1995.
Vol. 2, ed. J. Burnet 1922.
Vol. 3, ed. J. Burnet 1922.
Vol. 4, ed. J. Burnet 1922.
Respublica. ed. S.R. Slings 2003.

Complete Works. John M. Cooper (ed.). D.S. Hutchinson (associate ed.). Indianapolis: Hackett Publishers, 1997.
Plato in Twelve Volumes. Vol. 5–6, The Republic. Paul Shorey (transl.). London: Heinemann, 1969.

Sextus Empeiricus

M I–VI   *Against the learnt (Adversus Mathematicos)*
M XI   *Against Ethicists*
PH I–III *Outlines of Pyrrhonism*

Sexti Empirici Opera. H. Mutschmann and J. Mau (eds.). Bibliotheca scriptorum Graecorum et Romanorum. Lipsiae: Teubner, 1962.
Against the Ethicists. Richard Bett (transl.). Oxford: Clarendon University Press, 1997.
Outlines of Scepticism. Julia Annas and Jonathan Barnes (eds.). Cambridge: Cambridge University Press, 1994.

References

Annas, Julia. 1993. *The Morality of Happiness.* Oxford: Oxford University Press.
Asmis, Elizabeth. 1996. The Stoics on Women. In *Feminism and Ancient Philosophy*, ed. Julie K. Ward. New York and London: Routledge.
Inwood, Brad. 1997. Why do Fools fall in Love? In *Aristotle and After. Bulletin of the Institute of Classical Studies*, ed. Richard Sorabji, Supplement 68.
Reydams-Schils, Gretchen. 2005. *The Roman Stoic—Self, Responsibility, and Affection.* Chicago and London: The University of Chicago Press.
Schofield, Malcolm. 1991. *The Stoic Idea of the City.* Cambridge: Cambridge University Press.
Vogt, Katja. 2008. *Law, Reason, and the Cosmic City.* Oxford: Oxford University Press.

CHAPTER 13

Is It Possible to Marry and Be Happy? The Later Stoics on Matrimony and Modes of Life

Whereas the early Stoics would have abolished monogamy from their utopian state, the later Stoic sources praised it as an ideal mode of life. The Roman Stoics did not imagine any reconstruction of traditional cultural conventions or institutions, and some of them even explicitly argued against any such reforms. Their "marriage pamphlets" depart in many remarkable ways from the radical utopian ideals of their predecessors in the early school. Neither did the Roman Stoics voice any kind of political criticism or suggest alternative ways of living as the Cynics did. Somewhat surprisingly, however, in their praise of the traditional, institutionalized form of marriage, they mention precisely the unconventional union between the Cynic Crates and Hipparchia as a positive example. All in all, in Roman Stoic texts, marriage and family life occur frequently as topics worthy of serious philosophical concern.[1]

When Stoic views on gender have attracted systematic attention in the scholarship, it has mostly focused specifically on political philosophy, highlighting the roles of marriage and family. This is also the case in Elizabeth Asmis' article "Stoics on Women." She formulates her research problem in the context of the Stoic discussions on the cosmic city and family relations, and asks: "In general, are women viewed as morally or intellectually equal to men, or not?" (Asmis 1996: 75). However, as I

---

[1] Writings on marriage were so common that according to Elizabeth Asmis, these texts constituted a separate literary tradition in Antiquity (Asmis 1996: 76).

have demonstrated in the earlier parts of this work, it is not sufficient to pose this question solely in the context of ethics or political philosophy, since the relevant arguments for the Stoic views on female intellect and virtue are presented in their metaphysics and philosophy of education.[2] These views also form the theoretical foundation for the political and social discussions. Thus, my analysis on the Stoic views on marriage and family in this chapter builds on arguments that I have presented in the earlier parts of this work. Thereby I also wish to highlight the fact that the Stoic discussions on marriage and family life relate to many of their fundamental philosophical concepts.

Further, even though the Roman Stoic thinkers praise marriage as a perfect form of philosophical life, their discussions on the roles of the wife and the husband seem to emphasize differences more than similarities, and their views on division of labor still build on the Ancient dichotomy between the household (*oikos*) and the surrounding society (*polis*). This brings up a tension between the metaphysical arguments for equal capacities, on the one hand, and the unequal conditions people live in, on the other. This is a tension that, as I will demonstrate, the Stoic arguments are not able to solve.

13.1 Learning to Lose One's Love

One important context in which the Stoics discuss bonds with loved ones, paradigmatically with one's spouse and children, is in relation to their theory of indifferent things. This discussion, however, at least at first sight, is not very likely to support my previous claim that the Stoic thinkers placed great importance on close human relations, because here bonds with loved ones are used as an illustration of wrong kind of attachment, where one holds an indifferent thing to be intrinsically good. Thus, love of one's spouse or child exemplifies an extremely

---

[2] Gretchen Reydams-Schils dedicates an entire chapter to marriage and the family in her work, *The Roman Stoic* (2005). It is a great merit of this work that it gives these matters such an important role, but as her general project is an investigation of the later Stoics' views of the self (not of gender), she does not enter into a more substantial discussion on the connections between Stoic views on marriage and their metaphysics and philosophy of education. Neither does she pay any particular attention to the specific question concerning gender in the Stoic discussions on marriage.

common cognitive error that sets the source of one's happiness outside of oneself.

Epictetus repeatedly uses the image of losing one's spouse or child as a general cause of sorrow and distress. The third lemma of *Enkheiridion* states:

> In the case of everything that delights the mind, or is useful, or is loved with fond affection (*stergomenón*), remember to tell yourself what sort of things it is, beginning with the least of things. If you are fond of a jug, say, 'It is a jug that I am fond of'; then, if it is broken, you will not be disturbed. If you kiss your child, or your wife, say to yourself that it is a human being that you are kissing; and then you will not be disturbed if either of them dies. (*Ench.* 3, transl. Hard)

Although most of us would not be very happy likening our loved ones to jugs or other artifacts, Epictetus' point is to remind his audience of the fact that these people are, as humans, necessarily mortal. Their deaths belong to the material and inevitable order of the universe, and we should, therefore, accept these events as such (I would add, while still appreciating our loved ones while they are alive).[3] Seneca's consolation letters also approach close human relations from this perspective. In his attempt to console a person who is in mourning the death of a loved one, he repeatedly reminds his correspondent of the inevitability and naturalness of death (Cf. my discussion of Seneca's letter to Marcia in Sect. 9.3).

Thus, there is a tendency in the Stoic texts to discuss spouses and children as a matter of indifference—but yet as something we human beings, more often than not, tend to think as good and necessary for our happiness. Consequently, our happiness becomes fragile: its source is in something that is not up to us to have or to keep. This goes against both the Stoic thesis of the indifference of externals and their ideal of *autonomia*.

Epictetus captures the idea that the source of happiness is either inside or outside of the person's own control by stating: "Behold how

---

[3] As noted earlier, according to Stoic metaphysics, natural events are neither ethically good nor ethically bad, but indifferent. The only things with ethical value are our own evaluations, in other words whether we accept an outer impulse as inherently good, bad, or neither. Cf. Chap. 4 and 8.

tragedy arises, when everyday events befall fools!" (*Disc.* II.16.31, transl. Oldfather). A person who does not accept the mortality of the beloved one acts like a madman who becomes angry about not getting a harvest of figs or grapes in the winter—which, after all, is perfectly in accordance with nature (*Disc.* III.xxiv.86–87). A.A. Long condenses this part of the Stoic theory neatly: the goal of Stoic philosophy is to exclude tragedy, in other words, to help people to modify themselves so as to make them immune to a tragic faith (Long 2001: 24–25). Aristophanes' myth expressed the idea that our lives were dictated by a constant search for our "other half," which in my reading presents the human lot as vulnerable (cf. Sect. 2.1). I also quoted Aristotle's idea of the interconnectedness of characters and tragic faiths (cf. Sect. 7.1). The Stoics would agree, even though the idea of characters as fixed types obviously goes against the central Stoic idea of educating characters through philosophy. According to the Stoics, we are constantly on the verge of tragedy because of our erroneous beliefs and strong emotional attachments. The sage, however, has achieved a character that ensures that her life will never be tragic: she could never lose anything on which her happiness depends, given that it depends solely on her self.[4]

However, I would emphasize that even if the Stoics wished to protect people from experiencing a tragic faith, they did not fail to recognize the important value of other persons. Love relations are indifferent, but, finally, not in the same sense as a jug. As noted above, the Stoics admitted that there were qualitative differences between indifferent things. Furthermore, the principle of indifference does not lead the Stoics to conclude that it was indifferent whether or not one got involved in an intimate relationship such as marriage, or how one lived as a married person. On the contrary, these were utterly important matters of philosophical discussion.

---

[4]On the topic of tragedy and the good life in Ancient philosophy, see Martha Nussbaum's work *Fragility of Goodness* (2001/1986). On Stoic views on tragedy, death and suicide, see Malin Grahn (2014).

13.2 Not Every Wife Is like Hipparchia—Epictetus on Conjugal and Parental Responsibilities

In his commentary on Epictetus' *Encheiridion*, the Neo-Platonic commentator Simplicius (fl. 6th cent. CE) emphasizes the fact that the Stoic philosopher *was not against* family life or having children. He corrects this erroneous view by telling that the Stoic philosopher advised people how to deal with external things (Simplicius 33, 37). Indeed, as Simplicius' commentary indicates, Epictetus did not deny the possibility of living well *and* marrying—but he was nevertheless cautious about straightforwardly recommending marriage, either. This attitude is demonstrated in an encounter between the Stoic philosopher and a young man who was asking for guidance in taking up the Cynic way of life, as reported in Epictetus' *Discourses*. One specific question that arises in this discussion concerns whether it is appropriate for the young man both to pursue his philosophical goals and to marry and start a family.

Again, the question concerning characters is decisive. Epictetus states that the following words would be in concord with a Cynic's character (*kharaktêr*) and apprehension (*epibolê*):

> Look at me, I am without a home (*aoikon*), without a hometown (*apolis*), without possessions (*aktêmôn*), without a slave (*adoulos*). I sleep on the ground; I have neither wife nor children (*ou gynê, ou paida*), no fine residence, but only earth and heaven and a rough cloak. Yet what do I lack? Am I not without sorrow? Am I not free? (*Disc.* III.xxii.47–48, Hard's translation modified)

Epictetus emphasizes the autonomy of the Cynic, who apparently manifests the ideal shared by the Stoics that one can be happy in any circumstances whatsoever.[5] The Cynic is happy even when deprived of things that ordinarily are considered important for good life: spouse, children, and property. These were also the components of the Ancient art of *oikonomikê*, and thus, the Cynic's freedom straightforwardly opposes the freedom of the Greek freeborn man. (Cf. Sect. 11.2).

---

[5] Diogenes Laertius states that, according to Zeno, a Stoic sage could also be a Cynic, as Cynicism is a shortcut to virtue (DL VII: 121).

When asked whether or not a Cynic would prefer to marry and have children, the Stoic philosopher first states that in the city of sages, no one would become a Cynic in the first place: "For in whose interest would he take on this style of life (*diexagôgê*)?": (ibid. III.xxii.68). Epictetus' response highlights his conception of the Cynic philosopher as someone who acts for the public benefit: he frequently refers to the Cynic as a king (*basileus*), a messenger (*angelos*), and a scout (*kataskopos*). A Cynic, in his very way of life, manifests virtue and not only promotes his own happiness but also provokes other people into thinking about what they really need in order to be happy. This kind of provocative or pedagogic function would clearly be unnecessary in the community of sages.

Epictetus goes on to point out that if one nevertheless became a Cynic (in the community of sages, we are lead to believe), then "there would be nothing to prevent him from both marrying and having children, for his wife will be another person like himself (*allê toiautê*), and so will his father-in-law, and his children will be brought up in the same fashion" (ibid. III.xxii.68–69). This is another reference to Aristotle's famous description of friendship as "holding another person as another self," which, as we saw, was also an important aspect of the Stoic view of virtuous sexuality (cf. *EN* IX: 1166a31). In perfect circumstances, like in the Stoic utopia, one's spouse would be another sage and the partners would live together in a virtuous, mutually respectful erotic friendship. Furthermore, living among sages, one would not have to choose between family life and the more general goal of cultivating the mankind.

However, Epictetus claims, in the present conditions where the world "looks like a battle-field," it would be safer to stay outside of marriage. At least, the young man should seriously consider his abilities to live up to all the responsibilities awaiting him as a family man. Epictetus lists such duties: the husband has to provide for his family; get a bathtub for the baby and wool for his wife; provide beds, clothes, oil, and other household items, as well as take care of the children's education e.g. by getting them writing implement when they are ready to go to school (*Disc.* III.xxii.70–75). Thus, the fundamental problem concerning marriage and family life, for Epictetus, was not whether marriage itself was good or bad. It was rather about one's way of life and how one could, in the best possible way, live in accordance with one's philosophical principles. Epictetus' remarks about taking care of one's responsibilities are significant and allude to the point I am going to discuss later in more details: that the family forms a privileged place for the exercising of virtue. He reminds his audience that just as one should not become a Cynic if one is not able to live up to this demanding role, likewise one should not become a husband or a father on a similar basis. Marriage and family life bring duties one must take care of. To provide for one's family takes time, and Epictetus asks the young man to consider whether he, as a family man, would have enough time (*skholê*) for philosophizing.

Epictetus' interlocutor objects, pointing out that the Cynic Crates married. In response, Epictetus states that the marriage between Crates and Hipparchia was an exceptional case, since it arose out of erotic love (*ex erôtos*), and the wife herself was "another Crates" (*Disc.* III.xxii.76). Thus, this exemplary couple was able to live up to the mentioned ideal of holding one's spouse as "another self." Nevertheless, Epictetus claims, as the present discussion concerned "ordinary marriage" (*koinos gamos*), it would be a safer choice to stay outside of it.

The young man is still unsatisfied and asks how the Cynic can keep society going if he does not marry and start a family. Epictetus replies by alluding to the special role he assigns to the Cynic philosopher. He goes on to suggest that a Cynic does not need children of his own as he makes all mankind his children, and cares for all the men as they were his own sons, and women as they were his daughters (*Disc.* III.xxii.77–82). I refer above to the idea of feeling "paternal affection" toward all children, and ideal expressed in Plato's *Republic* and repeated in the early Stoic utopias. Epictetus brings it up again suggesting that the scope of the individual *oikia* is transgressed and replaced with concern and a caring attitude that stretches over a larger number of individuals than the inhabitants of one's own household. In the Cynic and Stoic cosmopolitan ideal, this encompasses finally the entire human race.

It is noteworthy, however, that the young man is precisely asking whether it was fitting *for a Cynic* to marry. Would Epictetus have given the same reply if his interlocutor had aspired to become *a Stoic*? As we have seen, Cynicism was a very distinctive and all-encompassing lifestyle, which presumably would be very difficultly connected with childcare and other domestic duties. Nevertheless, in terms of the ethical questions related to marriage, I claim that Epictetus would have given similar guidelines to a would-be Stoic interlocutor. In particular, it is significant that Epictetus connects marriage and the family to the more general question concerning an individual's bonds with the surrounding community and finally with the entire human kind. As I will show later in this and the following chapters, the idea of "making the whole of mankind one's family" is prominent also in other late Stoic sources. Thus, these aspects, as well as the list of conjugal and parental responsibilities, could as well have been addressed to someone aspiring to become a Stoic.

It is interesting to note, however, that despite his reservations about marriage, nowhere does Epictetus argue against it by appealing to the idea of indifference discussed in the previous section. He does not tell the young man that if he got married, he would run the risk of becoming emotionally attached to his wife and experiencing a tragic faith if she died. Instead of taking up the idea of indifference of other people as far as one's real happiness is concerned, Epictetus emphasizes the marriage as a chosen way of life. The philosophical question, then, concerns whether this way of life was a worthwhile choice for someone who was striving for virtue and the happiness. More specifically, are a philosophical and a conjugal life compatible? Another related question concerns the role of public duties or politics in the Stoic conception of a good life. Several Roman Stoic sources contain extensive discussions on these topics.

13.3 Marriage as a Natural Way of Life: Partnership and Sociability

In their lectures and pamphlets on marriage, the later Stoic philosophers Hierocles, Antipater (fl. 2nd cent. BCE), and Musonius explicitly direct their words against those who claim that a man was better off staying outside of marriage.[6] Their aim is to convince their unnamed opponents that marriage is a natural life choice and that it is in accordance with the ideals of political and philosophical life.

Some opponents had apparently criticized marriage by claiming that life with a wife was burdensome. Both Hierocles and Antipater argue against this statement by claiming that men who say like this are often unhappily married because they wedded their wives for wrong reasons in the first place, like for their beauty or the size of their dowry. Hierocles

---

[6] Seneca is also known to have written a treatise, *De Matrimonio*, but it has not survived. Some anecdotes about it are to be found in Jerome's *Adversus Jovianium* 1.41–49 (see also F. Haase, ed., L. Annei Seneca *Opera quae supersunt*, 1902). Given the little that is known of Seneca's work, I do not include it in my discussion in this chapter.

calls these men "too inexperienced in life" and "unprepared to wed"; according to Antipater, they are pleasure-seeking, licentious, and unable to control their lives. The philosophers conclude that these men are wrong in blaming their wives (or marriage as such) for their self-inflicted misfortune (Stob. *Anth.* 4.67.24, 3:8, 25 ff; SVF 3.254.23–257.10).[7]

In words closely reminding those of Xenophon in his *Oeconomicus*, Antipater also points out that these "bad husbands" are not able to teach their wives "about household-management (*mē didaskein peri oikonomias*), or the growth of the household (*mēthen mēde peri aukséseōs oikou*), or for what reason they came together in the first place." Similarly to Xenophon, Antipater presumes that it is the husband's duty to educate his wife in the things she needs to know in her role as mother, wife, and the keeper of the household. However, he adds philosophical teachings to this list, suggesting that the husband should teach his wife things that are "considered and recommended by the philosophers," which include doctrines such as "everything the wife desires cannot simply come about if only her husband will consent." Once educated, Antipater assures his reader, the wife will be "the lightest of all possible burdens." (ibid.).

Musonius, too, combines his defense of marriage with the topic of philosophical education, but proceeds to a different type of an argument. He directs his words expressly against men who question the compatibility of marriage and practicing philosophy. Musonius argues that marriage provides the optimal conditions for philosophizing, both for the husband and the wife. However, similarly to Antipater, Musonius refers to traditional gender roles in mentioning that a philosophically educated wife will be a virtuous keeper of the household.

To show that marriage and philosophy indeed fit together, Musonius appeals to the examples of Pythagoras and Socrates, both of which married "and yet one could not find better philosophers than these." Although the Cynic upheaval of traditional sexual norms seems to be very distant from Musonius' monogamous ideals, he refers to Crates as a case in point: "Even though Crates had no home, property, or money, he nevertheless married, and since he did not have a place of his own, he

---

[7] For an English translation of Antipater of Tarsus' *On Marriage*, cf. Will Deming 2004: 221–230, and Hierocles' *On Marriage*, cf. Ilaria Ramelli (ed.) & David Konstan (transl.) 2009.

passed his days and nights with his wife in the public stoas at Athens." (14:1, translation King, in King 2011: 59). The intended conclusion is that a person who has a house and property should not claim that taking a wife prevents him from practicing philosophy. It is noteworthy that Musonius (as Epictetus did in the passage discussed above) appeals to the case of the unconventional "dog-marriage" of the Cynic couple even though he is discussing a traditional, institutionalized form of monogamy. This is exactly the type of marriage Plato rejected in his *Republic*, the early Stoics in their utopias, and the Cynics in their very way of life.[8]

In their defense of marriage, the Roman Stoics frequently appeal to the idea of natural human sociability, a doctrine that was formulated in the context of Stoic metaphysics. Deriving his argument from the Stoic conception of *oikeiôsis* (cf. Sect. 8.2), they claim that all animals are naturally driven toward what is appropriate (*oikeion*), and, therefore, humans too are rationally guided to choose to live in families. Nature has shaped the humans to be social (*synagelastikous*), live in couples (*syndyastikous*), and generate children (Stob. *Anth.* 4.67.22, 3:7, 13–19). They also defend this position by referring to the genital difference between men and women, as I showed in Sect. 4.6. Musonius Rufus, however, emphasizes that procreation should not be the only goal of marriage given that it can occur as a result of any sexual encounter between a male and a female, just as when animals mate. Marriage as a human institution is, therefore, about more than just reproduction (Lecture 13 in King 2011; cf. Nussbaum 2002).

The Roman Stoic texts are rich in both philosophical concepts and poetic metaphors in their descriptions of the content and goals of marriage. Antipater applies the concept of "total blending" (*krâsis*) in describing the union of man and wife. He even describes this *krâsis* through the analogy of mixing wine and water—the same analogy that was used in Stoic metaphysics to describe the inseparable blend of reason and matter in the cosmos.[9] Musonius Rufus compares the

---

[8] For Musonius Rufus' lectures on "Showing that women also should study philosophy," "Practicing philosophy," "Sexual matters," "What is the chief end of marriage?" and "Whether marriage gets in the way of studying philosophy," see texts 3; 6; 12; 13; 14 in King 2011; cf. Nussbaum (2002).

[9] Cf. Chap. 4, where I discuss the metaphysical notion of *krâsis*. In this context, I also showed why the Stoic view of matter and reason (and their relationship to one another) is very different to that of Aristotle's. In Aristotle's biology, these concepts also receive an explicitly gendered interpretation, which I suggest is not the case in Stoic metaphysics. I do

companionship of man and woman to two oxen in a yoke and calls it "breathing together," thus, choosing a metaphor that reechoes the fundamental importance of breath (and the concept of *pneuma*) in Stoic metaphysics. Hierocles compares the married couple to a pair of arms or legs, and calls marriage a beautiful (*kalon*) union of two spouses who "share each other's destinies" (*synkatheimarmenôn allêlois*), who live "in harmony with each other" (*symfônountôn allêlois*), and who "share everything in their bodies and particularly in their souls." In addition, he extols the sharing of everyday life: together the married couple takes care of their children and household (Stob. *Anth*. 4.67.24, 3:8, 25–11, 27; SVF 3.254.23–257.10).

In addition to arguments stemming from Stoic views on nature, and descriptions of the marital union as a perfect form of sharing, a common strategy was also to defend matrimony as a good political deed. As Malcolm Schofield argues, the Stoics support matrimony as a part of their general defense of political life: marriage and children are, thus, viewed as not only personal but also, and importantly, public choices (Schofield 1991: 119–127). Musonius, for example, emphasizes that marriage is necessary for the continuation of the society and the human race: "Clearly, families and cities do not arise from women or men alone, but their union with each other." (Musonius, Lecture 14:4, in King 2011).

Finally, the sources also provide practical arguments for marriage. Hierocles, for example, praises how wonderful it is to have a wife, since she "welcomes us when we are worn out with troubles outside the home, restoring us with her healing and refreshing us with every attention" and "instills in our minds forgetfulness of disagreeable things." With her, the husband can discuss his affairs, both concerning private and public life (or "outside" and "inside" of the home), relax, and be comforted in his troubles. She is helpful in performing rites and sacrifices, and taking care of the household in her husband's absence. All in all, Hierocles considers a wife to be so useful that "it would be a long story to go through everything one by one." (Stob. *Anth*. 4.67.24, 3:8, 25 ff).

Hierocles' list sounds somewhat disturbing from a female point of view. It seems like the role of a woman is primarily to be there for

---

not think that Antipater alludes to a gendered notion of "reason" or "matter" either, even though he applies the analogy to describe the union between male and female.

her husband, to take care of his needs and assist him, and to give birth. This part of his argument crystallizes a tendency that prevails throughout the Roman Stoic discussions on marriage: the texts are written by men, directed to other men, and women only appear as the objects of the conversation. The argument is not stretched out to even try to capture the female perspective. Furthermore, there seems to be a discrepancy between endorsing the view of marriage as a relationship between two equals who share their lives, bodies, souls, and everyday duties, on the one hand, and emphasizing the differences in their everyday spheres of life, on the other hand. This problem becomes particularly evident in the context of gender roles and labor division within marriage, which is the topic I will scrutinize in the last subchapter.

The later Stoics' praise of matrimony seems to clash also with some other central Stoic doctrines. The title of this chapter asked whether it was possible to marry and be happy, and the Stoics Musonius, Antipater, and Hierocles seem to uniformly answer "yes." The question remains, then, how this view goes together with the above-discussed notions of insignificance and autonomy. In making marriage a condition for the highest human way of life, do they not make happiness dependent upon this condition—an outer thing that is beyond our control? Why were they not concerned, as Epictetus was, that becoming attached to another person destabilizes happiness? (However, as I point out above, Epictetus did not use this as an argument against marriage as such, but against the erroneous ways of thinking that married people, more often than not, have.) It is true that there are certain differences in emphasis between Epictetus and the views of Hierocles, Antipater, and Musonius on marriage. Epictetus emphasizes the doctrine of autonomy, whereas the other three stress the idea of natural sociability. Nevertheless, I argue that in the end, their views are not in conflict with the ideal of *autonomia*. My argument for this position builds on the Stoic idea of "chosen roles".

13.4 The Roles of Wife and Husband

"It should be understood that nature has endowed us with two roles, as it were," Cicero writes (*On Duties* I.107, 110, 1; Panaetius fr.97). First comes the role that stems from common, rational human nature. The second one stems from our individual features. I discussed these two roles above in Sect. 9.4. These roles are supplemented with yet another two that depend on circumstances and choice. It is these last-mentioned roles that are relevant to the present discussion on marriage, one task in which is to analyze the roles of husband and wife.[10]

Cicero presents the third role or *persona* (possibly presenting Panaetius' position) as that "which some chance or circumstance imposes"; as examples he lists wealth as well as different offices and public positions. The fourth persona, however, is that which "we take upon ourselves by our own decision," for example, when we choose to study philosophy, or any other subject. Cicero ends his discussion by stating: "Above all we must decide who and what sort of people we want to be, and what kind of life we want to lead; and this is the most difficult question of all." (Cicero, *On Duties* 1.107,110,114–17, L&S 66E).

Although Cicero does not explicitly mention marriage, conjugal roles fit perfectly well into this framework and would seem to fall neatly under the above-mentioned third and fourth *personae*. Seen in this light, these roles appear as essentially social and situational, and, thus, different from one's "natural" roles as a member of the human species and as a unique individual.

The fourth role, however, seems to be a rather selective one as it only applies to those who have the opportunity to choose "the kinds of lives they want to live." A slave does certainly not choose a life of enslavement. Similarly, in terms of gender, the situation of men and women in Ancient society (whether Greek or Roman) was radically different on this point: women could not freely choose whether or not to get married or with whom. As we saw earlier, in the Greek art of economics, the wife was discussed among other parts of the freeborn man's property, alongside cattle, slaves, and material possessions. Therefore, for women, marriage did not appear as one way of life that was to be preferred or dis-preferred to other possibilities. Thus, in those cases that men could freely choose their marriage, their role as a husband would fall under the fourth persona, whereas for women, it most likely would fit the third—a role that circumstances have imposed.[11]

Even if Greek and Roman customs on marriage were not quite identical, it still seems to me that Gretchen Reydams-Schils fails to take the

---

[10] Cf. Also the metaphysical categories of "disposed" and "relatively disposed" discussed in Sect. 4.3.

[11] On the history of marriage in Antiquity, see, e.g., Cynthia B. Patterson (1991): 48–72.

female view into account in claiming that Roman Stoics saw marriage precisely as *a choice*, and that they challenged the values of their contemporary audience in emphasizing "selective criteria," in other words, criteria to be used by both men and women, in choosing a good spouse. I claim that this reading is highly optimistic, and that Reydams-Schils fails to provide her readers with sufficient evidence for accepting it. Quoting how Marcus Aurelius and Musonius Rufus considered character and not only wealth or social status when selecting husbands for their daughters is unlikely to support the claim that the Stoics referred to *women themselves* as the ones who chose their husbands based on certain philosophical criteria (Reydams-Schils 2005: 152–253). However, although Reydams-Schils' reading is clearly optimistic, her main conclusion would seem to fit with certain premises generally accepted by Stoic thinkers, such as universal rationality, as discussed above, or their ideal of cosmopolitanism to be discussed below.

Leaving aside, for a while, the point that the third and the fourth *personae* were in fact very different for men and women in the times of the Stoics, I will consider what the idea of personas brings to the present discussion of Stoic views on marriage. First of all, marriage appears either as a contingent situation or a choice to be made. Thus, in terms of roles, marriage appears in no way necessary and does not follow directly from one's human nature or one's existence as an individual. It is something one might end up living in, which then adds the role of "wife" or "husband" to the preexisting roles of a rational human being and an individual person. However, whether marriage is a result of a free choice or one is married off, in both cases, it importantly influences the immediate conditions of daily life. It brings certain people, most obviously one's spouse and children, inside of the sphere of one's everyday concerns.

From the perspective of Stoic ethics, one could argue that the choice of whether or not to marry is, in the end, ethically indifferent. It is not in any necessary relation to happiness. One can be happy and unhappy both inside and outside of marriage, and in both cases, happiness is finally an internal matter, and I claim that also Hierocles, Antipater, and Musonius would accept this. However, as noted, in the Stoic view of indifferent things, some things have more selective value than others and can be rationally preferred. One could, therefore, read Hierocles, Antipater, and Musonius as defending the position that marriage is a preferable choice that has a high selective value (in the same way as, say, taking care of one's health), because it is in harmony with the sociable part of human nature. In this way, it falls within the Stoic category of *kathêkonta*, acts that are naturally appropriate for a human being.[12] Thus, the views endorsing marriage are not necessarily in contrast with the ideal of *autonomia*.

The idea of marriage as a role is also compatible with the advices Epictetus gives the young would-be Cynic. He underscores the idea that getting married changes the conditions under which one exercises virtue in one's daily life. In another passage, Epictetus expresses a similar attitude by ordering a father to go home and take care of his sick daughter (*Disc.* I.xi.). Also, this story highlights the importance of moral deliberation and exercise of virtues. Although marriage in itself remains indifferent, from the point of view of virtue, it is highly significant how one treats one's spouse, whether or not one takes care of one's sick child, or whether or not one sends one's children to the schoolteacher with their little notebooks (to use Epictetus' own examples).

Thus, it seems plausible to suggest that one of the main reasons why the Stoics give so much attention to marriage and family is that the people of the household commonly represent a significant part of a person's everyday life, and, thus, it is of crucial importance in terms of being a well-functioning ethical agent how one fulfills one's duties as husband or wife. The Stoic ideal is, as indicated above, not to escape from the everyday sphere of life, but on the contrary to strive for happiness by staying where one is. In this respect, the Stoics also differ radically from their opponents in the Epicurean school, in which the ideal of a philosophical life is depicted as a community of like-minded people following their philosophical doctrines in a disciplined fashion and not having too much connection with the outside world.[13] In Stoicism, the ideal of being *autonomos* does not mean leading a life of a hermit: one can both be self-sufficient in terms of happiness and establish intimate human bonds, as this follows from one's sociable nature.

Sociability also explains the why the later Stoic marriage pamphlets attach so much significance to having children: through reproduction, a person contributes to the continuation of the community and the whole of humankind. This view is supported also by the above-discussed

---

[12] Stobaeus defines marriage as "an intermediate appropriate act," comparable to "serving as an ambassador" or "discussing matters (*dialegesthai*)" (Stob.7.8; SVF 3.494).

[13] Cf. DL: X; Nussbaum 1994: 102–139.

metaphysical notion of reproduction as one of the rational soul functions, even though the later Stoics do not use this exact argument. However, it is interesting to note the difference between Plato and the Stoics on this point: the Stoics do not consider the choice to procreate a lower level or less philosophical choice than a life dedicated to the love of wisdom, nor do they refer to it as irrelevant for one's highest capacities and goals as a human being. In short, the Stoics make no juxtaposition between "begetting and giving birth to" real versus eternal children, i.e., philosophical ideas.[14]

13.5 Should the Wife Stay by Her Loom? Gender and the Division of Labor

Even if "husband" and "wife" are only understood as roles in which one lives and that only show one aspect of the person, as I have suggested, in the Ancient society, these roles were drastically different for a woman and for a man. This difference is evident also in the Stoic texts. Furthermore, we already saw continuums of the art of economics, *oikonomikê*, in the Roman Stoic texts on marriage. The Stoic corpus does not include as extensive a discussion on this topic as Xenophon's or the Aristotelian corpuses do, but Hierocles dedicated his treatise "Household Management" (*Ek tou Oikonomikou*) on this topic. This context particularly highlights differences between the roles of the spouses, rather than fundamental similarities between the genders.

In this treatise, Hierocles makes the following statement about the division of labor: "(T)o the husband are referred tasks concerning fields, marketplaces, and city business, whereas to the wife are referred those relating to spinning of wool, bread-making, and, in general, domestic tasks." (Stob. *Anth.* 4.85.21, 3:150, 6 ff.). As in the context *oikonomikê*, here, too, the gendered division of labor corresponds to binary opposition between *oikos* and *polis*, or private and public, illustrated through the images of "inside" and "outside" duties. However, immediately after the above statement, Hierocles goes on to argue that these

---

[14]Cf. My discussion on Plato's *Symposium* in Sect. 2.1. The Stoic stance differs significantly also from Plato's *Republic* where reproduction is solely discussed from the point of view of what benefits the whole society, and the decisions concerning it are left outside of the individual's own deliberation.

tasks de facto often get mixed up, the wife mastering the household, or the husband taking on traditionally female duties. He claims that this changing of roles is beneficial because it enriches the communality (*koinônias*) between the spouses. He is aware, however, that the idea of blurring traditional gender roles might sound controversial and mentions that some might object the idea that the husband could take over tasks such as weaving. He gives the following account of common prejudices—and argues against them:

> For since for the most part shabby little manikins (*euteleis anthrôpiskoi*) and a tribe of weak and womanish types (*kateagotôn kai gynnidôn phylon*) rush headlong into wool-working in their zeal for femininity (*zêlô thêlytêtos*), stooping to these things does not seem to be in line with a true man (*alêthinoterôn andra*). Thus I myself would not advise any men who did not exhibit complete confidence in their own manliness (*arrenotêtos*) and self-control (*sôfrosynê*) to touch such a thing. If, however, through a life of this kind he should have rendered himself free of every absurd suspicion (*hyponoia atopos*), what will prevent a husband from sharing in these things with his wife? (Stob. *Anth*. 4.85.21, 3:150, 6–152, 3; in Ramelli & Kostan 2009, David Kostan's translation slightly modified)

Thus, here lies the problem as Hierocles identifies it: men generally have "absurd suspicions" about gender roles in the household, and they are afraid of appearing effeminate, as opposed to "true men." However, views on "true manliness" form the backdrop for the argument. Again, the figure of a *kinaidos* is lurking in the background, again the Stoic philosopher is warning about "physical signs of gender" such as textiles that might turn souls toward effeminate vanity. However, Hierocles claims, if a man had confidence in his masculinity, he would not feel ashamed even by the loom: he would know that weaving did not destroy his manliness, and that a man could have rational grounds for sharing in his wife's duties. Maybe he might even accept Plato's statement from the *Republic* that once people got used to the sight of traditional gender roles getting mixed, this would gradually becomes acceptable in the public opinion.

An aura of manliness unquestionably surrounds Stoicism. We have encountered this aura already in different contexts, and it is clearly present also in Hierocles' description. What is remarkable from a gender perspective, however, is that he does not claim that the different duties of men and women are absolute or definite. Admittedly, he does not quite encourage going against the traditional roles as radically as Hipparchia did when she stated that she would rather philosophize with her husband than stay by the loom, or the Cyrenaic Aristippus when he dressed in female clothes.[15] Hierocles admits, however, that there is something artificial about definite gender roles—and even about the traditional conception of masculinity. This idea gives further support to my above claim that, despite "the aura of manliness" of the Stoic ideal, it also questions certain traits of manliness that were endorsed at the time. After all, Stoic manliness is purely attributable to inner qualities such as self-control that can be achieved both by men and women.

The "absurd suspicions" against men sharing the women's place by the loom occurs also in Musonius' defense of equal education. As I noted above, Musonius anticipates that his imagined opponent would be shocked about the suggestion that men learnt to spin, or women started to do gymnastics with the men. In words echoing the "weakness argument" from Plato's *Republic*, Musonius states that since males are naturally the stronger gender and women the weaker one, their duties should be assigned accordingly. His answer agrees with the tradition of *oikonomikê* in suggesting that the traditional division of labor between "outdoor" and "indoor" duties corresponds with the physical capacities of men and women. In contrast to Plato, Musonius also counts physical exercise as better suited for men.[16] However, Musonius leaves room for individual variation and presents the different gender roles as conditional, not definite. He admits that sometimes when the circumstances so warrant, a man could take up the lighter tasks and the female the physically more demanding ones (Lecture 4:5 in King: 2011, transl. King; Stob. 2.31.123).

Musonius, thus, defends the separate spheres of life and division of labor by appealing to what he considers to be natural, physical differences, even if he admits that there can be exceptions to the general rule. But how plausible is this argument in the end, even within the context

---

[15] Cf. Sextus *PH* I: 155, DL VI: 97.

[16] One could object that the general physical weakness of women is attributable not only to natural capacities but also to their way of life and lack of exercise, and this is why engaging in physical exercise would make women less inferior to men in this respect. This problem is similar to the connection between coldness and idleness in Galen (are women cold because they lead idle lives? Or do they lead idle lives because this follows from their natural coldness? Cf. Sect. 2.3).

in which it was originally presented? As I have shown, in Ancient texts such as Xenophon, Aristotle, and Hierocles, "outdoor labor" refers not only to physical labor in the fields but also to public and political life. This latter aspect is obviously not related to physical power or body size—the Ancient societies did not prevent small-sized or physically weak men from engaging in political activity; it was gender, not physical size or strength, that was decisive for receiving the status of a citizen. Furthermore, Musonius argues that there are no natural differences in the rational capacities of men and women. This premise would clearly support the idea that political and public duties belong to both since, after all, these are linked much more to rational than to physical capacities. This is exactly what Plato states in *Republic*. However, Musonius gives no hint of this. Even though he argues for equal education, this does not imply equality in political roles.

However, it should be noted that Musonius' proposal is perfectly in line with the Stoic idea that true education aims only at happiness and has no other purpose—philosophical education is not intended, e.g., to facilitate functioning in public roles (cf. Chap. 8, where I contrasted the Stoics with Plato and Aristotle on this point). Thus, Musonius could consistently maintain that girls should be educated and that women should philosophize, on the one hand, and, on the other hand, fail to propose any political reorganization of the respective social roles of men and women. The Stoics would probably answer my critical comments by pointing out that a sage could be completely happy both on the agora and by the loom. Why should the social order be changed when the only change that really matters for happiness is an internal one?

My reading agrees here with Martha Nussbaum who argues that Musonius' position fails to fulfill the true requirements of gender equality. One major reason for this is that it does not resolve the problem of the separation between the female and male spheres of life. Nussbaum's reading shows how Musonius never seriously questions male authority over women in either public or private life, and he does not extend his argument to require complete symmetry in relations between man and woman. Nussbaum further criticizes Musonius for not discussing laws or institutions in his treatises, and for not suggesting that they should be changed even if they discriminate against women (Nussbaum 2002: 300–313).

Nussbaum's remarks point to a grave problem not only in Musonius but in Stoicism on the whole. Indeed, there is a strong reactionary tendency particularly in later Stoicism to discourage any social reforms.

Although Hierocles acknowledged that roles inside the *oikos* could be changed, in his treatise "How should One Behave toward One's Country?" (*Ek tou pôs patridi khrêsteon*), he exhorts his readers to respect the existing laws and customs (*ethê*). He explicitly rejects the idea of new laws and customs being introduced in the city. It seems unlikely that this conservative standpoint would allow him to approve of any reorganization of traditional institutions such as marriage, gender roles, or citizenship that was reserved only for men (Stob. *Anth.* 3.39.36; 3.733, 7). It is noteworthy that even when Hierocles encourages the mixing of traditional roles, and Musonius admits that this can sometimes be justified, their examples stem from the *oikos*, not from the *polis*. They speculate on the idea of the husband doing the spinning—but what about the idea of women taking on political duties? The Stoic thinkers fail to mention this possibility.

Even though the Stoics recognize all human beings as metaphysically equal, they do not formulate any arguments against any existing inequalities or institutionalized form of oppression. Most strikingly, this problem occurs in the context of slavery. For example, Hierocles argues that one should treat one's slave well and consider how one would want to be treated if one was a slave.[17] Obviously, treating slaves humanely does not do away with slavery—and it is precisely the existence of the institution itself that is the main ethical problem here. Rather than wanting to be treated humanely as a slave, one would not want to be a slave in the first place. The case of slavery illustrates clearly that for a philosophy to favor equality and freedom in the full senses of the terms, they must also be recognized as political and not only internal or personal issues.

It is for this reason that I think Reydams-Schils is too optimistic in her assessment of Musonius as a thinker who promoted gender equality. She writes:

> As a thought experiment, we could ask what would become of Musonius' injunctions in a cultural setting in which physical strength does not matter so much anymore. In such a context his views would allow for a very far-reaching gender equality. (Reydams-Schils 2005: 155–156)

I would be cautious about making any such conclusions since we should bear in mind that Musonius did not promote any ideas that would, at least as far as legislation is concerned, change any "cultural settings." How, then,

---

[17] Cf. Hierocles' treatise on siblings, Stob. *Anth.* 4.84.20; for similar arguments on slavery cf. Seneca, *Letter 47*.

could there ever be a culture in which physical strength no longer mattered? Moreover, as I have pointed out, in terms of being engaged in politics on the agora, physical size was not decisive even in Ancient times. Thus, for this reason, I read Musonius as a less radical thinker than Reydams-Schils, even though I agree that he presented powerful arguments in defense of equal educability of boys and girls, and women's inherent rational capacities.

However, the Stoic views on marriage and family life have still other significant consequences in their philosophy, and I show in the following chapter how, in the end, the ethical significance of the family lies in its function as the starting point of ethical development that ends up taking into account the whole humankind. Even if the Stoic arguments would not do much to change inequalities in the real, existing *polis*, when the discussion is taken to the level of *kosmopolis*, the Stoics formulate some of their most powerful arguments for unconditional, cosmic equality between all humans.

Appendix

Antipater of Tarsus

> *On Marriage.* In: SVF 3.254.23–257.10.

Aristotle

> EN   *Nicomachean Ethics*
> *The Complete Works of Aristotle.* The Revised Oxford Translation. Jonathan Barnes (revised). Princeton, NJ: Princeton University Press, 1984.

Cicero, Marcus Tullius

> *De officiis.* M. Winterbottom (ed.). Oxford: Clarendon Press, 1994.

Diogenes Laertius, *Lives of Eminent Philosophers* (DL)

> *Diogenis Laertii Vitae philosophorum.* Miroslav Marcovich (ed.). *Bibliotheca scriptorum Graecorum et Romanorum Teubneriana.* Vol. 1. Stuttgart-Lipsia: Teubner, 1999–2002.
> *Lives of Eminent Philosophers.* R.D. Hicks (transl.). Cambridge and London: Harvard University Press, 1995.

Epictetus

> *Discourses (Disc.)*
> *Encheiridion (Ench.)*

Discourses and Selected Writings. Christopher Gill (ed.). Robin Hard (transl.). London: J.M. Dent & Vermont, Tuttle/Everyman, 1995.
Discourses, Books I–IV. W.A. Oldfather (transl.). Cambridge and London: Harvard University Press, 2000.

Hierocles

Éthikê stoikheiôsis	*(Elements of Ethics)*
Éthikê stoikheiôsis	*(Elements of Ethics)*
Ek tou Oikonomikou	*(Household Management)*
Ek tou pôs patridi khrêsteon	*(How Should One Behave toward One's Country?)*
Ek tou pôs syngenesi khrêsteon	*(How Should One Behave toward One's Relatives?)*
Peri gamou	*(On Marriage)*

Corpus dei papiri filosofici greci e latini. Vol. 1 and 4. Guido Bastiani and Anthony Long (eds.). Firenze: Olschcki, 1992. (CPF)
Etische Elementarlehre (Papyrus 9780): Nebst den bei Stobaios erhaltenen etischen Exzerpten aus Hierokles. Hans Friedrich August von Arnim (ed.). Berlin: Berliner Klassikertexte 4, Weidmann, 1906.
Hierocles the Stoic, Elements of Ethics, Fragments and Excerpts. Ilaria Ramelli (ed.). David Konstan (transl.). Leiden and Boston: Brill, 2009.

Musonius Rufus

Musonii Rufi Reliquiae. O. Hense (ed.). Leipzig: Kessinger, 1905.
Musonius Rufus: Lectures & Sayings. William B. Irvine (ed.). Cynthia King (transl.). CreateSpace, 2011.

Plato

| *Rep.* | *Republic* |
| *Symp.* | *Symposium* |

Platonis Opera (Oxford Classical Texts):
Vol. 1, ed. E.A. Duke et al. 1995.
Vol. 2, ed. J. Burnet 1922.
Vol. 3, ed. J. Burnet 1922.
Vol. 4, ed. J. Burnet 1922.
Respublica, ed. S.R. Slings 2003.

Complete Works. John M. Cooper (ed.). D.S. Hutchinson (associate ed.). Indianapolis: Hackett Publishers, 1997.
Plato in Twelve Volumes. Vol. 5–6, The Republic. Paul Shorey (transl.). London: Heinemann, 1969.
The Symposium. Christopher Gill (transl.). London and New York: Penguin Books, 1999.

Seneca, Lucius Annaeus

Ad Marciam
Epistulae

Opera Philosophica. Louis Delatte (ed.). Olm, Hildesheim, 1981.
Moral Essays. Vol. I. John W. Basore (transl.). Cambridge and London: Harvard University Press, 1928.
Moral Essays. Vol. 2. John W. Basore (transl.). Cambridge and London: Harvard University Press, 1932.
Epistles. Vol. I–VI. Richard M. Gummere (transl.). Cambridge and London: Harvard University Press, 1917–1925.
Selected Philosophical Letters. Brad Inwood (transl.). Oxford: Oxford University Press, 2007.

Sextus Empeiricus

PH I-III Outlines of Pyrrhonism

Sexti Empirici Opera. H. Mutschmann and J. Mau (eds.). In: *Bibliotheca scriptorum Graecorum et Romanorum.* Lipsiae: Teubner, 1962.
Sextus Empiricus, *Outlines of Scepticism.* Julia Annas and Jonathan Barnes (eds.). Cambridge: Cambridge University Press, 1994.

Simplicius

Commentary on Epictetus' Encheiridion
Commentarius in Epicteti enchiridion, Theophrasti characteres. F. Dübner (ed.). Paris: Didot, 1842.
On Epictetus' Handbook 1–26. Tad Brennan and Charles Brittain (transl.). London: Duckworth, 2002.

Stobaeus

Anth. Anthology

Anthologium, Ioannis Stobaeus. Otto Hense and Curtius Wachsmuth (eds.). Weidman: Berolini, 1884–1909.

Arius Didymus: Epitome of Stoic Ethics. Arthur J. Pomeroy (ed. and transl.). Atlanta, GA: Scholars Press, 1999.

Stoicorum veterum fragmenta. Vol. I–III. H. von Arnim (ed.). Leipzig: Lipsiae, in aedibus B.G. Teubneri, 1903–1924. (SVF)

Xenophon

Oec.   *Oeconomicus*

Oeconomicus—A Social and Historical Commentary. Sarah B. Pomeroy (transl.). Oxford: Clarendon University Press, 1994.

References

Asmis, Elizabeth. 1996. The Stoics on Women. In *Feminism and Ancient Philosophy*, ed. Julie K. Ward. New York: Routledge.

Deming, Will. 2004. *Paul on Marriage and Celibacy. Society for New Testament Studies*, Monograph Series, 83. Cambridge: Cambridge University Press.

Grahn, Malin. 2014. Free Philosophers and Tragic Women—Stoic Perspectives on Suicide. In *Culture, Suicide, and the Human Condition*, ed. Marja-Liisa Honkasalo, and Miira Tuominen, 105–128. New York: Berghahn Books.

Long, A.A. 2001. Ancient Philosophy's Hardest Question: What to Make of Oneself? In *Representations* 74. Berkeley, Los Angeles, and London: The University of California Press.

Nussbaum, Martha. 1994. *The Therapy of Desire: Theory and Practice in Hellenistic Ethics*. Princeton: Princeton University Press.

Nussbaum, Martha. 2001/1986. *Fragility of Goodness*. Cambridge: Cambridge University Press.

Nussbaum, Martha. 2002. The Incomplete Feminism of Musonius Rufus. In *The Sleep of Reason - Erotic Experience and Sexual Ethics in Ancient Greek and Rome*, ed. Martha Nussbaum and Juha Sihvola, 283–326. Chicago and London: The University of Chicago Press.

Patterson, Christina. 1991. Marriage and the Married Woman in Athenian Law. In *Women's History & Ancient History*, ed. Sarah B. Pomeroy. Capel Hill and London: The University of North Carolina Press.

Reydams-Schils, Gretchen. 2005. *The Roman Stoic—Self, Responsibility, and Affection*. Chicago and London: The University of Chicago Press.

Schofield, Malcolm. 1991. *The Stoic Idea of the City*. Cambridge: Cambridge University Press.

CHAPTER 14

Gender and Stoic Cosmopolitanism

If it is true that Diogenes the Cynic called himself *kosmopolitēs*, then cosmopolitanism was already part of Cynic philosophy. The juxtaposition between citizenship of a particular state and citizenship of the entire cosmos became prominent in early Stoicism. The most famous argument for Stoic cosmopolitan ethics stems from Hierocles who illustrates the idea through the image of concentric circles. Even though cosmopolitanism is arguably one of the most well-known innovations in Stoic philosophy, it has attracted surprisingly little attention from the perspective of gender. In this chapter, I will show that the cosmopolitan theory offers particularly strong arguments in favor of equality between all humans, as both ethical agents and objects of moral action. From a feminist point of view, another interesting aspect of cosmopolitanism is the value placed on the "inner circles," in other words, our most immediate spheres of life. The Stoic ideal of cosmopolitanism would extend the focus of ethics from one's own *oikos* to cover the whole of humanity. Marcus Aurelius expresses this powerfully in comparing the entire cosmos to a great city in which existing states (*poleis*) are like households (*oikiai*) (*Meditations* III: 11).

As indicated earlier in this study, the traditional prioritization of the public sphere of life over the private sphere has been a common criticism among feminist readers of the history of philosophy (e.g., Lloyd 2002; Homiak 2002). I will show that this feminist criticism does not hit the mark as far as Stoicism is concerned precisely because the Stoic ethics accentuates the ethical importance of how one behaves not only in public but also within the walls of one's own home. Finally, the significance of family life is alluded to in the Stoic idea that intimate human bonds provide the ethical model that finally leads to cosmopolitanism: the realization of universal humanity. Yet, my aim is not to present the Stoic position as feminist as such, and one should not forget the criticism I presented in the previous chapter, that the gravest problem with the Stoic stance is that it fails to make equality a political issue.

14.1 A Spouse, a Human, a Citizen of the Cosmos— The Stoic Theory of Extending Circles

Hierocles' view of "extending circles" is one of the most influential and well-known sources to Stoic cosmopolitanism. The argument goes like this. Hierocles proposes that each person is "circumscribed as though by many circles, some smaller, some larger, some surrounding others, some surrounded, according to their different and unequal relations to one another." The person herself, her body and mind, equals the innermost circle that "all but touches its own center." One's immediate family (parents, siblings, spouse, and children) constitutes the second circle, after which the next one is formed by other family members (cousins, uncles, aunts, grandparents, grandchildren, etc.), whereas the next circle after this encompasses all the rest of the relatives. As the circles extend, more and more people are included: the people of one's deme, then the ones of one's tribe, then the fellow citizens of one's country, and so on. Finally, the uttermost circle that surrounds all the other ones consists of the entire human kind (Hierocles, *How Should One Behave toward One's Relatives?*; Stob. *Anth.* 4.84.23, transl. David Konstan).

This eloquent argument invites us to imagine how we, and all the people in our immediate surroundings, are connected with the rest of human population. The argument points to our fundamental affiliation even with people who live furthest away from our own sphere of life. The argument proposes an ethical model that is based on the idea that exactly our closest human relations serve as the point of departure for our recognition of the humanity of the people in the most remote circles. Hierocles suggests that, on the basis of his reason, he can infer that also everybody else is a person just like himself: it is true for each person to be the center of all of these extending circles, and to be included in the circles of other people. As mentioned previously, in the ideal community of sages, the inner circles would, in a way, disappear, given that the traditional family does not exist and the sage loves all children equally. Hierocles' account of different circles seems to require a similar movement such that the scope of one's ethical concern extends to cover humanity in its entirety.[1]

Hierocles model starts from the closest circle and moves on to draw the remaining circles in so that we bring the remotest people closer to our sphere of ethical concern. Interestingly, when Cicero draws a connection between close family members and cosmopolitan ethics in *De Officiis*, he proceeds the other way around and starts on the outmost circle. He first draws attention to the "fellowship and society that Nature has established among men," and the natural bond that exists between all the members of the human race by virtue of their rationality. He also connects the human rational capacities to educability and language skills. He then starts to narrow his scope down, paying attention to the relationship people have as citizens of the same city-state, and then to the even more intimate bonds of the family. Cicero concludes:

> Starting with that infinite bond of union of the human race in general, the conception is now confined to a small and narrow circle. For since the reproductive instinct is by Nature's gift the common possession of all living creatures, the first bond of union is that between husband and wife; the next, that between parents and children; then we find one home, with everything in common. (Cicero *De Officiis* I.50–54, transl. Miller)

---

[1] Hierocles' account is not unproblematic, however. For a critical analysis of his demand for impartiality, see Julia Annas (1993: 267–276). Hierocles' argument of extending circles is often quoted in Stoic scholarship. However, the passage continues, but with the exception of Annas (1993), the latter part has attracted much less attention. The second part of the argument discusses how different family members should be treated. This account seems to be, in many ways, incompatible with the argument of the extending circles because here Hierocles calls for different, not same treatment: he proposes, for example, that one should show more love for one's mother and the relatives on her side, and more honor with respect to one's father and the relatives on his side. However, the two views, that all people are circumscribed in extending circles, and that there should be different treatment for different relatives, do not seem consistent and they seem to have been placed after each other somewhat randomly. Indeed, neither of these arguments depends on the other, and one could perfectly well deny the latter but still support the former. For this reason, I also limit my discussion of the second passage to this footnote (Hierocles, *How Should One Behave toward One's Relatives?*; Stob. *Anth.* 4.84.23, transl. David Konstan).

Like Hierocles, Cicero uses the idea of circles of nearer and more remote human relations to illustrate the profound community of all humans. However, contrary to Hierocles, he starts from the cosmopolitan perspective and proceeds to defend the naturalness of marriage and family. In this way, Cicero's argument combines the Stoic arguments for family and procreation with the idea of universal cosmopolitanism.

Similarly, also Marcus Aurelius takes the view of universal human rationality as his point of departure for his cosmological argument.

> If understanding (*noeron*) is common to us all (*hêmin koinon*), then so is also reason (*logos*) which makes us rational (*logikoi*). If this is common, then also that reason is common which tells us what to do or not to do. If so, also law is common. If so, we are citizens (*politai*). If so, we are fellow-members (*politeumatos*) of an organized community. If so, the universe is as it were a state (*kosmos ôsanei polis esti*) – for of what other single polity can the whole race of mankind (*to tôn anthrôpôn pan genos*) be said to be fellow-members (*politeumatos*)? (*Meditations* IV: 5, Haines' translation modified)

Marcus refers to the commonness of humankind in its entirety which forms, as it were, a universal community in which all are "fellow-members." He, thus, puts a strong emphasis on the idea of a shared humanity, despite ethnic, gender, or individual differences. Also, the significance of a particular household or a particular state diminishes when one considers the entire cosmos as one community, and all humans as citizens of it.

However, this account (as also Hierocles') leaves one problem open, namely: if all humans have the same value, on which grounds should one take care of one's own children and spouse rather than somebody else's? Cicero's account offers an answer to this since his way of formulating the cosmopolitan ideal shows that we can both consider people to be, metaphysically speaking, equally rational and valuable, but admit that social roles such as husband or father carry specific duties involving particular persons—one's wife and children.[2] This idea is also inbuilt in the above-discussed notion of different "roles" or *personae* (Cf. Chap. 13).

---

[2] This would also be in line with Epictetus' idea quoted above according to which, as I read it, it is not a case that one man would belong to one woman. But even if we consider monogamy a practical arrangement (rather than, say, a law of nature), one should still be true to one's own spouse, just as one does not grab another man's pork at the dinner party (*Discourses*, II.iv.8–11, 235–7; cf. Chap. 12).

14.2 The Importance of the Inner Circle

I am now in a position to argue that Stoic cosmopolitanism carries the following implications for gender equality: first, women and men are equal as citizens of the cosmos, and as such have the same ethical value; and second, following from the idea of essential human rationality, women and men are also equal as ethical agents, which involves exercise of moral deliberation and choice. The Stoics do not explicitly draw these implications, but they follow naturally from their premises. Women, qua humans, are necessarily rational, and as such, they are focal points of all the extending circles described by Hierocles and Cicero. A woman's mind and body form an innermost circle that "all but touches its center" and which is further connected to other people who are, from her perspective, situated in closer and more remote circles. As a wife, mother, daughter, sister, cousin, aunt, and so on, a woman, too, takes her place within all these human relations, and it is also her duty to "draw in" the circles from the remotest to the closest. In terms of roles or *personas*, it is her duty to perform her different contingent roles well, and to assume the responsibilities that go with them—while still not limiting her ethical scope to the *oikos* in which she lives and remembering that each particular *oikos* is but a small part of the entire cosmos, which in itself is like a great city.

I note above that feminist readers of the history of philosophy have criticized Ancient thinkers and their evaluation of the public over the private, reason over emotion, justice over care, and generally the traditional male sphere of life over the traditional female sphere of life.[3] I have argued that this criticism should be considered critically in its own right: as feminist thinkers, we should be alert to accepting generalizations such as "women are naturally more prone to care and men to rationality"— which should be the object of feminist analysis, not the point of departure. Other feminist thinkers such as Martha Nussbaum and Susan Moller Okin point to the fact that even if political equality is a central goal of feminism, it is not enough if equality does not extend into the homes

---

[3] This is a paraphrase of Marcia L. Homiak's criticism, directed particularly at Aristotle, but given that she counts Kant and Hobbes as continuing the same tradition, she would probably also include the Stoics in this package; (2002): 80–81; cf. Lloyd (2002: 1–25).

and private partnerships of men and women.[4] As I have now shown, the Stoics consider the most intimate human bonds and everyday life of crucial importance for ethical development, which in the ideal case leads to cosmopolitanism.

Furthermore, Stoic ethics pays close attention to virtuous behavior within the home, and many of their examples of ethically relevant situations stem from the intimate spheres of life. The Stoics frequently criticize people who hold different moral standards in their public and in their private lives. Marcus Aurelius states that good people live virtuously "at home and outside their homes, night and day" (*Meditations* III: 4).[5] Likewise, Musonius criticizes the husband who puts his own concerns ahead of those of his wife, and who lives in the same household but concentrates on matters outside of it, unwilling to work together or to agree with his wife.[6] Cicero emphasizes that there is no phase or sphere of life that would not require morality: morally right and wrong is equally at stake in both public and private life, in one's business and at home (Cicero, *De Officiis*, I.4.2). Also, Seneca refers to the crucial task of philosophy to do away with the double standards of morality. As an example of different personality types with their respective vices, he mentions a man who is gentle in public but a brute in his own house (*De Ira* III: 10). He emphasizes that the road to virtuous action is the same both in public and in private, and that those aspiring to live well should pay attention to how they behave in the most intimate sphere of life (cf. e.g. *De Ira* III.7; III.28).

---

[4]For example, it is one of the main arguments in Susan Moller Okin's work *Justice, Gender, and the Family* that the family has not traditionally been seen as politically or even ethically important, that not even theories of justice have taken into account its importance, and that family as a social institution is significantly gendered. The sphere of the home, she claims, is typically considered unimportant and uninteresting. Okin herself, in contrast, stresses the importance of the family in any relevant theory of justice, first, because one cannot talk about an equal society if wives are not equal to their husbands inside marriage, and second, because the family is an essential environment in which children learn about justice (1989: 6–24). There is a similar focus on the family in Martha Nussbaum's well-established feminist work *Women and Human Development*. She analyzes several particular problems women have traditionally faced, and still face, when family life is left outside of ethical and political concerns, such as domestic violence (2000: 1–33).

[5]Cf. Plato's story of the ring of Gyge, the point of which is to illustrate the temptation of doing whatever one pleases if one could do so protected by a ring that makes one invisible and thus without running the risk of being caught (*Rep.* 359b–360d).

[6]See Musonius' lecture "What is the chief end of marriage?" (in King 2011: 57).

Seneca ridicules people who complain about the loss of liberty in the republic after having destroyed it in their own homes (*De Ira* III: 35).[7]

Thus, Stoic philosophy underscores the fact that the privacy of one's own home is not an ethical no-man's-land. Even if one can ignore public opinion and sometimes even existing laws there, the universal law of nature is just as binding when nobody is watching. The Cynic approach to virtue was to make the private public—their way of life was based on the idea that people do not need the privacy of a house or even of a bedroom in order to live virtuously and in accordance with nature. The Stoics would not have abolished traditional institutions such as households, but maintained that one should not use the privacy of the home or the bedroom to escape from the demands of reason.

The Stoic philosophy can, thus, hardly be criticized for overlooking the importance of the private sphere of life. There does not seem to be a juxtaposition between care and justice either: a father's care of his sick daughter is given as a case of virtue, and justice is obviously not only a political concept but also one of the most important virtues in Ancient ethics. The Stoics both theorize about virtue and discuss in detail practical ethical issues such as taking care of one's children and one's family responsibilities. There is a focus on both the universal and the particular, on ideals and everyday realism.

As noted, family and home life play a crucial role in Stoic arguments that place the family at the focal point of ethical development, which in turn stems from the notion of cosmopolitanism. It seems that according to Hierocles, it would be rather unlikely that cosmopolitan ethics could start from an ethical concern for somebody one has never even met. However, through reflection on the value one puts on one's own spouse and children, one can infer that other human beings are ethically equally important, since also they are somebody's children, siblings, spouses, and so on. This recognition is what I take to be the core of Stoic cosmopolitanism— and family relations gave the Stoics the model of how to extend the sphere of ethically relevant persons so as to encompass the whole of humanity. From the perspective of Stoic metaphysics, human kind is one great family: the children of Zeus all have the seed of universal rationality in them. As such, all humans are alike, akin, and each other's equals.

---

[7] According to Martha Nussbaum, the focus on the private sphere in Seneca's *De Ira* has important consequences for public action: "In a world in which emperors mutilate their enemies for fun, looking into oneself is an act of public courage, and of humanity." (1994: 426).

Appendix

Aurelius, Marcus

Tôn Eis Heauton
Marcus Antonius Imperator Ad Se Ipsum. Jan Hendrik Leopold (ed.). Leipzig: B. G. Teubneri, 1908.

Cicero, Marcus Tullius

De officiis. M. Winterbottom (ed.). Oxford: Clarendon Press, 1994.

Epictetus

Discourses (Disc.)

Discourses and Selected Writings. Christopher Gill (ed.). Robin Hard (transl.). London: J.M. Dent & Vermont, Tuttle/Everyman, 1995.
Discourses, Books I–IV. W.A. Oldfather (transl.). Cambridge and London: Harvard University Press, 2000.

Hierocles

Éthikê stoikheiôsis	*(Elements of Ethics)*
Ek tou pôs patridi khrêsteon	*(How Should One Behave toward One's Country?)*
Ek tou pôs syngenesi khrêsteon	*(How Should One Behave toward One's Relatives?)*

Corpus dei papiri filosofici greci e latini. Vol. 1 and 4. Guido Bastiani and Anthony Long (eds.). Firenze: Olschcki, 1992. (CPF)
Etische Elementarlehre (Papyrus 9780): Nebst den bei Stobaios erhaltenen etischen Exzerpten aus Hierokles. Hans Friedrich August von Arnim (ed.). Berlin: Berliner Klassikertexte 4, Weidmann, 1906.
Hierocles the Stoic, Elements of Ethics, Fragments and Excerpts. Ilaria Ramelli (ed.). David Konstan (transl.). Leiden and Boston: Brill, 2009.

Plato

Rep.   Republic

Plato in Twelve Volumes. Vol. 5–6, The Republic. Paul Shorey (transl.). London: Heinemann, 1969.

Seneca, Lucius Annaeus

De Ira (On Anger).

Opera Philosophica. Louis Delatte (ed.). Olm, Hildesheim, 1981.
Moral Essays. Vol. I. John W. Basore (transl.). Cambridge and London: Harvard University Press, 1928.

Stobaeus

Anth. Anthology

Anthologium, Ioannis Stobaeus. Otto Hense and Curtius Wachsmuth (eds.). Weidman: Berolini, 1884–1909.
Arius Didymus: Epitome of Stoic Ethics. Arthur J. Pomeroy (ed. and transl.). Atlanta, GA: Scholars Press, 1999.

REFERENCES

Annas, Julia. 1993. *The Morality of Happiness*. Oxford: Oxford University Press.
Homiak, Marcia L. 2002. Feminism and Aristotle's Rational Ideal. In *Feminism and History of Philosophy*, ed. Genevieve Lloyd, 80–102. Oxford: Oxford University Press.
Lloyd, Genevieve. 2002. LeDoeuff and History of Philosophy. In *Feminism and History of Philosophy*, ed. Genevieve Lloyd, 27–39. Oxford: Oxford University Press.
Moller Okin, Susan. 1989. *Justice, Gender, and the Family*. BasicBooks.
Nussbaum, Martha. 1994. *The Therapy of Desire: Theory and Practice in Hellenistic Ethics*. Princeton: Princeton University Press.
Nussbaum, Martha. 2000. *Women and Human Development—Capabilities Approach*. Cambridge: Cambridge University Press.

CHAPTER 15

Conclusion

This book has scrutinized Stoic philosophers' views on gender and sexuality through three different fields of investigation, which I named *Body*, *Character*, and *Community*.

Part I explored Stoic views on gender and sexuality in the sphere of human (and animal) bodies. A discussion on Plato, Aristotle, and Galen formed a backdrop for my analysis of the Stoic theories. The scope of my investigation was broad, encompassing myths, biology, medicine, metaphysics, physics, and cosmetics, and finally the Ancient discipline of physiognomy. Indeed, I found this broad scope necessary to build a comprehensive view of the subject.

My analysis has highlighted the originality of the Stoic position on gender and sexuality in relation to their predecessors' views. I showed that Stoic philosophy abandoned the idea of a natural and definite hierarchy between the two genders, in contrast to, for example, Aristotle's biology and certain philosophical myths that present the male (or men) as naturally superior to the female (or women). I also claimed that the "biological myths" in Stoic cosmology should be understood as analogies that aim at explaining the creation of the cosmos, not as suggesting that the cosmos had a sexual origin as such, or that the Stoics understood the active and passive metaphysical principles in gendered terms.

My reading of the roles of gender and sexuality in Stoic metaphysics underscored the inclusion of sexuality among basic human rational functions, and the difference between the Stoic, Platonic, and Aristotelian positions. Stoicism does not place sexuality on a "lower" level of the soul (the Stoics did not divide the soul into parts), or consider sexuality as less rational than other soul functions. I also showed that sexuality is considered an indifferent thing (*adiaphoron*) in Stoicism: something that is ethically neutral. This claim went together with my other central argument according to which the Stoics considered gender to be one of our basic human qualities (belonging to the category of "the qualified," *poion*), alongside the four senses and the capacity of speech, all of which are intrinsically connected to the soul's commanding faculty (*hêgemonikon*). According to my reading of the Stoic categories, genderedness should be understood as a common quality (*koinos poion*) but whether we are men or women is a matter of individual characteristics (*idiôs poion*). Consequently, one's gender does not appear to be any more significant for the functioning of the rational reproductive capacity (identified in the sources with the notion of *sperma*) than eye-color is for the functioning of the rational capacity of seeing.

From the perspective of present-day debates where the binary opposition between two separate gender categories is highly contested both in science, feminist philosophy, and liberal politics, it is interesting to note that the Stoic model does not confine us to thinking about the male and the female as the only possible variations of gender. Basically, the Stoic model only assumes that on the physical level, each of us has some features that correspond to the reproductive capacity. I don't see any reason why the theory could not allow that there was much more variation in this than just two categories. Neither does the theory rest on the assumption that every individual was able to use her or his reproductive capacities, whatever the gender (similarly as a blind person might not be able to use the capacity of sight, which certainly would not make her or him appear as less rational in the Stoic theory). The Stoic metaphysics thus suggests a way of seeing gender as just one of the many variables in the unique fabric that constitutes an individual person.

The idea of metaphysical sameness between men and women indicates that the Stoics attached very little (or no) importance to gender, and that they had an utterly equal view of men and women and their capacities. However, I contrasted this egalitarian picture with another one found in all the numerous passages in which the Stoics discuss bodily beauty, beautification and looks—particularly beards. In this context, Epictetus, for example, states that men and women have different natures (*physis*) and that hairiness (but not fancy hair-styles) is in accordance with a men's nature. Here, masculine and feminine characteristics are discussed in binary opposition to each other, and they are not evaluated equally. The ideal for both men and women is to get rid of certain "womanish" characteristics such as vanity. However, in the context of Ancient physiognomy it appears that womanish characteristics are not necessarily connected to the female sex in the biological sense.

How, then, do these two pictures fit together? How does gender influence what and who we are as human beings? Addressing these questions moved us away from the sphere of the body, and towards that of character and education. In fact, I had already stepped onto the threshold between these two fields of research in that the specific discussion concerning men's and women's bodily looks is not only about bodies as material entities, but also about taking care of the body, attaching meanings to it and making choices about one's appearance. These topics were essential to my analysis of gendered signs, which are embedded not only in the physical world but also in the world of cultural meanings, habits, customs, and social expectations. In this world, we grow up to understand ourselves as gendered beings, and the educational practices of our society have a great impact on the things we learn and the aspects of ourselves we will develop.

Part II explored gender and sexuality within the social world with its educational practices, paying also particular attention to the praxis and goals of Stoic philosophy itself. In this part, I demonstrated that the Stoic philosophy provides a solid theoretical foundation for constructing an argument that all children are equally educable. It follows from the Stoic view of preconceptions as starting points of knowledge that all children have exactly the same potential to develop into fully rational and virtuous adults because they, according to the Stoics, are all born with the ability to perceive the world correctly.

Stoic discussions on childhood give strong support to the suggestion, explicitly made by Musonius Rufus, that not only boys but also girls should be educated, and that not only men but also women should practice philosophy. This position, as I have shown, is based on genuinely Stoic premises. Also Seneca points to the metaphysical indifference of gender in his consolation letter to Marcia, where he (like Musonius) indicates that many gendered characteristics are due to habituation, not nature. All in all, the Stoics pinpoint the origin of bad characteristics in the cultural environment in which people grow up, together with the traditional education that, according to them, was not able to produce wisdom and virtue. Consequently, the Stoics viewed also many gendered characteristics as being socially and culturally constructed. The Stoics pointed out, for example, that if women seemed to posses less courage or practical reasoning skills, this was due to lack of practice and difference in education, not to an intrinsic difference between the genders. Even if the Stoics sometimes alluded to the idea that certain characteristics may have a natural origin, e.g. due to our elemental constitution, the philosophical weight was on habituation and cultural influence. Further, I argued that the Stoic philosophical education and therapy would transform also certain aspects of the traditional conceptions of masculinity and femininity.

Thus, the Stoic notion of reason, if correctly understood, does not favor men over women, and rather works to include than to exclude women. The Stoic ideal of a sage is built exclusively on human rational capacities, and thus individual features such as gender that do not influence rationality are irrelevant for the ideal of wisdom. Seneca's characterization of a sage could easily fit both genders: a person who is able to make the best out of any circumstances in the same way as the artist molds the clay into the best possible artwork. Thus, the Stoic position can be seen as radical in its own time, since it implies that women had much greater potential than their contemporary society allowed. This potential, by virtue of which women could become sages exactly as men could, never comes to light when women are denied access to education and philosophy.

In contrast to the metaphysical discussion of reproduction as a rational human capacity, the Stoics approach sexuality from another angle in their ethics and philosophical practice. Whereas the Stoic metaphysical texts did not give any particularly detailed account of how exactly sexuality functions in relation to the rational human nature, in the context of ethics the Stoics expressly connect sexuality to rational activities such as choice, deliberation, virtue, and acceptance or rejection of impressions. My analysis of Stoic philosophical exercises of sexual impressions and abstinence underscored the idea that this type of philosophical practice ultimately aimed at building well-functioning and virtuous sexual agency. The Stoic notion of erotic friendship indicates that sexual relations could and would exist also among sages and that there was nothing ideal about not being sexually active as such. Rather, I argued that these exercises were introduced to empower our self-control, inner freedom and ability to act virtuously in all of our human relations, sexual relations included.

Part II highlighted the importance of social relations for ethical agency as well as the idea of social and cultural impact on character-formation. I also claimed that whereas both Plato's *Republic* and Aristotle linked education to a certain social standing and the goal of exercising political power, the Stoics, by contrast, did not have such political goals in their educational or therapeutic programs, which aimed at the individual's happiness for its own sake and did not support any radical changes in the existing social order. It became clear that a critical scrutiny of gender and sexuality has to take place also within the fields of social philosophy and politics.

In Part III, I scrutinized gender and sexuality in both the early Stoic social utopias and the more conformist political philosophy of the Roman Stoics, and showed that gender played a remarkable role in both streams of Stoic political thought. I suggested that the early Stoic utopias should be read as thought experiments of what the society would be like if everybody were sages. This thought experiment produces a vision of a society in which institutional marriage and traditional moral codes concerning sexuality are unnecessary—as are many other customs and institutions of the existing societies. For the Stoics, virtue is entirely an internal matter, and thus the society of sages does not need any particular structures for producing virtue or for regulating the behavior of people who are, by definition, perfectly rational and well-functioning ethical agents. I defended the position that the Stoic utopia should be understood as promoting gender equality in the sense that both men and women are citizens of the utopian state, and given that both are sages, the same way of life applies to both—they are guided by natural laws laid down by the *logos*, not conventional laws or customs. Thus, I claimed that the early Stoic utopias provide an entirely different vision of ideal state than Plato's *Republic*, where the guardians live highly regulated lives and where women's bodies are primarily there to serve the needs of the society. Yet, I suggested that both Plato, the Cynics and the early Stoics can be read as proposing radical counter-arguments to the Ancient art of economics (*oikonomikê*) which treats traditional marriage as a form of private ownership and reserves the public sphere of life to men, and the private sphere of the household to women.

In contrast to the early school, the later Stoics such as Musonius, Hierocles and Antipater praised marriage as an exemplary form of life, which is in accordance with the naturally sociable nature of humans. According to my reading, the later Stoics favored marriage and procreation because they were conceived of as good political deeds that benefit the community, but also as choices that are appropriate (*kathêkonta*) to one's human nature. Musonius also defended marriage on the grounds that it provides exemplary circumstances for the exercise of virtue and ethical development of both husband and wife. Thus, philosophical life and family life are not seen as mutually exclusive. Throughout my analysis of the arguments found in Stoic social and political thought, I highlighted the connections between these arguments and the metaphysical views investigated in Part I.

In the final chapter, I showed how the ethical implications of the Stoic notion of universal human rationality are expressed in their cosmopolitanism, which treats men and women as equally capable of ethical agency. This point is illustrated in Hierocles' notion of extending circles, which highlights both the global scope of ethics and the importance of family as the starting point of ethical growth. Therefore, I argue against applying to Stoicism the common feminist criticism that past thinkers neglected the value of things that are traditionally associated with the female gender, such as emotions, care, family and home. As I have shown, the Stoics did not reject emotions because they were associated with femininity—they also considered men to be thoroughly emotional even if they sometimes discuss different emotions as typical of men or of women. Further, they did not see the public sphere of life as superior to the private sphere of the home when it comes to living virtuously and philosophically. By contrast, the Stoics gave close human bonds a privileged role in their philosophy as they view the family as the first and foremost place where virtue is learnt and practiced. The family also provides the model for ethical reflection that finally comprises the entire human kind.

However, I have argued that the gravest shortcoming of Stoicism from the perspective of gender is that it does not draw any political implications promoting the fundamental equality of all human beings. For this reason, I find it too optimistic to read the Stoics as feminist thinkers: a necessary requirement for feminism, I claim, is that equality must be understood also as a political concept. Musonius' proposal to educate boys and girls alike is perhaps the most radical suggestion to be found in sources in which a Stoic thinker promotes action against existing customs. Yet even Musonius, like other Roman Stoics, would for the most part have accepted the existing social roles of men and women as well as the division between their spheres of life. Seneca praised Marcia for continuing her father's writings and handing them down to future generations—but did he encourage her to write her own philosophical works? We saw that similar conformism existed already in early Stoicism: even if Zeno's and Chrysippus' utopias would have radically rearranged the position of gender as well as sexual norms, they did not encourage acting against the norms and customs of the real-life society.

Gender and sexuality are still among some the most controversial topics in today's political debates. As I am completing this book in New York City in Fall 2017, the news are loaded with gender-related controversies, whether they are related to same-sex marriage and LGBTQ rights, financial inequality between men and women, abortion rights, sexual harassment or male dominance in the positions of political and economic leadership. Given their persistence as problems in today's world and contemporary feminist philosophy, it is valuable to engage in a systematic scrutiny of how these issues have been viewed in the history of Western thought. An investigation like this makes us aware of the historicity of our own ideas. It helps us to understand where our present-day ideas concerning gender difference and sexual orientation stem from. Delving into Ancient theories can also make us realize that gender and sexuality could be conceived of differently today, too, and that we could imagine a future in which these very concepts denote something different than they do today. Perhaps they would no longer determine how we conceive of the world, other people and ourselves, and what we think that we are and what we can become. Perhaps they would not have any more political significance than being left-handed or small-sized do today.

At best, the scrutiny of past thinking creates something that, in the spirit of Michel Foucault, could be called a critical and historical awareness of the present. As I see it, such awareness is among the most valuable results research in the history of philosophy can offer. I hope I have been able to communicate something of this to the reader. I believe that critical and historical awareness of the present is of fundamental importance not only for our conceptions, ideas and values, but also for theory formation. My aim was to broaden the scope of what research in history of philosophy talks about, and show that gender and sexuality are crucial topics not only in ethics or political philosophy, but also metaphysics and physics. However, I have also criticized those feminist readers of past thinkers who group together emotions and the female gender, and rationality and the male gender. I have shown that Stoicism problematizes such overly simplified dichotomies, and thus warns us against taking them as premises for any present-day theory of gender, or allowing them to guide the way we inquire into history of philosophy. The Stoics show that the reality of human rational and emotional capacities, choice, character-formation and cultural impact is much more complex than juxtapositions such as emotion–reason and care–justice allow.

I have argued that Stoicism emphasizes the impact of the surrounding culture on both gendered characteristics and conceptions of masculinity and femininity. What is significant from the present-day perspective is that whatever the differences between men and women are on the level of body or social roles, for the Stoics they are metaphysically and ethically insignificant. These differences do not affect the assumptions that all human beings are equally rational or that they are equally responsible for their personal moral deliberation. Nor does gender, according to the Stoics, affect in any way the fundamental human goal of becoming happy, or our possibilities of achieving this goal. Further, I have shown that the Stoics challenge the very idea of understanding sexual ethics as a set of norms and rules, and open up the possibility of seeing it as a field of virtuous action in which essential issues such as choice, self-control and other-concern are at stake.

Finally, gender and sexuality are not only theoretical and political issues, but also practical and personal matters that affect intimate spheres of everyday life. It is also for this reason that the everyday-life-oriented scope of Stoicism seems to me still to be topical and thought provoking. Stoicism challenges us to critically reflect on our characteristics, including the traits that are commonly considered to be gender-specific; to accept the responsibility for making the best out of ourselves and our lives; and to act virtuously even in our most intimate human relations, as partners in life as well as in sexuality. As readers of Stoic philosophy we are faced with the ever relevant and profoundly human problem concerning the roles of love, lust and other emotions in our lives, and how we let them affect our choices and actions. If we logically follow the Stoic way of thinking, it also seems to warn us against uncritically accepting gender and sexual stereotypes, and of letting such categories affect our understanding of other people or of our selves, let alone of justifying our action and behavior as rational, emotional and sexual subjects, regardless of gender.

Index

A
Abortion, 26, 45, 48, 293
Abstinence, 11, 33, 55, 105, 121, 210, 212, 213, 290
Activity
  vs. passivity, 9, 35, 49, 60, 63, 71, 80, 85, 110, 287
  sexual, 20, 65, 66, 68, 82, 110, 195, 207, 210
Adiaphora, *see* Indifference
Adult, 21, 76, 91, 94, 116, 147, 154, 155, 160, 166–168, 170, 175, 187, 195, 289
Adultery, 203, 236
Agency, 168, 172, 277, 281, 291
  ethical/moral, 2, 11, 200, 204, 210, 267, 277, 281, 291, 292
  sexual, 195, 199, 209, 248
Air, 35, 38, 47, 63, 66–68, 71, 72, 86, 165. *See also* Element theory
Amazons, 162, 182, 190
Analogy
  agricultural, 36–38, 48, 49, 59, 62, 63, 66, 68, 140, 141, 149, 154, 162, 167, 169, 243–245, 287
  dog, 140, 143, 161, 162

  in epistemology, 59, 125
  medical, 125, 194, 206
  sexual, 60, 67, 69, 70
Andreia, 22, 41, 51, 110, 137, 138, 150, 151, 162
Androgyny, 18, 20, 22, 109
Anger, 105, 129, 130, 132, 172, 184, 194, 201, 256
Animal, 1, 6, 19, 24, 26, 27, 30–38, 41–48, 50–52, 81, 82, 85–90, 102–106, 110, 123, 124, 128, 152, 162, 165, 166, 170, 207, 208, 210, 228, 229, 241, 262, 287. *See also* Analogy, dog; Beauty, Cynics
  amoeba, 31
  birds, 27, 162
  cicada, 19
  dog, 87, 103, 162, 167, 262
  Generation of Animals, *see* Aristotle
  horse, 32, 37, 46, 86, 102, 103, 105, 167, 206
  lion, 47, 105, 108, 110, 112
Annas, Julia, 4, 55, 61, 81, 82, 87, 90, 107, 133, 140, 145, 170, 223, 225, 244, 248, 249, 252, 279

296 INDEX

Anthropophagy, 249, 250
Antipater of Tarsus, 260–264, 266, 273, 291
Apatheia, *see* Emotionlessness
Aphrodisia, 6, 63, 106, 107, 199, 210, 228
Aphrodite, 23, 37, 66, 202
Aristophanes, 18–23, 26, 35, 95, 186, 209, 256
Aristotle, 1, 4, 6–10, 26, 29, 46–50, 60, 61, 67, 69, 71, 76, 86, 88, 92, 93, 96, 110, 124, 129, 130, 137–139, 147–155, 159, 162, 186, 192, 201, 258, 287, 291
  biology of, 29–45, 60, 62, 64, 65, 68, 89, 92, 95, 108, 124, 153
  Economics (Pseudo-Aristotelian), 220, 225–228, 268
  Generation of Animals, 30–43
  metaphysics of, 30–32, 34, 37, 42, 64, 68, 148
  Nicomachean Ethics, 32, 44, 45, 104, 148–155, 161, 230
  on female monstrosity, 39–41
  Politics, 149–153, 155, 161, 225
Ascetics, *see* Philosophical exercises
Askêsis, *see* Philosophical exercises
Asmis, Elizabeth, 4, 235, 238, 239, 244, 250, 253
Ataraxia, 185, 209
Augusta, Julia, 191, 192
Augustine, St., 20, 21, 27
Aurelius, Marcus, 3, 45, 93, 107, 174, 184, 195, 207, 208, 212, 266, 277, 280, 282
Autonomy, 185, 208, 211, 213, 257, 264, 267. *See also Ataraxia*; Self-sufficiency

B
Baby, 76, 92, 167, 168, 226, 258
Beard, 9, 102, 107, 108, 110–116, 118, 127, 182, 288
Beautification, 2, 101, 103, 104, 118, 119, 126, 183, 288
Beauty, 1, 9, 25, 102–110, 119, 123, 125–127, 144, 186, 201, 202, 230, 260, 263, 288
Beauvoir, Simone de, 42, 43
Biology, 6–9, 19, 22, 29–31, 34, 38, 40, 42–45, 50, 59, 63, 67, 71, 92, 119, 125, 130, 172, 174, 188, 287, 289
  Aristotle's, *see* Aristotle, biology of
Blend, *see* Mixture
Body, 1, 10, 24, 32, 33, 41, 43, 52, 53, 76–80, 82, 83, 85–92, 94–96, 101–115, 118, 119, 123–128, 186, 194, 207, 226, 229, 237, 287–289, 294
  beauty of, *see* Beauty
  hairs, *see* Hair
  left and right sides, 38, 39, 41, 48, 293
Boy, 7, 10, 21, 24, 45, 47, 109, 110, 143, 144, 146–148, 159, 160, 164, 165, 167, 168, 171, 172, 228, 242, 246, 273, 289, 292

C
Cannibalism, *see* Anthropophagy
Capacity, 31, 35, 79, 80, 104, 105, 150, 154, 190, 192, 288, 290, 294
  rational, 9, 82, 85, 87, 94, 152, 166, 167, 173, 271, 273
  reproductive, 9, 34, 51, 64, 76, 80–82, 85, 88, 91, 94, 96, 288

INDEX 297

Castration, 33, 51, 52
Categories
  in Stoic metaphysics, 4, 60, 61, 67,
    69, 74–85, 88, 193, 262, 263,
    267, 288
Character, 2, 8, 10, 24, 25, 103, 112,
    113, 124, 125, 127–131, 137–
    139, 141–143, 145, 147–149,
    173, 174, 182, 184–187, 189,
    191, 193, 199, 203, 256, 257,
    266, 287–290, 294
Characteristic, 138, 142, 143, 160,
    162, 173, 174, 187, 194, 213,
    225, 289, 290
  gendered, 10, 101, 124, 130, 131,
    137, 143, 160, 165, 175, 195,
    289
Childhood, 10, 149, 159, 160, 164,
    165, 167–169, 172–174, 182,
    240, 289
Children, 8, 12, 46, 47, 90, 91,
    93, 96, 105, 107, 129, 130,
    138, 148, 150, 152–154, 159,
    160, 164–171, 173, 175, 220,
    221, 223, 225, 228, 236, 241,
    246, 247, 250, 254, 257–259,
    262, 263, 266, 268, 278, 280,
    282, 283, 289. *See also* Family;
    Generation; Offspring
  daughter, 23, 191, 248, 250, 267,
    283
  education of, *see* Education
Choice, 2, 6, 11, 12, 65, 69, 71, 76,
    80, 87, 94, 101–104, 107, 109,
    115, 117, 119, 131, 137, 170,
    171, 200, 203, 210, 212, 213,
    236–238, 249, 250, 259, 260,
    265, 266, 268, 281, 289, 290,
    294
Christianity, 20, 23, 27, 62, 204, 209

Chrysippus of Soli, 11, 64, 68, 75,
    79–81, 92, 94, 126, 131, 167,
    173, 219, 235, 236, 248, 293
Cicero, Marcus Tullius, 64, 86, 96,
    128, 131, 167, 183–185, 193,
    194, 207, 244, 247, 264, 265,
    279–282
Citizen, 21, 117, 147, 150, 151, 153,
    154, 195, 227, 230, 236, 243,
    249, 272, 278–281, 291. *See also*
    Cosmopolitanism
Cleanthes of Assos, 125, 126
Clement of Alexandria, 126, 127, 132
Clothing, 7, 110, 118, 173, 236, 270
Coldness, 29, 30, 38–43, 47–49, 52,
    86, 106, 124, 129, 270
Comedy, 22, 23
Communism, 239
Community
  of sages, 11, 12, 245, 258, 279
  of women, *see* Woman, common
    ownership of
Contraception, 25, 26
Corruption, *see* Culture, corrupting
    effects of
Cosmetics, 1, 9, 101–105, 118,
    127, 183, 212, 287. *See also*
    Beautification
Cosmogony, 9, 59, 68
Cosmology, 1, 9, 26, 59, 60, 62,
    67–69, 71, 75, 85, 287
Cosmopolitanism, 1, 11, 12, 96, 170,
    195, 208, 230, 236, 241, 250,
    259, 266, 277–283, 292
Cosmos, 1, 9, 59–62, 64–68, 70, 71,
    86, 87, 195, 208, 244, 262, 277,
    278, 280, 281, 287
Crates, 220, 228–230, 253, 259, 261
Culture, 1, 7, 17, 43, 115, 117,
    118, 142, 160, 174, 175, 221,

229, 250, 273, 294. *See also* Habituation
corrupting effects of, 117, 142, 174, 175, 236
Cynics, 11, 109, 110, 112, 117, 190, 219, 220, 225, 227–230, 236, 238–241, 247, 253, 257–259, 261, 262, 267, 277, 283, 291

D

Deliberation, 82, 94, 104, 107, 109, 115, 131, 138, 149, 170, 212, 229, 237, 267, 268, 281, 290, 294
Desire, 6, 19–22, 24, 27, 29, 51, 94, 95, 113, 172, 201, 205, 206, 211, 229, 261. *See also* Lust
Deslauriers, Marguerite, 34, 43, 44, 155
Dio Chrysostom, 59, 66, 67
Diogenes Laertius, 66, 69, 72, 92, 97, 101, 120, 125, 126, 132, 165, 170, 176, 196, 202, 203, 214, 228–230, 236, 238, 246–248, 250, 251, 257, 273
Diogenes of Sinope, 228–230, 236, 238, 277. *See also* Crates; Cynics; Hipparchia
Diotima, 24, 25, 29, 31
Doctor, 45, 54, 93, 194, 206. *See also* Medicine
Dressing, *see* Clothing

E

Earth, 18, 28, 35, 37, 38, 47, 49, 63, 68, 69, 71, 72, 86, 164, 250, 257
Economics, 11, 31, 53, 146, 150, 151, 155, 219, 220, 225–227, 229, 230, 236, 265, 268, 291, 293

Educability, 10, 139, 146, 164, 165, 171, 172, 175, 273, 279
Education, 4, 7, 8, 10, 45, 75, 83, 84, 91, 93, 107, 131, 137–150, 152, 153, 155, 159, 161, 162, 164, 165, 167, 169, 171, 172, 174–176, 182, 189, 193, 220, 227, 229, 237, 240–242, 246, 249, 254, 258, 261, 270, 271, 289–292
Element theory, 29, 35, 38, 47, 50, 67, 86, 124, 128, 129, 174. *See also* Air; Coldness; Earth; Fire; Hotness; Sun; Water
Embellishment, *see* Beautification
Embryo, 26, 35, 36, 37, 39, 41, 45, 46, 48, 49, 54, 62, 89–93, 166
Embryology, 2, 7, 19, 27, 29, 34, 45, 48, 50, 52, 62, 64–68, 71, 76, 79, 88–90, 92–94, 141, 166, 219
Emotion, 1, 6, 11, 17, 52, 124, 129, 130, 137, 138, 142, 144, 149, 168–170, 172, 181, 182, 187, 188, 191, 199, 201, 204–206, 209, 211, 213, 281, 292–294
Emotionlessness, 185–188, 209
Enjoyment, *see* Pleasure
Epictetus, 51, 102–119, 160, 167, 168, 171, 172, 177, 187, 189, 190, 196, 204, 205, 207, 209, 210, 213, 214, 220, 222, 229, 231, 241, 244, 245, 251, 255, 257–260, 264, 267, 280, 284, 288
Epicureanism, ix, 2, 7–8, 10, 110, 112, 182–185, 187, 208, 267
Epicurus, 7, 8, 184
Equality, 2, 12, 125, 145, 186, 195, 203, 222–225, 244–246, 271–273, 277, 278, 281, 291, 292
Erastés, 21, 24, 110, 146

Erômenos, 21, 24, 126, 146
Erôs, 4, 6, 18, 23, 24, 27, 28, 199, 201–203. *See also* Erotic love
Erotic images, 59, 60, 64–72. *See also* Analogy, sexual; Fellatio; Hera; Zeus
Erotic love, 7, 23, 24, 144, 199–202, 204, 211, 213, 230, 259. *See also* Friendship, erotic; Homosexuality; Pederasty; Sexuality
Erotic subject, *see* Agency; Friendship, erotic; Sexual
Ethical agency, 210, 291, 292
Ethics
  sexual, 2, 4, 7, 21, 110, 199, 210, 224, 227, 235, 242, 248–250, 294
Eudaimonia, *see* Happiness
Eugenics, 142, 143, 223
Exercises, 11, 199, 207, 209, 210, 212, 224, 229, 267. *See also* Abstinence; Gymnastics
  philosophical, 1, 11, 199, 206–210, 213, 290
  physical, 5, 212, 270
  on sexual impressions, 206, 210

F

Family, 4, 8, 12, 84, 96, 138, 142, 155, 219–221, 225–227, 235, 236, 239, 241, 248, 250, 253–273, 278–280, 282, 283, 292. *See also* Children; Father; Marriage; Mother; Relationship
  traditional, 235, 236, 241, 279
Father, 26, 35–37, 39, 47, 50, 84, 93, 150, 154, 174, 225, 228, 248, 258, 259, 267, 279, 280, 283, 292. *See also* Family
Fellatio, 64–66, 70

Female, 2, 6, 7, 10, 12, 18, 19, 21, 23, 27–30, 32–52, 62, 64–68, 70–72, 76, 79, 81, 82, 92–95, 107, 108, 115, 119, 124, 125, 139, 140, 143, 145, 147, 148, 151, 152, 154, 159, 161, 162, 170, 175, 182–184, 186, 187–191, 194, 195, 222, 226, 229, 242, 245, 254, 262–264, 266, 269–271, 281, 287–289, 292. *See also* Gender; Preformationism; Sphere of life; Testicles; Woman; Womb
  in Ancient biology, 29–52
  exemplifications, 2, 182, 189–191
  genitals, 18, 19, 27, 30, 69, 77
  happiness, *see* Happiness, of women
  as a hollow container, 37, 91, 93
  as material cause of generation, 49, 67, 68
  as a monster, *see* Aristotle, on female monstrosity
Femininity, 8, 10, 11, 32, 39, 62, 101, 102, 118, 124–126, 130, 137, 176, 181, 182, 184–186, 193, 195, 230, 269, 288, 290, 292, 294
Feminism, 2, 4, 7, 27, 36, 40, 42–44, 62, 142, 145, 147, 148, 175, 181, 182, 186, 187, 190, 222–224, 277, 278, 281, 282, 288, 292, 293
Fertilization, 35, 39, 41, 47, 49, 91, 93
Fetus, *see* Embryo
Fire, 35, 38, 47, 48, 63–72, 86, 129, 130. *See also* Element theory; Hot versus cold; Sun
Foucault, Michel, 5, 27, 110, 160, 174, 189, 204, 207, 209, 293
Freedom, 11, 171, 192, 200, 204–206, 211–213, 223, 257,

272, 290. *See also* Choice; Man, freeborn
from emotions, *see* Emotionlessness
Friendship, 200–203, 209, 212, 213, 227, 230, 258, 290
  erotic, 200, 202, 209, 213, 258, 290. *See also* Erotic love; Relationship

G

Gaca, Kathy, 4, 59–61, 64, 65, 68, 70, 81, 221
Galen, 1, 6–9, 26, 33, 37, 45–54, 79–81, 86, 87, 91–93, 95, 97, 112, 123, 124, 129, 132, 165, 166, 168, 177, 205, 214, 270, 287
Gender
  and characters/characteristics, *see* Characteristic, gendered
  cultural/social construction of, 7, 101, 113, 141, 142, 160, 164, 172–174, 176, 195, 290
  difference, 26, 28, 32, 34, 38, 44, 46, 71, 76, 81, 82, 91, 96, 109, 143, 160, 172, 175, 193, 290, 293
  dimorphism, *see* Sexual dimorphism
  education of, *see* Education, and gender
  equality, *see* Equality
  metaphysical insignificance of, 9, 75, 102, 111
  myths of, *see* Myth
  as a philosophical question, 2, 4, 22, 102, 260
  resemblance, 46–47, 50–52
  signs of, 9, 101, 102, 108, 109, 111, 117, 123, 269
Generation, 1, 8, 22, 29–32, 34–36, 40–43, 46, 47, 49, 50, 62, 64, 65, 67, 69, 70, 81, 89, 92, 93, 141, 184, 210, 293. *See also* Embryology; Fertilization
  Generation of Animals, *see* Aristotle
Genitals, 6, 18–21, 27, 30, 33, 47, 50, 51, 59, 62, 63, 69, 77, 79–82, 88, 91, 96, 112, 114
  female, *see* Female, genitals
  genital difference, 46, 94, 95, 262
Girl, 10, 26, 47, 53, 75, 110, 118, 139, 143, 146, 148, 149, 155, 159–161, 164, 165, 167, 169, 171, 172, 227, 242, 246, 271, 273, 289, 292
Gleason, Maud, 39, 110, 113, 114, 125, 126, 130
God, 18–20, 23, 24, 26, 28, 29, 44, 59, 63–67, 69, 70, 72, 94, 108, 163, 195, 225–227, 237. *See also* Hera, Zeus
  in philosophical myths, 9, 17, 18, 89
  in Stoicism, 2–6, 8–11, 26, 68, 76, 78, 81, 93, 96, 107, 112, 117, 124, 139, 169, 175, 182, 202, 204, 230, 241, 243, 244, 267, 271
Gordon, Pamela, 183, 184
Gymnastics, 141, 162, 270

H

Habit, 118, 149, 174, 211–213, 227, 245, 289. *See also* Culture
Habituation, 10, 52, 53, 131, 142, 148, 149, 162, 174, 192, 289, 290
Hahm, David E., 4, 59, 60, 67, 68, 70
Hair, 9, 19, 33, 101–119, 140
Happiness, 6, 10–12, 20, 22, 23, 101, 102, 125, 139, 143, 146–148,

INDEX   301

150–153, 155, 159, 171, 185, 192, 200, 208, 211, 240, 255, 258, 260, 264, 266, 267, 271, 294. *See also* Sage of women, 9
Heat, *see* Hotness
Hellenistic philosophy, 2, 3, 138, 184, 206, 219, 247
Henry, Devin, 35, 36, 40, 41, 43, 44
Hera, 9, 59, 64–67, 70–72
Heracles, 189
Heterosexuality, 22, 126, 242. *See also* Relationship, male–female
Hierarchy, 21, 22, 25, 27, 30, 31, 38, 41, 42, 44, 72, 86, 140, 154, 155, 226, 287
Hierocles, 49, 88–93, 98, 219, 260, 261, 263, 264, 266, 268–272, 274, 278–281, 283, 284, 291, 292
Hipparchia, 78, 82, 182, 190, 228–230, 253, 259, 270
Hippocrates, 26, 27, 37, 38, 48, 49, 79, 87, 123
Home, 27, 52, 53, 221, 226, 228, 257, 261, 263, 267, 279, 281–283, 292. *See also* Sphere of life, private
Homiak, Marcia L., 181, 183, 277, 281
Homosexuality, 21, 242. *See also* Relationship, male–male
Hotness, 29, 30, 38–43, 47, 51, 52, 86, 106, 128. *See also* Coldness; Element theory
Household, 114, 146, 150, 151, 155, 220, 221, 225–227, 254, 258, 259, 261, 263, 267, 269, 280, 282
Husband, 42, 66, 144, 146, 150, 151, 154, 187, 191, 192, 221, 222, 225–229, 254, 258, 259, 261, 263–270, 272, 279, 280, 292

I
Idealization
  female, 2, 182, 189, 235
Idios poion, *see* Quality, individual
Impulse
  sexual, 1, 199–201, 206, 213
Incest, 228, 246, 248–250
Indifference, 9, 76, 102, 111, 115–117, 199, 201, 203, 245, 254–256, 260, 266, 267, 288, 289. *See also* Gender, metaphysical insignificance of
Individual qualities, *see* Quality, individual
Inwood, Brad, 4, 98, 99, 121, 124, 132, 133, 167, 178, 197, 202, 210, 215, 239, 275
Insignificance, 9, 42, 77, 102, 111, 114, 115, 118, 140, 185, 209, 212, 237, 264, 294. *See also* Indifference; Gender, metaphysical insignificance of
Intercourse, 19–21, 65, 66, 199, 202, 205, 207, 208, 223, 224, 228, 249. *See also* Love, to make
Intimacy, *see* Relationship, intimate

J
Jealousy, 42, 223
Justice, 103, 140, 146, 150–152, 174, 181, 183, 223, 240, 248, 281–283, 294

K
Kalos, *see* Beautiful
Kinaidos, 109, 110, 118, 126, 187, 269
Koinos poion, *see* Quality, common
Kosmos, *see* Cosmos
Krâsis, *see* Mixture, in Stoic metaphysics

L

Labor
  division of, 163, 225, 230, 254, 268, 270
  indoor vs. outdoor, 44, 53, 163, 226, 270, 271
LeDoeuff, Michèle, 4, 222, 223
Levin, Susan B., 142, 143
Lion, *see* Animal, lion
Livia, *see* Augusta, Julia
Logos, 29, 33, 34, 61–64, 70, 71, 80, 81, 86, 113, 164, 166, 210, 213, 229, 237, 244, 280, 291. *See also* Rationality; Reason; *Spermatikoi logoi*
Long, A.A., 64, 72, 78–81, 83, 89, 90, 98, 106, 120, 131, 132, 170, 177, 194, 214
Love, 4, 6, 7, 12, 17, 18, 20–26, 66, 96, 124, 126, 144, 145, 170, 172, 174, 199–205, 208, 209, 211, 213, 228–230, 250, 254, 256, 259, 268, 279, 294. *See also* Intercourse
  to make, 8
Lover, *see* Love
Lust, 6, 17–21, 23, 24, 26, 28, 29, 50, 82, 84, 88, 142, 143, 200, 204, 210, 294. *See also* Desire

M

Make-up, *see* Cosmetics
Male, 6, 7, 18, 19, 21, 27, 28, 30, 32–52, 62–64, 67, 68, 70–72, 76, 79–82, 92–95, 107, 114, 124, 125, 140, 150, 153, 161, 162, 170, 183, 187, 188, 190, 195, 203, 206, 239, 242, 246, 262, 263, 270, 271, 281, 287, 288, 293
  male–female and male–male relationships, *see* Relationship
  perspective on philosophy, 12, 45, 119, 144, 222, 245, 246
Man
  freeborn, 146, 150, 152–154, 189, 227, 257, 265. *See also* Male; Gender
Manliness, 22, 51, 113, 114, 126, 130, 137, 182, 183, 188, 190, 269, 270
Marriage, 1, 4, 11, 12, 21, 26, 95, 96, 102, 190, 210, 219–223, 228–230, 235–238, 241, 245–247, 253, 254, 256–268, 272–274, 280, 282, 291–293. *See also* Relationship; Spouse; Wife
  institutional, *see* Marriage, traditional
  monogamous, 219–221, 235–238, 280
  polygamous, 219, 236–238, 247
  Roman Stoics on, 3, 4, 10, 12, 94, 102, 117, 118, 159, 171, 182, 188, 203, 210, 227, 244, 253, 254, 260, 262, 264, 266, 268, 291, 292
  traditional, 11, 17, 18, 36, 52, 72, 108, 110, 124, 140, 141, 146, 150, 163, 174, 175, 181, 185, 188, 195, 219–223, 228–230, 235–238, 241, 246, 249, 253, 261, 262, 269, 270, 272, 277, 279, 281–283, 289–292
Masculinity, 10, 11, 32, 39, 51, 52, 101, 102, 110, 111, 113, 124–126, 176, 182, 184, 185, 188, 193, 195, 269, 270, 288, 290, 294. *See also* Manliness
Matrimony, *see* Marriage
Medea, 138, 182, 190
Medicine, 29, 35, 45, 206, 287. *See also* Doctor; Galen; Hippocrates
  as analogy to philosophy, *see* Analogy, medical

Menstruation, 34–38, 41, 49, 50, 81
Metaphysics, 1, 2, 4, 9, 28, 32, 34, 37, 40, 42, 54, 59–64, 67–70, 75–77, 106, 148, 153, 155, 160, 169, 173, 182, 193, 199, 201, 254, 255, 262, 263, 283, 287–290, 293. *See also* Categories; Gender, metaphysical insignificance of
  Aristotelian, *see* Aristotle, metaphysics of
  Stoic, 4, 6, 9, 40, 59–63, 67–70, 75–88, 96, 169, 173, 182, 193, 201, 242, 255, 262, 263, 283
Mixture, 47, 49, 52, 53, 67, 93
  in Stoic metaphysics (*krâsis*), 61, 70, 77, 85, 87, 127, 262
Monogamy, *see* Marriage
Moon, 18, 36, 39
Mother, 26, 27, 35, 37, 47, 50, 68, 84, 90, 93, 168, 191, 192, 195, 224, 248, 249, 261, 279, 281. *See also* Earth; Family
  earth (Gaia), 28
Myth, 17–29, 36, 37, 63, 287
  Aristophanes', 18–23, 26, 35, 95, 256
  biological, 9, 59, 63, 67, 71
  philosophical, 9, 17, 18, 22, 24, 29, 89, 287
  sexual, 4, 29, 64, 65
Mythology, 17, 18, 23, 71

N
Nature, 2, 18, 19, 21, 22, 24, 25, 27, 28, 30, 31, 34, 35, 38–41, 52, 59, 67, 76, 82, 86, 94, 96, 102–111, 114, 115, 118, 119, 124, 128–130, 138, 140, 141, 149, 161, 169, 170, 172–174, 186, 192, 194, 195, 202, 203, 210, 211, 221, 226, 227, 229, 230, 237, 238, 241, 242, 244, 249, 250, 256, 262–264, 266, 279, 280, 283, 288–292
  hierarchic view of, *see* Hierarchy
  human, 27, 28, 102, 106, 161, 186, 194, 242, 264–267, 290, 292
Nussbaum, Martha C., 4, 18, 22, 25, 160–162, 169, 172, 173, 175, 190, 204, 207, 211, 224, 256, 262, 267, 271, 281, 283

O
Offspring, 18, 26, 30, 34, 38, 41, 47, 48, 50, 67, 96, 151, 170, 221, 223, 241. *See also* Children
Oikeiôsis, 88, 94, 169, 170, 262
Oikonomia/Oikonomikê, *see* Economic
Oikos, *see* Household; Home; Property
Okin, Susan Moller, 221–224, 281, 282
Other-concern, 12, 170, 294
Ownership, *see* Property; Woman, common ownership of

P
Panaetius of Rhodes, 80, 193, 211, 264, 265
Passion, 17, 18, 205, 206. *See also* Desire
Pausanias, 21, 23–25, 66, 68, 202
Pederasty, 21, 24, 25, 110, 111, 146, 203. *See also* Erastês; Erômenos; Homosexuality; Erotic love; Relationship, male–male
Penis, 21, 27, 46, 50
Perfume, *see* Cosmetics
Personae, *see* Roles
Philosophical exercises, *see* Exercises
Philosophy
  Aristotelian, *see* Aristotle
  contemporary, 2, 4, 7, 43, 150, 222
  Cynic, *see* Cynics

feminist, see Feminism
Hellenistic, see Hellenistic
  philosophy
Peripatetic, 104, 123, 131. See also
  Theophrastus
Plato's, see Plato
political, 11, 117, 225, 235, 236,
  246, 247, 253, 254, 291, 293
practicing, 116, 117, 164, 172, 212,
  213, 261, 262, 289
Stoic, see Stoicism
therapeutic, 6, 172, 189–191, 193,
  199, 204, 206, 207, 210, 213,
  290
Physics, 1, 2, 4, 95, 163, 287, 293
Physiognomy, 10, 39, 42, 87, 123–
  131, 137, 173, 287, 289
Plato, 4, 7, 8, 10, 12, 17–21, 25, 26,
  28, 46, 88, 92, 103, 104, 106,
  111, 138–147, 149, 150, 153,
  155, 159, 161, 163, 165, 199,
  201, 203, 219–223, 225, 227,
  236, 238–240, 243, 245, 262,
  268, 270, 271, 287, 291
  Gorgias, 104, 146, 147
  Meno, 139, 146, 147, 161, 162
  myths of, see Myths
  Republic, 12, 88, 111, 117,
    139–147, 150, 155, 161, 163,
    182, 193, 220–225, 237–241,
    243–245, 259, 268, 270, 271,
    291
  Symposium, 17–26, 35, 66, 95, 103,
    186, 202, 209, 239, 268
  Timaeus, 17, 18, 26–30, 36, 45, 50,
    62, 68, 92, 95, 144
Pleasure, 6, 10, 20, 24, 93, 94, 124,
  184, 188, 202, 204, 207, 209,
  210
Plutarch, 76, 91, 173, 188, 189, 219
Pneuma, 35, 64, 66, 67, 76, 78, 79,
  85–90, 92, 263

Politics, 4, 8, 11, 44, 45, 96, 147,
  149–153, 155, 161, 225, 260,
  273, 288, 291
Polygamy, see Marriage
Posidonius, 92, 123, 124, 165
Preformationism, 36, 37, 68, 92, 93
Pregnancy, 25, 38, 40, 48, 50, 70, 91,
  224
Procreation, 7, 30–32, 37, 43, 93, 95,
  143, 170, 210, 220, 262, 280,
  291. See also Generation
Prohairesis, 102–104. See also Choice
Property, 115, 150–152, 219–221,
  225–228, 241, 244, 257, 261,
  262, 265. See also Woman, common ownership of
  common, 221, 222, 226, 241, 244
  private, 219–221, 225

Q
Quality
  common, 11, 76, 78, 82, 85, 193,
    288
  individual, 9, 76, 78, 82, 85, 96,
    193, 246, 288

R
Rationality, 9, 10, 32, 34, 44, 71,
  76, 79, 82, 86–88, 94, 105,
  139, 165, 166, 172, 181–183,
  190, 192, 193, 201, 205, 236,
  246, 266, 279–281, 283, 290,
  292, 293. See also Logos; Reason;
  Spermatikoi logoi
  and children, see Children
Reason, 1, 9, 27, 34, 35, 39, 44, 47,
  51, 61–64, 68–71, 87, 90, 94,
  103, 109, 115, 116, 125, 127,
  143, 149, 153, 154, 164–166,
  169, 174, 175, 182, 206, 208,

212, 237, 239, 242, 245–247,
249, 261–263, 271–273,
278–281, 283, 288, 290, 292,
294. *See also Logos*; Rationality;
Spermatikoi logoi
Relationship, 1, 7, 11, 12, 21, 23–26,
39, 43, 64, 68, 70, 77, 79,
109, 110, 112, 125, 126, 139,
142, 144, 146, 154, 155, 173,
199, 202–204, 209, 222, 226,
228–230, 240, 245, 256, 262,
264, 279, 294
  erotic, 7, 18, 21, 110, 144, 200,
202, 203, 258, 294
  hierarchical, *see* Hierarchy
  intimate, 11, 12, 204, 256
  male–female, 21, 25, 144, 202, 203,
242
  male–male, 144, 203
  pederastic, *see* Pederasty
Reproduction, *see* Capacity, reproductive; Embryology; generation
Reydams-Schils, Gretchen, 4, 92, 113,
114, 170, 190, 199, 247, 254,
265, 266, 272, 273
Roles, 186, 187, 193–195, 229,
264–273, 280, 281, 294
  and social construction, *see* Social
constructionism
  gender, 4, 118, 128, 141, 143, 147,
165, 169, 175, 226, 227, 229,
236, 243
  reproductive, 19, 43, 50
  role models, 175, 182, 188, 192
  sexual, 5, 110, 114
  social, 6, 53, 117, 150, 186, 187,
194, 195, 227, 271, 280, 292
Rufus, Musonius, 4, 10, 75, 96, 111,
118, 161, 162, 165, 169, 172,
175, 190, 192, 199, 260, 261,
263, 264, 270–272, 282

S

Sage, 25, 107, 125, 126, 163, 182,
185–188, 189, 193–195, 201,
206, 209, 213, 236, 237, 240,
243, 245, 247, 248, 258, 290.
See also Wisdom
Sappho, 21
Schofield, Malcolm, 4, 126, 127, 219,
235, 239, 242, 243, 246, 247,
249, 263
Sedley, David, 64, 77–81, 83, 89, 90,
131, 170, 194
Self-control, 6, 103, 130, 137, 144,
185, 199, 204, 209–211, 269,
270, 290, 294
Self-sufficiency, 20, 21, 185, 240, 267.
See also Ataraxia; Autonomy
Semen, *see* Sperm
Seneca, 76, 90, 91, 105, 110, 123–
125, 128–130, 160, 167–171,
174, 183–188, 193, 194,
210–212, 260, 282, 283
  Consolation letter to Marcia, 105,
106, 184, 185, 192, 289
Sextus Empiricus, 31, 123, 166, 242,
248
Sexual dimorphism, 27, 29–31, 41,
108
Sexuality, 195, 199–213, 221, 224,
287, 288, 290, 291, 293, 294
  and agency, *see* Agency, sexual
  and ethics, *see* Ethics, sexual
  in philosophical therapy, 4, 10, 11,
191, 195, 199
  myths of, *see* Myths
  philosophical exercises on, *see*
Exercises
Slavery, 150, 152–154, 185, 195, 200,
205, 220, 225–227, 242, 265,
272
Society, 289–291, 293

ideal, *see* Utopia
Socrates, 23–25, 29, 31, 78, 82, 83, 96, 103, 113, 139–141, 145, 146, 160–162, 188, 189, 219, 220, 223, 240, 261
Soul, 8, 77, 113, 123, 124, 128, 181, 184, 287, 288
　Aristotle on, 30, 32, 35, 37, 43, 44, 47, 50, 89, 147–149, 152–155
　Plato on, 24, 25, 27–29, 103, 142, 143, 146, 155, 220, 225
　rational, 9, 10, 12, 59, 63, 76, 79–82, 86–88, 153, 268
　Stoics on, 11, 61, 62, 66, 75–79, 82, 83, 89, 90, 92–94, 102, 104, 125, 126, 128, 130, 164, 167, 172, 188, 201, 206, 263, 264, 269, 288
Sperm, 34, 35, 37–39, 41, 47, 49, 50, 62–64, 66–69, 79–81, 89, 91, 93, 288
Spermatikoi logoi, 59, 63, 79. *See also* Logos; Rationality; Reason; Sperm
Sphere of life, 43, 45, 53, 140, 151, 154, 155, 188, 194, 195, 199, 205, 220, 226–228, 267, 269, 271, 277, 278, 281–283, 291, 292, 294. *See also* Labor, division of
　private, 205, 209, 219, 221, 226, 228, 263, 268, 271, 277, 281–283, 292
　public, 118, 189, 205, 221, 223, 224, 226, 228, 244, 247, 258, 260, 263, 265, 268, 269, 271, 277, 278, 281–283, 291, 292
Spouse, 12, 102, 221, 225, 226, 254, 255, 257–259, 263, 266–269, 278, 280, 283. *See also* Family; Husband; Marriage; Wife
Stobaeus, 63, 64, 68, 107, 115, 116, 125, 161, 173, 174, 200–204, 212, 267

Stoicism. *See also* Cosmopolitanism; Education; Metaphysics; Philosophy, practicing; Philosophy, therapeutic; Politics; Utopia
　Early school, 12, 23, 64, 65, 68, 70, 71, 94, 102, 117, 203, 219, 220, 228, 230, 235–241, 244–247, 249, 253, 259, 262, 277, 291, 293
　epistemology, 59, 69, 125, 165, 169, 171, 185, 208
　ethics, 2, 4, 7, 10, 23, 75, 83, 203, 242, 250, 266, 277, 282
　Late school, *see* Stoicism, Roman
　Roman, 4, 10, 12, 94, 102, 117–119, 159, 171, 181, 188, 203, 210, 219, 229, 244, 245, 253–273, 291, 292
　theory of extending circles, 277–283
Sun, 18, 35, 38, 63
Symmetry, 222, 224, 244

T

Testicles, 38, 46, 48, 49, 51, 52, 80, 81, 112
Theophrastus, 104, 131
Thought experiment, 11, 117, 140, 209, 235–237, 240, 245, 247, 249, 272, 291. *See also* Utopia
Tragedy, 22, 23, 137, 138, 151, 255–256

U

Uterus, *see* Womb
Utopia, 1, 4, 225, 230, 235–237, 239–247, 253, 258, 291, 293. *See also* Thought experiment

V

Value, 97, 292, 293
  selective, 9, 115–117, 200, 209, 266
Vanity, 11, 117–119, 126, 127, 130, 187, 269, 289
Virtue, 1, 12, 22, 26, 39, 41, 69, 79, 85, 86, 94, 104–107, 125–127, 138, 139, 144, 146, 148–155, 161, 162, 164, 170, 171, 183–186, 188, 192–194, 201, 245, 258, 260, 267, 283, 289–292
Vlastos, Gregory, 25, 142, 143, 145, 223, 224
Vogt, Katja, 4, 237, 240, 246, 249, 250

W

Water, 35, 38, 47, 61, 63, 66–68, 71, 86, 212, 213, 228, 262
Weeping, 10, 160
Wife, 42, 84, 102, 118, 150, 151, 154, 187, 191, 195, 220, 221, 225–228, 244, 254, 255, 257–263, 265–269, 279–282, 292. *See also* Family; Husband; Marriage; Spouse
Wisdom, 1, 24, 144, 176, 185, 186, 193, 211, 245, 268, 289, 290
Woman, 9, 11, 18, 19, 21, 23–27, 35, 36, 44, 47, 62, 63, 66, 68, 76–78, 81, 82, 84, 90, 95, 101, 106, 108–110, 130, 138, 140, 144–146, 149, 151–154, 159, 161, 162, 184–186, 188, 189, 192, 193, 203, 222–226, 229, 230, 244, 250, 263, 268, 271, 280, 281, 288, 291, 292, 294. *See also* Female; Gender
  and her sphere of life, *see* Sphere of life
  common ownership of women, 220–223, 228, 236, 238, 240, 244, 245
  education of, *see* Education
  examples of, *see* Female, exemplifications
  in Plato's theory, 62, 145, 202, 223
  prone to weep, *see* Weeping
Womb, 27, 35–38, 40, 47, 49, 65, 68, 89–92
Work, *see* Labor

X

Xenophon, 8, 44, 55, 102, 105, 106, 122, 151, 157, 163, 220, 225–228, 232, 261, 268, 271, 276

Z

Zeno of Citium, 3, 10, 11, 68, 75, 101, 109, 113, 117, 118, 123–127, 219, 220, 235, 236, 238–240, 242, 243, 246–248, 257, 293
Zeus, 9, 19, 20, 23, 59, 64–67, 70–72, 283

The manufacturer's authorised representative in the EU is Springer Nature Customer Service Centre GmbH, Europaplatz 3, 69115 Heidelberg, Germany. If you have any concerns regarding our products, please contact ProductSafety@springernature.com

Printed and bound by CPI Group (UK) Ltd, Croydon, CR0 4YY
23/03/2026
02076662-0010